The Invention of Communication

Other books by Armand Mattelart in English

How to Read Donald Duck, with Ariel Dorfman (1975)
Communication and Class Struggle: An Anthology in 2 Volumes, with
   S. Siegelaub (1979 and 1983)
Multinational Corporations and the Control of Culture (1979)
*Mass Media, Ideologies, and the Revolutionary Movement: Chile
   1970–1973* (1980)
Transnationals and the Third World: The Struggle for Culture (1983)
International Image Markets: In Search of an Alternative Perspective,
   with Xavier Delcourt and Michèle Mattelart (1984)
*Communication and Information Technologies: Freedom of Choice for
   Latin America?* with Hector Schmucler (1985)
*Technology, Culture, and Communication: A Report to the French
   Ministry of Research and Industry*, with Yves Stourdzé (1985)
Communicating in Popular Nicaragua: An Anthology (1986)
The Carnival of Images: Brazilian Television Fiction, with Michèle
   Mattelart (1990)
Advertising International: The Privatization of Public Space (1991)
Rethinking Media Theory: Signposts and New Directions, with
   Michèle Mattelart (1992)
Mapping World Communication: War, Progress, Culture (1994)

The Invention of Communication

Armand Mattelart

Translated by Susan Emanuel

University of Minnesota Press
Minneapolis
London

The University of Minnesota Press gratefully acknowledges financial assistance provided by the French Ministry of Culture for the translation of this book.

Originally published as *L'invention de la communication* © 1994 Éditions La Découverte, Paris.

Published by the University of Minnesota Press
111 Third Avenue South, Suite 290, Minneapolis, MN 55401-2520
Printed in the United States of America on acid-free paper

Library of Congress Cataloging-in-Publication Data

Mattelart, Armand.
    [Invention de la communication. English]
    The invention of communication / Armand Mattelart ; translated by Susan Emanuel.
        p.   cm.
    Includes bibliographical references and index.
    ISBN 0-8166-2696-0
    ISBN 0-8166-2697-9 (pbk.)
    1. Communication—History.   2. Civilization, Modern.   I. Title.
    IN PROCESS
    302.2'09—dc20   96-14993

The University of Minnesota is an
equal-opportunity educator and employer.

Me parece a mí... que puesto que dice el refrán:
"Quien necio es en su villa, necio es en Castilla",
el andar tierras y comunicar con diversas gentes
hace a los hombres discretos.

Cervantes, Coloquio de los Perros *(1613)*

For it seems to me... that while there is truth in the old proverb
which says "He who is a fool at home will be a fool in Castile,"
travel in foreign lands and intercourse with various peoples
is nevertheless the thing that makes men wise.

Cervantes, The Colloquy of the Dogs

(1950 Viking edition of Three Exemplary Novels,
trans. Samuel Putnam)

Contents

Part IV: The Measure of the Individual

Preface to the English Edition

"If the cannon was the first of the modern space-annihilating devices by means of which man was enabled to express himself at a distance, the semaphore telegraph (first used in war) was perhaps the second." So wrote Lewis Mumford in *Technics and Civilization* in 1934. A seemingly peremptory and truly provocative statement of this kind had the merit of synthesizing what was original in the project of this historian of the machine: doing away with the separations between different areas and crossing the angles of vision of the disciplines in order to bring out the manifold logics by which the multiple forms of technology have molded, and in turn been molded by, the history of humankind, its mentalities, and its civilizations.

The problem is that the sociology of communications, which was also officially born in the 1930s, is far from having thrown itself into the cross-fertilizing approach and the attitude of intellectual openness proposed by Mumford. As the third millennium draws near, this conception of history is still very much in the minority, and indeed more and more isolated, when it comes to approaching the evolution of technologies and systems of information and communication. Just as it was hardly obvious in the 1930s to make a link between the cannon and the telegraph as instruments for vanquishing space, it is still difficult today to legitimate a transdisciplinary approach that, for example, does not hesitate to trace the possible kinship between the first attempts by topographers of routes and waterways to control territories in the seventeenth and eighteenth centuries, the normalization and classification of individuals and regions undertaken by the pioneers of "moral statistics" according to indices of social pathology during the nineteenth century, and the targeting of "consumption communities" by modern marketing in the twentieth century. Bringing together in a history of communication, in a single portrait gallery, as it were, the mathematicians and ideologues of calculation such as Vauban, the French fortifications engineer; Adolphe Quételet, the Belgian astronomer and statistician; and Paul F. Lazarsfeld, the Austrian-born founder of quantitative functionalist sociology, is still looked upon as an impertinent exploit.

Communication studies in this century's end pivot around a notion of communication confined to the area of the mass media. This particular meaning of the term is only the most recent in a long evolution, during which "communication" has known many other denotations and other supports. The mediacentric perspective causes us to forget that the history of communication possesses a trunk that existed long before the appearance of modern mass media. The media tropism engenders a reductive vision of the history of communication. Worse, it provokes a historical amnesia that prevents us from discerning where the truly important stakes lie in the current and rapid transformation of our contemporary mode of communication. It is this rejection of history that explains why the debates on contemporary communication are so meager, so banal, and so mired in dualistic visions and impossible dilemmas, in which one is obliged, for example, to make exclusive choices between opposite poles, privileging now free will, now social determinations; now the local, now the global; now the individual, now the collective; now abstraction, now lived experience; now culture, now nature. Here is the origin, no doubt, of a real incapacity to uncover subtle articulations and to treat these different levels as dimensions of processes and as phenomena that, after all, cannot but cohere.

In fact, nothing takes us further from the future than history caught in the obsessions of the present. Paradoxically, we learn more about the uncertainties of the future by asking why, four centuries ago, the modern notion of communication emerged alongside the ideals of Reason and Progress and how they became embodied in the visions of nineteenth-century utopian thinkers, than by listening to the latest speech on the thaumaturgic virtues of digital superhighways, arteries of twenty-first-century "Global Information Infrastructure," and to the latest manifesto for the conquest of the natural-technological frontier through the development of private enterprise. This is all the more true in that our contemporary era is pervaded by the crisis of the ideals of Reason and Progress, the offspring of both the Enlightenment and liberal capitalism.

The present research breaks decisively with the one-sided history of systems and theories of communication. It retraces the genesis of the uses of this term and the multiform realities it has been designating, revealing, or masking in each historical period. Rather than seek the remote sources of "communication" in Egyptian papyruses, cave art, and the Assyrian postal system, I have situated the long process of its invention at the moment when a field of practical and theoretical knowledge began to take shape around the notion of communication as a system of thought and power and as a mode of government. For this was the moment when the ideology of communication, which is at the heart of representations of modernity and postmodernity, took its first steps. For the present edition I have made various additions scattered throughout the book. On a more personal level, I wish to thank Susan Emanuel for the dialogue during the process of translation, and James A. Cohen for accompanying me in the patient work of revising.

Introduction: Flow, Bond, Space, and Measure

"Communication: a term with a great number of meanings" — this statement does not date from the end of our millennium but from 1753. So begins the article that Denis Diderot devoted to the term in the *Encyclopédie,* the Enlightenment opus edited by himself and Jean d'Alembert.

Already in that era communication spoke the language of several "sciences, arts, and crafts": literature, physics, theology, the science of fortifications, penal law, highways. Its polysemy refers to ideas of sharing, community, contiguity, continuity, incarnation, and exhibition. In the *Encyclopédie,* however, the negative often tells us more than the positive, as demonstrated by the article titled "Excommunication." Written by a clergyman, it has the double merit of making us realize how much the original matrix of "communication" owes to the language of the church, while not being confined to it. Excommunication is defined in this article as the "separation from communication or trade with a person with whom one previously enjoyed it." "In this sense," the author goes on, "any man excluded from a society or a body, and with whom the members of that body no longer have communication, may be said to be excommunicated." In addition, the bodily metaphor allows us to gauge to what extent the discourse of communication is already dependent on organic references in order to be understood.

The semantic scattering of the term does not prevent Diderot from privileging one meaning when it comes to naming the "science of communicating." In the ordering of different kinds of knowledge and their connections that provides the texture of the whole *Encyclopédie,* only rhetoric has the right to that title, the "mode of understanding through reason."

Each historical period and each type of society has the communicational configuration that it deserves. With its different levels, whether economic, social, technical, or mental, and its different scales (local, national, regional, or international), this configuration produces a hegemonic concept of communication. In the movement from one configuration to another, it is important to distinguish the continuities and breaks. In the course of the time period studied here, we will observe the concept being refashioned many times into an unprecedented figure, without cutting off all connections from the elements present in the preceding mode of communication.

This history of the invention of communication is an invitation to follow a different itinerary than the one marked out by communication in its media modality. Communication will be understood here from a wider viewpoint, encompassing the multiple circuits of exchange and circulation of goods, people, and messages. This definition simultaneously covers avenues of communication, networks of long distance transmission, and the means of symbolic exchange, such as world fairs, high culture, religion, language, and of course the media. It also evokes the diverse doctrines and theories that have contributed to thinking about these phenomena. By the light of communication we take a new look at authors as different as Vauban, Quesnay, Turgot, Adam Smith, Malthus, Saint-Simon, Comte, Fourier, Cabet, Proudhon, Enfantin, Darwin, Spencer, List, Ratzel, Marey, Taylor, Tarde, Le Bon, and many other authors as well.

This history begins in the seventeenth century, in a period in which neither the media nor freedom of the press existed, and ends in the third decade of the twentieth century, at a time when the terms *mass media, mass communication,* and *mass culture* had barely emerged. In the intervening period, the focus is on the long nineteenth century, which many historians date back to the 1789 Revolution and terminate on the eve of World War I (while others go so far as to extend it until World War II). The nineteenth century sees the founding of both the basic technologies of communication and the principle of free trade.

This book opens with the first strategic formulations about the mastery of movement by Reason and the structuring of a national mercantile space by establishing a system of communication routes, a framework of analysis that sees the light of day in the kingdom of France. It closes at the moment when Fordism, in launching the practice of market studies, inaugurates the segmentation of territory in the United States in order to better communicate with target groups. It was then incumbent upon communication to ensure the welding together of serial production and mass consumption, work and entertainment, and, more generally, to bring its contribution to the technical management of opinion. This was precisely the moment when New York took the lead over London, hegemonic since the 1780s, as the center of a new world-economy. With the economy changing its leadership and geographical base, the model of universality was shaken—and with it, the very notion of cosmopolitan culture.

This archaeology of knowledge about communication is organized around four parallel histories with numerous junctions and crossing pathways.

The first deals with the domestication of flows and of a society in movement. It seeks to understand how the ideas of progress and of a perfectible society accompanied the birth of modern communication, as well as how the latter is associated with the trajectory of the ideas of freedom and emancipation, but also with those of evolution and development. At the heart of this analysis lie political arithmetic and political anatomy, the Enlightenment, Physiocracy, liberalism, and evolutionism.

The second history examines the issue of the place occupied by communication in the conception and creation of a universal social bond. It goes back to the first formulations of networks of communication as an instrument of global solidarity, and analyzes the increasing gap between promises and facts, doctrines and policies. In this respect, Saint-Simon and Saint-Simonianism are the precursors. The Universal Expositions, which displayed many ideas upheld by the proponents of industrialism, were also sites where the notions of mediation and negotiation appear in the scenarios of international and intercultural relations. In the quest for the "Universal Association," utopias and dystopias of the communitarian city represent a singular moment in the reflection on the future of technical networks and machine civilization.

The third history is interested more particularly in space. In effect, this amounts to making a genealogy of the geopolitical visions of communication. It draws up an inventory of the networks of communication and culture that in the nineteenth century accompanied the formation of hegemonies in the era of empire. It then explains the genesis of a strategic thinking upset by the new means of mobility.

Finally comes the history of normalization, that is, the emergence of an individual who can be calculated, the "man-as-measure"—on three levels. First, there was invention of the "average man," forerunner of the debates on the "criminal man" and the irruption into the city of crowds and publics. Next, it covers the constitution of areas of knowledge about the body and its movements: from chronophotography, perfected to measure the performances of athletes, and which made possible the discovery of cinematography, right up to the time-motion studies and chronometric measurement of workers' gestures in the workshop. Finally, there is the quest for a definition of the profile of consumers of cultural productions addressed to the broad majority. This research was bound up with the first steps of the institution of advertising and the gradual shift from scattered cultures to a mass culture, centrally produced according to industrial norms.

This fourth area is also an outcome, since measurement, computing, and recording have been the recurrent traits of the long process of construction of the modern mode of communication, starting with the first manifestations of "statistical reason." Between the invention of the microscope and that of the public opinion poll—between astronomical observatories and statistical observatories of human multiplicity—unfolds this history of thought about calculation. It is not by chance that the second millennium is closing with the era of cybernetics, in which communication and information play a central role.

Ever since communication—above and beyond the different meanings each era confers on it—undertook its trajectory in pursuit of the ideal of reason, the representation that has been made of it has been torn between emancipation and control, between transparency and opacity. On the one hand, there is the logic of emancipation from all hindrances and prejudices inherited from dogmatic thinking. On the other, there is the logic of constraint imposed by a social and productive order. The means of decentralization that permit escape from confinement and from mental and physical barriers allow both the unleashing of movement and the consolidation of the center with the support of the periphery. The notions of freedom and liberation associated with communication appear in a paradoxical light. To paraphrase Norbert Elias, who coined the concept of "configuration," the history of the configurations of communication is that of the diverse modalities taken by relations of interdependence tying people to each other, and the forms of control of their emotions and their impulses required by the management of large multitudes.

Only an evolutionist concept of history as cut up into successive, watertight stages might deceive us into believing that the memory of centuries does not continue to condition the contemporary mode of communication. As proof, one need only point out the kinship between the messianic discourses on the networks of steam and electricity in the nineteenth century, and those that in the twentieth accompany the policies of economic and social recovery through information high tech. Through "communication" in all its technological forms, it has been a matter of nothing less than effectuating a return to a primary community. For a long time, a straight line has been traced between communication and religion, each rediscovering the other in order to bind human beings together (*religare*). Humanity has not waited for the crumbling of certain political utopias in order to invest communication with the function of warden against the threat of disaggregation, and to demand that it create a new social bond. The boundless hopes placed in communication, this technological idealistic determinism, existed long before the twentieth-century prophets of the information society.

The progression that led us to undertake this study, following in the footsteps of our preceding book *Mapping World Communication: War, Progress, Culture,* takes the present as its point of departure. It responds to the need to take distance from a double logic.

First, we wanted to escape from the tropes of a definition that sacrifices too much to the media sphere, since this field of academic knowledge and industrial activity has proven to be intoxicating. Like any emblem of modernity, this object has ceaselessly outmoded itself, giving rise to anticipations that constantly become depreciated, and so on in an unending race. The observer forced to reckon with a volatile object of study is often reduced to succumbing to his own "relentless forward march." A one-sided analysis of the media, made to play in turn the roles of demiurge, deus ex machina, and scapegoat, is often oblivious to the growing cultural complexity of our societies. It leads us to believe that everything happens in a sphere of high visibility, whereas in fact the major stakes of the new mode of communication are not necessarily decided there.

Our other concern has been to swim against the tide of a pragmatism influenced by the development of expertise and administrative research that since the 1980s has not ceased extending its hold on ways of perceiving and speaking about communication. Forms of thought and practices of communication inspired by managerial ideology have invested the most diverse institutions and social actors. The internalization of this new mode of managing "human resources" renders ipso facto more solitary the task of developing reflection about communication within the history of modes of social regulation that accompany the mutations of power.

PART I

The Society of Flows

Chapter 1

The Paths of Reason

In the course of the seventeenth century, intellectual reform placed on the agenda a program for a science both useful and factual, from which emerged the representation of a world in movement and open to change.

The advent of communication as a project and a realization of reason descended directly from the ideal of the perfectibility of human societies. A first constellation of ideas took shape around the communication routes and the link that united them to the formation of a national space. Its principal home was France in the seventeenth and eighteenth centuries, where the transport of people, goods, and messages and the formation of a unified domestic market both faltered on the poor development of canals and roads.

Revealing the new criteria of knowledge and action, metaphors of the organism and of mechanics, of the living and the machine, were mobilized by economic and political thought to represent the new modes of regulation and organization of society.

Philosophers of Doubt and Motion

The seventeenth century dawned under the sign of the ingenious Don Quixote of La Mancha, and it waned under that of the engineer Vauban (1633–1707). The former fought in bare fields against windmills, while the latter built strongholds and directed sieges. The errant knight, whose epitaph says "He...whose courser, Rosinante hight / Long bore him many a way," is the symbol of nomadic communication. By contrast, Vauban, the architect of fortifications, who also commissioned the drawing of maps, undertook population surveys, and inventoried the differ-

3

ent means of circulation, embodies one of the first attempts to master communication. Both prepared the way for the Age of Enlightenment.

What a striking contrast between Rosinante, the horse whose "bones stuck out like the corners of a *real*," and who proves, like her rider, always ready to succumb to enchantments, and the culture of the horse that then prevailed entirely under the aegis of Mars! The equestrian culture, which dated from far back, still had much time ahead of it. One hundred and forty years after the death of Miguel de Cervantes Saavedra, the *Encyclopédie* would still speak of the horse as an "animal gifted for war" and explain with a wealth of details how, since the book of Job, the *Iliad*, and the *Aeniad*, it has always been so. In the article on "Equitation," one could read that "the horse in a sense stimulates the man in the moment of combat; its movements and its agitation calm the natural palpitation that the bravest of warriors has difficulty preventing as the first apparatus of battle appears."

Despite appearances, we are indeed embarked on a history of communication. Let us recall the analysis by Paul Virilio, the theoretician of speed, on the invention of the animal as vehicle. "Man attains one of the very first forms of relativity," he writes, "his territory will no longer be what it has been, now that the swiftness of the courser has gradually detached him from it. Places will become points of departure and arrival, shores one leaves or approaches, and surface area will be merely the limits of equestrian navigation."[1]

From the steed to the iron horse appearing at the end of the nineteenth century, the true ancestor of the tank, a long history leads up to scientific equitation, hippology, the exact science of a horse's movements. The analytical geometry of a horse's gallop leads to the mechanical art of the motor. The translation into mathematics of the movements of a horse will accompany a great change in military strategy: the gradual emergence of the idea of mobility and the mobilization of armies in the field.

Descartes, who was twenty years old when Cervantes (1547–1616) died, liked to repeat: "Give me matter and movement, and I will make you a world." The author of *Don Quixote* might have replaced the word "matter" with "imagination." Both men were former soldiers, but more especially they were philosophers of doubt, as has been magnificently analyzed by a specialist in Cervantes studies, Jean Cassou. Cervantian doubt is both a "successor to the doubt of Montaigne, cousin to the doubt of Hamlet, older brother to the doubt of Sigismond, the hero of Calderón's *Life Is a Dream*, and forerunner of the methodical doubt of Descartes."[2]

In the second part of his *Don Quixote*, published in 1615, the Spanish author dramatizes an "enchanted head" made of bronze, which is said to have been invented by a Polish disciple of a Scottish astrologer, and which, fixed to a table, answers the questions posed to it. This experiment reminds us that Spain at the time was fond of those android automatons, distant ancestors of the computer, which will come into vogue in the eighteenth century. But it is not the technical aspect of the inventions of his day that captures Cervantes's attention. What interests him is the literary myth of Pygmalion. He was, after all, the author of *Galatea,* a pastoral romance in the taste of the time, written in 1584, twenty-one years before the publication of the first part of *Don Quixote.* Galatea was the "artificial woman" of Greek mythology to whom Aphrodite, not wishing to yield to Pygmalion, gives life by penetrating into an ivory statue that he had laid in his bed, begging her to have pity on him. What fascinates the Hidalgo in these "wonderful machines" that were hunted down by the Inquisition— "the always watchful sentinels of our faith" — are their powers of illusion. Moreover, the *Quixote* episode ends with the unmasking of the ruse. It is in fact the nephew of the innkeeper who answers the guests' questions, thanks to a brass pipe linking the bronze head to the chamber underneath. "Nevertheless," notes Cervantes, "in the opinion of Don Quixote and Sancho Panza, the head continued to be enchanted."[3]

If Cervantes had lived at the end of the nineteenth century, he would probably have belonged to that line of magicians and mediums of the Academy of Prestidigitators who, from Jean-Eugène Robert-Houdin (1805–71) to Georges Méliès (1861–1938), brought about the shift from the theater of illusions to the magic lantern. Inversely, too, if Méliès had lived at the beginning of the seventeenth century, the scenario of his *Voyage à travers l'impossible,* that "unlikely venture by a group of scientists from the incoherent Geographical Society" going off to discover the King of the Stars (the Sun), would not have been outshone by the knight-errant.[4] Nor should we forget that the French pioneer of special effects also had borrowed a story from ancient myth when he filmed *Pygmalion and Galatea* in 1898 (a work that had been thought lost, until a copy was found in a Barcelona attic in 1993!).

On the other hand, Descartes, in his search for universal truth and for an order of knowledge analogous to mathematics, exercised his imagination by conceiving automata in order to prove that animals do not have a soul, feelings, or thought, and are therefore merely machines, "animal machines," which function by automatic response. His view contrasted with that of Montaigne, who thought that animals made better use of reason than did human beings.

In this light, the expression "disenchantment of the world," coined by Max Weber (1864–1920) to designate the advent of scientific and rational thought in the West, acquires a very particular resonance.

Vauban and River Topography

In Vauban's time, the absence of a fluid and coherent system of communication was still a major obstacle to the organization of a French national space.

At about the same time as Cervantes was writing *Don Quixote,* the minister of Henri IV, the Duke of Sully (1560–1641), an advocate of the free circulation of grains, had no doubt tried to develop the bases of a policy. But the basis of a policy of communication at the level of the entire country appeared only in the 1660s with Louis XIV's comptroller-general of finances, Jean-Baptiste Colbert (1619–83). Moreover, this was the era when another minister, Louvois (1641–91), effected two other essential reforms: as secretary of state for war, he reorganized the army from top to bottom by introducing discipline, creating a corps of engineers, and restructuring the military transport service; as superintendent general of the post office, he instituted the full monopoly over the conveyance of correspondence, up until then divided between the state and private institutions such as the university. Colbert completed the reform of means of transport by taking measures to ameliorate the equine stock so as to counteract the increasing dependence of the kingdom at war on foreign horses. Three edicts organized the construction and administration of the national stud farms and created the label "royal stallion."

Cartographic surveys of the kingdom began when Colbert hired Jean Dominique Cassini (1625–1712), the first in a family dynasty of astronomers and geographers. The production of maps had been dominated since the second half of the sixteenth century by Amsterdam publishers and geographers. Vauban created the corps of geographical engineers and took stock of the need for and progress of communication routes, in particular waterways. Navigation projects were at that time the nearly exclusive responsibility of the military engineering corps.

In 1699, Vauban composed a memorandum on "river navigation"—he enumerated more than 190 routes—in which he evaluated case by case the possibilities for rendering navigable those rivers that were not yet so, by means of canals "to communicate the navigation of rivers one with another." This project was the crowning effort in his unceasing labors to improve river navigation, which, according to his estimates, was potentially twenty-five times more economical than land transportation.

Vauban insisted on the importance of better management of taxes with a view to providing the resources necessary for these large-scale projects, indispensable for commerce. He concluded:

If the king should take a liking for it and put some effort into it, the greatest good that could ever happen to this kingdom would ensue, thanks to easier circulation of foodstuffs, which would procure a considerable increase in them, and consequently a rise in well-being and convenience, and a very great ease for the provinces in helping each other in expensive years and in times of war.[5]

This idea of interprovincial solidarity had been in the air since its formulation by Antoine de Montchrestien at the start of the century. In his *Traité d'Œconomie Politique* (1615)—it was the first time this term "political economy" appeared—this mercantilist author advanced the necessity of an "intranational division of labor" (while refusing the idea of an international division).

As for the older and more general idea of reciprocal dependence, which one finds in Vauban and many others, it is by no means foreign to the meaning that for a long time was conferred on the word "communication" by reducing it to "commerce." In the article that the *Encyclopédie* devoted to this topic in 1753, we read:

By commerce we mean in a general sense a *reciprocal communication*. It applies more particularly to the communication that men have with each other in the productions of their lands and their industry. Infinite Providence, whose creation is nature, has willed, by the variety that It spreads, putting men into dependence on each other: the Supreme Being has formed links in order to bring peoples to preserve peace among themselves and to love each other...This reciprocal dependence of men, by the variety of commodities that they can furnish each other, extends to real needs and to the needs of opinion.

Did not Montesquieu also say that "the history of commerce is that of communication"?

Colbert's policy was in harmony with Vauban's judgments. It grants priority to inland navigation routes. The invention of locks by two Italian engineers from Viterbo, in the sixteenth century, had made possible the creation of canals. The first test of a lock—the idea of which had been brought to France by Leonardo da Vinci—took place on the Vilaine River in Brittany in the period 1538–75. The first great canal, running from Briare on the Loire, the foremost French river, was to Buges on Seine, a distance of fifty-nine kilometers. Although its construction began at the start of the century under the auspices of Sully, it would not be inaugurated until 1642.

The first stroke of the pickax in the building of the Midi canal was struck in 1663; this "canal for the junction of seas" was completed in 1684. It ran 240 kilometers, with a width of thirty-eight meters. It was the first canal of such a magnitude constructed in Europe. To achieve it, the supervisor of the project, Pierre Paul Riquet (1604–80), applied for the first time a complex hydraulic mechanics. Another innovation was the use by civil engineering of gunpowder to dig a tunnel. These great projects could not have been carried out without a meticulous method of personnel management. In contrast with the usual labor situation of the time, under Riquet fixed wages, benefits, and even retirement plans ensured a spirit of emulation. At the origin of this great royal project was a strategic aim: the navy had to be able to move from the Atlantic to the Mediterranean while avoiding Gibraltar. Ultimately, however, the canal would not prove wide enough to allow warships through and it could only transport equipment, arms, and troops.[6]

Vauban himself drew up the plans for four other canals, notably that of Orléans (begun in 1679 and finished in 1690). Nevertheless, all this work amounted to little with respect to the infrastructural needs of a domestic market. But it was enough for the German historian of transportation, Richard von Kaufmann, in a book published in the last years of the nineteenth century, to see in it, retrospectively, the birth of the star-shaped network that will mark networks that come later:

> The examination of the configuration of France, which would later suggest to the government the best plan for the establishment of a network of railways, already indicated to [Vauban] the importance of the country's natural navigable waterways, their extension, and their junction by canals. And thus a network of interior navigation was established, radiating from the center of the country just as the great railway lines were to do.[7]

Whether or not it was a structuring effect of a natural configuration, Paris for Vauban could only be the "true heart of the kingdom," the "common mother of Frenchmen and the summation of France." "If the Prince is to the state what the head is to the human body, which cannot be doubted," he wrote in 1689,

> one could say that the capital city of this state is what the heart is to this same body, since the heart is considered the first organ to be alive and the last to die; the principle of life, the source and seat of natural warmth, from whence it spreads to all the parts of the body, which it animates and sustains until the body has totally ceased to live.[8]

The Bridge Engineers

Meanwhile, the construction of roads throughout the national territory met with abundant administrative resistance. Colbert created the Ponts et Chaussées, which was entrusted in 1669 with the building and maintenance of "bridges, roads, canals, rivers, and ports." The engineering corps of Ponts et Chaussées, organized in the form of a pyramid as civil servants of the state, would be definitively constituted in 1716.

Since the beginning of the sixteenth century, jurists had recognized the public character of routes, bringing them into the "domain of the sovereign." But it was only in 1705 that a royal writ began to lay the foundations of a normalization of the layout and traffic (via expropriation, alignments, duties and obligations of bordering residents, weights, and types of means of transportation, etc.). In 1720, another ruling fixed the width of routes and the planting of their banks. In 1731, road police became necessary

> to prohibit all rubble collectors, plowmen, wine growers, gardeners, and others from filling in the ditches and cutting down the embankments that line the major routes, and along this distance to prevent them, in their plowing or otherwise, from dumping any rubble, dung, refuse, and other impediments to public passage, . . . from digging up the cobblestones from Paris streets, and likewise from the roadways of the faubourgs, suburbs, and public lanes.[9]

It was not until 1738 that the century's great founding document for the policy of road systems was formulated (the equivalent of which in the following century would be the 1842 law on the construction of the railway network). These instructions from the comptroller-general, Jean Orry, also established the use of forced labor [*corvée*] for the "building of roads." But the introduction of this use of forced labor, in fact, dated back further, that is, to the last years of Louis XIV's reign (1661–1715), when it was necessary to make the routes practicable for the transport of munitions in the provinces affected by war. Certain intendants drew lessons from this experience and extended it to peacetime. But the first road administrations were not able to shield their management from the control of treasurers. This would not occur until 1743, with the creation of the Détail des Ponts et Chaussées, entrusted to Daniel Trudaine (1703–69), who maintained the separation of technical services from financial services.

In 1744 began a systematic charting of the national territory, as large-scale topography made its appearance. A central bureau of draftsmen, the embryo of the future École des Ponts et Chaussées, was created by Trudaine "for the supervision and inspection by geographers and draftsmen of maps for the routes and great avenues of the kingdom."[10] The grandson of Colbert's geographer, César Cassini de Thury (1714–84), relying on a vast triangulation of the country, made the first large-scale map (at 1/86,400). This effort was achieved thanks to voluntary contributions and under the auspices of the Académie des Sciences. The gradual replacement of Cassini's atlas by the map of the general staff of armies was not complete until 1831, when the corps of geographical engineers founded by Vauban was in fact incorporated into the general staff. (The publication of this topographical map, with a scale of 1/80,000, would last from 1832 to 1880.)

In 1747, Trudaine presided over the creation of the École des Ponts et Chaussées (which did not, in fact, take this name until the early 1770s). Seventy to eighty students were trained there at a time. The most advanced ones taught the others skills including arithmetic, hydraulics, drafting, stonecutting, and the calculation of the pavement area. All students learned architecture, physics, chemistry, and mineralogy from the foreign professors at the school. Then they were all sent into the field to "become educated in the practice of constructions: drafting of plans, surveying, and so on."[11]

In their actual practice, these engineers, in attempting to master the different phases in the development of a construction project, questioned the old mode of labor organization through corporations and guilds. At the same time as an "esprit de corps" was formed, the foundations of a new ideal were developed, guided by technical and economic rationality and an ideology of the relation of communication with Nature and Reason.

Communication had the mission of bringing about a rational and "good" nature—since there was also such a thing as irrational and "bad" nature, a nature that separates, interposes itself between men, and lies at the root of prejudices. This point is clearly explained by Yves Chicoteau and Antoine Picon, historians of the École, in the conclusion to a groundbreaking study of the dissertations ("the style competition") organized for the bridge-building pupils under the Old Regime:

> By introducing a distance between terms that Reason nevertheless
> ought to bring together, this fundamentally bad nature ought to be
> combated. This is the whole meaning of an engineer's deeds,
> establishing communication routes, building bridges across
> precipices to bring men together. To illustrate this viewpoint, the
> metaphor of famine was very frequently used by engineers of the
> Ponts et Chaussées. By separating men, nature creates the

conditions of scarcity, since it allows one province to overflow with grain while another lacks everything. The engineer is therefore invested with a mission to "correct" these inequalities by allowing the circulation of commodities. Transposed, this conception makes the engineer the privileged servant of Reason since he combats prejudices by making men communicate. The eighteenth century considered, in effect, that prejudices were born of isolation, whereas Reason fought them by making possible the coming together of individuals.[12]

For these engineers, this coming together, which corresponds to an ideal nature, becomes identical with the map as a projection of a rational system in which everything should communicate.

Thus, in France under the Old Regime the basis of a body of ideas on "communications" began to be formed, that is, a proper mode of thinking about the relations between movement, the economy, and society, between "networks," the state, and national unity. As Fernand Braudel would point out at the end of the 1970s:

> Given the huge dimensions of France, it is clear that progress in transportation was crucial to the unification of country, though it was by no means adequate at this stage, as has been pointed out with reference to periods closer to our own time by the historian Jean Bouvier (who maintains that the national market did not exist in France before the completion of the railway network) and the economist Pierre Uri (who goes even further, claiming categorically that present-day France will only be a true economic unit when the telephone system has reached "American-style perfection"). They are no doubt right. But the admirable engineers of the Ponts et Chaussées who built the eighteenth-century roads were certainly responsible for progress towards a French national market.[13]

In contrast, in England at the beginning of the eighteenth century, the question of circulation and communication was no longer the subject of theoretical debate. It was already anchored in the reality of a domestic market, generator of exchanges and ties, whose formation had been accelerated by the Irish expedition and the victory over Scotland. The kingdom rid itself very early of many of its tolls and other internal barriers, and its system of communication was national. The attraction of the capital, a sole and enormous head (with 10 percent of the population), and a network of coastal navigation and waterways were combined in the establishment of the national space. Substantial investments in the first quarter of the eighteenth century brought to completion a network of navigable rivers extending 1,160 miles, which put the greater part of the country at no more than fifteen miles from water transportation.[14] This was facilitated by considerable advantages: not only a more compact territory and, unlike the continent, a nobility of gentlemen-entrepreneurs experienced in pecuniary rationality, but also very regular rivers, easy to deepen, which did not wash along alluvial deposits and which were separated by level surfaces that were easily cut through by junction canals.

France, on the other hand, was a giant divided against itself, always torn between Lyons and Paris, and was still in search of its unification via the market. Five-sixths of its population lived in the countryside, and the other sixth originated from it or lived off it. England, strengthened by its conquest of its domestic market, and whose cities contained about 30 percent of the population, had already begun to dream of making itself the center of a new "world-economy." But she would still have to wait until the 1780s to supplant Amsterdam.

Toward a Useful Science

"Social evolution is becoming oriented toward a structure based on calculation."[15] This was Vauban's conviction. His goal was to organize a new order in which the handling of numbers would make possible a "more regulated conduct" that "would overcome chaos and confusion." In addition to the "routes of communication" dimension, this general project included two others.

It began with the construction of strongholds. After the construction of the fortress of Lille, begun in 1667, Vauban, who served successively as commissioner general of fortifications (1678), lieutenant general of the army (1688), and marshal of France (1705), built thirty-three others and restored ten times that number in the four corners of a national territory that, from 1667 to 1689, would change borders three times (with the treaties of Aachen and Nijmegen and the truce of Ratisbon).

In an opuscule published in The Hague in 1685 entitled simply *Le Directeur général des fortifications,* Vauban recorded his experience with the architecture of fortresses:

> It is necessary to establish a uniform order in all places that one fortifies, which establishes and separates the functions of those who are in charge of them, and who organize and distribute their tasks according to the needs of the project, and the capacity of each, so as to employ only useful and necessary people, and not to entrust anyone with what he does not do, nor what he cannot do; this fault of not taking care being customarily the origin and the source of all disorders in the supervision of fortifications.

And he continued: "To achieve the establishment of such an order, it is necessary to go into detail concerning the major positions, and to provide an idea of them, so as to make known to those who occupy them what should be the duties of their charge, and up to what point their function extends."[16] These were the tasks Vauban tried to accomplish in his instruction manual.

Some two hundred years before Taylor, this forerunner of the scientific organization of labor invented the system of the "route card" for each "function," each "job," and each "task." Prefiguring the work of the American engineer with a view to suppressing "systematic soldiering" (loafing) by workers in the workshops of the great steel mills, he hunted down "mischief" and tried to remedy it: "The worker who is assured of his wages never hurries, whereas the one who earns only as much as he works for never needs any other carrot than his own interest."[17] In this rationalization of work, it is difficult for Vauban not to question forced labor:

> One must avoid all work by forced labor if it demands some skill and promptness, given that diligence and expertise are never found among people who work only by force and try only to make the time pass; but when one is obliged to use it for moving earth, one must impose the quantity that one wants moved, and distribute it by community.[18]

This director general of fortifications who initiated the chronometric measurement of excavation also had the idea of implementing systematic timing of cannon shooting, as Michel Foucault notes.

Another field of calculation and evaluation dear to Vauban was the survey. In 1686, he wrote a "Méthodologie générale et facile pour faire le dénombrement des peuples" (General and simple methodology for counting populations), and in 1696 he levied a "counting of the populations, land resources, woods, and beasts of the fiscal subdivision of Vézelay," the region of his birth; he followed this by commissioning a vast survey from intendants between 1697 and 1700. He even produced a text on "pig breeding, including estimates of the potential production of sows in ten years' time."[19] He also attempted to calculate the chances for the growth of families populating the Canadian colonies up to the year 1970! Vauban proposed generalizing his counting projects. He indicated the path to follow in creating a corps of "officers or commissioners for the counting of peoples," and conceived the "tabular forms" to realize this operation. The organization of such operations at a national level must, according to him, obey a military principle. He proposed "dividing people into groups of one hundred [décuries], like the Chinese, or into companies, like our regiments, and creating parish captains, who would have under them a lieutenant for each fifty or so houses, who would in turn be under the orders of the commander, where commanders are present." In each division, the captain and his two lieutenants were to visit the fifty families four times a year, going from house to house. They were to have each member of the family—men, women and children—introduced to them and would "be informed about changes and new events that occur and would record these in a register, to be renewed every year."[20]

This meticulous description of the procedures of counting appears in *La dîme royale* (The royal tithe), a book printed without the king's knowledge in 1707, the date of its author's death, but it had been finished eight years previously. It was written in support of a vigorous appeal to reevaluate the system of a tax imposition that would weigh the heaviest on that "portion of the people so useful and so despised, who have suffered so much, and who suffer still." Vauban's proposals were backed up by figures worthy of a modern conception of taxes, with each person paying "in proportion to his income."[21]

The historical period in which Vauban's research manifested a "structure based on calculation" as a way of escaping from chaos was the moment of the emergence of utilitarian science.

In 1667, Colbert founded the Paris Observatory, whose organization he entrusted to Jean Dominique Cassini. The previous year, the king had authorized a group of scholars to meet in his library at the Louvre; they formed the embryo of the Académie Royale des Sciences. In England, Charles II had chartered in 1662 the Royal Society of London for Improving Natural Knowledge by Experiments. As Lewis Mumford reminds us, this scientific institution was founded under the impetus initially provided by the merchants of the City of London. The new instruments for scrutinizing the universe of constellations and for determining the planets' laws of motion accompanied the struggle for the conquest of foreign markets and naval hegemony.

In France, the merger of the interests of the state and those of science, which opened the way to modern cartography, triggered the first geodesic study and the first detailed survey of the country's coasts, as a prelude to a vast plan of naval expansion.

In 1676, five years after the perfection of Newton's telescope, England built an observatory. There was nothing innocent about its location in Greenwich Park, which dominates the mouth of the Thames.

A quarter century earlier, Oliver Cromwell, by means of the Navigation Act, had opted for customs and maritime protectionism. This policy, inspired by mercantilism, liberalized trade within the national perimeter, while foreign trade was protected, sustained, and propelled by the state. Passed by the Rump Parliament, which was later dismantled as a result of the English victories in Scotland, the Navigation Act stipulated that any European ship landing in England could bring in only the products of its own country; the merchandise of other continents could be imported only by English vessels. These measures would not be abolished until the second half of the nineteenth century with the rise of free trade, when the British Empire reinforced, over its home territory first, the bases of its world hegemony and constructed its naval strength.

One of the first missions entrusted by the king to the English Observatory was to resolve the old problem of the measurement of longitudes at sea, that is to say, the calculation of the position of ships in relation to east and west. David S. Landes, the American historian of machines to measure time, observes:

The pernicious effects of ignorance of longitude were multiplied by the consequences for cartography. The map, after all, was the primary medium for the transmission of information and experience in matters of navigation—just as the book was in other areas of knowledge. In the international contest for access to the riches of the Indies, maps were money, and secret agents of aspiring powers paid gold for copies of the carefully guarded Portuguese *padrons*. Bad measurements made bad maps, though, and many a ship spent precious days searching for land that showed only on paper. Cartographers had a dearth of accurate information and a plethora of guesses to go by, so that even contemporaneous maps differed in detail... Cartographic inaccuracies, with all the dangers they entailed, persisted into the nineteenth century, largely because astronomical methods of ascertaining longitude, the only ones then available, were so unreliable.[22]

It was only in the nineteenth century that this enigma would finally deliver its secret, with the invention of the marine chronometer and the drawing up of detailed tables of the moon's positions. Its resolution would mobilize numerous clock makers and scientists, astronomers and mathematicians. Their experimentations would mark not only the progress of inventions of "automatic machines to measure time" more and more precisely, but more generally mark the history of thought about calculation.

Discovery of Circulatory Movement

The philosopher and Lord Chancellor of England, Francis Bacon (1561–1626), established the principles of a science based on facts. His *Novum Organum* (1620) is a plea for a theory of scientific progress, and for progress itself through science—a science founded on experiments and observation and capable of inventing the means of "making us better and more happy" and "making human life gentler." In this era, the secular inertia of dogma was challenged and people began to believe in the virtue of movement. The world came to be seen as perfectible.

The idea of circulation, to which the genesis of the modern concept of communication was indissolubly linked, saw the light of day in the laboratories of this scientific Reformation. It was the "first biological revolution" that caused it to flourish.[23] The method of microscopic observation contributed to the constitution of human anatomy and comparative anatomy as well as early physiology.

In 1628, the work of William Harvey (1578–1657), *Exercitatio anatomica de motu cordis et sanguinis in animalibus,* overturned millenarian ideas about blood circulation. The ancient theory of Claude Galien (131–201) asserted that only the veins contained blood, product of a transformation of the chyle formed from digested food. The English doctor discovered the mechanism of circulation and described the heart's movements: blood arrives in the heart by the veins and leaves by the arteries, with heartbeats producing a perpetual movement in the closed circuit. This was the first representation of the mechanism of an organic function.

Some forty years later, the Italian naturalist and physician Marcello Malpighi (1628–94) completed this physiological discovery by showing how the passage of the blood from the arteries to the veins takes place. This founder of microscopic anatomy, the future histology, performed the first complete anatomical study of an invertebrate (the silkworm) and proceeded to a systematic and comparative study of different animal and vegetable tissues. On this occasion he imported into science the word "network," which until then had been reserved for lace making. Malpighi's "network" was at first the "reticulated matter of the skin," only observable thanks to the new microoptics. The microscopes that appeared around 1615 in fact remained prototypical until around 1660.

To express his discovery of the blood's circulatory movement, it is true that Harvey drew on the mechanical image of the lift and force pump. But he also had recourse to an astronomical image in which he compared the heart to the sun as that which occupies the central place in the water cycle, with its evaporation and its condensation into clouds and rain, and then the return of water to the earth, renewing the cycle. This metaphor indicates that before this revolution in knowledge affecting physical bodies, there had been another that had changed the understanding of celestial bodies. In 1543, Nicholas Copernicus's essay *De revolutionibus orbium coelestium* had undermined the scholastic dogma of geocentrism, the belief in a cosmos formed around the earth, with the latter at the summit of the celestial hierarchy. In less than a century and a half, an epistemological upheaval took place: from the closed world to an infinite universe. This shift began with Copernicus, and it continued with Johannes Kepler (1571–1630), author of *Mysterium cosmographicum* (The secret of the world) (1596), who in 1611 perfected an astronomical telescope.[24] It culminated with Isaac Newton (1642–1727), who in 1687 assembled into a coherent whole the vision of a homogeneous and infinite universe. It was through its application to Copernican cosmology that the term "system" would make its breakthrough at the end of the seventeenth century, and become common in the philosophical discourse of the eighteenth century.[25] It was also via this science that the term "revolution" would make its entry into political vocabulary.

Meanwhile, we owe to the discovery of blood circulation the paradigm of bodily mechanics, with its law of functional physiological necessity from which the discourses on communication and society would never cease to draw metaphors.

Political Arithmetic and Anatomy of the Social Organism

Vauban put the bodily analogy to work to express the bonds that organically unite a sovereign power and its subjects—in other words, the center of the map and the flows emanating from it and draining toward it. Flow starts from the center and ends up there.

Some fifty years after the death of the author of *La dîme royale,* Jean-Jacques Rousseau (1712–78) would provide, in the article "Économie publique ou politique" (Public or political economy) written for the *Encyclopédie,* an actual working drawing of the bodily metaphor to express a kind of communication that gives life and confers unity on the body politic as an organized body and as a "moral being."

> The laws and customs are the brain, point of origin of the nerves, and seat of understanding, the will, and the senses; hence the judges and magistrates are the organs; commerce, industry, and agriculture are the mouth and stomach that prepare communal subsistence; public finances are the blood that a wise economy, in performing the functions of the heart, sends out to distribute the nourishment of life throughout the body; the citizens are the body and the members that make the machine move, live and work . . . The life of both is the "I" common to all, reciprocal sensibility, and the internal correspondence of all parts. Does this communication cease, the formal unity disappear, and do the contiguous parts cease to belong to each other except by juxtaposition? Then the man is dead or the state is dissolved.

These are indices, among many others, of the fact that the organism is on its way to imposing itself as a matrix of understanding among thinkers and rulers. The metaphor serves to shape the scenario of a world perceived in its systematicity.

In a reference work entitled *Les Métaphores de l'organisme* published in 1971, Judith Schlanger studied the role of *analogon* played by the idea of the organism at the end of the eighteenth century and in the nineteenth. Before this period, she observes, one could say that political analogies remained "most naively anthropomorphic," but also "most rigorously methodological and positive, since from knowledge of the living to the knowledge of political society there is no transposition of intuition but a transfer of procedures and norms of scientific knowledge."[26] This observation applies perfectly to the first attempts to formulate a science of the economy under the sign of mercantilism.

The precursors of political economy and statistics spoke of "political anatomy," an expression coined by Sir William Petty (1623–87) and developed in his *Political Anatomy of Ireland*. This frontier of Europe, subjected in 1641 to fire and blood by Cromwell, had since then been totally subjugated to the English market and was on the way to becoming the first peripheral country of the future British Empire, the first link in its "world-economy"; the weapons and prejudices of colonial oppression were sharpened there. With its production oriented to the needs of the metropolis, Ireland specialized in raising livestock and the export of salted beef and pork, to which the indigenous people never had access. In his satire *A Modest Proposal for Preventing the Children of Poor People from Being a Burden to Their Parents or Their Country*, the Irishman Jonathan Swift (1667–1745) proposed in 1729 that to solve the problem of begging, the children of beggars be exported like butchers' meat. As for Petty, he quite seriously expressed the wish that all the inhabitants of Ireland (and Scotland) be transported to England and that these countries then be submerged in the sea.

In the preface to his book, sailor and military doctor William Petty explicitly invokes Francis Bacon in order to establish a parallel between the natural body and the body politic, and thereby justify his scientific enterprise.

As students in medicine practice inquiries on cheap and common animals, and such whose actions they are best acquainted with, where there is the least confusion and perplexure of Parts, I have chosen Ireland as such a Political Animal, who is scarce twenty years old, where the Intrigue of the State is not very complicate, and with which I have been conversant from an Embryon state . . . 'Tis true, the curious Dissections cannot be made without variety of proper Instruments; whereas I have had only a common knife, and a "Clout", instead of the many more helps such a Work requires: however, my rude approaches being enough to find whereabout the Liver and Spleen, and Lungs lye, tho' not to discern the Lymphatick Vessels, the Plexus, the Choriodus, the Volvuli of vessels within the Testicles.[27]

Money is envisaged as the "fat of the Body-Politick...that lubricates the motion of muscles, feeds in want of Victuals, fills up uneven Cavities, and beautifies the body," in the same way as a state's money "quickens its Actions, feeds from abroad in the time of Dearth at Home, even accounts by reason of its divisibility, and beautifies the whole." In excess, it wears down agility. Tradesmen, in this bodily economy, fulfill the "role of veins and arteries, to distribute in a circulatory movement the blood of the nourishing sap of the Body-Politick."

In 1698, the Englishman Charles Davenant (1656–1714) would write that "commerce and industry are the only intermediaries that can assure the digestion of the gold and silver by which the body of the State is nourished."[28] And he would cite the example of colonial Spain where "the stomach of the State's body" — that is, the consuming population — could not "digest" overabundant silver from the mines. The Scot John Law (1671–1729), comptroller-general of finances in France, would make money the blood of the body-state and would define the bank as "heart of the kingdom where all money must return to recommence circulation."[29]

With Petty, the metaphor of the bodily economy serves to articulate a project of constructing a science of measurement. Diagnostics are allied with therapeutics.

To assert the necessity of developing "appropriate instruments" so as to "know the symmetry of the body politic, its structure and its proportions," he wrote, and thus to "treat" it, means to adopt a method: "to express my Self in Terms of *Number, Weight* or *Measure,* to use only Arguments of Sense, and to consider only such Causes as have visible Foundations in Nature; leaving those that depend upon the mutable Minds, Opinions, Appetites and Passions of particular Men to the Consideration of others."[30] Petty placed this manifesto for a science of social observation at the beginning of his essay on *Political Arithmetick,* whose classic edition appeared in London in 1690, but which had largely been written in 1671. The subtitle indicated the breadth of the project: "Discourse concerning the extent and value of lands, peoples, buildings, husbandry, manufactures, commerce, fishery, artizans, seamen, soldiers, publick revenues, interest, taxes, superlucration, registeries, banks, valuation of men, increasing of seamen, of militia's, harbours, situation, shipping, power at sea, etc." We are witnessing the first steps of mathematical economic reasoning, the faltering beginnings of demographic research.

Historians of statistics situate the birth of probability calculation, as a "procedure aiming to lay the basis for rationality of choices in situations of incertitude,"[31] between 1650 and 1660. In 1654, Blaise Pascal (1623–62) invented the "geometry of chance" in response to a question from the chevalier de Méré regarding how to share a stake equitably among players in case of the game's being interrupted. Three years later, the Dutch physicist and astronomer Christiaan Huyghens (1629–95), following up Pascal's analyses, published his *Calculation of Games of Chance* and formulated, with the help of his brother, the first table of mortality.

The question of human multiplicity in relation to subsistence—already present in the works of Machiavelli, Thomas More, Thomas Hobbes, and Francis Bacon—gave rise to research on laws governing population changes.

In 1662, a London merchant, John Graunt (1620–74), published his *Observations upon the Bills of Mortality,* based on the city's civil registers, which he compared with those of a Hampshire parish.[32] In 1693 appeared extended mortality tables calculated by the astronomer Edmund Halley (1656–1742), whose major concern was actuarial: to determine scientifically life insurance premiums, which at first were accessory to maritime and fire insurance. He was trying to derive, from what was still just a series of game combinations or bets on human life, a means of measuring probability for those whose work relied on the fundamental notion of risk and the magnitude of the chances to which they were subject. But the first life insurance company relying on scientific calculations would not be founded until 1762 in England; known as the Society of Equitable Insurance, this company modulated the annuities of its insurance in proportion to life expectancy and age groups. The long tradition of maritime insurance had placed England in the lead of research on the extension of the formula to other domains, notably fire insurance. The first company to insure against this risk was founded in 1696, also in London. The Great Fire that had ravaged certain parts of the city for four days in September 1666 seems to have been crucial in the launching of this policy.

The first works of political arithmetic, the first demographic and statistical studies, and even the first calculation of the country's national product by Gregory King (1648–1712) linked theory to practice. This is not surprising when one knows that men like Locke and Newton were technicians of the monetary problem.[33] Thus a new social role took shape. With Graunt, Petty, and Davenant, we have the birth of "expertise," as the historian of "statistical reason" Alain Desrosières notes: "The expert with precise skills proposes his techniques to the rulers and tries to convince them that, in order to realize their plans, they must go through him. He offers a precisely articulated language."[34]

Despite the omnipresence of the organic metaphor in the analyses offered by this embryonic political economy, one of the future central concepts of communication, the network, still remained outside this language of the living. In the seventeenth century, as in the following one, the term "network" did not leave the orbit of medical language, where it had been introduced, as mentioned earlier, by Malpighi in transplanting a term found in lace making. Thus, in the *Encyclopédie* the word maintained no relation to communication, not even in the article that treated "routes, byways, and paths" on the same footing, insisting on the importance of the heritage of the infrastructure and construction techniques of the Roman Empire. Network still spoke exclusively—the article dates from 1765—the language of thread and silks. It was defined as a "work of simple thread, gold or silver or silk thread, woven in a way that has meshes and openings." The age of the network is not yet born.

In her critical work on organic totalities, cited earlier, Judith Schlanger writes: "Representations linked to the notion of the political organism were situated in a complex intellectual space in which the historical state of biological concepts interpenetrated with political convictions and feelings in search of justifications and formulations."[35] To this it could be added that there was also an interpenetration with the state of and trends in techniques of communication, especially when one measures the role of *analogon* that would be played by the idea of the organism, from the nineteenth century onward, in the formation of the ideology of communication, which is also that of the network.

A completely different signifying environment of metaphors would then appear: "The notion of the organism, in its diverse elements," notes Schlanger,

became generalized and absolutized into the archetype of rationality. The organism then no longer designates an important but localized order of phenomena that are the object of a body of knowledge: it refers to a complex of meanings on the basis of which all knowledge is organized by right. The term "organism" becomes endowed with a power of rational integration to which one could only feebly compare the current role [the author is writing in 1971] of the notion of *structure*: it is no longer one of the natural phenomena, it is the very *type* of rational reality. In this sense one could speak of a true organic rationality.[36]

Vaucanson, La Mettrie, Sade, the Machine, and the System

Another metaphor beside that of the living organism also flourished in the eighteenth century: that of the mechanism, which was fed by the automatic machine, that ancestor of the programming that "enchanted" Don Quixote and his squire. This theme of the machine should not be understood in opposition to organic thought, since "one and the other are figures of organization, and hence of harmony."[37]

Jacques de Vaucanson (1709–82) undertook to construct living anatomies reproducing the principal vital functions of respiration, digestion, circulation. He invented in succession a mechanical flute player and an artificial duck, exhibited in Paris in 1738. In 1745, he imagined the first automatic loom, without, however, being able to realize it, and then tackled the conception of an "automatic speaker." The *Encyclopédie* celebrated the drawing of the inventor who, as a worthy representative of the Enlightenment, allows for the viewing of mechanisms in the digestion process of his glass duck, in order to "demonstrate rather than simply show a machine."

"Automatic machines for measuring time"—pendulum clocks and watches—had also made considerable progress. In 1637, Galileo had conceived of the pendulum clock, without, however, succeeding in making one work. In 1656, Christiaan Huyghens made the first clock with a hanging pendulum. In 1673, the same Huyghens published *The Pendulum Clock (Horologium oscillatorium)*. In 1690, the Englishman John Floyer added the second-hand needle, in order to count arterial pulses with precision. In the 1760s, the Englishman John Harrison and the Frenchman Pierre Le Roy, each on his own, perfected a first marine clock.[38] With the clock mechanism began a theory of the "production of regular motion," which led in the eighteenth century to the idea of applying automatic devices moved by springs to industrial production processes.

The *Encyclopédie* devotes an article to clocks in 1765. Relying henceforth on the "theory of the body in motion" that includes what "geometry, calculation, mechanics, and physics possess of the most sublime," its author stresses that their great contribution is to have turned a mechanical art that "required only manpower" into a science in which manpower is no longer necessary. The metaphor of the clock, the emblematic figure of "the machine of machines"—*machina machinarum*—serves for Denis Diderot (1713–84) to illustrate the concept of "system."

> A *system* is nothing more than the arrangement of the different elements of an art or a science in an order that makes them mutually dependent; the primary elements lead to and account for

the final ones. Those which explain the others are called *principles,* and the *system* is all the more perfect as the principles are fewer in number: it is even to be desired that they be reduced to one. For just as there is a principal spring in a clock on which all the others depend, there is also in all *systems* a first principle to which the different elements that compose it are subordinated.[39]

Others claimed authority from this knowledge of the mechanisms of these automatic machines in order to draw an equivalency between them and the human body and to speak of a "man-machine." Vaucanson's innovation constituted a key moment in the development of this mechanistic materialism.

In 1747, the year before the publication of the first volume of the *Encyclopédie,* the doctor Julien Offray de La Mettrie (1709–51) published anonymously in Leyden, the high spot of "iatromechanicism" (a doctrine that reduced the body's vital functions to physical and mechanical phenomena) a work bearing the precise title of *L'Homme-Machine* (Man a machine). "The body is but a watch, whose watchmaker is the new chyle," he postulated.[40] And more explicitly:

> The human body is a watch, a large watch constructed with such skill and ingenuity that if the wheel which marks the seconds happens to stop, the minute wheel turns and keeps on going its round; and in the same way the quarter-hour wheel, and all the others go on running when the first wheels have stopped because rusty or, for any reason, out of order.[41]

Thus an intellectual link can be traced from the technician Vaucanson and the physician-philosopher La Mettrie, who saw in the creations of the former the first work of a "new Prometheus." "In its perception of Vaucanson's automata," explains Paul-Laurent Assoun, an exegete of *L'Homme-Machine,*

> the scientific perspective sees not only the workings of a mechanics that imitates the living, but also the living itself, long identified as mechanical, that avows its truth. Reality admits itself as fiction in the intuition delivered by the automaton... Not that the automaton would itself give the idea of the man-machine; but as soon as the man-machine is allowed to be *seen* in its own guise, a necessity is imposed on philosophical discourse to *name* it — a task long postponed — and to ground it in discourse.[42]

The individual body is a machine and the collective body is a machinery whose organization responds to a mechanics of the same nature. According to La Mettrie, "organization is the prime merit of man, the source of all others; instruction is the second."[43] This book of the classical age delivers, then, an organic vision of social mechanisms. This leads Michel Foucault to note that it is written in two registers,

> the anatomico-metaphysical register, of which Descartes wrote the first pages and which the physicians and philosophers continued, and the technico-political register, which was constituted by a whole set of regulations and by empirical and calculated methods relating to the army, the school and the hospital, for controlling or correcting the operations of the body... La Mettrie's *L'Homme-Machine* is both a materialist reduction of the soul and a general theory of *dressage*, at the centre of which reigns the notion of "docility", which joins the analyzable body to the manipulable body.[44]

La Mettrie is located in a historical trajectory that extends from the sixteenth century to the nineteenth, the establishment of a new "anatomy of power" by means of the technologies of surveillance, a set of minute procedures for classifying, controlling, and measuring individuals. In the course of this history, the economy of power based on the flexible "discipline mechanism," unlike the old "discipline-blockade" composed of prohibitions and interdictions, finds itself invested with a function: "to guarantee settling and to allow circulation." The exercise of this new way of producing collective will presupposes a mechanism that constrains by the gaze. It is the building of "observatories of human multiplicity":

> Side by side with the major technology of the telescope, the lens and the sight beam, which were an integral part of the new physics and cosmology, there were the minor techniques of multiple and intersecting observations, of eyes that must see without being seen; using techniques of subjection and methods of exploitation, an obscure art of light and the visible was secretly preparing a new knowledge of man.[45]

But there is more to La Mettrie: his machine thinking grounds a "sort of imperialism of pleasure." The thesis of man as machine has as its obverse side the thesis of hedonist determinism. Pleasure is commanded and ordered by the machine. While it makes individuals the "target of power," it transforms them at the same time into a "target of pleasure," indissolubly linking the one to the other.[46]

One finds in the practical approach of Vaucanson numerous elements that together constitute the notion of system as a "tool of action," such as it will emerge in the twentieth century from the works of Ludwig von Bertalanffy or other precursors of systems theory: the system as a "set of elements in interaction, oriented toward the realization of objectives." He develops a global project, a model of the whole, that isolates certain functions whose interrelations are to be organized. The latter obey a rule (command) that in certain cases is formulated with the help of a code (programming), a line of continuity discerned by Jacques Perriault in 1982. Retracing the genesis of notions of "system" and "machine," this historian of technology has not only dissected the intellectual project of the father of automata, but has identified the common points that unite him with the project defined a generation later by the Marquis de Sade (1740–1814).[47]

Roland Barthes had in 1971 already underlined the numerous references in the libertine's project to mechanics, or even to formulas close to algorithms, and went so far as to evoke programming to explain the division of roles between partners in the arrangement of the love machine, a "total machine." Employing the symbols A and B to designate these partners who have become rods and pistons, Sade grounded their identity in that of an automatic group: "The Sadean machine," notes Barthes,

> does not stop at the automaton; the whole living group is conceived, constructed like a machine...what defines it is the interlocking of all the parts...which interconnect as though they knew their role by heart and without any improvisation being necessary...Once in operation, it shakes and makes a bit of noise, owing to the convulsive movements of the participants. There remains but to look after it, like a good unskilled worker who paces along, lubricating, tightening, regulating, changing, etc.[48]

The Sadean scene and practice are dominated by a "grand idea of order" in which "deregulations" respond to this principle, too. It is a universe of "precision timing" and "performance," the permutations determined by an organizer: schedules, rites, and hierarchies make for a very closed and measured-off space, and functions governed by a set of rules that anticipate interactions.

More than just metaphors, notes Perriault, these schemas of relations are the principles of the apparatus. In the programmed environment of exchanges, the Sadean discourse thus reveals that "the project of the machine is conscious in the one person who articulates the organization, and consequently in Sade himself." But nothing authorizes us to conclude that in Sade, or even in Vaucanson, "is there a consciousness of an underlying abstract concept that could be compared with that of system in its contemporary definition."[49] Only Denis Diderot attained this level of abstraction.

Chapter 2

The Economy of Circulation

Some forty years before the fall of the Old Regime, the school of philosopher-economists known as Physiocracy discovered the mechanisms of
the flow of wealth and attempted to represent it geometrically. It was
the first system of laws of modern economics. Faithful to Enlightenment philosophy, its exponents postulated that exchange had a creative
power. Therefore they advocated the free-flowing circulation of goods
and labor power as well as a policy of constructing and maintaining paths
of communication. For a brief period, their doctrine inspired a strategy
of building roads and suppressing hindrances to exchange. On the other
hand, the corollary idea of the role of the circulation of opinion as the
foundation of a true public sphere would remain marked by ambiguity.

The unifying schema of territory, arising from the Revolution of 1789,
called for the harmonization of the norms of exchange (weights and
measures and statistical information) and the implantation of a national
system of semaphore telegraphy, in a scenario in which Reason acted as
arbiter of the tensions between universalism and local interests. But it
would have to wait until the arrival of the locomotive coupled with the
electrical telegraph for a complete upheaval in the mode of circulation
to occur.

François Quesnay and the *Tableau Économique*

In 1758, the philosopher-economist François Quesnay (1694–1774) published his *Tableau Économique* (Economic table), followed by his *Explication* (Explanation) and *Maximes générales du gouvernement économique* (General maxims of economic government), in which he offered
a macroscopic and materialist vision of the economy. The table is a geo-

metric figure, albeit still very elementary, in which zigzag lines expressing flows cross and intermingle, allowing us to visualize the circulation
of wealth. As a genealogical tree of the functioning of incomes, it constitutes a prototype of a method of national income accounting, involving a conception of the total annual output of a country. And this is how
it would be interpreted by Karl Marx (1818–83) nearly one hundred
years later. For he devoted a long commentary to the table and recognized
in the originator of Physiocracy one of the founders of modern political
economy.

Before publishing the table, Quesnay had laid the basis of his philosophy of the economy in the *Encyclopédie*—not in the article devoted
to the term "circulation," which remained centered on the circulation
of the blood, but rather in two others titled "Farmers" and "Grains,"
published, respectively, in 1756 and the following year. At the time, the
question of free trade in grains occupied an important place in the debate over the liberalization of the regime. These two articles constitute
the first work on economic matters by Quesnay, a physician, already sixty
years old and known until then for his treatises on the effects of bleeding (1730), animal economy (1736), suppuration and gangrene (1749),
and chronic fevers (1753).

In the physiocratic conception of the circulation of wealth, the circuits of the economic world were apprehended as a unified system. Circulation was seen as double, just like that of the blood. One circuit exists
between nature (the land) and man; the other between the three social
classes that compose society. The *productive class* is at the origin of the
"net product" or the "disposable agricultural product," a surplus
wealth. The *class of owners* includes the sovereign, the landlords, and
the collectors of the tithe; this class lives on the net product of cultivation paid to it every year by the productive class. Finally, the *sterile* or
nonproductive class is that of artisans, manufacturers, and merchants,
all the citizens engaged in other services or employment than those of
agriculture, and whose expenditures are paid for by the two preceding
classes.

These analyses were formulated in the context of a nation that was
largely agricultural. The most populous country of Europe, France was
confronted with the dilemma of population versus subsistence, following a large demographic growth due to a declining death rate—the dis-
appearance of two major plagues, pestilence and war—and thanks to
the progressive attenuation of "famines," the joint result of climatic
chance and economic expansion. In less than a century, the population
had grown by five to seven million people, in addition to the twenty million or so who inhabited France in the era of Vauban's studies. More-

over, it was around the mid-century that the expression "population" acquired its modern denotation and ceased to be synonymous with "small tribe" [*peuplade*].

People multiply in proportion to land; in the Physiocrats' view, the employments in industry that occupy men at the expense of the cultivation of the soil damage the population and hinder the increase in wealth: this is what Quesnay suggested, reacting to the bankruptcy of mercantilism and its industrial and commercial system, rife with regulation and protectionism. He risked everything on agriculture, which seemed to him the only *productive* form of labor, and the sole source of wealth. Its fate decides that of society. The arts and "manufacture and sale" include merely the sterile work that only the product of agriculture — "foodstuffs and raw produce" — can pay for and sustain. Now peasants cannot get rich except by the freedom and security of their persons, their labor, and their goods. Hence one must consider that forced-labor teams, militias, and the rules that prescribe one kind of cultivation rather than another, the impediments and prohibitions in the commercialization of production, are all "public scourges." And for this reason all circulation must be liberalized.

In this first theoretical sketch of the circulation of wealth, circulation was considered in a broad sense. There is the "imperfect" circulation that takes place between two classes only, and the "perfect" sort that unfolds among the three classes. Circulation encompasses production, consumption, and distribution. "As goes the flow, so goes the reproduction": breaking with the ideas of his day, Quesnay postulated that only by "guaranteeing circulation," that is to say, by developing consumption, will wealth be perpetuated and reproduced. This thesis was so novel that the historian of economic doctrines René Gonnard would write in the 1920s, the great period of the "consumptionist" doctrine in the United States: "This is one of the characteristics that have allowed us to speak of the 'modernity' — I would almost say the Americanism — of the French economist."[1]

Domestic and foreign free trade, free labor, freedom to cultivate one's field, unregulated prices, unregulated profits: such are the physiocratic laws of the circulation of wealth. An originally physiocratic maxim, "laissez-faire, laissez-passer," would be taken up later by liberalism. "Let, therefore, the complete freedom of trade be maintained because the policing of interior and exterior trade that is the surest, the most accurate, the most profitable to the state and to the nation consists of the full freedom of competition." This is maxim 25 of the economic government of an agricultural kingdom according to Quesnay.[2] In his memorandum "Despotism in China," we further read: "The natural policy for commerce is therefore free and broad competition, which procures to each nation the greatest number of buyers and sellers, in order to assure it the most advantageous price in its sales and in its purchases."[3]

The liberalization of flows obviously involves the circuits that raw foodstuffs must follow. A long note on the state of roads is devoted to this subject in the article "Farmers," while maxim 17 proclaims: "The outlets and transport of the products and the commerce of manpower should be facilitated, by repairing roads and by the navigation of canals, rivers, and the sea."

To back up his thesis, Quesnay took his examples from distant civilizations. In his analysis of the government of the Incas (1767), Quesnay celebrated their "routes of communication." In his memorandum on China, composed the same year, he confessed his admiration for the organization of its rivers, lakes, and canals. In a chapter entitled "Trade Considered as Dependence on Agriculture," he devoted long sections to the transport facilities of this empire: "Circulation and flow are very prompt; self-interest, which is the dominating passion of the Chinese people, holds them to continual activity; everything is in motion in the cities and in the country; the highways are as crowded as the streets of our commercial cities, and the whole empire seems to be nothing less than one vast fair."[4] He never tired of praising the "magnificence of the construction" of roads, the "particular attention to their maintenance," the "police admirable for ensuring their safety"; he spoke of the rest areas that border them, the free distribution of tea offered to travelers, and the exemplary punishments that await those mandarins who fail to repair or maintain the great roads.

To express his economic analyses, Quesnay indeed resorted to the anatomical metaphor of blood circulation. But inversely, the metaphor of the circulation of rivers from his early medical treatises also serves to describe the changes that occur in blood circulation during bleeding.[5] From his writings on hygiene as "the art of healing through a good diet" to those in which he elevated the principles of a "science of government" to a universal hygiene, the transition is quite gradual. Quesnay applied to the latter the same general rules he had followed with the former. He advocates an inductive method of experiment and observation. Without theory, there is neither science nor art; this leitmotif was first put to the test in his polemics against the surgeons of his day. The introductions to certain of his medical treatises are thus transformed into veritable dissertations on the paths of science and the advancement of the Enlightenment.

Moreover, Quesnay justified the legitimacy of recourse to analogy. In his "Memoirs of the Royal Academy of Surgery" in 1743, he asserted:

Where certitude abandons us, there remain to guide us only
conjecture and *analogy* . . . [These] are the sources of light;
verisimilitude and comparison of like objects lead to research; and
from this research is sometimes born knowledge of the truth . . .
[But] it is a delicate step that may throw into one's path many
errors and dangers. It must therefore be forbidden to closed or
unenlightened minds[6]

— a precaution not always taken by some of his disciples who, more inclined to the speculative than the inductive approach, would take this
to an extreme. Inviting "anatomizing" of economic values (flows, flux,
reflux, exhaustion of arteries, and their engorgement), they would impart
a new vigor to social applications of anatomy and physiology.[7]

A Space for an Enlightened Public

What confers a coherence on the two lives of this physician turned
philosopher-economist, in his move from the "animal economy" to "political economy," is above all his philosophy of nature and of the natural order. His pathological observations lead him to establish an axiom: "Nature is universal hygiene; it is she who wounds and she who
heals."[8] Each attack on this code of nature provokes regulative measures;
this law applies as much to the body politic as to the physical body. It is
the specific property of a "crisis," the eruption of a previously existing
morbid state, to make this known. Quesnay returned constantly in his
medical reflections to the theory of bleeding and the theory of fevers as
"arts of healing." Thus he combats the idea that a fever is something
bad in itself, and that it ought to be suppressed, whereas often it is the
means by which nature can help itself.

Nature, with its curative power, is the great instructor of humanity.
Starting with his *Essai physique sur l'œconomie animale* (1736), Quesnay defines the economy as a "natural organization."[9] One of the principal missions he assigns the proponents of the new political economy
is to instruct the "moral body of the nation, that is to say, the thinking
portion of the people," on knowledge relative to the laws of this natural
order. "The first political decision of government should be the institution of schools to teach this *science* . . . Evident and general knowledge
of the natural laws is therefore the essential condition of a combination
of wills."[10] Where there is absolutely no instruction of this kind — both
public and private — then everything is just darkness, since knowledge
of the common interest is the only "social bond." This brings us back
to Physiocracy's conception of the functioning of the public sphere.

"The particulars of Chinese doctrine merit serving as a model to all states": these words appear at the beginning of the conclusion to the memorandum "Despotism in China," which bears the title "Comparison of Chinese laws with the constituent natural principles of prosperous governments."

For Quesnay, the Chinese journey, through the tales of "travelers and historians, eyewitness accounts, for the most part," is naturally a pretext to speak more freely about the institutional blockages of the French kingdom—as, for example, when he marvels at the "gazette of the internal government of the empire" and its veracity. Thanks to it, "in China, books containing the fundamental laws of the state are in everyone's hands; the emperor must conform to them. In vain would an emperor desire to abolish them; they would triumph over tyranny."[11] Hence the "principle of publicity" is advanced here as one of the guarantees of democracy in a "nation educated in natural laws." "In this immense empire," he writes later on, in a general summary,

all errors and all embezzlements of the leaders are continually divulged in the public writings authorized by the government, in order to ensure, in all the provinces of such a large kingdom, the observance of laws against the abuse of authority, always informed by a free right of complaint, which is one of the essential conditions of a sure and inalterable government.[12]

Thus in France in the second half of the eighteenth century one witnesses the slow and contradictory emergence of a theory of the public sphere that Habermas, following Marx, has judiciously analyzed: "Only when the physiocrats ascribed it to the *public éclairé* [enlightened public] itself did *opinion publique* [public opinion] receive the strict meaning of an opinion purified through critical discussion in the public sphere to constitute a true opinion. In *opinion publique* the contradiction between *opinion* and *critique* vanished." But although the Physiocrats were the first to defend the idea of a public making political use of its reason and, thereby, the idea of the legislative autonomy of civil society with respect to state interventions,

in relation to the absolutist regime they acted as apologists. As Marx said, their doctrine amounted to a bourgeois reproduction of the feudal system. In the transition from mercantilism to liberalism they continued to affirm the basis of feudal domination, that is, agriculture as the single productive labor... According to them, the function of the monarch was to watch over the *ordre naturel*; he received his insight into the laws of the natural order through the *public éclairé*.[13]

Physiocratic doctrine did not succeed, however, in transcending the limits of the established regime in a France where the isolation of society in relation to the state was constantly growing. With the impossibility of sharing legislative and executive power, the "nation as a body," the assembled nation, could under no circumstances be the possessor of the power to legislate. This situation is very different from that of contemporary England, where *public spirit* is "an authority that could compel lawmakers to legitimize themselves."[14]

Moving beyond the scope of the philosopher-economists' agricultural kingdom, one gets a hint of the uncertainties of this historical period by glancing through the *Encyclopédie* in search of an archaeology of the terms that accompanied the emergence of a public sphere.

In the article entitled "Opinion," there is no trace of a definition of a concept approaching that of public opinion. The subject is treated only in the framework of individual opinions. Although there is no "popular or general opinion," there are, in the articles entitled "People" and "Popular," remarks about the ambivalent character of these notions. The rubric "people" stresses the difficulty of defining this "collective noun" because one forms of it "different ideas in different places, different eras, and according to the nature of different governments." The approach to the word "popular(s)" is twofold: in the singular, via the "Popular State" or "Democracy"; and in the plural, via "those who seek to attract the benevolence of the people" in order to dupe them. It is through amusements, bread, and spectacles that the most odious tyrants in history have succeeded in making themselves "popular." What stands out here is a very negative portrayal of entertainment and the popular.

Everything that has some relation to an "opinion" expressed by the common people (*le vulgaire*) has pejorative connotations: irrational, inept, and impulsive. This is not surprising when one considers that in 1776 Condorcet would go so far as to define popular opinion as "that of the most stupid and most miserable part of the people." But a different reality emerges from a study by Arlette Farge on the existence of a popular public opinion in the eighteenth century — that is, the "plebeian public sphere," which Jürgen Habermas deliberately left aside in order to concentrate exclusively on the formation of enlightened opinion and the lettered critical sphere. Using several types of sources containing "popular views" (chronicles, newspapers, memoirs, police investigations, handbills, the archives of the Bastille), Farge tries to pinpoint the political forms of popular acquiescence or discontent in the face of events — visible, real, and daily — and of the spectacle of the monarchy. "Devoid of existence or status," she notes, popular speech is a political nonplace and yet at the same time a common site of social practice. Harried by political power, it takes shape and existence and develops in the heart of this system that contradictorily denies it and yet takes it into account, and hence, to a certain extent, creates it. Existent and nonexistent, popular speech on the affairs of the time lives in an in-between world: between the political out-of-bounds and the common site of an always suspect practice.[15]

Since the *Encyclopédie* lacks an entry on the topic "Public Opinion," let us consult the article on the term "public," which designates either the political body formed by all the subjects of a state, or the citizens of the same city. "Public" in the sense of "audience" (a term that would be used only much later) is not present among the definitions in this entry. On the other hand, it is used several times by Diderot in the forewords to certain volumes of the *Encyclopédie,* where it refers to the future reader of this work, written by "men of letters": "the public who reads, and who thinks." As for notions of "mass" and "crowd," strictly speaking, they have no relation to the people, opinion, or the public. Mass belongs above all to physics or economics, whereas "crowd" (*foule*) (defined in the singular) is one of the operations in the manufacture of cloth, and, in the plural, refers to one of the peoples of Africa.

It fell to Voltaire (1694–1778) to present in 1757 one of the institutions that popularized an embryonic public sphere. In the article "Gazette" (or "Relation of Public Affairs"), he relates the history of this "useful object." Invented in Venice at the beginning of the seventeenth century, at a time when Italy was still at the "center of European negotiations" and the Doge's City "was still the asylum of liberty," it owes its name to a small coin, the gazetta, which was the price of the weekly paper. The argument of liberty recurs, provocatively or in veiled terms, several times in his presentation of gazettes, relying when necessary on international comparisons. The Chinese example, here too, is taken as evidence, because if Venice is the cradle of such newspapers in Europe, remarks Voltaire, they have been a fact in China since time immemorial. There, a daily gazette of the empire was printed by order of the court. (In the eighteenth century, it is probable that more books were printed in China than in all of Europe; Chinese civilization was at its apogee in cities like Beijing.)

Voltaire alludes to the obstacles to free public speech. He recalls that the doctor Théophraste Renaudot (1586–1653), who gave France the first gazettes in 1631, for a long time kept it a family privilege. He also remarks that although London boasted no less than a dozen of these "political gazettes" per week, they could only be printed "on stamped paper, which is not a negligible tax for the State." As for France's gazettes, they "have always been reviewed by the Minister." On the other hand, all these French newspapers "have never been soiled by scandalmongering and have always been well written" — which is not the case with foreign gazettes, such as those published in the English capital. And unlike those of China that "concern only that empire," the gazettes of Europe "embrace the universe."

Diderot takes up the same matter in the entry "Journalist," and very probably also the unsigned one titled "Newspaper" (1765). The newspaper is defined as "a periodic work that contains excerpts from newly printed books, with details of the discoveries made every day in the Arts and Sciences." It should be the "work of a society of scholars," as illustrated by the founding in France in 1665 of the first of them, the *Journal des Savants,* which was "imitated in the majority of countries under an infinity of different titles," such as *The History of the Works of the Learned* (1699) in England.

These two entries express the skepticism of the Enlightenment regarding this new form of dissemination of knowledge. Newspapers were invented

for the comfort of those who are either too busy or too lazy to read entire books. It is a means of satisfying one's curiosity, and of becoming a savant on the cheap... One buys or rejects a book according to the good or ill they [journalists] say about it: a sure means of having in one's library almost all the bad books that have appeared, which they have praised, and of not having the good ones they have ripped apart.

Diderot ends the article on journalists with a proposition for a code of professional ethics. Not only does he plead that the interest of the latter "should be entirely separate from the interests of the bookstore or the writer," but he insists on the journalist's pedagogic mission. "His art is by no means that of making us laugh but rather of analyzing and instructing. An amusing journalist is a laughable journalist."

Turgot and the Construction of the Road Network

Regarding political life in France toward the middle of the eighteenth century, Alexis de Tocqueville (1805–59) noted the following:

In England, political writers and political actors were mixed, one set working to adapt new ideas to practice, the other circumscribing theory by existing facts; whereas in France, the political world was divided into two separate provinces without intercourse with each other. One administered the government, the other enunciated the principles on which government ought to rest. The former adopted measures according to precedent and routine, the latter evolved general laws, without ever thinking how they could be applied. The one conducted business, the other directed minds.[16]

The reformer Turgot (1727–81), an independent Physiocrat, was possibly the exception that confirmed Tocqueville's rule, first as intendant of the Limoges province from 1761 to 1774, and later as minister of finance to Louis XVI, comptroller-general of France from 1774 until his disgrace two years later. With Turgot, the ideas of the philosopher-economists were converted into an art of governing. From his first public trust, Turgot would learn to hold in suspicion orders and prohibitions in which everything becomes a pretext for the collection of taxes and the constitution of exclusive concessions. Perhaps his suspicion was not great enough, because he would never be able to thwart the maneuvers of the privileged, even once he was at the summit of the state administration.

His practical activity during his intendancy would make him very knowledgeable on problems of public works. It was under his provincial management that a new system for graveling roads would be invented and applied. The foundations of the Roman-paved roads that still served as standard references were composed of one or two layers of flat stones, then smaller stones nearer the surface. In 1770, the chief engineer in Limoges, Pierre-Marie Trésaguet (1716–96) proposed the innovation of using gravel unmixed with sand and with an arched foundation and surface. This procedure would be generalized throughout the kingdom five years later. (The next technical leap in paving would not occur until 1815 and would be the work of the superintendent of roads in Bristol, John McAdam [1756–1836], who would popularize the use of a single layer of broken stones, an intermediate step that would lead to asphalt pavements around 1850. In 1860, the steam compression roller would make its appearance.)

Overcoming the isolation of the provinces was the order of the day in France, where tolls were gradually disappearing. One thing is certain: it was at this time that the star-shaped network centered on Paris was conceived. What is less certain is the number of kilometers of roads opened in the course of the last forty years of the Old Regime. Historians are extremely cautious about the generally quoted figure of forty thousand kilometers built or improved, stone-covered or paved, bordered with ditches and trees and lined with stone markers. A great transformation

of roads in France in the eighteenth century, or a limited change?" asks
Bernard Lepetit.

The quantitative data for deciding are lacking. The waning Old
Regime offers only a handful of overall estimations, which tally
but are crude: about six thousand leagues, or a little more than
twenty-six thousand kilometers of roads, opened in the entire
kingdom at the beginning of the 1780s. But, to be more precise, a
supposedly open road is not necessarily finished or in a "state of
repair": not until 1855 would the two notions of openness and
perfection coincide in almost all cases.[17]

And the same author goes so far as to speak of "impossible national
coverage" to characterize the period from 1775 to 1800 and the context in which Turgot assumed his function of inspector general of the
kingdom's roads: the coffers were empty, and forced labor resisted dra-
gooning more and more.

The project managers of the road network at the time were far from
believing that they had attained their basic objective. In his *Traité de la
construction des chemins* (Treatise on the construction of roads), published in 1778, M. Gautier, architect, engineer, and inspector of major
routes, bridges, and roads in the kingdom, still felt obliged, when addressing the sovereign, to demonstrate the usefulness of a suitable road
network. "The channels of communication in a state, as well as the great
roads that traverse it, if they are well maintained, bring abundance to
every region of a kingdom, and maintain the whole economy by circulation."[18] He further recited the advantages a road system in good repair would bring: for example, allowing someone with too much wheat
but lacking in wine to acquire the latter and vice versa. Carriages would
require fewer horses, and men and the vehicles would be lighter and
hence cheaper. In winter there would be one-half more useful voyages
and fewer disabled horses. The king would save a sixth of the transport
costs for the supplying of troops stationed on the borders, plus another
quarter, given the overpricing on merchandise by suppliers on account
of impracticable roads. There would be more people on the roads—
coaches, carriages, horses, poste chaises—and hence more innkeepers,
"earning more by the great number, who would give better service and
at a cheaper cost." These "conveniences" would attract more foreign
travelers, who would bring still more money into the kingdom. In short,
the "prodigious multitude of small exchanges among sellers and buyers
would be half again as great in the six winter months if buyers and sellers did not have to fear bad roads, and if merchandise could be carried
easily to fairs, markets, ports, and cities."

But in a situation where roads were scarce, the real novelty of Turgot's work was in the protest against forced labor and the search for another way of financing public works. This was a step he had already taken in his Limoges intendancy and that would earn him the admiration of foreign travelers such as the Englishman Arthur Young.[19]

In January 1776, comptroller-general Turgot submitted to the king a memorandum proposing the abolition of forced labor throughout the kingdom (as well as the suppression of taxes levied in Paris on grains, flours, and essential foodstuffs for the population, and that of duties on the ports, docks, halls, and markets of Paris, known as *jurandes*). The preceding year, Turgot had created an administration of "coaches and parcels," abrogating concessions to individuals, and taken a series of measures to assure the regularity of traffic (including establishing schedules, routes, departure and arrival points) and the security of passengers and merchandise (fixing the number of places available and designating coach conductors). He also codified the instruction dispensed in the École des Ponts et Chaussées, establishing the school's name definitively and instituting most notably a "style competition" for its students.

The project of suppressing forced labor gave rise to a long epistolary exchange between Turgot and the minister of justice, Jean de Maurepas. Three-quarters of a century after *La dîme royale*, Turgot adopted the same tone as Vauban in denouncing the inequalities of the king's subjects with respect to numerous taxes, charges, and other "burdens." Turgot spoke of the inequality of benefits and called for "a return to justice, which ought to burden with the expense those who have an interest in it." This was not the opinion of the justice minister, who resisted the idea of a new tax on landowners to finance the construction of thoroughfares and objected that everyone profited to the same degree from well-maintained major roads. This earned him an ironic reply from Turgot:

Travelers gain from the beauty of the roads by going faster. The roads' beauty attracts travelers and increases their number. These travelers spend money, consume the country's foodstuffs, which always runs to the advantage of property owners. As for wagoners, their carriage rates are less dear in proportion to the lesser time they spend on the road and their better management of equipment and horses. From this reduction in the costs of carriage results the ease of transporting foodstuffs farther and selling them at a better price. Thus the entire advantage goes to the owner of lands who sells his foodstuffs at a higher price. Monsieur the Minister of Justice will grant me my belief that the pleasure of walking on a well-graveled road does not compensate people for the pain they have suffered in building it for no wage.[20]

This debate is doubtless one of the first in history in which the problem of communication—a field from the start so propitious for the myth of sharing and communion—is posed in terms of inequality and social injustice. Less than a century later, a new myth of equality before the rail would be flourishing.

In February 1776, a royal edict in accord with the principle that "roads ought to be made at the expense of those who profit from them" eliminated forced labor in peacetime.[21] The financing of roadworks, henceforth granted to a firm selected after a tendering procedure, would come from the contributions of landowners.

In the long preamble to the edict, Physiocratic doctrine on the preeminence of agriculture and the virtues of circulation has a place of honor: "The protection that we owe to agriculture, which is the veritable basis of public abundance and prosperity, and the favor that we wish to grant to commerce as the surest encouragement of agriculture, made us seek to link more and more by facilitated communications all parts of our kingdom, be it among each other or with foreign countries."[22]

A decision by the council of state divided roads into four categories, fixing a width for each one. The judgment explained why the major roads have been assigned a lesser width than before: "It was justice to leave to the industry of farmers, now become free, and to the reproduction of foodstuffs, everything that it would not be absolutely necessary to confer on the roads in order to facilitate commerce."[23]

Until the end of his term as minister, Turgot's policy thus remained faithful to the agrarian orthodoxy of Physiocracy. Roads were conceived for the transport of "raw foodstuffs," and the tax proposed to substitute for forced labor burdened principally the owner-cultivators, since manufacturers and merchants were clearly defined as the "sterile class."

The year of the enlightened public servant Turgot's downfall was also that of the decline of agricultural liberalism and Physiocracy as tools of government. There is a coincidence and a contrast here: in this year of 1776, in London, appeared the masterwork of Adam Smith, *An Inquiry into the Nature and Causes of the Wealth of Nations,* which would herald the industrial and commercial liberalism of the following century. In his youthful writings, outlines of a universal history and a "political geography" dating from the 1750s, Turgot had proposed a first theory of the "stages of progress," that is, the successive phases of development through which human societies pass in the course of their history: hunting, pasture, agriculture, commerce, and industry.[24] The Scottish economist, in his turn, proposed a logico-historical approach to the evolution of societies. But he clearly distinguished the industrial stage from the agricultural kingdom, in an England where, according to Fernand Braudel, domestic transport was multiplying and "the precocious Industrial Revolution is directly linked to an active economy of circulation."[25] The year of Smith's book was also that of the United States' Declaration of Independence.

With Turgot ousted by the taxed property owners, the "perpetual and irrevocable" edict—terms that figure in its preamble—would be considerably watered down. Starting in August 1776, the "statutory [i.e., forced] labor" option was reestablished, opening up a period of uncertainty and hesitation in which taxes and work gangs coexisted. In 1786, forced labor was even considered as conferring the right to a wage.

To Circulate Is to Measure: The Adoption of a Single System of Weights and Measures

The debate over how to finance public works required a knowledge, with figures, of roads to be constructed, and of the degree of progress of each regional project. Three years before the end of the Old Regime, the administration of Ponts et Chaussées undertook the first major statistical inquiry into the state of the roads. With the Revolution of 1789, the work of unifying the territory was inscribed in a larger framework, with a central role attributed to the improvement of communication and the fluidity of exchanges: suppression of interior customs barriers and of tolls, standardization of the tax system, elaboration of a single legal code, a new administrative partitioning of the national territory, and the obligation to use the French language for public acts.

"Language is an obstacle to propagation of the Enlightenment," declared the abbot Henri Grégoire (1750–1831) in June 1794, in presenting before the deputies of the National Convention a report, the fruit of a long study launched four years previously, by the Committee of Public Instruction on the "necessity of means of abolishing patois, and universalizing the use of the French language." At the time, there were still about thirty patois dialects in use in France. "The Republican regime," we read in the report,

> has effected the suppression of all the parasite castes, inequalities among fortunes, the leveling of conditions . . . In order to extirpate prejudices, promote all truths, all talents, all virtues, and in order to blend all citizens into the national mass and simplify the mechanism and facilitate the workings of the political machine, language must become a means of identity . . . The new partitioning of territory established new relations contributing to the propagation of the national language. The suppression of tithes, feudalism, and customary rights, and the establishment of

the new system of weights and measures, brought about the
abolition of a multitude of terms that were only of local usage . . .
Let us encourage everything that may be advantageous to the
country; that from this moment the language of liberty may be the
order of the day, and that the zeal of citizens may proscribe regional
jargon — the last vestiges of feudalism destroyed — forever.[26]

This founding text fixed the cultural centrality of the state at the expense of a "plural culture," in the expression of the historian Michel de
Certeau. It was in the name of the urgent destruction of the age of tyranny
that the authorities rejected the survival of "particularisms."

In 1794, the École Centrale des Travaux Publics (Central School of Public Works) opened its doors. A year later, it was renamed the École Polytechnique. Its direction was entrusted to the director of the École des
Ponts et Chaussées, founded nearly fifty years earlier, after a long and
vigorous debate on the necessity of creating a single school for "national
engineers," bringing together the corps of military engineers and the corps
of bridge and road construction.[27] In 1795, a new École des Ponts et
Chaussées was founded; field training in the provinces for future engineers, as practiced under the Old Regime, was suppressed.

The public authorities also attacked the problem of the unity of the
"language" of commercial exchanges posed by diverse systems of weights
and measures, an old problem if there was one. In his "Questions intéressantes sur la population, l'agriculture et le commerce" (Interesting questions on population, agriculture, and commerce), Quesnay, recommending a national study in this area, noted under the heading "Usages":
"Measures of a region; their variety for all the different foodstuffs; the
weights, ell-measures, land measures, grain measures, etc., giving the detail in pounds, ounces, feet, and inches."[28] This recommendation was preceded by another: "What is the character of the inhabitants, where does
it come from, what determines it?" This contiguity is not fortuitous: it
indicates the great degree to which the problem of weights and measures was experienced at that time as a cultural question. The ancient
measures had an unconventional but "significant" character: they signified or expressed man, the conditions of his life, and his work; they had
a social significance, they were signs endowed with meaning.[29] Thus anthropometric measures (linked to the foot, elbow, arm, or thumb) referred
to the specific character of each action. Thus, too, the value of measures
of content was determined by the dimension of means of transport.

Hence the extreme diversity of weights and measures (linear, square
area, cubic capacity). The *Encyclopédie* had even reproduced equivalency tables. A measure called by the same name might assume a differ-

ent value according to the place, inside the frontiers as well as outside. One hundred pounds in Amsterdam had the same value in Paris, La Rochelle, Saint-Malo, and Besançon, but was worth 89 in Geneva, 105 in Bourges and in Brussels, 109 in London, 114 in Lille and Madrid, 118 in Toulouse and in the Haut-Languedoc, 123.5 in Marseilles, 143 in Florence, and 182 in Venice. In Spain the "quintal-macho" reached 150 pounds, that is, fifty more than the common quintal. Taking into account the difference in calculating the pound, this measure from across the Pyrenees amounted to a little less than 140 pounds in Paris.

What is even more complex, the standard could fluctuate according to the place in the social ladder occupied by the purchaser and vendor. The weight of a sack of grain was not necessarily the same for the commoner and his lord, or for country and city. Notwithstanding, the revolutionary notebooks of grievances attest to the number of cases under the Old Regime where the measure of reference was transformed into an "instrument of trickery."

Over the course of the centuries since Charlemagne's reforms, royalty had tried to remedy the drawbacks for commerce posed by such an assorted collection of standards, but none of the attempts at unification of weights and measures had succeeded in vanquishing the weight of cultural traditions. The watchword attributed to Louis XI— "A state needs only one law, one weight, and one measure"—still seemed wishful thinking, while across the Channel such a decision had been in force since the twelfth century. The situation was still being deplored in 1765 by the author of the article titled "Measure" in volume 10 of the *Encyclopédie*:

> One well imagines that people will never agree to adopt in concert the same weights and measures, but the thing is possible in a country subject to the same master. Henry I, king of England [from 1100 to 1135], established the same weights and measures over all his estates, the work of a wise legislator, which he saw through in his kingdom and which has been fruitlessly proposed in our own ... Do not object that this idea is merely a specious project, full of inconvenience in its execution, and that in the end it is futile, a mere dispute over words, because the price of things soon follows their weights and measures. But would it not be still more natural to avoid this step, to forestall it, to simplify and facilitate the course of interior commerce that is now done with difficulty, when one must constantly have in one's head or before one's eyes the tariff of weights and measures of different provinces of a kingdom, in order to adjust one's operations to them?

The article was cataloged as referring to the subject of "government."

It was in December 1799 that the law fixing the meter and the gram, the fundamental units of the metric system, was promulgated. This law was the institutional result of a decree of May 1790 by which the National Constituent Assembly gave birth to the decimal system. For nine years, commissions composed of eminent scholars—geographers, astronomers, philosophers, and physicists such as Cassini, Condorcet, Laplace, Lavoisier, and Monge—had labored over an essential idea: "to borrow the units from nature." From their work on measuring the meridian between Dunkirk and Barcelona, their observations of the pendulum, and their study of the weights of distilled water was born a common denominator: the meter as a fraction of the terrestrial meridian (1/40 million). Undertaken separately in the same era, the work on the new standard measure to determine the weight of the kilogram (18,827 grains) recalled, in passing, the long history of the wheat trade that had accompanied the progressive liberalization of commerce and circulation.

The new nomenclature met resistance for a long time. In order to manage the transition, a decree of 1812 even had to authorize the use of certain old denominations, while adapting them to the new measurements. It was not until 1840 that the metric system was made exclusive and mandatory.

The new metric standard was one of the basic elements of the apparatus of fiscal reform. It facilitated the calculation of the assessment of property taxes, a question that had haunted both Vauban and Turgot in their search for a more equitable tax system. In 1803, the Administration of Direct Taxes ordered from six mechanical engineers some surveying instruments so that the land surveyors could establish a cadastre (property register). This monumental labor of mapping took nearly forty years. In 1811, instructions on the method to follow in executing such an operation were assembled into a *Recueil Méthodique*. In composing it, the French technicians of the First Empire took inspiration from the experience of the Hapsburgs in a province of the Austrian monarchy, the Milanese, where the cadastral survey had begun in 1719 was finished in 1760. Unlike the other territories of the Hapsburgs, where the reform of land taxes did not encounter the same success, the Milanese lent itself to the ideal way of establishing a cadastre. Two reasons for this were offered by a specialist in financial history: "its geographical characteristics—a plain checkered by canals—and its development, the traffic occasioned by the activity of the main city and secondary ones."[30]

A product of the Enlightenment idea of the equality of all before the law, the intellectual process of abstraction incarnated by measurement was presented by its initiators as one of the symbols of national unity and of progress. Here is how the Polish historian of weights and measures Witold Kula summarized in 1970 the structuring effect of this new "system":

It was their steady, enduring labors that enabled the ideas of the *philosophes*, so beautiful in their rationalist purity, to materialize in daily practice and to permeate the very thinking of the entire nation. And thanks to this, gone are the countless, daily opportunities for the strong to injure the weak, for the smart to cheat the simple, and for the rich to take advantage of the poor... Through this innovation, moreover, the whole nation was made to acquire common ways of thinking, to share the same perceptions of space, dimensions, and weights, and to grasp — albeit with the greatest difficulty — the principles of decimal division... And to have imposed upon men common ways of perceiving, and thereby to have enabled them the better to understand one another, was surely an admirable accomplishment.[31]

This observation should be placed alongside the analyses of Georges Canguilhem on the genealogy of the "norm" and "normalization." "In this respect," he wrote, "there is no difference between the birth of grammar in France in the seventeenth century and the institution of the metric system at the end of the eighteenth century... One begins by grammatical norms and ends up with morphological norms for men and horses in the interests of national defense, as well as industrial and hygienic norms."[32]

As a fruit of reason, the decimal system for counting weights and measures could only have a universal vocation. In the early years of its formulation, Talleyrand had proposed to collaborate with the Royal Society in London in this enterprise. Declining the offer, England would resist the adoption of the metric system for more than a century and a half. Meanwhile, it was exported to most European countries and Latin America. By the end of the nineteenth century, in Europe only Great Britain and Russia had not rallied to the norm. In other latitudes, the United States, China, Japan, and Persia continued to hold out. From 1875 on, the meter had its international organization — the International Bureau of Weights and Measures, with its headquarters near Paris in Sèvres, in the pavilion of Breteuil, depository of the metal standard of the "international meter" and the "international kilogram."

Mathematicians had less success in their reform of time. Their calendar of 1793, divided into twelve months of thirty days, and their decimal system of decades and hours, with the year beginning the day of the autumnal equinox, with perfect equality between day and night, did not manage to gain acceptance, and so disappeared twelve years later.[33] The calendar of Gregory XIII (1582) reassumed its preeminence.

"Statistical Reason"

In his *Esquisse d'un tableau historique des progrès de l'esprit humain* (Sketch for a historical picture of the progress of the human mind), published in 1793, Marie Jean Antoine de Condorcet (1743–94) made a fervent appeal, in the name of the fight against inequalities, for the institution of a "universal language" that would be the fruit of the "application of methods of mathematical science to new objects" — a language of "geometrical certitude" that, reserved exclusively for the sciences, expressing only the combinations of those simple ideas which are the same for every mind, and used only for the reasoning of strict logic, for the precise and calculated operations of the understanding, would be understood by people of every country, and could be translated into every vernacular and would not have to be altered, as happens now, when it passed into general use.[34] This universal language would be learned along with science itself and along with the language of algebra, in such a way that "the sign would be learned at the same time as the object, idea, or operation that it designates."[35] The philosophy of exact measurement, which inspired the reform of the system of weights and measures, also guided the organization of a statistical system.

At the end of the eighteenth century, the apparatus for assessing demographic trends was generally lacking. The contrast is striking between the progress made in the measures of mortality and the lag in studies of the fecundity of marriages. Until this era, only mortality was considered of importance — for the insurers, as we have seen, but also for the process of secularization. "In studying mortality," explains the demographer and historian Hervé Le Bras, "the men of the eighteenth century appropriated their destiny, one that is no longer fixed arbitrarily by God but bends to the calculation of probability. By contrast, birth, their birth, occurs in any event."[36]

Measurement had nevertheless made a breakthrough since the 1740s in certain European countries. In 1741, the Prussian pastor J. P. Süssmilch produced the first significant book of mathematical statistics, entitled *Die göttliche Ordnung in den Veränderungen des menschlichen Geschlechts* (The divine order manifested by population movement). It was also a German, Gottfried Achenwall, who, toward the middle of the century, inaugurated the word "statistics," defined as "the detailed knowledge of the respective and comparative situations of states." In 1746, the Frenchman Deparcieux published new mortality tables in an *Essai sur les probabilités de la vie humaine* (Essay on the probabilities of human life). In 1755, Richard Cantillon's *De la nature du commerce en général* (On the nature of trade globally considered) appeared in France. Written some fifteen years earlier, this book, apparently a translation of an English manuscript that has disappeared, is the posthumous work of an author who was Irish by origin and French by adoption. It directly inspired the Marquis de Mirabeau, disciple of Quesnay, whose *Traité de population* appeared in 1757.[37] With Marshal Maurice de Saxe, and his two works, *Réflexions sur la propagation de l'espèce humaine* along with his *Mémoires militaires,* the latter published seven years after his death in 1750, demography encountered with strategic thought.

In 1776, the magistrate Jean-Baptiste Antoine de Montyon published under his secretary's name the first systematic evaluations of the French population and its evolution (*Recherches et considérations sur la population de la France*). Between 1776 and 1786, he ventured onto the terrain of "criminal pathology" in urban areas. He conducted a survey of convictions of criminals in the Paris jurisdiction and classified them according to gender, age, professional occupation, nature and site of the crime; from this work resulted, three years before the Revolution, his *Observations sur la moralité en France.*

In the years preceding the fall of the Old Regime, mathematicians like Condorcet and Laplace had started to apply the calculation of probabilities to problems that were soon to become essential for government: determining more equitable ways of conducting elections, and the influence of the plural composition of court juries on verdicts.

The nations that had already begun in this era to count their populations were rare: Sweden and the two other Scandinavian countries had conducted a census in 1749, as had the United States of America in 1790; they were the exceptions. England conducted its first census in 1801. The English Parliament, having previously refused any such counting in the name of individual freedom, this time bowed to a general movement favored by the climate of fear created by the publication of Thomas R. Malthus's book, to which we shall shortly return.

In France, following the pattern of weights and measures, statistics became a tool for unifying the nation. At the turn of the century, at the initiative of the minister of the interior, a "Bureau of Statistics of the Republic" was created. Alain Desrosières notes:

> At this time, statistics moved from manuscripts locked up in administrative archives to printed publications destined in principle to a wide public. This shift is linked to the fact that the *republican* state, having become *something belonging to everyone,* represented the whole society, by means of electoral

representation, but also through statistics, now the "mirror of the nation" and not just the "mirror of the prince." This ambition to offer society a reflection of itself, through a network of enquiries commissioned from local prefects, constituted the first orientation of the new bureau.[38]

Shaky until the 1830s, this type of institution for the collection and processing of statistics, which all European states developed during this period, then began to acquire its full legitimacy as an art of governing.

Since the last decades of the eighteenth century, as Montyon's preoccupation about the city as the source of crime and Malthus's book both demonstrate, the question of the situation of the "lower classes" haunted the field of statistical knowledge. Setting the tone in the 1830s, the mathematician and astronomer Adolphe Quételet (1796–1874) tried to deduce, from the calculation of certain averages on criminal trends in the population, some laws of a moral order parallel to the physical order. A conceptual framework on the notion of the "average man," as the standard molecule of the social order, began to gain prominence. Later on we shall see how, before the end of the nineteenth century, this type of research would have a direct influence on the formulation of debates on the character of average parameters such as: crowds, masses, public(s), and collective opinion.

The Central Commission of Statistics in Belgium, founded by Quételet, became an institutional model for other countries. In 1832, Quételet proposed to the British the creation of the future Royal Statistical Society. Its statutes would be approved two years later. The Statistical Society of Paris came into being in 1860. In 1853, again under the influence of the Belgian statistician, the first international statistical congress was held in Brussels, as suggested two years earlier in London during a meeting organized as part of the first Universal Exposition. In 1885, ten years after the creation of the International Bureau of Weights and Measures, statistics would have its own transnational body: the International Institute of Statistics. The first great phase of modern internationalization of nomenclatures was then at its height, and the technical methods of processing large numbers were undergoing changes. In 1880, the American statistician Hermann Hollerith (1860–1929), inspired by the weaving loom of Joseph-Marie Jacquard (1752–1834), invented the perforated card machine. Its first wide-scale application was for the exploitation of data from the United States census in 1890. Six years later, the statistician would found his own society to produce and market his invention (in 1924, Hollerith Tabulating Machines would become International Business Machines, the future computer giant).

Telegraph and Railway: Toward a New Use of Time

Necessity knowing no law, it was the revolutionary authority that in 1793 launched a French network of long-distance or "instant" communication. Here again, the context was the vast enterprise of rationalizing and mastering space.[39]

Taking up a modality of communication that went back to the dawn of time, the abbot Claude Chappe (1763–1805), engineer and physicist, arrived at an opportune moment for the application of his optical or semaphore telegraph. The logic of war made this technology an auxiliary of armies in the field. Its codes were stamped with state secrecy, just as Napoleon shortly afterward imposed secrecy on Cassini's topographical maps, reserving their use for strictly military purposes. The fear of plots and conspiracy also inspired the restoration of the "Black Cabinet," the administration's practice of violating private correspondence, which had been abolished by the 1789 Revolution. As Yves Stourdzé notes:

> With this telegraph system, we can already observe the distinction that will be found again later between sign and signal, semantics and "signaletics," meaning and identification, since, for example, the content of messages is not known by the telegraphists who transmit them from post to post (they do not understand what they are transmitting), but on the other hand they understand perfectly well the signals (for instance, whether to go fast, stop, begin again, etc.). Basically, there is a double level of language comprehension: an operating language that is comprehensible to those who make the apparatus function, and a language of the content that is in the sole command of the administration.[40]

This use of the telegraph oriented to an obsession with internal security did not prevent certain revolutionary thinkers of the time from placing all their democratic hopes in this first means of long-distance communication. It would be sufficient, they reckoned, to increase the number of lines and to liberate their coded language so that all citizens might "communicate their news and their desires to each other." Thus there would be reproduced on the national scale the conditions of the Greek agora and, by the same token, Jean-Jacques Rousseau's reservations about the possibility of "great democratic republics" would be overcome. Here the technology of instantaneous communication as the eternal promise of a liberated public space took its first steps in the history of utopias of communication.

Between 1793 and 1855, the country would be covered with the longest telegraphic network in the world, under the supervision of the ministers of war and the interior. Constructed in a star shape like the road network, it linked the capital to the great fortresses at the borders and coasts and to the strategic cities. The Napoleonic period (1799–1814), and more particularly the First Empire (1804), constituted a decisive moment, not only from the viewpoint of the international extension of the telegraph (which would be extended to Turin, Milan, Venice, Mainz, Tilsitt, Antwerp, and Amsterdam), but also for the overall planning of the communications system, with the creation of a general post office under the aegis of the finance minister (1804), a service of mounted couriers on a European scale (1805), a reform of the Ponts et Chaussées (1805), and restructuring of national stud farms (1806). The couriers conveyed orders and urgent dispatches in saddlebags to which only the sender and receiver had keys; they also served as informers.[41]

The telegraph would not leave the bosom of French national security and its secret codes until, with the invention of electric telegraphy by Britons William Cooke and Charles Wheatstone and the American Samuel Morse (1837), access to the telegraphic service was authorized to railroad companies, commodity markets, press agencies, and the public. Gradual liberalization — still within the framework of state administration — would not begin until 1851, when England, which for nearly ten years had allowed anyone who so desired to set up a telegraphic link, already boasted 6,500 kilometers of lines[42] (a density of coverage equaled only by its railroad system).

From 1800, the revolution in steam began to be more increasingly applied to transport, an application that had been in the making since the sixteenth century. To overcome a lack of wood, England, unlike France or the Low Countries, began very early the large-scale use of coal. This combustible would eventually feed not only the boilers of trains; its early use in English factories was one of the elements favoring the takeoff of an industrial infrastructure in an increasingly lively domestic market. Thus a process of innovation involving steam began to develop around coal, all the more so since the mines were located in basins exceptionally saturated by rainwater, and a solution had to be found for pumping them. The pump became one of the first areas of application of steam (as was noted by the novelist Herbert George Wells [1866–1946], who was also a perceptive historian of communication technologies).[43]

Here more than elsewhere, one is reminded of Fernand Braudel's explanation for the appearance of continual innovation in the Industrial Revolution: "Inventions tend to come in clusters, groups or series, as if they all drew strength from each other, or rather as if certain societies provided simultaneous impetus for them all."[44] The invention of the railroad is one illustration among others of this.

Since the seventeenth century, English mines had used rails—at first simple wooden bars on which tubs with wooden wheels rolled, allowing horses to pull three times heavier a load. Starting in 1767, wooden rails were replaced with cast-iron ones. Twenty-two years later, the Englishman William Jessop perfected the protruding rail and the wheel with a projecting edge. The principle of rolling movement had been found for a locomotive that had yet to be invented. (Soon there would be viaducts but no rolling stock! In 1779, the first cast-iron bridge was built in Coalbrookdale.)

Road tests had already taken place: in 1771, the French military engineer Joseph Cugnot invented the steam chariot, which was the first steam-driven automobile; in 1784, the Scot James Watt, father of the condenser, perfected three earlier inventions (the cylinder-and-piston steam mechanism of the Frenchman Denis Papin [1690], the water-raising fire engine first conceived by the English military engineer Thomas Savery [1698], and the atmospheric engine of the Englishman Thomas Newcomen [1705]) and took out a patent; in 1804, the Englishman Richard Trevithick made an inconclusive test of the locomotive, at first on the road, then on rails, and tried it again four years later with success; in the same year, the American Oliver Evans's engine crossed a mile and a half of Philadelphia. However, it was not until 1829 that the Englishman George Stephenson succeeded in combining the escape of steam via a smokestack and the tubular boiler invented by the Frenchman Marc Seguin. The steam locomotive could now begin its race. The gauge railway corresponded to the horse-cart gauge of the time (4 feet, 8½ inches, or 1.435 meters). It would still take seventeen years before this standard was adopted by Parliament (the Gauge Act of 1846) in the country of the locomotive's inventor, and equally long again before it became the norm shared by the majority of the Western world's networks. In Europe, only Russia and Spain, for reasons of national defense, would remain resolutely on the margins of this community of rail.

From the horse to the train, from organic speed to mechanical speed, a new way of moving arose, and it would determine a new way of organizing society. "With the steam engine," notes Paul Virilio, "we are in the presence of a weapon of movement that extends the weapon of war. Throughout technical evolution, moreover, we find this archetype, the 'firing tube' capable of directing both the power of the energy source (powder, steam, gasoline...) and the movement of the vector (projectile, vehicle...)."[45] The facts assembled by this author are quite convincing.

In 1673, Christiaan Huyghens borrowed from the cannon—the

"monocylindrical internal combustion machine"—the model for his "gunpowder machine," ancestor of the combustion engine. When Cugnot invented his steam chariot, it was at the request of an inspector of the royal artillery and in order to replace draft horses for pulling heavy arms. A century after Huyghens's experiment, it was a rifle sealed up and filled with water that inspired in the boilerman Evans the idea of using high pressure—feared by Watt because of the risk of explosion—and led him to build a boiler in which the steam was produced at a pressure of eight or ten atmospheres. The multitube system, which would make possible the development and refinement of locomotives with tubular boilers, had existed since the seventeenth century in weaponry, since armies were always on the lookout for methods to increase the rhythm of firing. Samuel Colt's barrel revolver (1832) would serve as model for the photographic revolver of French astronomer Jules Janssen (1873), then for Étienne-Jules Marey and his chronophotographic rifle.

Since the military revolution, which, according to historians of strategy, had taken place between 1560 and 1660 (with the emergence of professional standing armies, the introduction of discipline, and the increased effectiveness of cannon, both for offense and defense), the needs of armies had found solutions among men of science. A good example is Galileo's discoveries in dynamics (the principle of inertia, the law of freely falling bodies, and the principle of the composition of velocities) and his experiments on the trajectory of a projectile, which would accelerate progress in ballistics.[46]

Huyghens, as we know, was the inventor of the spiral spring, a key moment in the development of the clock. The railway was the culmination of a rationality in which the ordering of time on a large scale is allied with the institution of security systems calling for the military mode of organization. Before designating applications of the new technologies, and even before the invention of the locomotive or the telegraph, the term "line of communications" had been used in the treatises of war academies. Its transfer to civilian vocabulary by no means took place metaphorically. It was the expression of a regime of organization. "The operating rules of railways," observes Virilio, "would be copied from those of the military. The cult of exact schedules would be that of a strategy of tension necessitated by the requirements of traffic safety."[47]

Here we can situate the series of inventions for the transmission of signals, or "information," as one would say later, that led to the automatic systems of regulation of rail flows. The electric telegraph played a determining role in this, since, as a chronicler of the first great international exhibition of electricity, organized in Paris, noted in 1881:

The development of the operation of railways could not really become possible, and the admirable activity that was its consequence could not take off, until the electric telegraph, whose aid arrived at the right time and has constantly gone hand-in-hand with steam locomotion. The considerable increase in traffic, the resultant difficulties for the operators, the insufficiency of the initial installations, which had no doubt been improved since, but were conceived on the basis of forecasts that have been greatly outstripped by the facts; the requirements of a new and unexpected situation, whose progressive and inexorable character is better appreciated today: such are the determining causes that have decisively opened the vast field of practice in this new science.[48]

One of the early uses of the electric telegraph was in fact to signal trains. This occurred in 1840 in England on the London-Blackwall line. Four years later, the first application of the principle of the "block system" was made on a section of single track. Each stationmaster could read on a dial with needles invented by Wheatstone the section of track on which the train to be signaled electrically was engaged, as soon as it entered this section.

From this time on, the principle of the "block system" was constantly perfected. In 1835, the Germans Wilhelm Weber and Carl Friedrich Gauss narrowly missed beating the English to the first experimenting, with a procedure in which "every break in the rail would be automatically signaled by the telegraph." Their idea of using rails as telegraphic conductors would come to fruition in 1880 in the United States with an electroautomatic block system named the Union Automatic Electric Signal, which engineers described as follows: "The interruption of the current automatically halts the signals, so well that every break in the rail or failure by isolated vehicles (which derive their current from the line) on a section of the 'block' gives rise to an interruption or weakening in the current, and consequently provokes a 'danger' warning in the signal protecting that section."[49] This was a decisive step in the science and practice of signals, whose purpose was to suppress human intervention in matters of protection and prevention of collisions, catastrophes, and crises.

Ever since the advent of the mechanistic model of organization, notions of crisis and management of crises in complex situations had been linked to those of communication and information. They would become more and more central to the degree that the informational model was approached, with the latter ultimately supplanting the former at the end of World War II. The origin of the shift from the mechanistic model to the model characterized by electronic transport of information and action, or the "control revolution," lies precisely in the fact that the techniques of information and communication instituted in the course of the nineteenth century proved insufficient to administer accelerated circulation of production and distribution.[50]

The new temporality of the railway universe had been the starting point for a new temporality altogether. Through rail time there began the process of harmonization that before the end of the century would lead to world time, a process the American historian David S. Landes has explained in his study of clocks, time measurement, and the formation of the modern world. In 1847, the British Railway Clearing House recommended to various companies the adoption of Greenwich Mean Time in all stations. What made possible the adoption of a "legal time" was the refinement of electric timekeeping, which permitted the creation of a national time service. The signals transmitted at regular intervals to clocks and stations throughout the country unified the measurement of time over the whole British network. Synchronization, which did not proceed without resistance from defenders of the "local time" to which stagecoaches had long accommodated themselves, aligned all activities depending on rapid transport with the new norm. In 1884, despite opposition from the partisans of a broad range of "national times," Greenwich time would become the parameter for defining a universal time.[51]

In the *Grand dictionnaire universel du XIXe siècle,* begun in 1865 under the editorship of Pierre Larousse, the network became "the entanglement of objects disposed in lines" and the term would be applied essentially to railways, roads, and canals as well as the telegraph. Its meaning became fixed around 1849.[52]

Communication was to be the sacred standard by which the power of a people is measured, along with its social well-being, its prosperity, its civilization, and the degree of civil and political liberty that it has attained: "In our modern times," stated the *Dictionnaire,*

> the freest and most civilized nations — that is to say, France, England, Belgium, Holland, Germany, and the United States — are also those that possess the best means of communication. The lack of success of former Spanish colonies in establishing freedom in their territories and in developing their civilization after having conquered their independence, has as its cause, according to most of the renowned publicists who have visited these countries, the new governments' profound negligence regarding the means of communication.[53]

And finally, the French economist Paul Leroy-Beaulieu (1843–1916) could write in 1890: "The construction of roads and railways is one of the most belated results of the principle of the division of labor, one of the most recent applications of the idea of capitalization."[54]

Toward 1825, military engineers had approved the term "network" to designate the connections among fortifications, subterranean galleries, and routes of communication. In 1802, the future General Pierre-Alexandre Allent (1772–1837), an engineering officer, had, in his "Essai sur la reconnaissance militaire," inaugurated the modern representation of the network, referring, for example, to the hydrological network whose topography recalled the ramifications of a tree.[55]

From the nineteenth century on, the concepts of network and the reticular metaphor would know an unparalleled good fortune in French, in comparison to their uses in other languages.

Chapter 3
The Crossroads of Evolution

The discourse that nineteenth-century society accepted as true and brought up to date is based on the biological paradigm. This regime of truth began to predominate in the second half of the century, via a circuitous route. Biology borrowed from political economy, which in turn appropriated tools forged by the life sciences. The objects of these transactions were the concepts of development and growth and the division of labor. The mutual borrowings gave birth to the first sociological theory that explicitly defined communication as a component of "apparatuses" in a "system."

Adam Smith and Theorizing the Division of Labor

"The greatest improvement in the productive powers of labor, and the greater part of the skill, dexterity, and judgement with which it is anywhere directed, or applied, seem to have been the effects of the division of labour."[1] Thus begins the first chapter of book 1 of *The Wealth of Nations* by the Scot Adam Smith (1723–90).

An example follows this abrupt opening statement: workers engaged in the manufacture of pins. One worker draws out the wire; another straightens it; a third cuts it; a fourth sharpens it; a fifth is employed in grinding the end that receives the head, which in turn requires three distinct operations (cutting, softening, striking). Then, successively, the pins are yellowed, whitened, slaked, dried, pierced into the paper to package them, and lined up. Making pins into objects of consumption requires eighteen distinct operations. In fact, all the objects in our everyday environment presuppose an incredible variety and quantity of labor. Without a division of labor, "the very meanest person in a civilised country could not be provided, even according to, what we very falsely imagine, the easy and simple manner in which he is commonly accommodated."[2] The course of the production of a woolen jacket is another proof of this: there is the shepherd, the sorter of wool, the wool comber or carder, the dyer, the scribbler, the spinner, the weaver, the fuller, the dresser, the merchant, and the carrier, plus shipbuilders and sail makers, and mariners bringing back different dyes from the four corners of the world, and so forth.

Smith infers a law from the example of pin manufacture: the higher the degree of perfection of a country, the greater the extent of the separation of jobs and tasks. What in a "rude state of society" is the work of a single man, in "every improved society" is the job of many. Three factors explain the gain in productivity to the degree that labor is divided: the increase in dexterity in each individual worker, the saving of time that was previously lost (in the shift from one task to another), and the invention of a great number of machines that shorten and facilitate tasks, and that allow one person to fulfill the functions of several. This labor of invention has engendered a particular profession that we call "philosophers or men of speculation, whose trade it is not to do any thing, but to observe every thing; and who, upon that account, are often capable of combining together the powers of the most distant and dissimilar objects." This work is also subdivided into a great number of different branches, each of which affords occupation to a particular "tribe" or class of philosophers.

Smith was certainly not the first to speak of the principle of the division of labor. Before him, philosophers such as Plato or political economists such as William Petty and Turgot had sensed the importance of this notion, but he was the first to use it to build a scientific system.

This conceptual revolution involves a strange paradox. To substantiate the concept, Adam Smith does not turn for his example to a manufactory in his own country, which was beginning its Industrial Revolution with a lead of several decades over continental Europe, but to an "allemanderie" (needle factory) in Laigle, thirty leagues from Paris, in Normandy.

In fact, Smith borrowed his example, while neglecting to cite his sources, from the article on pins published in 1755 in volume 5 of the Encyclopédie.[3] It was signed by M. de Laire, who had just published a book on the philosophy of Francis Bacon. This extremely well researched study of the pin, defined as "the thinnest, commonest, least precious of mechanical objects and nevertheless one of those that demand perhaps the most combinations," is illustrated in a separate anthology by three plates of which two double ones describe the eighteen operations through which this tiny object passes, starting with the "thick copper wire" imported from Germany and Sweden.[4]

The article in question even earned a commentary on its final page from Diderot, who seized the opportunity to recall that the philosophy of his great encyclopedic project was to ally technology and theory: M. de Laire's book on Bacon,

> joined to the preceding description, will prove that a good mind may sometimes, with the same success, both elevate itself to the highest contemplations of philosophy and descend into the most minute details of mechanics. Moreover, those who know a little of the views held by the English philosopher in writing his books would not be astonished to see his disciple pass without scorn from the search for the general laws of Nature to the least important use of its productions.[5]

As for the three factors advanced by Smith in his analysis of the impact of the division of labor on the increase in productivity and wealth, their resemblance to the argument contained in the article titled "Art," published in 1751 in volume 1 of the same *Encyclopédie,* is not fortuitous either.[6] All this suggests how much the idea of the separation of tasks was already in the spirit of the times, as is further shown in the *Encyclopédie*'s article titled "Function." Initially defined strictly according to "animal economy" ("an action corresponding to the object of the organ that executes it, as respiration is the function of the chest"), the term then turns toward a more general meaning: "actions, insofar as they are carried out to fulfill a duty in which their structure and position engage them." This meaning of the word is illustrated by the "arrangement and preparation each worker in a printing shop is obliged to make, according to the task to which he is assigned."

Still, Adam Smith was the first to make the connection between the small Normandy factory so minutely examined by a French philosopher and a search for the general laws of nature as they operate in the economy of nations.

The division of labor is not the product of "human wisdom." It is the "necessary, though very slow and gradual, consequence of a certain propensity in human nature which has in view no such extensive utility; the propensity to truck, barter, and exchange one thing for another."[7] The problem is that the universal propensity of human nature to barter — the power to exchange that gives rise to the division of labor — is limited "by the extent of that power, or, in other words, by the extent of the market." An exiguous sphere of exchange is incompatible with the "separation of different trades and employments from one another."

It is here that Smith takes up the theme of routes of communication. They constitute in his view essential elements in the extension of markets, the progressive complication of the division of labor, and, as such, they are at the root of civilization. This subject occupies the whole of chapter 3, preceding another devoted to money, that other means of exchange whose origin and use are situated within the same framework.

In a world acted on by coexchanging producers and consumers who are all responding solely to self-interest, communication contributes to the organization of collective labor (within the factory, but also in the structuring of economic spaces).

In trade between village and town, among towns, between London and Calcutta, between the colony and the metropole, Smith insists on the role of domestic and foreign navigation. His history is river-oriented. He attributes to the Nile and its canals the "great opulence" of ancient Egypt, skips to the multitude of canals in the civilizations of China and Bengal in order by contrast to note the "barbarous and uncivilized" state in inland parts of Africa, a whole part of Asia Minor, and Siberia, deprived as they are of means of communication. He indicates in passing the role of the Maas and the Rhine in Holland, and the scant utility of the Danube for Bavaria, Austria, and Hungary.

His history of the English economy is also principally a maritime one. The slow process of formation of the domestic market is seen through this lens. "As by means of water-carriage," he writes,

a more extensive market is opened to every sort of industry than what land-carriage alone can afford..., so it is upon the sea-coast, and along the banks of navigable rivers, that industry of every kind naturally begins to subdivide and improve itself, and it is frequently not till a long time after that those improvements extend themselves to the inland parts of the country. A broad-wheeled wagon, attended by two men, and drawn by eight horses, in about six weeks' time carries and brings back between London and Edinburgh near four ton weight of goods. In about the same time, a ship navigated by six or eight men, and sailing between the ports of London and Leith, frequently carries and brings back two hundred ton weights of goods... Since such, therefore, are the advantages of water-carriage, it is natural that the first improvements of art and industry should be made where this conveniency opens the whole world for a market to the produce of every sort of labor, and that they should always be much later in extending themselves into the inland parts of the country.[8]

In spite of his laissez-faire vision, Smith was so convinced of the strategic importance of this opening to the entire world through mastery of the seas that he did not hesitate to support the Navigation Act, a manifestation of the old protectionist regulation inspired by mercantilism, in the name of the "defense of the Country," indissociable from that of naval trade and the fleet. (He is more consistent with his doctrine of governmental noninterference when he asserts, with reference to the construction of roads, that it is better not to build a road or a bridge with public money if the tolls collected from users do not cover the original outlay and maintenance costs.)

In the commercial cosmopolis of the laissez-faire vision, the division of labor and the routes of communication rhyme with opulence and civilization. They are indices of "growth," another word that began its ambiguous career in Smith's century. They also coincide with peace. The universal economic republic leads the civilized world toward a "single workshop" and a "single market." The abolition of borders via the extension of the market eliminates the hostile forces that pit nations against each other. The merchant is a citizen of the world. "A merchant is by necessity not the citizen of any country in particular. He does not care in what place he has his business."

Wakefield and Babbage: Cooperation and Division of Mental Labor

The English school of classical economics would continue to relay Smith's analyses while correcting and adapting them. It accentuated them in conjunction with the rise of England's maritime hegemony. Reviewing the "causes of a superior production strength," John Stuart Mill (1806–73) wrote in 1848 in *Principles of Political Economy* (book 1, chapter 7):

> Perhaps a greater advantage than all these [fertility of the soil, the climate, the abundance of mineral deposits] is a maritime situation, especially when accompanied with good natural harbors; and next to it, great navigable rivers. These advantages consist indeed wholly in saving of cost of carriage. But few who have not considered the subject, have any adequate notion how great an extent of economical advantage this comprises; nor, without having considered the influence exercised on production by exchanges, and by what is called the division of labor, can it be fully estimated. So important it is, that it often does more than counterbalance sterility of soil, and almost every other natural inferiority; especially in that early stage of industry in which labor and science have not yet provided artificial means of communication capable of rivalling the natural.[9]

Mill in this chapter approaches the tone of the military strategists of the period and prefigures the future analyses of the new "political geography" at the century's end.

In book 4 of the *Principles*, in which he treats the "influence of progress," in particular in a chapter devoted to the "consequences of the tendency of profits to a minimum," John Stuart Mill devotes much attention to the "conversion of circulating capital into fixed, whether by railways, or ships, or canals, etc.," and analyzes the role played in crises by wild speculations, as in the English railway gambling of 1844 and 1845. He concludes his observations as follows:

> The railway operations of the various nations of the world may be looked upon as a sort of competition for the overflowing capital of countries where profit is low and capital abundant, as England and Holland. The English railway speculations are a struggle to keep our annual increase of capital at home; those of foreign countries are an effort to obtain it.

Another of Mill's contributions to thought about "communication" appears in his comments on the role of information flows, notably in book 5, where he deals with "taxes on commodities" and especially "taxes on communication which are taxes on information" (the postage tax, taxes on advertisements and on newspapers). When government is the sole authorized carrier of letters, demands a monopoly price, and causes the chief burden of taxes to fall on business letters, this, he notes, runs counter to a free system. By increasing the expense of mercantile relations between distant places, it

> obstructs all operations by which goods are conveyed from place to place, and discourages the production of commodities in one place for consumption in another; which is not only in itself one of the greatest sources of economy of labor, but is a necessary condition of almost all improvements in production, and one of the strongest stimulants of industry, and promoters of civilization.

The same type of objection can be made to taxes on advertisements. If such taxes are high, this seriously discourages advertising, whose function is to facilitate "the coming together of the dealer or producer and the consumer," and one runs the risk of seeing a prolongation of the period "during which goods remain unsold, and capital locked up in idleness." As for taxes on newspapers, they should not exist in any country, since they "render this great diffuser of information, of mental excitement, and mental exercise, less accessible to that portion of the public which most needs to be carried into a region of ideas and interests beyond its own limited horizon."

Mill's focus on information does not stop at these isolated examples. One cannot understand his preoccupation with this subject outside the context of his overall conception of information as an agent in the dynamics of the market. As the American historian of communication James R. Beniger noted in 1992, Mill's classic economic theory, extending the earlier analyses of Quesnay and Smith on the "generalized symbolic media of exchange," is an attempt to treat this sphere of symbolic exchanges "in a cybernetic model of material flows with feedback flows of money *qua* information."[10]

But renewal of thought on the division of labor came in England from two authors: Edward G. Wakefield (1796–1862) and Charles Babbage (1792–1871), whose ideas would be taken up and integrated by Mill into his *Principles of Political Economy.*

Wakefield would revise the founding concept by adding another, that of cooperation, invoked as a reference point in the configuration of modern communication in the nineteenth century. The division of labor is just one aspect of things; it is merely a part of the more general principle of political economy: cooperation, which may be simple or complex. Simple cooperation is the union of several workers who help each other in particular labor situations (work aboard ship to raise or furl the sails, moving loads, erecting scaffolding, etc.). It is the first step in social progress. The product of this shared labor is proportional to the mutual assistance. Those who cooperate are conscious of the assistance they lend each other. Complex cooperation is a different situation, when a group of workers from different specialties aid each other through the division of operations. They work separately and require a mental effort to realize that they are in fact cooperating.

From this principle, Wakefield constructed a theory and practice of the management of territory in the colonies, advocating what he called "systematic colonization." The mode of colonization practiced up to that point was to place families, each on its own piece of land, one next to the other. However, nothing, in his view, was more harmful to progress and commerce. He recommended that instead, in every new colony, an urban population equal to the agricultural population should be made to settle so that the two together could constitute a market. Indeed, it was the lack of urban population that limited the productive forces of a country, as illustrated by the case of India, where the "few wants and the unaspiring spirit of the cultivators (joined until lately with great insecurity of property, from military and fiscal rapacity) prevent them from attempting to become consumers of town produce."[11] An urban population spurred on the nearby agricultural centers. Wakefield and Stuart Mill thus clearly connected the question of the division of labor to a theory of the organization of society.

Mathematician Charles Babbage's contribution to the conceptualization of the division of labor is of another kind. His work is intimately connected to the history of information-computing machines. His book *On the Economy of Machinery and Manufactures,* published in 1832, is one of the first to explain to the general public the efficiency of machines for deploying strength beyond that of man or performing tasks too delicate for the hand—the third element in the division of labor, which Smith had merely touched upon.[12] Babbage's thought on the "division of mental labor" led him to observe, for the first time, that the division of labor allows the classification of workers according to their capabilities, a point that had gone unnoticed by Smith.

As an inventor, Babbage would devote much effort to mechanizing the operations of the intelligence. He devised two projects for calculating machines: the "difference engine" and the "analytical engine," or "number mill." Only the first was realized. For the second, he imagined combining a broad variety of existing technologies (steam engine, windmill, programmed automata, mechanics); this aborted project was one of the ancestors of the great calculators that preceded the advent of the computer. Shifting large series of numbers from a manual mode of processing to a mechanical mode would preoccupy Babbage until the end of his life; he had undertaken this task in 1820, with the explicit object of facilitating the calculation of the actuarial tables of insurance companies. Babbage, who occupied Newton's chair of Lucasian Professor of Mathematics at Cambridge and was appointed first President of the Statistical Section of the British Association, had entitled his first book, published in 1826, *A Comparative View of the Various Institutions of the Assurance of Life.*

What is interesting about Babbage is how he arrived by his own intellectual path at the notion of division of mental labor, and how he saw his immediate predecessors. He reports how reading the works of Smith had inspired the research of the Frenchman Marie Riche de Prony (1755–1839). This engineer of Ponts et Chaussées and director of the school from 1815 to 1839, had been asked in 1791 by the Commission of Weights and Measures to draw up, for the geodesic department, logarithmic and trigonometric tables (at 14, 19, and 25 decimals) required to establish the metric system. It was while skimming the first chapter of Adam Smith that de Prony had conceived the idea of "manufacturing logarithms like pins."[13] The French engineer divided the task into three sections. A first group, composed of five or six specialists in geometry, was charged with searching among the analytic expressions for a single function that could be the most easily adapted to simple numerical calculations. The second, made up of seven or eight mathematicians, translated these formulas into numbers. The last group of sixty to eighty calculators, of whom nine-tenths knew only the two first rules of arithmetic, performed the indicated operations and drew up the tables. The resulting tables filled no less than seventeen large folio volumes.

The influence of Smith's analyses would also be felt throughout the whole European continent. After *The Wealth of Nations* it became difficult to ignore what one historian of economic thought, Melchior Palyi, much later, in the 1920s, would call "historical economism":

> All manifestations of social life, the development of the whole social organism and of every part of it, according to some page or other of *The Wealth of Nations,* can be explained in terms of the underlying economic necessities and interests. It was this aspect of the doctrine which was adopted by the French, underlying the liberal *historicisme* since de Tocqueville as well as the historical philosophy of Saint-Simonisme and the sociology of Auguste Comte.[14]

But before entering into this discussion, and before judging the pertinence of this assertion, which may seem peremptory, we must first explain another thesis of English political economy.

Malthus and Vital Competition

Condorcet's theory of "continuous progress" and the unlimited "perfectibility of human societies" had made the suppression of inequalities, social and natural, the surest guarantee of equilibrium between means of subsistence and population. Demographic thought in mercantilist and then Physiocratic France had espoused the adage. "There is no other wealth or strength than men," seeing in the population increase a source of prosperity and power. On the other hand, in England at the end of the eighteenth century there began to appear doctrines that rejected the optimistic hypothesis of a natural equation between the growths of resources and numbers of inhabitants, considering that one progressed arithmetically and the other geometrically, hence the struggle for survival within the framework of a natural selection. On the basis of this demographic question, a larger debate on the paths to progress would develop.

It is on the determinism of this "natural law of population" that in 1798 the pastor Thomas R. Malthus (1766–1834) centered his pamphlet

An Essay on the Principle of Population, as It Affects the Future Improvement of Society, with Remarks on the Speculations of Mr. Godwin, M. Condorcet, and Other Writers. Published anonymously, this edition is now usually known as the *First Essay*, an octavo of fifty-five thousand words. Late in 1803 appeared a second edition, a quarto of two hundred thousand words with the new title *An Essay on the Principle of Population, or a View of Its Past and Present Effects on Human Happiness with an Inquiry into Our Prospects Respecting the Future Removal or Mitigation of the Evils Which It Occasions.* In his preface, Malthus considers the new edition a "new work." The *First Essay* had a polemical purpose; the second had the appearance of a treatise emphasizing empirical observations. In this second edition and subsequent ones (1806, 1807, 1817, and 1826), chapters and appendices were added and passages were excised or substantially rewritten. Despite these alterations, the central thesis remained unchanged and largely controversial.

Malthus's verdict allows for no appeal. In the second edition he wrote:

> A man who is born into a world already possessed, if he cannot get subsistence from his parents on whom he has a just demand, and if the society do not want his labor, has no claim of *right* to the smallest portion of food, and, in fact, has no business to be where he is. At nature's mighty feast there is no vacant cover for him. She tells him to be gone, and will quickly execute her own orders.[15]

In 1806, this famous paragraph was omitted.

Malthus's book takes as target the "systems of equality" defended by his compatriot William Godwin (1756–1836) in his *Enquiry Concerning Political Justice and Its Influence on General Virtue and Happiness* (1793) and by Condorcet in his *Sketch*. He also refutes the defenders of the English Poor Laws, arguing for "less state" and a restructuring of social expenditure. Malthus took aim not just at the French thinker but at all systems postulating the organic perfectibility of man and society, as embodied in particular in the French Revolution and its belief in infinite progress. To speculations on the building of an alternative society, he opposes the principle of self-interest or self-love as the "mainspring of the great machine of society," the only motive capable of inspiring action by the mass of society. To all those who accuse institutions of being the cause of the people's misery and poverty, he retorts:

> The principal and most permanent cause of poverty has little or no *direct* relation to forms of government, or the unequal division of property; and [since] the rich do not in reality possess the *power* of finding employment and maintenance for the poor, the

poor cannot, in the nature of things, possess the *right* to demand them; [these] are the important truths flowing from the principle of population.[16]

A precursor of the "crowd psychology" so dear to conservative thought starting in the late nineteenth century, which was to write an important chapter in the doctrines of mass communication, Malthus expressed fear of the "mob," which he made responsible for the return to despotism:

> A mob, which is generally the growth of a redundant population, goaded by resentment for real sufferings, but totally ignorant of the quarter from which they originate, is of all monsters the most fatal to freedom. It fosters a prevailing tyranny, and engenders one where it was not; and though, in its dreadful fits of resentment, it appears occasionally to devour its unsightly offspring; yet no sooner is the horrid deed committed, than, however unwilling it may be to propagate such a breed, it immediately groans with the pangs of a new birth.[17]

To the revolutionary model, synonymous for him with anarchy and usurpation, Malthus opposes that of evolution and order, the "mode of bettering that is prescribed to us by nature." To egalitarian utopia he opposes the progressive reality of a society in which the middle classes are destined to become larger and larger. Only the "middle parts of society are the most favorable to virtuous and industrious habits, and to the growth of all kinds of talents." The social success of this middle class will impose itself, he believed, as a model to be emulated by the lower classes, provided that the "hope to rise" and the "fear to fall" in society be maintained, and that the "animated activity in bettering our condition, which now forms the master-spring of public prosperity," be also allowed free play. Provided as well that two major institutions, private property and marriage, indispensable in the development of a sense of responsibility, be allowed to exercise their regulatory function. Both institutions served as "preventing checks" on population. (Delayed marriage and the observance of strict sexual continence during the waiting period constitute the check of "moral restraint.") All this is to be desired even, he admits, if "all cannot be in the middle; superior and inferior parts are in the nature of things absolutely necessary: and not only necessary, but strikingly beneficial."[18]

In accordance with this "rational expectation" of capillary movement and social mobility, Malthus, ferociously opposed to any intervention by the state in favor of the poor, proposed instruction in the principle of population through a "system of parochial education." The internalization of this dynamic principle by the lower classes would cause them to choose "moral restraint" and allow them to accept their misery with patience, before benefiting from the "gradual reforms" that the elites would not fail to promote. Education and propagation of these truths, touching closely on their happiness, while producing new means of advancement for all, should create the consensus necessary for evolution. "If these truths were by degrees more generally known (which in the course of time does not seem to be improbable from the natural effects of the mutual interchange of opinions)," he writes in the final chapter, "the lower classes of people, as a body, would become more peaceable and orderly, would be less inclined to tumultuous proceedings in seasons of scarcity and would at all times be less influenced by inflammatory and seditious publications, from knowing how little the price of labor and the means of supporting a family depend upon a revolution."[19]

Malthus believed, then, in the force of persuasion, that is, in both its virtues and its vices. According to him, only manipulative actions by opinion leaders, "the ambitious demagogues," "the discontented and turbulent minds who, born into the middle classes, seek to agitate the people," can explain social unrest.[20] In the same way, he is convinced that only a counterstrategy of propagation of the "population principle" as the explanation of its situation can check the "false expectations and extravagant demands" of the people. Thanks to his model of a society regulated by the "middle estate," Malthus is without a doubt the first to link the demographic question, as a tool of government, to a coherent strategy of communication, the formulation of which owed much to his experience as a preacher in the Lambeth parish.

All these antecedents make the *Essay* an essential core in the formation of a theory of the regulatory function of institutions or of social equilibrium. This was well understood by the founder of the structural-functional school of American sociology, Talcott Parsons, who considered Malthus an early precursor of an "equilibrium theory" of regulation, or better, of social self-regulation.[21] In stressing the need for the lower classes to internalize the population principle as a guide to social behavior, Malthus's doctrine represents a turning point in the legitimation of a form of power that Gilles Deleuze, in the lineage of the Foucauldian idea of the "discipline mechanism" as the internalization of constraint, calls "bio-power" or the "bio-politics of populations": life as stake and object of power.[22]

A century after the publication of the *Essay*, Malthus's fear of crowds in movement would be revived in Victorian England, under the effect of a phenomenon that Malthus, in promoting the behavior of the cultivated classes as a model, had scarcely foreseen: the declining fecundity of the marriages among elites. This was a time when the sociologist Herbert Spencer was expounding his law of individuation opposing sex and brain: the more the intellect develops, the more the reproductive functions dwindle.[23] It was also in this context, at the end of the nineteenth century, that English mathematical statistics—biometry—was born; it constituted an important milestone in the progress of high-quantity counting methods and social regulation by figures.

Having examined two major premises of English political economy, the division of labor and the struggle for existence, we shall now observe how each of them contributed to a theory of the evolution of human societies.

Laws of Development and the Positivism of Auguste Comte

The concept of division of labor theorized by Adam Smith combined with another theoretical tradition, articulated around the conceptual pair of growth and development arising from the life sciences.

In 1759, a German scholar living in Russia, Caspar Friedrich Wolff (1733–94), published a treatise entitled *Theoria generationis*. This book—followed by another, *De formatione intestinorum* (1768)—initiated a questioning of concepts that would result, about a century later, in the Darwinian theory of descent conditioned by natural selection. In the course of the eighteenth century, the "epigenetic" position took the lead over the "preformationist" position. According to the former perspective, the living being constructs itself after fertilization, with the different parts forming themselves progressively into the whole. The latter position holds that the living being is already constructed and merely develops after fertilization.

The concepts of development and evolution became a polemical stake in the understanding of organic generation. Embryology as a theory of development began to achieve its autonomy with respect to anatomy. Studying by microscope the development of the chick in the egg, Wolff proved that its intestine is at first a simple membrane, which then folds, forming a drain, then a tube. Refuting the idea that this intestine existed fully formed beforehand, Wolff showed that the anatomy of adult beings, the system formed by their structures, is only the end product of a more complex and basic system of embryonic structures. The concept of development was opposed to the mechanistic explanation of the origins of a living being as a juxtaposition of elements not originally organized into a totality.[24]

In 1828, another German also residing in Russia, Karl Ernst von Baer (1792–1876), introduced new concepts that would support that of development or evolution. In development, according to von Baer, there is an initial generality of typical characteristics, with the general ones appearing before the particular ones. There is a primordial homogeneity; differentiation is progressive and heterogeneity is the terminal state. Forty years later, the German biologist Ernst Haeckel (1834–1919) will call this idea the "basic law of biogenetics."

Development, homogeneity, differentiation, heterogeneity: these concepts would emigrate outside their realm of origin and serve as the bases of a nascent sociology, which would mix them with the notion of division of labor furnished by the political economy of both Smith and Turgot.

The first person to appropriate and systematize these concepts was Auguste Comte (1798–1857) in his *Course of Positive Philosophy,* which appeared by intervals from 1830 to 1842. His project was to build the foundations of a "true science of social development," a social physics modeled on the biological approach. The scientific matrix that made possible the interdisciplinary encounter around the sociological project in the nineteenth century was the organizational conception of life proposed by the life sciences. As François Jacob, historian of biological thought, explains:

> The organization was identified with life because it constituted a meeting-point for three interdependent variables: structure, function and what August Comte called "milieu" (environment). Life could exist only insofar as these three parameters remained in harmony. Any variation in one of them influenced the whole organism, which reacted by modifying the others. In a defined environment, wrote Comte, "given the organ, [it] finds its function, and vice-versa." This interaction was henceforth to provide the basis for the analysis of the functions and properties of living systems.[25]

Moreover, this idea of organization was indissolubly linked to that of history. The history of an organized system became the successive stages it had gone through or the series of transformations by which the system was progressively formed. Thus all ingredients were assembled to produce a theory about the history of human societies as a process of development.

"Progress is the development of order," Comte wrote. The notions of order and progress that became the bases of his social physics were as indivisible as are those of organization and life in biology. Progress is predetermined; it cannot transgress certain limits. The collective organism that is society obeys a physiological law of progressive development.

"The qualification of *development*," the founder of positivism specifies, "has by nature the precious advantage of directly determining what the real *perfecting* of humanity necessarily consists of; because it quickly indicates the spontaneous spring, gradually seconded by a suitable culture, of the always pre-existing fundamental faculties that constitute the whole of our nature, without any introduction whatever of new faculties."[26] This law of development or of the continuous progress of humanity was formulated thanks to "research into ovology and embryology" suggesting that "the perpetual accordance between the chief phases of the individual evolution and the most marked successive degrees of the organic hierarchy [constitutes] one of the most constant laws of biological philosophy."[27] As progress and order, movement remains subordinate to equilibrium, with social dynamics founded on social statics. Human history becomes the history of human nature. This history of the fundamental and necessary development of humanity obeys the "great law of triple intellectual evolution."

This latter idea first appeared as an intuition by the young Turgot. In the 1750s, the independent Physiocrat, in his lectures at the Sorbonne on the fundamental principles of a "political geography," had identified the increasing complexity of forms of social organization, insisting on the great law of progress in knowledge. According to him, the intellectual evolution of humanity, "the successive advances of the human mind," had passed through three phases: theological, metaphysical, and scientific. These observations by Turgot constitute, in Comte's view, "the precious early insights into the general theory of human perfectibility that no doubt usefully prepared the way for Condorcet's thought"[28]—and thereby that of the positivist philosopher himself.

Already, in the early eighteenth century, the philosopher and philologist Giambattista Vico (1668–1744), in his major opus *Scienza Nuova* (*The New Science*) (1725), had expressed his view of the pretension of Enlightenment political rationalism to enclose history within philosophical reason. Opening the path for a philosophy guided by the idea of progress, he had drawn up a chronological table of the three ages in the "march of nations": the divine or mythical age characterized by theocracy; the heroic age, or age of aristocratic government; and finally, the human age of freedom and reason. Each age was defined by different types of natures, manners, natural rights, governments, languages, and characters. But while he had insisted on an "ideal history of eternal laws that govern all nations, at their *birth,* in their *progress,* and their current *state,*" he had added "in their *decadence* and their *end,*" breaking with the idea of exponential human perfectibility and progress. For the author of *The New Science,* one of the first great modern critics of modernity, the history of the past that gives meaning to the present is that of the cycle, "corsi e ricorsi"—a movement in spirals and not in a unidirectional line.

Comte's "philosophical law of progress" conceived human history as the constant and inexorable succession of three general stages—primitively theological, transitionally metaphysical, and finally positive—through which our intelligence always passes.

This law explains both general history and the history of each individual. In the theological or imaginary stage, the human mind seeks a First Cause. It attributes all phenomena to supernatural agents and mysterious forces. It is as true for societies that live this stage as it is for children. There are child-peoples just as there are children. Both need a sense of the marvelous, fetishism, and chimerical beings. The metaphysical stage is that of adolescence, of personified abstractions, with naturalism being the extreme limit of this stage's development. The adult or positive stage relies on observation aided by calculation. It is the scientific age—that of reality, the useful, and organization. The positivist ideal is to be able to consider the diversity of observable phenomena as particular cases of a single general fact, such as gravitation, for example. In its theological or metaphysical stage, a society is conquering and then defensive. In its final positive stage, it is industrial.

The law of three stages is also a key to understanding the successive appearance of the various sciences, a history that began with calculation, geometry, and rational mechanics from which the first scientific category was formed: mathematics. This in turn allowed the study of stars (astronomy), analysis of the terrestrial environment—heat, light, atmosphere, electricity (physics)—and of substances (chemistry). It finally results in the two sciences of the industrial age: one that explains the organization of plants and animals, biology, from which in turn arises the second, sociology. In the conclusion to the portion of his course devoted to biology, where he reviews the notions of structure, apparatus, organ, tissue, function, and property, Comte writes:

> Social physics, the truly definitive science, which necessarily takes its immediate roots from biological science properly speaking, will therefore constitute the whole of natural philosophy into a corpus of doctrine, complete and indivisible, that will then allow the human mind to proceed always according to uniformly positive conceptions in whatever mode of its activity, causing the intellectual anarchy that characterizes our present state to cease.[29]

This conclusion also serves as an introduction to the fourth and final part of the course, which takes this "social physics" as its subject.

Unlike the theoretical formulation of positivism in its English version represented by Herbert Spencer, one finds in the Comtean history of the three stages no sketch of a general application of the notions of systems and apparatuses to the phenomena and processes of communication. Here is how, in his *Autobiography,* Spencer would characterize his own scientific project in relation to that of the Frenchman:

> What is Comte's professed aim? To give a coherent account of the progress of *human conceptions.* What is my aim? To give a coherent account of the progress of the *external world.* Comte proposes to describe the necessary, and actual, filiation of *things.* Comte professes to interpret the genesis of our *knowledge of nature.* My aim is to interpret, as far as it is possible, the genesis of the phenomena *which constitute nature.* The one end is *subjective.* The other is *objective.*[30]

In these years when the founder of sociology exercised his magisterial influence, the contrast was striking between the febrile activity of Saint-Simonianism in the area of technical networks of communication, and the philosophical project of positivism. The former draws a tight link between industrial organization and scientific organization. Comte, persuaded that only an "immense philosophical development arising from a single fundamental law" could prepare the "rational reform of a society in crisis," dissociated the two and dedicated himself unilaterally to achieving a city of the Learned. Moreover, he attributed to this deliberate choice his estrangement from Saint-Simon in 1822. Aged twenty-four at the time, he proposed a "plan of scientific work necessary to organize society." "Having pondered for a long time the generative ideas of M. de Saint-Simon," wrote Comte, "I applied myself exclusively to systematizing and developing and perfecting that part of the philosopher's insights pertaining to scientific leadership. This work resulted in the formation of a system of positive politics that today I begin to submit to the judgment of thinkers."[31]

In 1848, nine years before his death, while the fate of the Republic was being played out, Comte would invoke this city of the mind, which renounced all temporal power, to justify the universal vocation of his positive system. Prefacing a report on the reorganization of the French Republic within the framework of an "Occidental Republic of Order and Progress," he would write: "The philosophy that conceived of it [the Republic] can all the better recommend its adoption, in France first of all, and then in the rest of the Occident, if it finds itself politically disinterested, since the preachers of Humanity cannot today obtain their le-

gitimate spiritual ascendancy except by their fundamental renunciation
of all temporal authority, local or central."[32]

Comte is not exempt from a long French tradition of divorce between
society and technology. He was a practitioner of those "silences" vigor-
ously criticized by historian of technology Bertrand Gille:

> We see the French technological world taking shape progressively.
> Technology is not what people wish for: it offers few intellectual
> satisfactions; they think that at the very least it sullies one's
> hands... There is no technology in Balzac, who even ignores the
> railway, nor in Stendhal nor in Flaubert nor in Victor Hugo... But
> in English literature, people spin, weave, forge... Everything holds
> together, the system is entirely constructed.[33]

Throughout its history, French social science, descended from positivism, would accept only with difficulty the responsibility of accounting
for the essential part of the regulative apparatus of industrial societies
consisting of technical networks and material objects of communication.

This did not prevent Comtean positivism and its organic theory of
society from exercising a profound influence on future theoreticians of
communication. And today there are scarcely any serious studies in this
field of the social sciences that leave out this first stratum of sociological knowledge inspired by a functionalist vision, *avant la lettre*, of social institutions.[34] If this is true, it is because the notion of communication
has progressively converged with notions of development and growth.
Communication, which was only one indicator among others of the development of human societies, had in the course of time become one of
the most manifest expressions of a certain conception of progress, and
even became confused with it.

Herbert Spencer and "Organic Society"

> We must not overlook the greatness of the step made by M.
> Comte... Apart from the tenability of his sociological doctrines,
> his way of conceiving social phenomena was much superior to all
> previous ways; and among other of its superiorities, was this
> recognition of the dependence of Sociology on Biology... A
> society as a whole, considered apart from its living units, presents
> phenomena of growth, structure and function, like those of
> growth, structure and function in an individual body; and these
> last are needful keys to the first.[35]

This assertion by Herbert Spencer (1820–1903) is quoted from *The
Study of Sociology*, published in London in 1873. At the time, the work

of Auguste Comte continued to have a strong impact in English intellectual circles. John Stuart Mill had devoted a flattering book to him eight years previously, even though he was far from sharing Comte's ideas and hopes regarding the equation between progress and democracy.

Spencer, however, does not really belong to the lineage of the French philosopher: in his *Autobiography*, Spencer confessed that the word "sociology" was virtually the only thing he had borrowed from Comte. The English positivist left things up to individual initiative, denying the state the right to interfere in commercial transactions or in the managing of industry, education, or aid to the poor; he denounced the "adoration of the legislature" by men of his time and associated it with fetishism. Comte, by contrast, fed into the historical tradition of a state culture when he drew up projects for reorganizing society. Thus, on the one hand, we have "administrative nihilism," according to the expression of the naturalist Thomas Huxley (1825–95), and, on the other, social planning or the public management.[36] For Spencer, state constraints block differentiation and paralyze the law of vital competition and natural selection.

This was not the only major difference between the two. There was another of an epistemological nature. Both Spencer and Comte, it is true, adopted an evolutionary perspective, starting from the same embryological law of von Baer and his predecessors. But Comte founded his "social physics" by transforming the social mathematics of the eighteenth century (Turgot, Condorcet, etc.) into physics. By referring to physics broadly defined as master-discipline of the natural sciences, Comte marks his break with the philosophers of a theological and metaphysical bent, and lets it be understood that observation of social phenomena must prevail over sensory experience and logical/mathematical methods as well as the search for general laws. As for Spencer, he creates his "social physiology" by taking up the mechanical model of energy physics. His principle of "persistence of force" for explaining the process of evolution is synonymous with the conservation of energy. The universe is governed by "forces." Life consists of an incessant action and reaction of different forces, which tend everywhere to attain an equilibrium; but from the moment that, for whatever cause, this tendency to equilibrium is perturbed, the vital forces gain in energy. This is the law of the instability of the homogeneous. In his *First Principles* (1862), Spencer defines the evolution as an "integration of matter and concomitant dissipation of motion; during which the matter passes from an indefinite, incoherent homogeneity to a definite, coherent heterogeneity; and during which the retained motion undergoes a parallel transformation."[37]

The mechanistic principles of force—the physical aspect and not the biological side of Spencerian evolutionism—would attract the attention of Henri Bergson (1859–1941), who in 1907 would devote the end of *Creative Evolution* to it. He reproached Spencer's method for not keeping its promises, eliminating duration by reconstituting movement from static states, that is, from immobile results. Spencer, he says, "recomposes consolidity with consolidity, instead of discovering the gradual work of consolidation that is evolution itself."[38]

Social physiology brings to an extreme the hypothesis of a continuity between the biological order and the social order. Society is an organism, and the law of organic development is valid for all progress, "whether of the development of the Earth, the development of life on its surface, the development of society, of government, of industry, commerce, language, literature, science, or art." Division of labor and progress go hand in hand. Progress is a necessity, as sure as the fact that human beings must "become perfect." Civilization is a phase of nature, like the "development of the embryo or the opening of a flower."

From the homogeneous to the heterogeneous, from the simple to the complex, from concentration to differentiation, "organic society" or today's industrial society—as opposed to yesterday's "military societies"—is a society that is more and more coherent and integrated: its functions are more and more clearly defined. "If organization consists in such a construction of the whole that its parts can carry on mutually dependent actions, then in proportion as organization is high, there must go a dependence of each part upon the rest so great that separation is fatal, and conversely. This truth is equally well known in the individual organism and in the social organism."[39] Having defined the term "development" as the passage from the homogeneous to the heterogeneous, Spencer refuses to assimilate it to "growth" because, in his view, growth does not imply modification of the structure. On the other hand, "evolution" encompasses both "development" and "growth."

Spencerian evolutionist sociology proposes to study the development of social organisms, their apparatuses, their systems of organs, and their functions, drawing inspiration from the description of biological organisms. In *The Principles of Sociology*, his mature work published in three volumes (1876–96), Spencer thus distinguishes between three great "systems of organs" in society: the productive, the distributive, the regulative. Communication is a basic function of the latter two; mutual dependence implies intermediation and the development of the "apparatus for exchanging products and influences," both in defensive and offensive contexts.

The productive apparatus resembles the system that accomplishes the feeding of the living body; these are the productive industries that sustain the social body. The second type of system assures the distribution of the nutritive matters. Just as the gelatinous protozoans, the lowest major division of the animal kingdom, show scarcely any trace of ramifications running throughout the body to carry nutritive fluid, the "lowest types of societies" have no systems of distribution: "no roads or traders exist." Spencer retraces the long evolution of communication routes "necessitated by increase of size, resulting in the massing of groups" and the concomitant emergence of a "complex mercantile agency of wholesale and retail distributors": hunting tracks, country paths, toll roads, finished roads, highways, railways. The contrast between "undeveloped and developed societies" arises from the fact of this increasing specialization of functions. "Beginning as a slow flux to and reflux from certain places at long intervals," the movement of commodities passes "into rhythmical, regular, rapid currents, and material for sustentation distributed hither and thither, from being few and crude become numerous and elaborated."[40] The gradually formed channels of sending the bought and sold commodities fulfill a function similar to that fulfilled in a living body by the tortuous channels of the vascular system and its blood vessels.

The regulative apparatus is what makes possible the management of relations between a dominant center, increasingly voluminous and complex, and subordinate centers. The main agent of regulation is information. The body politic and the structures of its great "centers of control" are guided by information that arrives by means of petitions, the press, inquiries, commissions, intelligence, advisers, and informers. These data allow it to make decisions and have its commands carried out by subordinate centers. In the human body, this function springs from the nervous system, with the brain sifting information brought by the sense organs to determine which actions should be stimulated by the motor centers. The spinal cord, motor and sensory ganglia, medulla oblongata, cerebrum, cerebellum, and so forth, are all given specialized missions as receivers of stimuli and conveyers of impulses in this evolutionist cartographic analogue to information.

The "apparatuses" by which central control is exercised are the "media of communication" through which the center may affect the parts, to "propagate its influence," "communicate intelligence" (via messengers, couriers, newsletters, newspapers, and, finally, long-distance transmission). Spencer writes:

> There arises a far swifter propagation of stimuli serving to
> coordinate social actions, political, military, commercial, etc.
> Beginning with the semaphore telegraph, which, reminding us in
> principle of the signal fires of savages, differed by its ability to
> convey not single vague ideas only, but numerous, complex, and
> distinct ideas, we end with the electric telegraph, immeasurably

more rapid, through which go quite definite messages, infinite in variety and of every degree of complexity. And, in place of a few such semaphore telegraphs, transmitting, chiefly for governmental purposes, impulses in a few directions, there has come a multiplicity of lines of instant communication in all directions, subserving all purposes. Moreover, by the agency of these latest internuncial structures the social organism, though discrete, has acquired a promptness of coordination equal to, and indeed exceeding, the promptness of coordination in concrete organisms. It was before pointed out that social units, though forming a discontinuous aggregate, achieve by language a transmission of impulses which, in individual aggregates, is achieved by nerves.[41]

Messages conveyed by this "molecular continuity of wires" are compared with a "nervous discharge" that communicates a movement from any citizen of one town to any citizen in another. As for the postal apparatus, it is "bringing those impulses by which the industry of the place is excited or checked." The cardinal law is that as "organic evolution shows us more and more efficient internuncial devices subserving regulation, so, too, does social evolution." For example, sponges, which have no coordinating centers of any kind, are also without "means of transferring impulses from part to part" and without the possibility of "cooperation of parts to meet an outer action."

Spencer's scientific work was significantly influenced by his early career as an employee of the London and Birmingham Railway. As Joseph Needham noted in his book *The Sceptical Biologist* (1929): "Spencer's system of ideas is a philosophy which, well articulated and riveted firmly together in every part, seemed to spring fully armed from the brain of a master engineer."[42] Despite his engineering background, his conceptual scheme reserves no place for the figure and concept of "network" to express what he called the "apparatus of major and minor channels through which the necessaries of life are drafted out of the general stocks circulating through the kingdom."

Nothing escapes the scalpel of the former engineer's theory in this quest for symmetries between the human body and the body politic — between Adam Smith's economic division of labor and the "physiological division of labor." This latter concept had been forged in 1827 by the French physiologist Henri Milne-Edwards (1800–1885). Reading, in 1851, a textbook by this French zoologist prominent in comparative anatomy and physiology, Spencer had found the theory that thereafter was to play a crucial part in his thought. In March 1852, he published a famous article, "The Development of Hypothesis," in the *Leader* about his project for an organicist science. The same year, he gave his own interpretation of Malthus's principle in a brief essay titled "The Theory of Population," extending it in an evolutionary direction by making the struggle for existence the starting point of his theory of progress in human society.

Seven years later, the concept of the "physiological division of labor" was taken up by the naturalist Charles Darwin.

The Decisive Influence of Darwinian Evolutionism

"Natural selection," wrote Darwin,

acts exclusively by the preservation and accumulation of variations, which are beneficial under the organic and inorganic conditions to which each creature is exposed at all periods of life. The ultimate result is that each creature tends to become more and more improved in relation to its conditions. This improvement inevitably leads to the gradual advancement of the organization of the greater number of living beings throughout the world. But here we enter a very intricate subject, for naturalists have not defined to each other's satisfaction what is meant by an advance in organization... Von Baer's standard seems the most widely applicable and the best, namely, the amount of differentiation of the parts of the same organic being, in the adult state as I should be inclined to add, and their specialization for different functions; or, as Milne-Edwards would express it, the completeness of the division of physiological labor.[43]

When he spoke of the broad differentiation of the parts of the same being, the specialization of these parts for different functions and the perfecting of the "physiological division of labor," Darwin was renewing the thought of von Baer with his own theory of progress in the organization of the animal kingdom, the living in movement. These theories are developed in a major book, *The Origin of Species*, published in 1859, which proposes to study the nature of characters, whether innate or acquired by variation, that is to say, in the course of gradual evolution, as opposed to the change in the form of a jump or brutal leap.

The research that provided Darwin (1809–82) with the basis for this book bore, strictly speaking, on the raising of pigeons.[44] In the same way, based on his observation of an order of crustaceans, the cirripedes (including barnacles and acorn shells), living and fossilized, he set up a perfectly coherent system of classification that served him as the methodological foundation for his entire opus following his voyage around the world between 1831 and 1836 on board the *Beagle*.[45] Although he seldom wrote about humans the way he wrote about the animal kingdom, he offered multiple reference points for an anthropomorphic under-standing of his analyses. In any case, many readers of this astoundingly successful book—the first edition was published in November and the second only a month and a half later—did not hesitate to extrapolate to the human being the principle of "natural selection." (This principle, established by Darwin after a minute genealogical classification of or-ganized beings, is a "natural system" in which the degrees of acquired differences are expressed by the terms varieties, species, genera, families, orders, and classes.)

The Spencerian framework for interpreting *The Origin of Species,* moreover, would clearly foster a social use of Darwinian theory that moved in the direction of a sociological evolutionism. Darwin himself wished such a cross-fertilization. "In the future, I see open fields for far more important researches. Psychology will be securely based on the foundation already laid by Mr. Herbert Spencer, that of the necessary acquirement of each mental power and capacity by gradation. Much light will be thrown on the origin of man and his history."[46]

In addition, having made political economy a source of inspiration, Darwin, in one way or another, had to account for it. On the one hand, it was reading Malthus's *Essay on the Principle of Population* that launched the theorization of Darwin's long-term observations. As he acknowl-edged in his introduction, he would consider "the Struggle for Exis-tence among all organic beings throughout the world, which inevitably follows from the high geometric ratio of their increase...This is the doc-trine of Malthus, applied to the whole animal and vegetable kingdoms."[47] On the other hand, as we have already seen, there are borrowings from Adam Smith. The Malthusian iron law discernible behind the principle of natural selection orients his work toward what S. S. Schweber calls a "determinist, quantitative, mechanistic and Newtonian conception of the world." Along with Smith's theories comes the entire Scottish school's principle of divergence and its representation of market operations as a free and open process. Darwin effected a curious amalgam between a static vision and a dynamic explanation.[48]

But Darwin was, after all, a man of his time, a subject of the Victo-rian Empire, that paragon of "progress." As he wrote in *The Voyage of the Beagle,* "It is impossible for an Englishman to behold these distant colonies without a high pride and satisfaction. To hoist the British flag seems to draw with it as a certain consequence, wealth, prosperity and civilization."[49]

The Origin of Species was rapidly taken up by a broad range of opin-ion of his time. The industrial bourgeoisie sought in it a legitimation of its historic mission as the bearer of progress. Social Darwinism sought his scientific warrant for an inegalitarian organization of society, and even for a frankly oppressive conception of relations among individuals, races, and cultures. At the other end of the political spectrum, the theoreticians of socialism would see in Darwin the confirmation of their critique of religious obscurantism and the static vision of the world. Not to mention the aberrations of a Marxist Darwinism allying biological determinism and social determinism and equating the Struggle for Life with the Class Struggle.[50]

With the theory of evolution by natural selection, scientific research that did not take as its direct object the study of human societies would thus decisively influence later thinking about the social. Certain techniques and procedures for obtaining the truth were hereafter valorized, and the status of those responsible for defining the truth was redefined: "It is no doubt with Darwin," observes Michel Foucault,

> or rather with the post-Darwinian evolutionists, that the "specific intellectual," the "expert scholar," begins clearly to appear. The stormy relations between evolutionism and the socialists, the very ambiguous effects of evolutionism (for example, on sociology, criminology, psychiatry, eugenics), signal the important moment when it is in the name of a "local" scientific truth — as important as it may be — that the scholar makes interventions in contemporaneous political struggles. Historically, Darwin represents this turning point in Western intellectual history.[51]

Diffusionism and the Spreading of the Ideology of Progress

At the end of the nineteenth century, the evolutionist model of the social seen through biological lenses would become common sense when it came to labeling new systems of communication. The following quote from a geography treatise of the day illustrates this clearly: "The terrestrial globe today constitutes a vast organism all of whose parts are in solidarity; any change occurring in one of these parts affects all the others: it is the effect of the routes of communication; their development is perhaps the characteristic trait of the contemporary age."[52]

Communication became "one of the principal agents of civilization" in a geography whose ideal was defined by "the harmonious determinism of natural life." The globe as an organized body explained the new international division of labor and the growth in "reciprocal dependence of nations," and at the same time obliterated the new hierarchies of the world economy and universalized a particular idea of history: the catechism of free trade. We know how much the latter was combated by Karl Marx even before the abolition of protective measures and the universalization of competition. "We are told, for instance," he wrote in 1848,

> that Free Trade would create an international division of labor, and thereby give each country those branches of production most in harmony with its natural advantages. You believe perhaps, gentlemen, that the production of coffee and sugar is the natural destiny of the West Indies. Two centuries ago, nature, which does not trouble itself about commerce, had planted neither sugar-cane nor coffee trees there...If the Free Traders cannot understand how one nation can grow rich at the expense of another, we need not wonder, since these same gentlemen also refuse to understand how in the same country one class can enrich itself at the expense of another.[53]

"The theory of evolution by natural selection," writes Eric Hobsbawm, "reached out far beyond biology...It ratified the triumph of history over all the sciences, though 'history' in this connection was generally confused by contemporaries with 'progress.' "[54] This statement applies not just to the work of Darwin, but to the entire evolutionist mentality. Having rejected the search for the First Cause proper to the theological age, that mentality lost its way in the quest for the Final Cause.

In this perspective, history unfolds according to the "slice model," to use Braudel's felicitous expression. To attain this "progress," backward societies or those deprived of the support and the revelation of the Enlightenment must mount one by one the several stages of history. The path that leads upward is a straight line, without loops, detours, steps backward, regressions, or intersections with paths already taken. The golden rule of this irresistible and "necessary" movement forward is the imitation of the models of perfectibility symbolized by the societies that have already achieved this most advanced stage. This was the theorization espoused, starting in the third quarter of the nineteenth century, by a certain anthropological approach known as diffusionism.

This incarnation of the evolutionist schematics proposes a scale of values for different cultures. "As *Homo sapiens* was zoologically at the peak of the animal kingdom," explains the historian of ethnological theory Robert H. Löwie (1883–1957),

> so Western Europe in 1870 marked the goal of civilization. As the single cell was the hypothetical starting point for evolution, so a savage hovering on the border of bestiality must serve as the point of origin for culture. Since, however, that primeval man could no longer be observed, modern savages were lightly substituted insofar as they differed from Victorian Europe. On the other hand, usages of modern Europeans not in keeping with their advanced

status were like those rudimentary organs of animals which Darwin had compared to the letters of a word that are no longer pronounced. A fatal fallacy of all this reasoning lay in the naïve equation of modern primitive groups with the primeval savage.[55]

The vision of a history in slices also infused economic science. Even before Spencer and Darwin had published their books, the historical school of German economists — launched in 1843 with the book by its leader, Wilhelm Roscher (1817–94), entitled *Grundrisse zu Vorlesungen über die Staatswirtschaft nach geschichtlichen Methode* (the 1877 edition is translated as *Principles of Political Economy*) — adopted the viewpoint of evolution and was constructed around a concept of the development of a nation's economic life envisaged as a succession of stages. Bruno Hildebrand (1812–78) synthesized this program in the title of a work published in 1876, *Die Entwicklungsstufen der Geldwirtschaft* (The phases of economic development), in which he defines political economy as the "doctrine of the laws of economic development of nations."[56] Germany, along with England, was the seat of one of the two great diffusionist schools at the end of the century, and it gave rise to Albert Schaeffle (1831–1903) and his *Bau und Leben des Socialen Körpers* (Organization and life of the body social) (1885), one of the most systematic expositions, besides that of Spencer, of the organicist method. Before the century was over, the German diffusionist Friedrich Ratzel laid the foundations of the new political geography or "geopolitics" with the concepts of "life space" and "natural borders."

The biomorphic notion of development, heir to the nineteenth century, would inspire the politics of the League of Nations after World War I. In the Covenant of this international organization, approved in 1919, one could still read under article 22 concerning the establishment of the "Mandate System":

To those colonies and territories . . . which are inhabited by peoples not yet able to stand by themselves under the strenuous conditions of the modern world, there should be applied the principle that the well-being and development of such peoples form a sacred trust of civilization and that securities for the performance of this trust should be embodied in this Covenant. The best method of giving practical effect to this principle is that the tutelage of such peoples should be entrusted to advanced nations who, by reason, of their resources, their experience or their geographical position, can best undertake this responsibility, and who are willing to accept it, and that this tutelage should be exercised by them as

Mandatories on behalf of the League. The character of the mandate must differ according to the stage of development of the people.[57]

Thus the "Mandate System" naturalized the international regulation efforts resulting from the economic imperialism of the great powers, in particular France and Great Britain, in the so-called backward countries. The evolutionist model was one essential component of the first sociological formulations of communication. It would remain so during the following century.

In 1959, the centennial year of the publication of *The Origin of Species*, Georges Canguilhem justified in the following terms the work he had undertaken with a multidisciplinary team to retrace the genealogy of the concepts of "development" and "evolution":

The subject was chosen because of the current interest in the concept of development. In psychology and education, it is taken as a foundation for the practices of a new technocracy. In politics, and especially in the international sphere, the concept of underdevelopment tends to give a good conscience to ex-colonizing nations. Thus, a historical study of the elaboration of concepts of development and evolution seems worthy of being attempted other than as futile erudition or a scholastic exercise.[58]

It could not have been said better. The following year, Walt W. Rostow published *The Stages of Economic Growth*, in which he drew from the history of industrial development in England a universal model of the trajectory toward modernization and the supreme phase of high consumption that he offered as a path for the "Wretched of the Earth."[59] In these same years appeared revamped diffusionist theories that saw in the mass media the agents of this modernization modeled on the historical experience and the values of Western centers. But the day came in the late 1970s when these ideologues of linear and vertical progress through the "revolution of rising expectations" were exposed for their inability to assure the transition to development for the great majority living in the periphery, while at the same time protecting the biosphere.[60] In an ironic twist, the "living systems," on the basis of which the evolutionist model had claimed to make "natural" its rationalist idea and productivist ideology of progress, made an abrupt return to the scene.

PART II

Utopias of the Universal Bond

Chapter 4
The Cult of the Network

"Everything by steam and electricity"; "Replace the exploitation of man by man with the exploitation of the globe by humanity": these slogans sum up the doctrine of the school of Saint-Simonianism. Starting with the utopia of an egalitarian society advanced by Saint-Simon, this ideal became among his disciples a reality principle for a way of reorganizing society, and a philosophy of enterprise in a France that was seeking its path toward industrial society. With the appearance of the railway, the image of the network served as a guide for the first formulation of a redemptive ideology of communication. Networks of communication were envisaged as creators of a new universal bond.

Saint-Simon, Organism and Organization

In the genesis of the vision of society-as-organism in the nineteenth century, there is an essential link in the chain of thought that we have not yet examined: the one Comte called the "mother ideas" of Claude Henri de Saint-Simon (1760–1825). These ideas are the point of departure for a renewal of the framework of understanding borrowed from the living world. "The philosophy of Saint-Simon," notes Pierre Musso,

> appearing at the start of the nineteenth century after the French Revolution, assembled symbolic images of the body as a state, identified with an equivalence between the organism and the network, and mobilized them to develop a theory of administration thought of as transition/mediation between social systems: the celebrated passage from the "government of men" to the "administration of things."[1]

Saint-Simon's purpose was indeed to supply the tools for administering the organic economy of society, seen as a great body or as a "veritable being whose existence is more or less vigorous or faltering according to whether its organs each perform more or less regularly the functions entrusted to it." This metaphor of the organism fits together neatly, moreover, with that of the mechanism: society is a "veritable organized machine" in which the lives of individuals constitute the "cogs" and whose harmony depends on that of all the "springs" that compose it, each of them having to furnish "its necessary contingent of action and reaction."[2]

The metaphor of the organism considered as a tangle or web of networks refers to a project for an exact and applied science of social organization, or better, the "reorganization of the body politic," a key phrase in the philosopher's work. The science of organized beings and of their relations considered as physiological phenomena, for which he aspired to lay the foundations, was called by Saint-Simon "social physiology" — a term directly linked to the advances in medical research at the start of the century.

In 1801, in his book *Anatomie générale appliquée à la physiologie et à la médecine* (General anatomy applied to physiology and medicine), the physiologist Xavier Bichat (1771–1802), founder of modern histology, had inaugurated a century in which physiology would "take off" and define its methods. During this century, the establishment of the life sciences was accompanied by a definitive challenge to the image of an eternal Nature and a living world conceived as "a system regulated from without, as long as it was presumed to be administered externally by a supreme power."[3] In scrutinizing this "logic of life," the life sciences excluded any recourse to extrascientific considerations of a metaphysical or theological order. No more God the supreme watchmaker, no more deus ex machina operated by a machinist in the wings of the theater of life. With the help of new techniques like desiccation, putrefaction, maceration, and coction, the French physiologist extracted from his observations the notion of tissue, and discovered that life is constituted by the tissues' vital properties and their specific activities. These histological observations went beyond the conception of the organ to demonstrate the elements that compose it, the basic structures of its organization: anatomy has its simple tissues, which, through their combinations, form organs.[4]

Saint-Simon, likewise freed from the idea of a "system regulated from without," transferred this vision of combinations and entanglements from anatomy to the social, from the natural organism to the social organization as the production of an artificial network.

Each historical epoch of the life of the human species, each "age of the social body," produces a "sanitary regime" corresponding to its needs. In this "biographical" perspective of civilization, in which history is conceived as a "physiology of different ages," if a society conserves "hygienic habits" that no longer correspond to the new physiological stage, it risks functioning with institutions proper to the age of "childhood" when it has reached the "adult" stage.[5] Therefore, a "hygienic system" suitable for the new social configuration must be found.

Social physiology, the "science of man" in the service of politics as "social hygiene," offers, precisely, to help this great social body — which maintains its health when at work, and when lacking work languishes in sickness — to surmount its crises. Saint-Simon criticizes Condorcet for not having taken this notion of crisis into account and having too easily believed in a fulfillment of the "progress of the mind" by simple, continuous accumulation. The fundamental cause of the crisis was the "total change of the social system that tends to take place today within the most civilized nations." Affecting the body politic for the preceding thirty years, it expressed the "passage from a feudal ecclesiastical system to an industrial and scientific one."[6] Failure to check the crisis, warned Saint-Simon in 1821, would create the risk of a "veritable and immense retrogression toward barbarism," since the crisis was the stumbling block for the "division of labor, spiritual as well as temporal," that was trying to establish itself. The relation of the individual to the mass — the interdependence of parts — was blocked. Society, prey to disorder and the confusion of ideas, was living only on its acquired momentum; it was a mere agglomeration of isolated and competing individuals. The escape from this critical state and the passage to an organic state could only be managed if society defined its "goal of activity."

In the front rank of factors responsible for the persistence of the crisis stood, in Saint-Simon's view, the ideas of jurists and metaphysicians, "littérateurs" and men of letters. Although their influence had been decisive in the birth of a new system, thereafter it risked being useless or even harmful to a regime entering the adult stage, since, in his words, "the vague and metaphysical idea of freedom, as it is held today (if one continues to take it as the basis of political doctrine), will eminently tend to hinder the action of the mass on individuals."[7] The "negative ideas" that had helped the Encyclopédistes to undermine the old order no longer sufficed. It was urgent to replace these destructive and disorganizing kinds of knowledge, this "scientific insurrection," with a positive and practical kind of thought. The world needed a "New Encyclopedia," a "new alliance between Newton and Locke."

Starting at the end of the eighteenth century, Saint-Simon constructed the foundations for this new kind of knowledge—a new Enlightenment combining the science of observation with the science of organization. The period of theoretical incubation lasted nearly eighteen years, during which time he tried to forge a new synthesis of contemporary knowledge. He turned successively to the physical and mathematical sciences, to the physics of simple bodies and the physics of compound or organized bodies, by following the course of study at the École Polytechnique and the École de Médecine. From the engineers and mathematicians he adopted the law of universal attraction that, in his view, ought to replace God and "deism." "In stating that this law governs all natural phenomena," observes Judith Schlanger, "Saint-Simon offers a physicist's interpretation of gravitation: everything is understood on the basis of relations of struggle, equilibrium, and reciprocal action of solids and fluids in the universe."[8] We have already seen what he owes to physiology and the physics of organisms through his borrowings from nascent histology.

To form a synthesis from this confused mass of knowledge with a view to formulating a doctrine capable of satisfying the needs of men, a philosophy for constructing the "industrial system": such was the task that Saint-Simon set himself starting in 1814, when he published *De la réorganisation de la Société européenne* (translated as *On the Reorganization of the European Community*), right up until his last book *Le Nouveau Christianisme* (The New Christianity) appeared in 1825. Writing letters to politicians, legislators, captains of industry, and workers, and creating organs of expression such as *L'Industrie, Le Politique*, and finally, in 1819, *L'Organisateur*, to which his disciple of the period, Auguste Comte, actively contributed, Saint-Simon embraced the cause of the "industrialists," who were the "real center and home of civilization," inciting them to gather together and mobilize themselves to make history. The first volume of his major opus on the subject, *Du système industriel* (On the Industrial System), appeared in 1821; it is a collection of disparate writings—letters, tracts, and brochures—written between June 1820 and January of the following year.

The industrial class (farmers, manufacturers, and the merchants) are "all those who work to produce and to put into the hands of all members of society all the material means of satisfying their needs or their physical tastes." But only "positive experts" are called upon to bring their contribution to the forming of the theoretical core that gives coherence to the new system. "To admit collaborators of lesser ability," he wrote, "would be an infallible way of denaturing the work and rendering it as incoherent as the *Encyclopédie*."[9] For the propagation of these new ideas, a different idea applied: it was a duty of all to be transformed into apostles.

· Saint-Simon drew inspiration from the church's model of propagation. "The era that offers the best analogy with ours," he wrote, "is the one when the civilized portion of the human species moved from polytheism to monotheism through the establishment of the Christian religion...In this memorable moral revolution, we can distinguish very clearly the two types of action I have just indicated: on the one hand, Christian doctrine was systematically coordinated by the philosophers of the Alexandrine school; on the other, it was preached and spread by men from all classes, even those whose particular interest was most opposed to the new system."[10] In "The New Christianity," faced with the industrialists' slowness in mobilizing around the edification of the new "system," Saint-Simon again praised Christianity and the virtues of Christian fraternity for having succeeded so well at creating a popular morality.

This work of propagation of industrial doctrine must spill over borders, since "industry is one, all its members being united by the general interests of production, and by the need they all have for security and freedom of exchange."[11] A coalition must be made of the different political forces of industry, the union of national industries; this is one of the conditions for guaranteeing peace in a Europe emerging from the Napoleonic wars of conquest. In "On The Reorganization of the European Community," he proposes forging a tight alliance between France and England by establishing a common currency, a common bank, and a permanent commercial dialogue. For the entire continent, grouped into a "European Confederation," he suggests the establishment of a "general parliament" that would be entrusted with treating the "common interests of European society," as well as alignment around a "single code of general as well as national and individual ethics" that would be taught everywhere and reflect the system of "positive demonstrations."[12] "On the Industrial System" insists anew on the fact that a temporal European bond—the community of interests—that would result from the industrial development would in no way exempt the Continent from forging a spiritual bond made of "common moral ideas."

The Nation as a Large Industrial Company

The constitution of the industrial system was inconceivable for Saint-Simon without an ambitious system of credit and the establishment of an industrial parliament.

The circulation of money gave industry a unitary life, which Saint-Simon expressed by the old metaphor of blood circulation: "Money is to the body politic what the blood is to the human heart. Any part where the blood ceases to circulate languishes and is not long in dying." Thus, in his reorganization scheme, the "administration of the budget" is the crucial task of any government seeking to "maintain security and freedom in production." Industry would develop spontaneously thanks to a steady flowing of credit. Moreover, this was one of the few roles conceded to government. The nation being nothing but a "large industrial company," the government could be only its chargé d'affaires or representative.

But for this to be accomplished, it was also necessary to institute an "industrial parliament" with three chambers.[13] The representatives who would sit there were to belong to the useful social categories, precisely those that Saint-Simon contrasted with the "idle ones" in his famous pamphlet *The Parable* ("Suppress the nobility, officers of the crown, bishops, etc., and no political harm would result for the state. But lose the fifty foremost physicists, physiologists, poets, etc., and France would need at least a generation to recover").

The *chamber of inventions,* with three hundred members, is divided into three sections: one with two hundred civil engineers; another with fifty poets or other "inventors in literature"; the third, with twenty-five painters, fifteen sculptors or architects, and ten musicians. Their mission would consist of presenting a program of public works (drainage, clearance, road building, canal building); of perfecting a program of public holidays of a new kind: the "festivals of hope" (where citizens would view exhibitions covering the proposed projects and be made to see how much their lives could be improved by them) and "festivals of memory" (where they would be shown how preferable their fate was compared to their ancestors'). The nucleus of this chamber of inventions was to be composed of eighty-six chief engineers who are directors of Ponts et Chaussées in the various geographical departments, and forty members of the French Academy, as well as painters, sculptors, and musicians belonging to the French Institute. This nucleus would select the other members of this chamber, including up to fifty foreigners.

The *examining chamber,* composed of scholars, would establish "the hygienic laws of the body social." It would include a hundred physicists specializing in compound bodies, a hundred physicists specializing in simple bodies, and an equivalent number of mathematicians. It would recruit its core from among members of the Institute. Its functions were to examine the programs of the first chamber, to establish a vast project of public education so as to render "young people as capable as possible of conceiving, directing, and executing useful work programs," and to administer the "public holidays" (festivals of men, of women, boys, girls, fathers and mothers, children, shop foremen, workers). To celebrate these festivals, orators were to be sent everywhere to deliver speeches on the social obligations of the groups being celebrated.

Finally, the *chamber of commons* was the third and executive branch. Invoking the phrase "to make and unmake nature according to our taste," Saint-Simon thought that "the entire French territory should become a superb English park." He situated himself in the direct lineage of the engineers of Ponts et Chaussées and their ideology of struggle against irrational and "bad" nature.

In the planning of roads and canals, Saint-Simon specified that it was indispensable to join the useful and the agreeable by facilitating transportation and by making voyages as pleasant as possible for travelers. Sites that are among the most picturesque would be chosen along these routes and land would be devoted to "rest spots for travelers, and recreational sites for inhabitants of the area." Each of these gardens would contain a museum of natural and industrial products of the surrounding countryside and dwellings for artists. "Luxury should be made national," taken out of royal courts, townhouses, and châteaus. The customary sight of fine arts should stimulate the faculty of imagination and intelligence among those who up until now were riveted to material labor. At these sites, there would always be musicians who "will inflame the inhabitants of the canton with passion when circumstances require it for the greater good of the nation." Here one finds Saint-Simon's constant concern to make music a means of popular education (he even set up a working-class choir in a wool factory and asked the author of the "Marseillaise," Rouget de Lisle, to compose words and music for a "First Song of Industrials": "Honor to us, children of industry!").

The importance Saint-Simon granted to public works and to their engineers also had to do with an old dream that he had once tried to convert into reality, as he recalls in his autobiography:

I entered military service in 1777. I left for America in 1779; I served under M. de Bouillé and under Washington. At the peace, I presented to the viceroy of Mexico a project for establishing communication between the two oceans, which is possible by making the river Inpartido navigable, since one of its mouths opens onto our ocean, while the other flows into the southern sea. My project being coldly received, I abandoned it.[14]

That was in 1783, when Saint-Simon was only twenty-three years old. Returning to France in 1786, he began again and presented to the Spanish government a plan for financing and recruiting military manpower for its projected canal to join Madrid with the sea, but Spain lacked workers and funds to execute it. The French Revolution would prevent the realization of this project. Nine years later, Saint-Simon, struggling for his own subsistence, created a public transport firm in Paris. This would be his last incursion into an enterprise related to the routes of communication — and the beginning of his career as philosopher and future exponent of the industrial system. From there on, communication would appear only as part of his plans for recovering from crisis.

From the philosopher of industrialism's doctrine on the production of artificial networks as a means of relieving the crisis in the body politic his disciples would primarily extract a discourse on the redemptive virtues of new technologies, and secondarily a strategy of transition to the positive age by means of networks of communication and of finance.

The Preaching of Saint-Simon's Idea

Saint-Simon, as the author of "The New Christianity," the only true one, and as founder of a new theocracy, had conceived of three high priests: the priest of science, the priest of industry, and — overseeing these two sacerdotal functionaries — the social priest, representing the new "social religion," source of sanction and order.

When Saint-Simon died, the Church of the Saint-Simonian cult was born. In this church, the polytechnician Barthélemy Prosper Enfantin (1796–1864) was one of the two Supreme Fathers and Michel Chevalier (1806–79) was one of the cardinals, a member of the sacred college of the Father. Their venture would end before the criminal court in July 1832 with these leaders' conviction and sentencing to prison terms for violation of article 291 of the penal code prohibiting immortality and meetings of more than twenty people. In November 1831, there was a schism between these high priests and the other Supreme Father, Saint-Amand Bazard (1791–1832). However, disagreement over questions of the emancipation of the flesh, the new morality, and the "priest couple" — an idea dear to Enfantin (who would boast the title of "liberator of womanhood") — concealed a more profound disagreement. Bazard cultivated a conflictual vision of society and necessary social change, believing in an irremediable opposition among classes. By contrast, Enfantin, while just as critical of those "privileged by birth who are crushing the worker," thought in terms of harmony; he believed it possible to bring peacefully "into the *holy human Family* all those who until now had been *excluded* or treated only as *minors*"[15] — above all, proletarians and women. Enfantin was convinced of the force of "preaching Christian fraternity." When the schism was consummated, he found himself the sole pope of the Saint-Simonian religion. Throughout these years, the apostolate was a central concern. Publications for the faithful were, first, *Le Producteur,* founded in June 1825 and liquidated at the end of the following year; then *L'Organisateur,* launched in August 1829; and finally, *Le Globe: Journal de la doctrine saint-simonienne,* from 1830 until its termination two years later. Between 1828 and 1830, Bazard organized lectures that were compiled by the youngest members of the school into *L'Exposition de la doctrine saint-simonienne.* In April 1830, preaching by the Saint-Simonians began in their Parisian headquarters. In July of the following year the "General Communion of the Saint-Simonian Family" was born and propaganda for the working class was organized district by district. For the purposes of "propagation of the Saint-Simonian faith among industrialists," Paris was divided into four sections. These initiatives did not last long — the district organization was dissolved in November 1831 as a result of the schism within the school — but long enough nevertheless to see a scheme for apostolic militancy emerge.

Members and potential followers of the propagation were ranked into visitors, aspirants, and staff.[16] The highest position was granted only to those who were recognized as worthy of taking part in apostolic work, after a more or less lengthy novitiate. They received a diploma and were authorized to work in the Family's workshops. Each apostle filed a daily detailed report on people who had been contacted to the director or subdirector of these section offices (which stayed open every day from 5 A.M. to 10 P.M.).

People of modest means, most often artisans of the capital, visited these offices: wheelwrights, seamstresses, cobblers, doormen, laundry-women, sand quarrymen, locksmiths, linen maids, saddlers, day laborers, engravers, vest makers, carpenters, and so on. Here are four reports extracted from the section covering the first and second districts of Paris:

> Monsieur Bottier, florist working at rue St.-Honoré. Material circumstances: husband and wife both work. The husband is a very good worker in his field and could, if necessary, make shop foreman. They appear to keep a good house and have a gentle character.

> Madame Rondet, midwife, has become well known in her field thanks to several important discoveries. Separated from her husband for eight years, she has since obtained two invention patents. She is constantly engaged in the perfecting of devices

useful to humanity. She has had to struggle against the envy customarily harbored against women who have the courage to raise themselves above their sex, as the phrase goes. She has embraced the new faith with joy and spreads it passionately.

Monsieur Knobel, blacksmith, one child, rue du Rocher. He wants to keep his membership card, pretends to be a Saint-Simonian, but I know that he mocks it. He is selfish. His wife has the same sentiments as he does.

Mademoiselle Bourgeois, Amélie, dramatic artist, is a very interesting young person. She made an early debut at the Odéon in a child's role and was then admitted to the theater of M. Comte, who, it appears, cruelly exploited his *young actress*. Serious complaints forced the mother to make her quit her house. At the moment she is without work and, with her mother, occupies a very humble lodging. She is a musician and did seven years at the conservatory. Mlle B. is not pretty but she has the freshness of springtime, and is perhaps also pure, despite her somewhat indecent profession. The two women know our doctrine.[17]

Evaluations of the often disastrous financial state of the Saint-Simonian journals shed a stark light on the other side of proselytizing. They attest to the hesitations in the organization's approaches to the "enlightened public." In 1826, in his report to shareholders, Father Enfantin retraced the fluctuating fortunes of *Le Producteur,* then in the process of liquidation despite an attempt to adjust to a different type of readership:

Some of our readers reproached us for being too serious, others for being too removed from the facts, still others for being obscure ... Profiting from these complaints to better choose our readers ... , we became still more serious, increasing the volume of *Le Producteur* and only appearing once a month. We neglected detailed facts as much as possible in order to concern ourselves with generalities; these changes may also have made us seem more obscure to those people little accustomed to philosophical studies; but, on the other hand, they put us into easier direct contact with people who create new ideas and with those who conserve deposits of intellectual riches. In other words, *Le Producteur* became a journal for philosophers and scholars. Hence our financial success was necessarily delayed.[18]

In 1831, a year of the great religious effervescence, the director of the *Globe: Journal de la doctrine saint-simonienne,* Michel Chevalier, had no doubt about the strategy to follow. The Saint-Simonians, in his view, should return to the old Jesuit model, infiltrating the breeding grounds of future elites and reaching "influential people." In a circular to members of the Family asking them to cooperate in establishing a list of those to receive free copies of the paper, this former student of the École Polytechnique et des Mines observed:

> Indicate to us, then, for the department you inhabit and for those you know, the persons and the meeting places you believe we ought to choose. In particular, point out to us former students of the École Polytechnique, doctors, lawyers, engineers . . . On your list you should indicate succinctly the reason you think it suitable to send the *Globe* to so-and-so . . . You should make efforts so that these people study it and have others around them read it.

He concludes that it is a matter of "the propagation of our faith," "a labor that in this respect is eminently religious."[19]

A year later, Enfantin and Chevalier, as well as Charles Duveyrier, were sentenced to a year in prison and a fine of one hundred francs. Until his death in 1864, well after the stormy years, Enfantin would maintain this pastoral relationship with his disciples and followers. Here is an excerpt from a personal letter addressed to the Father by M. Soulard on 29 February 1862, shortly after the publication of *La Vie Eternelle* (*Life Eternal: Past-Present-Future*), his religious and political testament:

> The confines of a letter are too narrow for me to tell you of all the impressions I felt upon the attentive reading of *La Vie Eternelle*. May it suffice you to know that I entered at full gallop into the course of love that you opened to my soul, and that having moved suddenly from a simple disciple into the apostolate, I do not waste any occasion to evangelize.[20]

A case of church against church, this encroachment of Saint-Simonianism into the realm of spiritual power would never be to the Vatican's taste. And with good reason: had not Saint-Simon himself accused the pope and his church of heresy for offering human beings only the happiness of a paradise in the kingdom of heaven and not on this earth? In 1837, the Jesuit priest Cornelius Everboeck, with a mandate from the Sacred Roman Congregation of the Holy Office, suggested that the pope send out an encyclical against the "sect" and its doctrine, whose influence was already being felt in the Italian peninsula. The Holy Father did not go that far, but he did forbid the circulation of Saint-Simonian brochures in Catholic schools.

Embrace the Universe: Enfantin and the Suez Canal

"Hope, our nation's sons, that / The hand that breaks our curse / Braids the network of industry / That will embrace the universe," sang the Saint-Simonian songwriter Louis Vinçard in 1835 in "The Future is Here," at events such as "industrial and pastoral tournaments." He crisscrossed France with a repertory that included other songs such as "The New Faith" and "The New Man," sung to the tune of the "Marseillaise."[21]

While the Family was officially dissolved in 1833, the Saint-Simonian heritage remained. For some, this heritage, when divested of its religious chimeras, became a doctrine of industrial development, a doctrine of power, and, as a corollary, a breviary for their own careers as managers or captains of industry. For others, Saint-Simon's ideas remained an essential moment in the formation of a socialist consciousness. These ideas lent themselves, it is true, to alternate and shifting interpretations; the famous "Saint-Simonian model" was not one-sided. The utopian desire for community and the thirst for justice convey the profoundly subversive character of the author of "On the Industrial System," who never stopped contrasting "liberalism," as a political force founded on private capital and on the class of jurists employed to defend its rights, with the new potential of "industrialism." What was common to both tendencies was the belief in "progress" as well as in the approaching advent of a "Universal Association" that would replace universal antagonism: for some, through the intervention of technical networks of free trade in commodities and ideas, and for the others, through networks of social solidarity.

In 1833, upon his release from prison, Enfantin embarked for Egypt, where the "Companions of Womanhood" had prepared his arrival; he was still on the mythic quest for a feminine messiah, the "Mother" coming out of the Orient whose vacant seat symbolized her place at the side of the Supreme Father, with whom she would one day be united. In this quest, Enfantin was accompanied by several polytechnicians, architects, draftsmen, farmers, workers, doctors, and men of letters. All were joining the project for the "communication of two seas," which already occupied the engineer M. A. Linant de Bellefonds, who had revived two Napoleonic projects: digging a canal and damming the Nile.

It was the era of viceroy Muhammad Ali (1769–1849) and the major general of the Egyptian armies Octave de Sèves, alias Suleiman Pasha, a Napoleonic officer converted to Islam. In this era, French experts helped to professionalize the Egyptian military establishment, creating an École Polytechnique and an artillery school, and reorganizing the

École de Médecine. Enfantin dreamed of setting up a pacific army of workers charged with building the canal and the dam: "A corps of twelve thousand regular workers regimented, ranked, disciplined, dressed, and nourished and housed like army regiments, commanded by engineers, composed of men and children with music in their heads, pickax and ax on their shoulders, compass and T-square at their sides, while the company and field officers have surveying meters in hand."[22] But an epidemic of cholera, together with pressures from England, which was doing everything in its power to have the concession refused, combined to finally defeat the grand projects so dear to the Saint-Simonians. Enfantin returned to France in 1837. The project for a union of the two seas was dropped. It would be taken up later by Ferdinand de Lesseps (1805–94), who would bring together a multinational team and lead it to complete the canal inaugurated in 1869.

In 1845, Enfantin wrote to the Egyptian authorities:

We are conscious of having prepared this grand project as no other has ever been prepared; it remains to us to achieve it with you as no other great enterprise has ever been, that is, without national rivalries, with the cordial cooperation of three great peoples who have often been divided by politics and whom industry must unify. It remains to us, the industrial society, to accomplish what diplomacy would attempt in vain without us; it remains to us to trace across this very globe the *sign of peace* and to truly forge the link between two parts of the Old World, the Orient and the Occident.[23]

Taking charge of the project nine years later, de Lesseps did not call upon Enfantin to collaborate when he set up a Universal Commission for the Suez Canal. The former Supreme Father was very piqued about this. But Saint-Simonian ideas had a place of honor in the editorial of the first issue of the *Isthmus of Suez*, subtitled *Journal of the Union of Two Seas*, launched on 25 June 1856 by the builder of the future Suez Canal.

Organ and representative of a universal interest, and a stranger by the goal it sets itself to any spirit of exclusive nationality, this journal has nothing and wants nothing in common with the politics of international and domestic rivalries ... It will make a rule of avoiding anything that might embitter and divide the great interests whose mission is to conciliate and to unify in a work of labor and peace.[24]

Henceforth, Saint-Simonian doctrine would be part of the natural landscape of great interoceanic projects.

In 1841–42, Enfantin turned into an ethnographer. We encounter him again in the Scientific Commission of Algeria, created four years previously, where he studied the "indigenous populations of the province of Constantine," classifying them according to "differences in language, habitat, and uses of culture" and identifying "everything that could enable or else form an obstacle to the progress of civilization"; he gathered his insights on this subject into a book published in 1843, *De la colonisation de l'Algérie* (On the colonization of Algeria), in which he pleads for a form of political association. Saluting this study, the correspondent of the *Daily National Intelligencer* in Washington noted:

> A most able and excellent volume, whether as regards science or politics, has been lately written upon Algeria; but, because it is full of common sense and just views, not a single French journal has taken the least notice of it. The volume is written by Enfantin, *quondam* high priest of the St. Simonians. It is astonishing how almost all the men first enlisted in this monstrous absurdity have turned out since to be most clever, sensible, and able.[25]

This ability would be recognized by his former apostles turned railway industrialists. The Polytechnician Enfantin would end up as administrator of the PLM company, the future "imperial line" that linked the three largest French cities, Paris-Lyons-Marseilles, and would later connect France with Switzerland, Italy, and other Mediterranean countries. It hastened the formation of this network by negotiating the merger of several companies that served the diverse branches of the line.

"Spiritual" and "Material" Networks

In 1832, Michel Chevalier had written:

> Industry, leaving aside the industrials, is composed of production centers tied to each other by a relatively *material* link, that is to say, by the means of transportation, and by a relatively *spiritual* link, that is to say, by banks... The relations are so tight between the banking network and the transportation network that, when one of them traces a suitable pattern for exploiting the globe effectively, the other thereby finds itself subject to the same essential determinations.[26]

This assertion foreshadowed a whole program for Saint-Simonian industrialism. Once it had escaped from the straitjacket of its militancy, Saint-Simonianism embodied the vigorous spirit of enterprise of the time. At the PLM company, Enfantin came back into contact with Paulin Talabot, a Polytechnician like himself, pioneer of railways in the southeast of France, and the author of a project for a canal between Alexandria and the Red Sea.

Two other Saint-Simonians, Emile and Isaac Pereire, had since the end of the 1830s participated in the construction of rail lines in the north, east, and southwest of France, and were beginning to undertake interoceanic links. In 1855, they founded the Compagnie Générale Maritime. For fifteen years, British steamers had dominated the sea lanes toward the United States, Central America, and Brazil. French trade was dependent on the Royal Mail steamship line for receiving orders from overseas. Aside from establishing postal services, its main goal, the brothers' company, soon renamed Compagnie Générale Transatlantique or the French Line, took advantage of a new international division of labor. The mission they explicitly assigned the company left no doubt on this subject:

> To bind the colonies to the mother country by more numerous ties
> and to open up an unlimited horizon for the energy and powers of
> expansion of the national genius... To contribute to the
> equilibrium between the needs of consumption and the resources
> of production, not only by the transport of foodstuffs and raw
> materials, but also by the moving of laboring populations and a
> better division of human labor.[27]

In their fashion, the company's ships did weave a network of industry and embrace the universe, as the song would have it. Sailing out from France, they exported large quantities of French merchandise and transported emigrants. On the way back, they took on guano from Peru and nitrates from Chile as fertilizers for French agriculture; they made available to consumers the meats of the River Plate region by developing local industries for preserving and packaging beef derived from cattle purchased by the thousands of heads. Tanned hides, also prepared locally, served the leather industry of the old continent, as waste products did the fertilizer industry—all part of a tight synergy between maritime lines, rail transportation, and the agro-industrial complex. In times of war, steamships were converted into an auxiliary flotilla of the French navy, transporting and supplying troops. Their baptism of fire was the imperial military expedition against the Republic of Mexico between 1864 and 1867.

There was also a synergy with credit, the nervous system of all construction enterprises for the great technological networks. Credit was the "instrument of modern times, comparable to the fulcrum of Archimedes' lever for lifting the world," according to a popular expression among entrepreneurs at the time.

At the end of 1852, the Pereire brothers created the Société Générale de Crédit Mobilier. Their network of agents and partners grew rapidly abroad. Soon, they participated in the building of more than ten thousand kilometers of rail in Austria, Spain, Switzerland, Russia, and the Ottoman Empire. They had a stake in the Royal Society for the Canalization of the Ebro, the Madrid Lighting Company, not to mention the Paris Omnibus—to the chagrin of their rivals, the Rothschilds, the other chief architects of routes of communication, who feared the abuses of a double monopoly over finance and transport and looked on the Pereires as speculators. The response of the traditional world of high finance symbolized by the Rothschilds—who in the 1830s had nevertheless backed the Pereires by supporting their first railway construction efforts in the north—would come in 1864 with the creation of the "Société Générale pour favoriser le développement du commerce et de l'industrie en France." Paulin Talabot and the industrialist Joseph-Eugène Schneider were among its chief figures. On the list of shareholders of this financial institution was Father Enfantin.

Why was there a coalition of the established banking houses against the Pereire brothers? The Société Générale's own answer was as follows:

> The constitution of a vast financial conglomerate on a European scale is leading the Pereires to dismantle the traditional high finance network of agents, without which they can no longer benefit from a monopoly in public loans. A reaction from the main representatives of traditional finance is inevitable. It is the coalition of interests threatened by the Pereires that unites the principal promoters of the Société Générale.[28]

In 1879, Marx would make his own assessment of this alliance between "spiritual networks" and "material networks." In a letter to Nikolai Danielson, the historian, economist, and translator of the Russian edition of *Capital* (whose first volume had come out in Hamburg twelve years previously), Marx, no doubt considering that he had not insisted enough on this point in his book, wrote:

> The railways sprang up first as the *"couronnement de l'oeuvre"* [crowning glory] in those countries where *modern industry was most developed*, England, United States, Belgium, France, etc. I call them the *"couronnement de l'oeuvre"* not only in the sense that they were at last (together with steamships for oceanic intercourse and the telegraphs) *the means of communication* adequate to the modern means of production, but also in so far as they were the basis of the immense joint-stock companies, forming at the same

time a new starting point for all *other sorts* of joint-stock companies, to commence with banking companies. They gave in one word an impetus never before suspected to the *concentration of capital* and also to the accelerated and immensely enlarged *cosmopolitan activity of loanable capital,* thus embracing the whole world in a network of financial swindling and mutual *indebtedness,* the capitalistic form of "international" brotherhood.[29]

We know that, for Marx, the deployment of means of communication is indissociable from the modern world market, since the transformation of all capital into industrial capital entails the rapid circulation (the perfecting of the monetary system) and centralization of capitals. It was not techniques of communication, thought Marx, but rather the commodities on the world market, that were indifferent to religious, political, national, and linguistic barriers. To believe the contrary was equivalent to turning reality upside down, to metamorphosing men into things and things into animate beings—in other words, giving way to fetishism or, as Barthes will put it later, producing a "mythology." The commodity form is the general form of exchange. The universal language is the language of commodities, as expressed by price. With everything to be sold and bought, the common link is money, the symbolic medium and mediator par excellence, the *perpetuum mobile.*

The German term *Verkehr,* which at the end of the nineteenth century would be used by the strategists of the Kaiser's empire as a synonym for what the French called "communication(s)," was used by Marx either in the larger sense of the word "commerce," or in the sense of "social relations" (as in *Verkehrsform* and *Verkehrshältnisse,* which will become in the Marxian opus the "relations of production," or *Produktionsverhältnisse*). Thus, if one is bent on finding in Marx the traces of the term "communication" in its current meaning, one would have to include all the forms of relations of work, exchange, property, consciousness, as well as relationships among individuals, groups, nations, and states. Just as much as Marx believed in the social determination of communication technologies, so did the Saint-Simonians espouse a determinist conception of such technologies, which they saw as agents for transforming the world.

Chevalier and Salvation through Railways

Of his twelve-month prison sentence, Chevalier served only six, following which Adolphe Thiers, then minister of the interior and public works, sent him to the United States to study the organization of the routes of communication.

The Saint-Simonian took advantage of this trip to extend his field of observation to Mexico and Cuba. No sooner were the results of this mission published under the title *Lettres sur l'Amérique du Nord* (*Society, Manners and Politics in the United States*) in 1836 than he began a second assignment, this time to England to observe the "industrial crisis" raging there, and in particular its repercussions on the railway sector. In that year, a first panic took hold among savers who fell victim to the "Railway Mania," judging the railways sure enough for prudent investment. (Other shocks would occur after the railway speculation of 1844 and 1845: the famous "Black Friday" of 1866 on the London Stock Exchange, and another around 1880, all of which would temper this enthusiasm but never quench it.) On the basis of his British mission, Chevalier published in 1838 a comparative study entitled *Des intérêts matériels en France: travaux publics, routes, canaux, chemins de fer* (Material interests in France: public works, roads, canals, railways).

In France at that time, capital still proved cool toward railways and the government hesitated to get involved. Some people thought that priority should go to roads, others to canals. This was a new manifestation of the old problem lingering in France since Vauban's day: the incapacity to conceive and realize a nationwide system distributed among the different modes of transport. A historian of roads has seen in this the effect of the "persistence of neo-Physiocratic thought," which had "durably anchored the country in the ruralism of the gentry and independent producers."[30] Joining the polemic on the comparative advantages of rail and road, *Le Journal des Économistes* could still write in 1842: "Let us strengthen our roads. Let us tie our innumerable villages lost in the countryside to these highways. Only then let us experiment with railways."[31] In any case, this seems to be the dominant reasoning that maintained France in backwardness regarding railways, after having long prevented the realization of a dual and complementary network of canals and roads.

In the years when Chevalier was carrying out his assignments abroad, one single experiment proved to be conclusive, that of the mining of the basin of Saint-Étienne, cradle of the French rail network. England was already in advance by several leagues. The Pereire brothers and another Saint-Simonian, Adolphe d'Eichtal, were inspired by the principles of the Manchester-Liverpool line, opened by Stephenson in 1829, to build some eighteen kilometers of a suburban line from Paris to Saint-Germain, completed in 1837. Minister Thiers himself, who called the train a "plaything for the curious," cared little about main lines and saw utility only in local rail. On his trip to England at the end of the 1830s, Tocqueville noted his interlocutors' astonishment at the meager enthusiasm for the train demonstrated by an official delegation led by a Polytechnician. In an official 1838 report that has remained famous, the great astronomer and physicist François Arago (1786–1853) mocked the hopes of those who believed that "two rods of parallel iron would give a new face to the landscape of Gascony." He went as far as to dispute the strategic advantages of troop movement by rail, and even speculated on whether "our generals would not decide that transport by rail carriage would make the troops effeminate and cause them to lose that ability for great marches that has played so important a role in the triumph of our armies."[32]

Here is yet another contrast with England, where the father of the free-trade regime, the prime minister Robert Peel (1788–1850), had proclaimed since 1834 at a meeting in Tamworth: "Let us make haste, let us make haste; it is indispensable to establish from one end of the kingdom to the other communications by steam, if Great Britain wishes to maintain its rank and superiority in the world." Meanwhile, in France, his colleague Thiers "would feel happy if twenty kilometers of railways were completed per year."[33] In January 1848, France had only 1,830 kilometers of tracks, while Great Britain had nearly 6,500. Moreover, in the 1840s, almost half the capital of concessionary private companies came from London.

The "unparalleled pusillanimity of French capitalists," denounced by a chronicler of the day who stigmatized their "lack of audacity and intelligence," would start to be a bad memory only after the law of 1842.[34] This law, a kind of transaction between the defenders of private companies and those of the state, instituted a mixed system and gave the starting signal for the race to construct major railway lines arranged in a star-shaped and centralizing network. Still, it would be nine years before an actual process of catching up began.

What enabled Chevalier to secure his transatlantic assignment was an article he published in *Le Globe* in February 1832 under the headline "The Mediterranean System." There he broke with the predominant moroseness. Against the pessimism of the apocalyptic visions of the damaging effects of rail and tunnels burrowing into the countryside and turning it into Swiss cheese, he offered a deterministic optimism about new networks—an optimism of an openly religious nature, since, in his view, the function of railways was assimilable to that of religion: "If, as we are assured, the word religion comes from *religare,* railways have more relation to the religious spirit than we think. Never has there existed an instrument of such power to link together scattered peoples."[35] This would be his conviction well beyond 1832, even though at the time little was known about the consequences of the advent of these transportation technologies.

"The Mediterranean is going to become the nuptial bed of the Orient and the Occident"; the great historic struggle and field of continuous battle are going to be transformed into a "vast forum in which peoples until now divided on all points will communicate" — such is the leitmotif of Chevalier's future vision of the "Mediterranean System" in 1832.[36]

The confederation of peoples organized in a Mediterranean system encompassing the Black and Caspian seas was for Chevalier the first step toward a *Universal Association*. A major instrument of this plan for pacification would be the means of communication. Technical questions had been overemphasized, according to Chevalier, and speed had been addressed only "in relation to merchandise." The introduction of steam on the continents and the seas "will be not only an industrial revolution, but a political one." Hence it was necessary to attract "men who have the faith that humanity is marching toward the Universal Association." Railways would play a primary role among the means of transportation that would link the various points of the "Mediterranean System," with a complementarity between rail and the great waterways. Railways, which were to run alongside the routes of navigation, were to specialize in the transport of people and light products. Waterways should be reserved for heavy and cumbersome goods.

From Sebastopol to Gibraltar, from Carthage to Smyrna, from Venice to Alexandria, from Constantinople to the Persian Gulf via Baghdad, Basra, and Mesopotamia, Chevalier projected the ramifications of this imaginary system of rail, water, and sea routes—what he called "circulating civilization"—that would "awaken slumbering countrysides from their torpor." Italy and Spain would shake off their lethargy. The cities of Greece and Asia will escape their sepulchre. Even deepest Russia would lose the "numbness of a people bound in by snows." Agriculture would flourish; mineral riches would be exploited in accordance with a grand design; factories of all sorts would make the products necessary for the well-being of mankind. In this gigantic construction, a vast system of banks would spread a "salutary chyle into all the veins of this body, with its devouring activity and its innumerable articulations." In the face of such prosperity, bellicose fevers would disappear from the surface of the earth. No more wars, nor destruction, nor "starving populations who could be persuaded to riot." It would be the "consecration of peace on earth."

How to execute this plan for a Mediterranean confederation? Thanks, notably, to the conversion of enormous sums of money formerly consumed by the construction of fortresses, the purchase of war materials, and the upkeep of soldiers. Here we see the resurgence of an old project of Saint-

Simon's, also dear to Enfantin, for redirecting armies to peacetime tasks. With conquest belonging resolutely to another age, prophesied Chevalier in another work,

> we will no longer recruit men in order to teach them the art of *destroying and killing,* but in order to have them learn *production* and *creation.* Regiments will become schools of industrial arts and crafts to which everyone can be admitted from the age of sixteen. Artillerymen will be mechanics and metal foundrymen; cannon foundries will produce furnaces and steamships; the cavalry will form the corps of plowmen, and the fleet of carts, postal vehicles, and public carriages.[37]

And so on, up to and including a change in the attributions of the Ministry of War—then responsible for the École Polytechnique, the Saint-Cyr military academy, and other officer academies—which would become instead a "Ministry of Industry."

Although this utopian confederation by rail is composed of multiple interconnecting and crisscrossing networks, thus blurring the topography of empires of the old warrior age, it still has a center, since one virtue of new means of communication is, after all, to constitute a new mode of governing. On this point, Chevalier was a realist, drawing early lessons from a France that at the time was the only country to dispose of such a vast network of semaphore telegraphs:

> By the railway and steamships, and with the help of some other modern discoveries such as the telegraph, it will become easy to govern most of the continents that border the Mediterranean, with the same unity and the same instantaneousness as exists today within France. Among all countries with the exception of England, France is far and away the one in which it is easiest to communicate an impetus from the center out to the extreme circumference.[38]

Chevalier would come back many times, in other texts published during the same period, to the necessity of centralization around a hub: "There is no middle way between centralization (that is to say, unity) and anarchy... It is a matter of transforming centralization in such a way that it allows for movement, spontaneity, and life in a circumference that is today inert and passive around the center."[39]

Chevalier displayed the same pragmatic realism when his reveries led him to anticipate the origin and flow of the "advance of civilization":

> Let us imagine that Europe extends little by little into Asia, via the Russians in the north, the English in the south, the Turkish in the West, and the Americans rushing in from the east; and that in

order to accelerate the double current moving from America and Europe toward old Asia, one pierces the two isthmuses of Suez and Panama, and let us then imagine, if possible, the ravishing picture the old continent would then offer.[40]

We are, let us recall, back in 1832! The Suez Canal would not be open to navigation until 1869, nor the Panama Canal until 1914.

The contradictions of the myth of equality via the means of communication appear here for the first time at a global level, but also at the level of the social classes. From London, Chevalier writes in 1833:

> To better communications is therefore to work for real, positive, and practical freedom; it is to allow all members of the human family to enjoy the possibility of traveling across and exploiting the globe that has been left to it as an inheritance; it is to extend the franchise to the largest number as much and as fully as possible by elections. I would go farther, and say that it amounts to making equality and democracy. Perfected means of transportation have the effect of reducing the distance not only from one point to another, but also from one class to another.[41]

The anarchist thinker Pierre-Joseph Proudhon must have gone pale reading these lines—he who railed against "the trains of princes" reserved for "the privileged of fortune" in contrast to "the beggars' trains" in which travelers were herded standing "like pigs" on bare platforms.[42] Even in England, Parliament had to intervene in favor of popular trains and to impose on private operators the obligation to provide a minimum standard of comfort compatible with the technical progress of the time. It was, in the words of a historian, the "first democratic victory concerning the railways."[43]

In 1860, Napoléon III (1808–73) signed, without the approval of the legislature, an Anglo-French commercial treaty. Free trade was in full bloom. The principal negotiators were, on the English side, Richard Cobden, and on the French, Michel Chevalier, who meanwhile had been named professor of political economy at the Collège de France and adviser to the emperor and had become a caustic critic of egalitarian theories.

In the eighteenth century, the road network had obsessed the French ruling establishment and the engineers of Ponts et Chaussées. In the nineteenth, the railway network mobilized public authorities, engineers, and philosophers. Drawing up a list of important books published on railways since 1824, Pierre Larousse's *Grand dictionnaire universel du XIXe siècle* could assert without too much exaggeration at the end of the century that it is in France that the greatest share of these books have seen the light of day. British or American engineers have generally little time or taste for writing, and so the works published in England or America are relatively few in number... As for Germany, she understood early on the usefulness of railways, and she has produced works in great number, several of which are excellent and in which the question is studied in all its aspects, theoretical as well as practical.[44]

Compared with the abundant reflections on railways, other means of Universal Association would claim less attention from French engineers and philosophers. One indication of this, among others, is that in the personal archives of Enfantin there is only a single reference to underwater cable and to the telegraph—and this is just a press cutting, an article published in 1858 in the *Journal des travaux publics, de l'agriculture et du commerce, chemins de fer, mines, industrie*. Here is an excerpt:

News dispatches announce the success of the operation to lay an electric cable between Ireland and Newfoundland. It is a great step toward the direct establishment of a telegraphic link between Europe and North America... Here is a fact of a certain importance from the international point of view. The relations between America and Europe will be profoundly altered. We hope that they will be much improved from the day when it is possible to correspond at any hour and at short notice between the industrial centers of our hemisphere and the markets of consumption on the other side of the Atlantic, and vice versa.[45]

This has nothing to do with Michel Chevalier's utopian dreams about encircling the universe with rail networks or with singing the tomorrows of humanity's exploitation of the world. Only in Jules Verne's tales of social anticipation written between 1860 and 1906—the exploits of Captain Nemo, the engineers Robur and Smith in *The Mysterious Island*, and the adventures of polytechnicians, veritable Promethean heroes of progress, in the *Voyages Extraordinaires*—could one find steam and electricity allied with each other and speaking to the imaginary. As Jean Chesneaux tells us,

It is legitimate to place Jules Verne in the distant lineage of utopian socialists of the first half of the nineteenth century. From a distance of fifty years, the generous and confused dreams of Saint-Simon, Fourier, Enfantin, and Dr. Guépin are one of the sources on which he drew to design his vision of *Mondes Connus et Inconnus* [Worlds known and unknown].[46]

Advertising: The Legacy of Saint-Simonianism

Proclaimed Chevalier in the *Globe* in 1832:

> The cleverest person will be he who embraces in his solicitude the interests of the *master* and the interests of the *workers*, those of the *rich* and the *poor*, those of the *idle* and the *laborer*, and assumes the mission of conciliating all interests and blending them together, dissipating the alarm of one group and tempering the ardor of the other. He who, thus animated by the sentiment of the Universal Association of peoples, classes, parties, and individuals, has the power to keep his language within the understanding of the greatest number, and makes his ambition consist of the simplicity and popularity of his discourse—that person will have prodigious success.[47]

This manifesto, calling for the overcoming of political and social divisions, was coherent with Enfantin's harmonious vision of Saint-Simonian society, but it had practically no time to be put into practice.

Thirteen years later, the self-styled "poet of God," Charles Duveyrier (1803–66), former contributor to the *Globe* where he signed two lyrical articles entitled "On Women" and "To Women," reflected back on the great principles of this period of fervent militancy. Having converted to business, he and some sympathizers of the doctrine created the Société Générale des Annonces (SGA), a firm that lasted four years. It would be liquidated in 1849, in the trough of the first "Krondatieff wave"—the very same one that led to economic crisis and contributed to the Parisian insurrection of 1848 and the proclamation of an ephemeral republic.

The ambition of Duveyrier's company was to become a kind of intermediary wholesale purchaser of advertising space, to gather for itself the advertising potential of the capital's daily newspapers, and by playing on advantages of scale, to secure the exclusive right to place advertisements. There was nothing entirely new about this aspect of a project for a monopoly, which had manifested itself before Saint-Simonianism came on the scene. The process had begun when advertising became a means of financing the press, that is, in the 1820s, even before Emile de Girardin had launched *La Presse* (1836).[48] It continued with Charles Louis Havas, who in 1832 founded an office that translated foreign papers for his French clients, and who progressively extended his areas of competence, composing bulletins, news-sheets, and reports on the stock market, and news items and summaries of ministerial activities, thereby laying the foundations for both the formula of a centralized purchasing firm for advertising space and for his own great future international news agency—in a France where the development of advertising and large newspapers was slow in comparison to England. In the course of the two decades from 1830 to 1850, the *Times* created in 1785, consisted of first eight, then twelve, and then sixteen pages, plus occasional supplements devoted solely to advertising, while the French dailies never surpassed an average of four pages throughout the nineteenth century.[49]

What was new, however, in the advertising landscape of the Parisian press of the time was the project for a new type of advertisement, known as "omnibus," consisting of classifieds at reduced price, presented in monotone fashion according to a classification useful to the working classes: rentals, jobs offered and sought, secondhand items for sale, and other diverse notices. Inspired by the experience of London "coffeehouses," Duveyrier opened local offices, usually installed in reading rooms, in the forty-eight neighborhoods of the capital so as to facilitate clients' placement of their ads. At that time, significantly, such classified ads were often called "annonces anglaises." To justify this service offered to the public, the Saint-Simonian resorted to an argument about the "democratization of advertising." In a society in which the humblest advertisers—housewives, boarding-house keepers, and so on—in search of a "good deal" disposed of limited means of public exchange, and in which ordinary Parisian servants and workers were seeking contacts with "producers," the SGA proposed to furnish them.

This purpose did not lead Duveyrier to forget the central axis of his SGA project, which remained the concentration of the advertising space in the large dailies. The first wave of the concession of the railway networks helped him greatly. In a climate of financial speculation, the major contending companies were converted into a lucrative source of advertisements. The adjudication of lines to private firms that constructed and operated them forced the candidates to chase after shareholders and the small depositors whose number and magnitude determined whether contracts would be secured. Advertising was used to help mobilize opinion. In this task, Duveyrier turned once again to the network of Saint-Simonian entrepreneurs and engineers, including the Pereire brothers. But what made possible the SGA's dazzling expansion was also the cause of its setbacks. Already slowed down by the crisis of 1847, railway construction came to a halt during the February 1848 revolution. The value of rail stock followed the general decline. The Paris-Orléans line belonging to the Pereires, for example, which already offered a 12 percent dividend, fell from 1,410 to 420 francs on 10 April. From 23 February to 12 April, shares in railways lost more than 315 million francs.[50] On top of the interruption of traffic, the acts of sabotage, and the strikes by workers demanding major wage increases came the claims of railwaymen insisting on the firing of English mechanics brought over to train them. More fundamentally still, the Republic of 1848 challenged the law of 1842 by seeking to nationalize the whole railway system.

From this pioneering attempt to rationalize advertising transactions, Gérard Lagneau and Marc Martin, authors of many books and articles on the history of the French advertising industry, draw two conclusions. First, although it was brief, the experience of the SGA was sufficient to leave as a legacy an organizatonal matrix for the advertising business that would mark the industry in France in the decades to come. Duveyrier's company furnished a pattern of relationships between the media, the advertiser, and the consumer. This formula of advertising management would recur in 1865 when another Société Générale des Annonces was born and gathered under one umbrella all the brokers who controlled the French market for advertising space—this time under the aegis of the powerful Havas agency, which would dominate both the news and advertising sectors until the end of World War II. Second, these historians judge that the "Saint-Simonian advertisement," an institutional expression of the French model of advertising that attempted to harmonize and articulate the interests of ordinary people and those of large enterprises, combining an idea of public service with the business spirit of competition, would be largely responsible for France's backwardness in the later development of its advertising market and industry.[51]

Meanwhile, Charles Duveyrier's advertising company had scarcely folded when the "poet of God" launched himself into another venture, again taking up a central idea dear to Chevalier in 1832: the reconciliation of social antagonisms. On 1 November 1848, he founded Le Crédit and became its editor in chief. Enfantin joined, and the publication lived for twenty-one months, five more than Le Globe. The editorial policy of this new press organ proclaimed: "Neither the republic of the heartless, nor the republic of the rebellious mob [sans-culottes]. We want a humane, intelligent, industrial, liberal, and magnanimous republic, one that proletarians defend, bankers give credit to, kings respect, the people envy, women and priests bless, and that poets one day will sing to."[52]

Le Crédit would publish in installments such novels as La Petite Fadette by George Sand (1804–76). To an editorial colleague of Duveyrier's who had asked her to soften the preface to her work, Sand replied:

As for toning down my thought to bourgeois taste, I have never known how to do this and I do not wish to learn it at the age of forty-five...I am truly angry that you are taking this paper in the direction of M. Cavaignac [the general who repressed the Parisian insurrection of June 1848]. You have a lovely soul and a noble character, so you will later regret your misplaced trust, as well as all the attention you pay, and that you advise me to pay, to the *bourgeois,* since you yourself call them such. They are stronger. This should be one more reason to tell them the truth, since when they become weaker your frankness will have no great merit.[53]

(George Sand never spared her criticism of what she considered Father Enfantin's autocracy.) In this passage, the woman who founded the weekly *La Cause du Peuple* (9 April 1848) portrays the profound ambiguities at the heart of the Saint-Simonian doctrine: born with the generous idea of liberating women and the proletariat, it finds itself constructing the hegemony of the rising industrial bourgeoisie.

"The Saint-Simonians," Walter Benjamin would observe in 1939, "foresaw the development of world industry; they did not foresee class struggle. This is why, with respect to participation in all industrial and commercial enterprises toward the middle of the nineteenth century, one must recognize their powerlessness in matters concerning the proletariat."[54] The Frankfurt School philosopher was writing about the way in which the Saint-Simonians, Michel Chevalier at their head, in their projects to exploit the planet, "became carried away with the idea of Universal Expositions." These great events displaying technologies of steam and electricity for the masses constituted, in the second half of the nineteenth century, "a school in which crowds forcibly excluded from consumption became impregnated with the exchange value of commodities, to the point of identifying with them: 'It is prohibited to touch the exhibited objects.'"[55]

Chapter 5
The Temple of Industry

The Golden Age of Universal Expositions lasted throughout the second half of the nineteenth century. Their key idea was to "show the degree of civilization and progress the various nations have attained."[1] In the beginning, the term "universal" simply meant openness to all the "products of human labor," to all branches of economic activity. But the adjective quickly became inseparable from the fortunes of universalism in the ideology of progress, and the nations that embodied it. These events, which placed steam and electricity on display, soon became showcases for the whole world, and already constituted a new medium in themselves. But there was more to it: they led photography, underwater cable, animated images, the telephone, telegraph, and other nascent techniques of communication in cross-fertilizing the grand narratives of the advent of "Universal Association."

These periodic events also welcomed congresses and conferences organized around the most diverse topics and protagonists. Thus they gave an opportunity for the contradictory quest for new forms of international mediation and negotiation, among states as well as among civil societies, to express itself.

Genesis of the Industrial Exposition

The first international industrial exposition in history took place in London in 1851, at the dawn of the Victorian era, in an England that had only recently opted for free trade. This "Great Exhibition of the Works of Industry of All Nations" was housed in the Crystal Palace. "All Nations" amounted then to twenty-four countries, invited by diplomatic avenues to exhibit there.

In 1837, the architect of the Crystal Palace, Joseph Paxton, had already constructed a greenhouse at Chatsworth where tropical plants were acclimatized. To come up with the structure of the palace, Paxton, in phase with a decade that would see the ascendancy of naturalists, let himself be guided by the organic world, and took his inspiration from the veins in the leaf of a giant Amazonian water lily christened *Victoria regia*,[2] so that the structure became an intricate network of slender iron rods. It was a symbol of a new era opening up, but another underlying symbol was the desire for transparency. The building opened to the daylight.

Not only is the very theme of the Exhibition universality and unification — ("Gentlemen! The Exhibition of 1851 will be a faithful witness and a living image of the stage humanity has reached along this great path toward *unification*...") — but the architecture of the building, because it was based on the use of iron, wood and clear glass, seemed to dissolve classical forms, those of closure and fortification. Here "no vantage point allows the evaluation of...real distances and dimensions, and so *everything becomes immaterial.*"[3]

These were the germs of what Yves Stourdzé calls the "crystalline paradigm": the glass construction that ensured light a continuous presence prefigured the electric light and its technical network. This paradigm signified "luminosity, transparency — all the processes by which flows traverse space without being interrupted — in short, continuity (sound and light are propagated everywhere and destroy the zones of obscurity and silence)."[4] Before electricity, there were the immense glass windows of the department stores, built by French engineers who were also exploding the dichotomy between interior and exterior.

After the first International Exposition, the largest ones would take place in Paris (1855, 1867, 1878, 1889, 1900), once more in London (1862), and once each in Vienna, Philadelphia, and Chicago (1873, 1876, and 1893, respectively). The seventeen thousand exhibitors at Crystal Palace had attracted six million people over a period of 141 days. The Paris Exposition that closed the century would last 205 days and attract eight times as many visitors to its eighty-three thousand exhibitors. In the meantime, the "International Exposition" formula would enjoy a vogue in the four corners of the world, even if this appellation referred to many different contents. Sydney, Calcutta, Buenos Aires, Rio de Janeiro, Bogotá, Amsterdam, Brussels, Bombay, Melbourne, Barcelona, Edinburgh, São Paulo, Moscow, and many other cities organized such events. Among the world powers at the time, only China and Japan proved resistant to this new form of contact among nations via industry — which did not prevent these two countries from being present in the expositions organized in other countries, where they nourished the imaginary of extreme Orientalism.

If England was the first to internationalize the formula of the industrial exposition, she was not its inventor. In fact, it was in France, in the late eighteenth century, that this new form of communication — which would be referred to as a "below-the-line medium" by the advertising industry of the twentieth century — was conceived. In 1798, the French Directory's minister of the interior, François de Neufchâteau, decreed an "annual public exposition of the products of French industry" and assigned it a double goal: to provide an overview of national production and to stimulate French entrepreneurs in the struggle against monarchic England. Many elements converged to give this first industrial exposition (properly speaking) the aspect of a war campaign. In the opening parade there were a school of trumpeters, a detachment of cavalry, the first two teams of ushers, drummers, military orchestras, a squad of infantry, heralds, the master of the festivities, the competing artists, and the jury. Neufchâteau reserved the gold medal for the exhibitor "who did the most harm to English industry."[5]

During the first half of the nineteenth century, ten such events were organized in Paris. The 1849 Exposition was meant to be international in scope, but the frank opposition of manufacturers and chambers of commerce to a broadened participation defeated the government's proposal: the majority of them felt that they were not in a position to confront foreign competition on the domestic market.

The emergence of the "industrial exposition" formula coincided with the suppression of barriers of all kinds that stood in the way of trade under the Old Regime. Its genesis thus has little to do with the great fairs that reached their culmination in the sixteenth century (in cities such as Antwerp, Bergen op Zoom, Frankfurt, Leipzig, Medina del Campo, Lyons, Besançon, Beaucaire, and Nijni-Novgorod). These festive crossroads of commerce had put the consumers into contact with producers, and buyers with vendors, compensating to some degree for the paucity of avenues of communication and means of exchange. In an economic space protected by tolls, taxes, and privileges, the fairs appeared as "free-trade zones" or "territories of exception," enjoying fiscal advantages from which ordinary forms of commerce in no way benefited. Beginning in the seventeenth century, this old institution lost its importance in Europe and was replaced by other, more permanent circuits of exchange: stock exchanges, money markets, and, of course, shops. The new world-economy centered in Amsterdam, seat of the prestigious Dutch East India Company, chartered in 1602, with its virtual monopoly of the European trade in spices and coffee, was built on a financial market characterized by volume, fluidity, publicity, and the speculative freedom of transactions. A continuous flow of trade began to prevail over episodic encounters.[6]

Within the grounds of the industrial exposition nothing was sold and nothing bought. Exhibited there were industrial machines, and in turn the means of production used to manufacture them. In this way, exhibitions sought to promote technological innovation, bring industry closer to society, and stimulate industrial patriotism and simple national pride. The first such event already announced these ritual jousts of emulation: at the Champ-de-Mars, scene of French national celebrations since the Revolution, a temple of industry was erected in the center of a square courtyard bordered by a gallery of sixty-eight arcades, where industrialists, scientists, engineers, and workers were recompensed by medals, citations, and honorable mentions. In addition, this site of initiation to scientific and industrial progress was freely accessible to visitors (admission was not charged until the internationalization of these events).

The same minister of the interior who inaugurated the formula of the industrial exposition between 1797 and 1799 also began to lay the foundations for a future service of general statistics, by regularly sending forms to municipalities to obtain various kinds of data. The chemist Jean Chaptal, who would pursue this project under the empire, gave the inaugural speech at the first national exposition. Nothing appeared more logical than to ally the "overview of national production" with the search for nomenclatures. Expositions were, from this viewpoint, a life-size laboratory: the greater and greater complexity of the classification of production was the material proof that the division of labor, recently theorized by Adam Smith, was gaining in perfection. Starting with the London Exposition, the international community of statisticians, under the presidency of Adolphe Quételet, would be one of the first professional bodies to organize and to devote meetings to standardizing its instruments of observation and analysis. At the same event there began definitive discussions about the internationalization of the metric system.

At the beginning of the century, the national industrial exposition included only four sections: mechanical arts, chemical arts, fine arts, and textiles. In 1867, the Universal Exposition in Paris would include ten groups and ninety-five classes of exhibits. The principle of classification would be translated into the exhibition space itself. It was the first time that the "theory of universal space" was applied: the building should be as flexible as possible, and capable of housing content of any kind. The result was the building of a palace on the Champ-de-Mars to serve as a terminus and tax-free station for merchandise coming from around the world. It was composed of two semicircles with 190 meters of counter, linked by a rectangle 380 meters long and 110 meters wide. Designers applied a principle of classification into abscissas and ordinates adapted to a circular figure. Each ring contained a branch of production; each sector displayed the production of a nation. By following a concentric gallery, visitors could pass in review the products of the same group from different countries; and by following one of the sectors from the middle to the periphery, they could pass in review exhibits about a country's labor history, applied arts, liberal arts, housing, clothing, the products of its extractive industries, the instruments and procedures of its everyday crafts, and fresh and conserved produce. Outside the perimeter of the central palace were erected brightly colored pavilions in the various national styles, authorized for the first time in an event of this kind.

The major planners of this 1867 Exposition, a key moment in the history of calculation, were Frédéric Le Play (1806–82) and Michel Chevalier. Le Play, general commissioner of this exposition and the one in 1855, devised the mode of classification of exhibits and carried it out with the architects. A specialist in ethnographic methods, he was a notable pioneer of the collection, storage, and processing of empirical data on industry. Chevalier, as editor in chief of the Exposition's official reports, developed its underlying philosophy. He had already taken part in juries and official delegations in the three previous Universal Expositions organized in London and Paris.

The British authorities decided in the 1870s to change the rules of the universal exposition formula by organizing a series of annual exhibitions by industrial branch. The experiment was inconclusive and was suspended after four years. Thus, the last great industrial exposition in nineteenth-century London was that of 1862. At least the Crystal Palace Exhibition had given the world the first museum of science and industry of the industrial age: the Science Museum, founded in 1857.

Paris, Capital of Universal Culture

The Crystal Palace Exhibition took place thanks to private initiative under royal patronage. The one in Paris, by contrast, was designed under state auspices and steered by distinguished civil servants in association with heads of enterprise, engineers, and scholarly institutions. In France the exposition carried a greater symbolic charge, and doubtless this is one of the reasons the discourse accompanying it occupied such an important place. This discourse matured as Paris adopted its role as the "capital of the nineteenth century," in Walter Benjamin's phrase. While the Victorian Empire egregiously dominated the networks of technical communication throughout the world, a reflection of Great Britain's industrial and commercial hegemony, Paris would continue to set the norms for "legitimate culture."

A French consul in Argentina understood this well and did not mince words in a report to the minister of commerce and industry on the occasion of an International Exposition held in Buenos Aires, during which a statue by Rodin of Domingo F. Sarmiento, an Argentinean statesman, writer, and educator, was unveiled. "The taste for French culture," he wrote to his minister, "has gotten the upper hand, among the elite of society, over all foreign productions. Our writers, our dramatic authors, our thinkers find faithful readers and listeners down there . . . So let us maintain the lead acquired over other nations thanks to our artistic supremacy. It is an easy thing to do."[7] But as always since the Crystal Palace Exhibition, the first to celebrate France's luxury industries, her delegates had constant need to reassure themselves concerning the other function of expositions, which was to conquer markets. "Other successes are reserved to us," continued the consular functionary,

> which will be no less useful than those of yesterday for our country and its commercial and industrial expansion, which must go hand in hand with the prestige of French thought. We have in fact struck a major blow in showing, by the part we have taken in exhibits of railways, agriculture, and hygiene, that we are capable of equaling and, on many counts, surpassing our rivals thanks to the excellence of our products, the quality of our inventions, and the perfection of our manufactured goods.[8]

Argentina's geographical location was particularly strategic for this commentary: its economy, the trade in meat and wheat, and rail and telegraph lines were at the time largely in the hands of British companies.

The tendency of the national elites of Latin America to focus on the European countries was undeniable. There is no better example of this than the fact that Brazil, which, having overthrown its emperor in 1889, hastened to inscribe on the flag of the new republic the motto of positivism, "Order and Progress." In that country, the philosophy of Comte became the object of a cult to the point that the Brazilians would in 1903 buy the Parisian home of his lover and spiritual guide Clotilde de Vaux and convert it into a temple of the "Religion of Humanity," inscribing on the frontispiece: "Love as principle. Order as base. Progress as goal." The "love as principle," belatedly added by Comte to his doctrine under the influence of Clotilde, was often eclipsed in the successive transplantings of which his conception of universal progress became the object. Under foreign skies, Comtean thought indeed knew a strange destiny. Merging with political liberalism, it served to combat authoritarian regimes and the power of the clergy, but dictatorships also called on it to establish domestic order when choosing to embark on a forced march toward industrial progress. The most convincing illustration of this is Mexico under the iron rule of General Porfirio Díaz between 1884 and 1911.[9] As a Latin American historian notes: "This long government of Porfirio Díaz and his positivist advisers made possible the last great offensive against the world of the Indian."[10] The countershock was not long in coming. In 1911, the first indigenous and peasant revolution of modern times broke out.

The great wave of "Europeanization" has been much studied by South American historians. It was the era of transplants of the Cartesian models of teaching and schemas of organization of justice then current in France, as well as the decisive influence of the Paris architect Haussmann's urbanistic models, that helped to refashion great capitals like Buenos Aires, Rio de Janeiro, and Santiago de Chile. Here is how Uruguayan historians Gustavo and Hélène Beyhaut describe these one-way flows:

> The Europeanization of Latin American civilization was the fruit of both outside imposition and a greater receptivity on the part of local groups. As to the former, one must insist on the standardizing role played by the application of technology to production and communications. Latin America focused principally on England and France. The appeal of the former was its technical progress and growing economic power. As for France, it seduced by virtue of its ways of life (doubtless more adapted to the aspirations of local elites than were the norms of British behavior), and dazzled outsiders by its intellectual progress and the refinement of its luxury industries.[11]

Brazilian economist Celso Furtado defines this attraction of France among elites as a "Bovaryste attitude," that is, a mode of behavior that induces them to turn toward the latest artistic novelties of the Parisian season and to disdain other forms of cultural expression born within their own country and linked to the popular classes.[12]

These are the indispensable elements for understanding the role of Parisian expositions in the maintenance of a cultural hegemony, as witnessed by the major participation of the Latin American countries in those events and the interest the organizers took in these countries. The official reports of French commissioners are prolix about that region of the world, even venturing forecasts of their future. Here is an excerpt from the official report of the 1889 Exposition, where the American sections grouped together were christened "Exposition of the New World":

The study of present and especially the future resources of promising countries such as the Argentine Republic should command all our attention, since it is indisputable that the axis of the world is shifting. Civilization penetrates everywhere, and brings along with it perfected industry and rapid means of manufacture and production. Soon all these new countries of South America, yesterday states of the fourth rank, following the example of the United States on the path of constant progress, will achieve a power equal to the secular states of old Europe. The sap drawn from our side of the Atlantic will germinate in an astonishing fashion on the other side.[13]

This sample of the assessment of intercultural relations can be compared with another, drawn from the same report, concerning the probable impact of the Exposition not on sovereign nations, but rather on colonies:

It is to be feared that the consideration enjoyed by the humble and the great during their stay in France may have spoiled those we administer or protect overseas, and will have made them more demanding than usual. In any event, it may be asserted that their stay will have had many advantages alongside some slight inconveniences. They have certainly gained something from their contact with us; their minds are opened to new ideas, and the moral leadership of France among these peoples still so distant from our civilization will become easier than in the past.[14]

The 1889 Exposition was in fact the first to organize an "Exposition of French colonies and countries of the protectorate."

The Grand Naratives of General Concord

"To tour this palace, circular like the equator, is literally to take a turn around the world, since all peoples are here: enemies live in peace side by side. As it did over the orb of waters, in the origin of things, so the divine Spirit floats over this orb of iron." This passage appears in an international publication authorized by the Imperial Commission of the Universal Exposition of 1867.[15]

Pacification and reconciliation of social antagonisms is a recurrent theme of the imaginary of Universal Expositions. On the occasion of the one in London, two dramatists in a Parisian theater sang out: "Each industry, showing its trophies / In this bazaar of general progress / Seems to have waved the fairy wand / To enrich the Crystal Palace . . . Rich men, scientists, artists, proletarians, / Each works for common well-being; /

And, uniting like noble brothers, / They each want the happiness of the other."[16]

During the exposition to commemorate the first centennial of the French Revolution, we read in another official report:

> You have in these galleries, in these monuments, under these domes, a kind of representation of the material unity of the human species, of the union in labor, in the struggle for existence, in the struggle against misery and hunger, and here you have the representation of the moral unity of humankind. What these things exhibited before our eyes teach us is the fraternity of humankind, and we come here from all corners of the world to proclaim it.[17]

The Universal Exposition shared with the communication network a common imaginary, a common quest for a lost paradise of human community and communion. Both of them reinvigorate and take mutual comfort in the construction of the myth of this transparent universal bond.

The promises of innovations in communication punctuate these great events. The 1851 Exposition cut the ribbon on the first telegraphic link by underwater cable, between Dover and Calais. The one in 1855 featured an early teleprinter invented by the Anglo-American David Hughes. In 1867, underwater cable again occupied the place of honor, some few months after the first transatlantic cable began operating. In 1876, at the United States Centennial Exhibition in Philadelphia, Graham Bell's telephone worked for the first time in front of a general public. The 1893 event in Chicago featured the first intercity telephone line, from Chicago to New York. By 1851, interoceanic canals were part of the landscape of universal communication. In 1889, the Suez Canal and the projected canal through Panama occupied a pavilion, as did the Compagnie Générale Transatlantique. And it was doubtless thanks to "communication" that the Eiffel Tower, hotly contested at the time of its inauguration, was not razed once the festivities of the centennial of the Revolution were over. Some years later, the tower was called on to play an important role as a radio transmitting station, first for military and then for civilian purposes.

As for steam, it was everywhere, right up until electricity burst onto the scene at the International Exposition devoted to it at France's initiative in 1881, barely three years after the invention of the incandescent lamp by Thomas Edison (1847–1931). But unlike the others, where, except in case of war, all sovereign nations were generally invited, only fifteen were summoned to the gathering to celebrate electricity—mostly European countries, along with Japan and the United States—and with good reason, since it was the first international meeting with the explicit purpose of "codifying electrical science and sounding out its depths."[18] Thus it involved only scientists and manufacturers from the countries that produced its applications. Progress in several areas — telegraph, underwater cable, railways, navigation, phonograph, and so on — was passed in review by the participants at scientific congresses that complemented the 1881 Exposition, which, moreover, played the role of laboratory. The major electrical units like the ampere (after André Ampère, French physicist) were agreed upon. The Chicago Exposition of 1893 would see the triumph of Edison at the Palace of Electricity; he had already made a sensation in 1889 with his phonograph, invented in 1877.

Nor were technologies of image reproduction neglected. Photography and its successive advances were a guiding thread of all the universal expositions. The first international exposition in Paris had dazzled visitors with its special section on photography. Forty-five years later, out of every one hundred people passing out of the turnstiles of the exposition, an average of seventeen possessed a "portable photographic chamber."[19] The saga of animated pictures began in 1878, when the praxinoscope — a device relying on a drum of mirrors around which a strip of images turned, creating the impression of animation, invented by Emile Reynaud — enjoyed lively success as a curiosity. The Paris Exposition of 1900 featured the triumph of the Lumière brothers' cinématographe on a huge screen, five years after the first public projection of moving pictures at the Grand Café. At the beginning of the twentieth century, film became the very symbol of universality. "Animated images," remarked novelist Jack London (1876–1916),

> tear down the barriers of poverty and of the environment that barred the route to education, and distribute knowledge in a language that everyone can comprehend. The worker with a poor vocabulary is equal to the scientist . . . Universal education is the message . . . Time and distance have been annihilated by the magic film to bring together the peoples of the world . . . Gaze horror-struck at war scenes and you become an advocate of peace . . . By this magic means, the extremes of society take a step closer to each other in the inevitable readjustment of the human condition.[20]

The introduction to the official reports on the 1867 Exposition, composed by Michel Chevalier, is beyond doubt the document that combines the most clearly the universalizing virtues of Communication with those of the Exposition. Chevalier, at that time an adviser to Napoléon III,

describes in this document how the horizon had enlarged since the beginning of the century through communications, which brought the
"genius of Europe to regions relegated to an inferior rank"; and how
steam, the telegraph, and migrations had permitted the expansion of
the "great triad of modern Europe—France, England, and Germany."
To these countries, which constituted for Chevalier the "pedestal of Western civilization," and where the "forces of the human spirit have reached
their highest development, and where morality, science, and industry have
assumed a form superior to anything seen before," the Saint-Simonian
added the United States, because it was living "on the same foundation
of religious, moral, social, political, and scientific ideas."[21]

Thirty-five years after his article in the *Globe* on the subject of a
Mediterranean confederation through rail, Chevalier speculated this time
on a possible combination between rail and the interoceanic canal in
Panama in order to link the Pacific with the Atlantic and North America with South America. An inveterate utopian of communication, Chevalier sometimes recovered the lyric accents of his youth to celebrate the
blessings of means of shortening distances:

> The need for exchange leads all peoples to draw closer to each
> other. The sentiment of unity among the human family excites
> them to this, like a natural instinct that never slumbers. Their
> reciprocal relations are activated by politics, which, despite itself,
> under pressure of public opinion, frequently takes on a humanitarian
> character, by the ascendancy the race of Japhet has acquired over
> the whole world. The new means of locomotion strengthen these
> contacts more and more. One may consider, as of today, that the
> moment of triumph is at hand for the principle—equally dear to
> philosophy and religion—of the solidarity of peoples and races.[22]

But this time Chevalier was not entirely duped. His conclusion evokes
the antagonism that subsisted in Europe between two tendencies: the
"idea of harmony" and the "right of the saber and the cannon," between industry and military organization. He even saw in this a source
of a decline that might favor a future world hegemony of the American
"colossus."

> Europe, whose children, united on the grounds of the Exposition,
> seem ready to grasp each other in their arms, appears much more
> like a camp than like a group of communities of industrious and
> enlightened men, honoring God, loving their fellows, keen to
> facilitate universal and individual progress by the development of
> general liberty and individual freedom. As far as one goes back in
> history, one will never find such a collection of armed men, such
> an accumulation of instruments of war.[23]

Until the eve of World War I, this tension between war and peace, between the grave tone of threats and the hubbub of the universal festival, constantly characterized the great expositions, despite the predominance of the pacific discourse of the organizers of these industrial gatherings. Within their grounds, machines of destruction were exhibited in the same way as those of production. Referring to the 1867 Exposition, Émile Zola in *L'Argent* denounced the curious crowd who pressed in to touch the famous Krupp cannons displayed at this "imperial festival," this "extravaganza of lies." (In 1889, the Exposition would include an entire military section.)

The year 1867 was also the date of the execution of the Emperor Ferdinand-Joseph Maximilian, who had been placed on the throne of Mexico by Napoléon III, then at war against the Republic and its president Benito Juárez. The French authorities did everything in their power to suppress the news of the execution until the end of the closing ceremony of the Universal Exposition! Chevalier, a specialist in American issues, was one of the principal advisers for this imperial policy. He had launched the idea of "Pan-Latinism" in response to the "Pan-Americanism" promoted by Washington, bent more than ever on defending the principles of the Monroe Doctrine (1823) that guaranteed its control over the countries of the South in the name of safeguarding its own national security. The Saint-Simonian even took part in the auxiliary corps of scientists and engineers that accompanied the French military expedition to Veracruz, in an effort to repeat Bonaparte's Egyptian expedition of 1798 and to establish a Catholic and Latin empire in Mexico.

The legitimization of this imperial adventure led Chevalier to write a geopolitical essay on Mexico where he went so far as to advocate a strategic use of the train:

> The most dangerous adversary that our valiant soldiers had to encounter on the way was yellow fever... To combat this plague... one of the means is the construction of a railway over which troops, as soon as they have disembarked at Veracruz, can cross the infected zone in a few hours... This railway would render the expedition another service, that of assuring its communications with Veracruz, from which reinforcements, munitions, matériel will necessarily come, and even a portion of their provisions — everything that cannot be taken from the country itself.

He concluded: "Moreover, for an army, the speed and the security of communications and the facility of contact with its base of operations are advantages of inestimable value."[24]

"Pan-Americanism," for its part, would find in the World's Fair of 1876 in Philadelphia, the nation's original capital, and especially in the one in Chicago to honor the fourth centennial of Columbus's landing (which was inaugurated in 1892 but opened to the public only in the following year), two occasions to reaffirm its claim to a geopolitical space encompassing the countries of Central and South America.

An International Public Space in Formation

From the first Universal Exposition on, through the congresses that took place within them, these events became a site of international agreements. We have already noted the examples of the harmonization of statistics and weights and measures.

These congresses and conferences were informal until 1878, but they would be officialized in that year by decree in the Paris expositions. In the others they remained informal, and in the 1870s their number grew. The world context of the time was favorable to contacts across borders. An evaluation of the frequency of appearance of international associations and agreements drawn up by the historian Werner Sombart (1863–1941) at the turn of the century is, in this light, more than eloquent: before 1850, only seven were realized; in the twenty subsequent years, seventeen; from 1870 to 1880, twenty; and from 1880 to 1890, thirty-one—a figure that doubled in the final decade of the century.[25]

Tied to the expositions, the congresses played a decisive role, notably in the creation of several institutions charged with regulating international relations in this area of communication.

At the Vienna Exposition of 1873, the congress on industrial property proposed the first international convention on patents. At the Paris Exposition in 1878, under the presidency of Victor Hugo, a congress on literary property took place. Eight years later, the International Union of Bern was created for the protection of literary and artistic works, although this convention was signed by only ten states.

In 1878, too, a congress held in Paris revised the first treaty of the General Postal Union, signed at Bern four years previously, and changed its name to the Universal Postal Union, reiterating the foundations of its civilizing mission:

> The postal service should not be considered a financial institution . . . Masses of people, by the force of circumstances, remain tied to their place of birth—*glebae adscripti*; proportionally few are able to make purchases and sales in their respective places, or to see up close the great progress that characterizes our era, or the results of industry brought together in

the expositions of the world capitals and offered to the gaze of
spectators. This bringing together of the guardians of thought and
the industrialists of different countries in a common purpose,
toward which economic development and development in general
strives, is manifest first along the great artery called the postal
service. Progress of whatever kind — political, moral, or
material — imprints an ever stronger movement along this artery
and accentuates even more the importance of the complete
freedom of correspondence.[26]

Twenty-two countries, all European with the exception of the United
States, ratified this agreement. The institution's first decisions aimed to
guarantee respect for the right of correspondence and to facilitate the
delivery of parcels of declared value and money orders. The adhesive
postage stamp was then already forty years old, and its inventor, the
English educator and father of postal reforms Sir Rowland Hill, would
soon have his statue in bronze on a granite pedestal before the City of
London's Stock Exchange. Before the signing of the accord creating the
Universal Postal Union (UPU), relations among the postal services of different countries were regulated by bilateral treaties. France had thus subscribed to sixteen agreements of this type, Germany to seventeen, and the
United States to at least nine. The result was a jungle of rules for dis-
patching mail (regarding rates, weights, letter sizes, and routes). The same
confusion reigned concerning telegraphic communications, at first also
subject to bilateral agreements.

The Postal Union was not the first example of an international regulatory body to use Universal Expositions to bring members together. It
had been preceded by the International Telegraph Union (ITU), founded
in 1865 during a congress convened by Napoléon III and attended by some
twenty countries. This union is the first international organization of the
modern era, the first intergovernmental initiative that transforms the
territories of various nations into a single unit for the exchange of electrically transmitted messages.[27]

Aside from hosting meetings among governmental delegations, the
Universal Expositions above all played the role of a forum for the most
diverse groupings: social movements, scholarly societies, and all sorts
of associations.

In 1878, thirty-two international congresses met at the Paris Exposition; in 1889, no less than sixty-nine, including scientific congresses (in
the areas of geography, aeronautics, criminal anthropology, legal medicine, chronometry, meteorology, ethnography, veterinary medicine, statistics, zoology, physiological psychology, mental health, teaching, the bibliography of the mathematical sciences, etc.); congresses by professional

or amateur activity (architects, photographers, stenographers, electricians, firemen, bakers, but also pigeon-fanciers, specialists in lifesaving, homeopaths, and people of letters); congresses on social issues (alcoholism, a reduced workweek, public assistance, provident institutions, low-cost housing, the welfare of the blind, profit sharing, etc.); congresses on peace, currency, the study of colonial questions, consumer cooperatives, artistic property, industrial property, the protection of works of art and monuments, and the conservation of popular traditions. Some examples may suffice to illustrate this movement.

The 1862 Exposition in London, in which working-class delegations participated, was the prelude to the founding two years later of the International Workingmen's Association. The address by the Parisian workers' delegation even served as a reference point in the formulation of the statutes of this First International.

The 1889 Exposition was also host to the creators of the modern Olympic Games, whose original rationale was educational. Pierre de Coubertin (1863–1937) organized a congress on the "propagation of physical exercises in education," the first step toward internationalization of the project to reestablish the Olympic Games. Another form of universal concord by emulation was appearing on the horizon:

> It is not fitting that any race or era hold an exclusive monopoly... Olympianism overturns barriers. It demands air and light for everyone... Let us export rowers, runners, fencers: this is the free trade of the future, and the day it is introduced into the customs of old Europe, the cause of peace will have received a new and powerful support.[28]

Above all, however, this Exposition of 1889 was the affirmation of the disciplines of ethnography and ethnology, coupled with the colonial exposition. It was the era of justification for colonial conquest, marked by evolutionist theory.[29]

The ethnological preoccupation was also present in the Chicago World's Columbian Exposition of 1893, which confided to anthropologist Franz Boas the task of organizing anthropological expositions commemorating Columbus's voyage of discovery. In Chicago as well, one of the first congresses on the international role of the press was held; it ended with a declaration of intent: "The press should seek to dissipate misunderstandings among nations. With the telegraph now present in principal centers of human activity, one can enlighten public opinion and unmask the selfish and corrupting intrigues of the servants of monarchies—intrigues whose result has been to incite nations to kill each other."[30]

Still in Chicago, feminine organizations made their breakthrough. The World's Fair included a "Board of Lady Managers" that had its own pavilion and organized separately a Congress of Women. What was discussed there was not to the taste of the French general commissioner, Camille Krantz, who registered his disapproval of a "long series of panegyrics of women and violent criticism about modern society and men" and objected to the "very regrettable intemperance of language."[31] The female delegation from France received honorable mention for the precision of its statistics on the condition of women.

In 1900 in Paris, the "international feminist congresses" debated the conditions of employment of domestic maids. The comparison with the United States, prefiguration of the future, was inevitable:

> Never will a young girl enter a home to be its servant . . . Shortly machines will replace human labor: machines for washing and drying the dishes, for waxing and shining shoes, for sweeping and beating carpets; communal stoves will heat the whole town; communal kitchens and restaurants will provide the family's nourishment, when the family does not live in hotels. According to the Americans, these are the conditions in the great civilizations of the future and especially for the emancipation of women. Continental family habits lead us to believe that we will not see the ideal of the New World realized very soon in Old Europe.[32]

In 1889, twenty thousand people attended the congresses organized within the Exposition, and the official spokesman assessed their efficacy:

> First of all, one must consider the very real advantage that results from the encounter of people concerned with questions of the same order, who often were not previously in direct relation and who are now in a position to discuss things without intermediaries. Often many misunderstandings are thus dissipated . . . As for the results of congresses from the standpoint of their work, these are very real in some cases: they may reach an agreement on a common effort, on rules to follow in nomenclature, on the path to follow in future research on a given question. In other cases, the congresses have furnished precious information that, combined with information already possessed, will allow the summing up of the subject in collective work, or will contribute to completing an investigation . . . [However], certain congresses have resulted only in the expression one more time of worthy and just ideas that are generally accepted, but without offering the means of achieving their practical realization.[33]

If the Universal Exposition is a site where an international public space is formed, it is also a place around which the fear of the other becomes crystallized. The bringing together of people, international communication, was also seen by some as the site of contamination across borders. Starting with the Crystal Palace Exhibition, the detractors of the exposition formula did not fail to brandish the risk of an epidemic posed by the invasion of crowds it occasioned in a major capital that concentrated 10 percent of the population of England and Wales. Very symbolically, the question of "hygiene" became a science in the process of internationalization at the same time as statistics. In fact, at the request of the French government, a first conference on international sanitation gathered in the same year of 1851, with a view to codifying measures to take against cholera, yellow fever, and other epidemics. But in contrast to the success of specialists in moral statistics, the representatives of the twelve countries invited there did not manage to reach agreement on a minimal code. It was not until the beginning of the twentieth century that an International Office of Public Hygiene would be created. At each Universal Exposition, however, this piercing issue would come back onto the agenda.

Post-Darwinian anthropology, as Alain Corbin notes, would lead increasingly to emphasizing "the specific odor of different races or ethnic groups," with certain commentators finding "offensive" the odor of Negroes at the Exposition crowded onto the Champ-de-Mars.[34] As late as 1889, the official chronicler of the Exposition felt obliged to detail in his report the measures taken by the commissioners to combat "the danger of epidemic from the congestion of natives, in general of doubtful cleanliness": airing by fanlights, reserved toilets, urinals with running water, taps with springwater "to avoid typhoid," Pasteur filters for drinking water, and an employee assigned throughout the exposition to "maintain the different hygienic installations, washing down, disinfecting, and watching over them."[35]

The hygienic preoccupation evidenced in these international microcosms was consistent with the concerns guiding the sanitary strategies of governments vis-à-vis the laboring populations of urban metropolises since the beginning of the century. (Robert's *Dictionnaire historique* dates the rise of the word "hygiene" in the sense of "preventive medicine" to 1803, and the expressions "mental hygiene" and "public hygiene," respectively, to 1808 and 1833; this indicates how novel Saint-Simon had been in using this metaphor in his social physiology!) During the course of the century, measures to deodorize public space and private space were constantly refined, through ventilation or "control of the circulation of aerial flows," or by creating a vacuum, "disinfecting," and the immediate evacuation of refuse.[36] The first laboratories for this strategy of deodorization, starting at the end of the eighteenth century, were soldiers' tents, naval vessels, hospitals, and prisons.

At the moment when the first international sanitation conference was taking place, London already offered a model. In 1848, England created a Ministry of Public Health to fight against "filth." Twelve years later, its engineers undertook the construction of the great network of sewers in London, a system soon adopted by Brussels and several major cities in the Germanic confederation. The French administration, on the other hand, long rejected them. Another network, that of the freshwater supply, would soon complete the range of public sanitation measures in industrial countries.

These strategies of social hygiene and of the struggle against socially disseminated odors — and the image of the popular classes that they promoted — would serve in part as the background to the first debates over the nature of crowds.

The Buffalo Bill Syndrome:
Progress Undermined by Spectacle

The Paris Exposition of 1900 marks the apogee of the ascending curve of Universal Expositions. It was the most cosmopolitan and the most "universal" (in the original sense of the term, referring to the variety of products exhibited). But it was also the moment when the model fell into crisis.

Talk began of the perversion of the exposition formula by the logic of the spectacle: "More and more," wrote the economist G. Gérault in 1902, "Universal Expositions have lost their original character and become enterprises for pleasure. Interest in industry and commerce is only a pretext, and amusement is the aim...In order to foster the commercial expansion of the country, it will be necessary to resort to other, less expensive but more productive means."[37] People of this opinion thought that only specialized expositions were still in a position to produce effects in terms of discoveries and innovations.

Numerous exhibits were devoted to "animated pictures." The Lumière brothers installed in the Gallery of Machines a giant cinema that projected scenes onto a screen twenty-five meters wide and sixteen meters high. Georges Méliès perfected a rotating tripod for shooting panoramic shots; the result was seventeen filmstrips, which were hand-colored.[38] But the Cinéorama, the circular cinema invented by Raoul Grimoin-Sanson, which was supposed to project them and to provide spectators with extraordinary sensations, notably during a scene of ascension in a hot-air balloon, ran up against "various defects concerning both the hall situated at the foot of the Eiffel Tower and the projector," and it was soon shut down.[39]

The general public could admire at the same 1900 Exposition a variety of automobiles. The fifth anniversary of the birth of the motor vehicle was celebrated there, in the presence of the manufacturers of Benz automobiles (founded in 1883), Daimler (1890), Peugeot (1885), Renault (1898), Ford (1892), and Fiat (1899), not to mention the tire manufacturer Michelin (1895), which on this occasion issued its first travel guide. Races and parades were organized to commemorate the first automobile race (1895, from Bordeaux to Paris). Competitive sports also made their appearance: championships in fencing, shooting, cycling, aeronautics (competitions for altitude, speed, distance, length of flight, direction, and balloon photography). The noticeable presence of large department stores like Le Bon Marché (founded in 1852), Le Printemps (1865), and La Samaritaine (1869) indicated not only the tendency to commercialization but also the pressure exerted by their market-oriented distribution model on the conception of the Exposition itself.[40] These innovations disturbed those who continued to think in terms of a pedagogical purpose and of the initiatory quest for knowledge.

Already in 1889, the general chronicler was concerned about the drift toward "amusement." Criticizing the "excessive acrobatics" similar to those of the fun fairs, and even to the Folies-Bergères, he called for "more decency": that the exposition

> seeks amusements and curiosities and everything that can attract
> and hold provincials and foreigners in a city—nothing is more
> natural and proper. But there must be enough tact, and we would
> even say enough respect, for oneself and one's country not to
> resort to overly rude "attractions." This is especially true when an
> international festival is combined with patriotic celebrations. The
> contrast shocks honest people.[41]

In 1889, gaudy attractions from the United States created an element of disruption. The walls of Paris were covered with gigantic posters for William Cody, alias Buffalo Bill, the "Napoléon of the Prairie." With his "redskins" and buffaloes, he made the front page of *L'Illustration*. The issue of 22 June contrasted on the same page an enactment of an attack on a settlers' wagon train by Indians and a Gobelin tapestry portraying Henry IV—a metaphor for two types of distraction. The journalist Rastignac exercised his wit by contrasting two types of visitors: the "grumpy ones" who reacted by saying that

Buffalo Bill has licked Corneille. People have no use for the paintings of Corot and Delacroix, and rush to the rue du Caire [a "theme street" composed of the facades of Egyptian houses from various eras, two mosques, a school, a minaret, and portals, inhabited by some 160 natives — including merchants, workers, donkey drivers, cafe owners, and dancers]. Everything is transformed into a great bacchanalia. People care nothing about industry, progress, and they pounce on pleasure. Crowds eat sausages on the lawns, and loll there as if at a bazaar. And the Eiffel Tower [built as the central attraction of the exposition], the hateful Eiffel Tower! When will I no longer have to see, when seated on the gravel or under the trees, this immense asparagus, this iron triumph of idle curiosity?

Meanwhile, the "satisfied" visitors say:

What life, what joy, laughter, movement, a happy fever... Every place is full — the cafés, restaurants, theaters. And what a century this is that has produced in art and industry what we see displayed on the Champ-de-Mars! Oh, the Delacroix, the Millet, the Corot paintings! And Edison on top of it! The crowd is in a good mood, sees everything, goes everywhere.[42]

In short, with its "ardent tones," its "extraordinary fantasy," the Buffalo Bill spectacle directed by the journalist Crawford with the collaboration of the actor Note Salsbury brought back the "infernal gallop of legends." "How can you expect the theater to struggle against these realities in which the readings of Fenimore Cooper or of Gabriel Ferry are portrayed, materializing the very imaginations of novelists?"[43] In order to rival such spectacles, or even that of the Eiffel Tower illuminated by electricity or lit by fireworks, the classical actress Sarah Bernhardt, "to make money, would have to die on the second level of the Tower."[44]

Thus a process of deritualization may be observed here. The well-marked path of the ascetic apprenticeship to progress, work, and high culture, which was still untouched in the 1870s, now entered into conflict with the undisciplined uses of festival, leisure, and the "right to be lazy," in Paul Lafargue's expression of 1880. "Sybaritism had permeated practically all the classes. The popular classes no longer like to wait too long for pleasure," argues the reporter of L'Illustration.[45] In pushing gigantism to its extremes and in multiplying the number of spectacles, the Chicago World's Fair of 1893 played a major role in undermining the foundations of the temples of industry.

Many years later, the echo of the first steps of the American dream would still resonate in the imaginary of the French: "Sun / Buffalo Bill / Barnum / You go to our heads / Like opium," wrote poet Jean Cocteau.

Chapter 6
The Communitarian City

The utopian visions of the first half of the nineteenth century contain an implicit reference to the *Discourse on Inequality* and the "natural man" of Jean-Jacques Rousseau, whose own work is a locus in which Plato (*The Republic*), Tommaso Campanella (*Civitas Solis*), and Thomas More (*Utopia*) converge, diverge, and intermingle. Each utopia in its fashion incorporates ideas of a community of goods, and of universal equality, harmony, and fraternity.

Before the end of the century, communitarian thought guided the first representatives of a self-managed and antiauthoritarian socialism in their proposals for reform of the juridical regime of the means of communication. Under its insignia, a first notion of "public service" made its appearance, pitting—already in this period—the partisans of "everything to the state" against those of "everything to the market."

Opening the way to another view of the management of society and the world, communitarian thought built the foundation for doctrines that in the following century proclaimed the liberating virtues of technical civilization and its networks. Not until the 1920s did skepticism about the emancipating potential of neotechnics and electrical communication begin to penetrate into speculations about the society of the future.

From the New Atlantis to Charles Fourier's Phalanstery

Communication did not wait for a precise definition to become part of the utopian narrative of the new scientific age. One could even say that it was born alongside it. In an unfinished text begun in 1623 and published in 1627, one year after his death, Francis Bacon imagined an ideal city based on science, *The New Atlantis*.[1]

This first work of "science fiction" takes place on the island of Bensalem, which resembles the Atlantis imagined by Plato. Bacon assumes that in this utopian society the most significant progressive factor is its technological power. Vegetable species are bred there for medicinal purposes; experiments are done on animals before being conducted on the human body. Bensalem is rich in precision instruments and tools designed to produce movement of all kinds: they fly or imitate birds' flight; they navigate under the sea; they produce perpetual motion. But this arsenal of inventions inviting one to travel contrasts with the natural geographical closure of the New Atlantis, the refusal of the foreign, the prohibition on communication with the outside, the imposition of a strict secrecy, and with major restrictions placed on the movements of its insular inhabitants. The scientific community is organized according to a rigorous division of labor. In the headquarters of the scientific body known as the "House of Solomon," only certain handpicked scholars are authorized to travel abroad and inform themselves about scientific discoveries that might be useful to their compatriots; some search in books for useful experiments; others do research in the mechanical arts; still others classify experiments; as for the "interpreters of nature," they systematize these experiments and endeavor to draw principles from them.

The utopian Charles Fourier (1772–1837) took the exact opposite position to Bacon's communicational closure. The territory of Harmony has worldwide dimensions, a world whose geography he redesigns as he pleases, imagining the planet of the future. He makes the polar ice cap melt and give birth to a polar "ring" or a "boreal crown" that distributes the double fluid of heat and light. Under the effect of the general softening of the climate, new lands offered for cultivation allow humankind to burgeon "to its full size of three billion inhabitants," the necessary condition for "harmonic creations." The earth, an immense vital organism, in fact has not yet finished creating herself.

> All creations take place through the conjunction of a northern fluid, which is male, with a southern fluid, which is female. A planet is a being that has two souls and two sexes and that procreates, like animals and vegetables, through the meeting of two generative substances... To believe that the earth will not produce new creations, that it will limit itself to what it has already accomplished, would be like believing that a woman who has had one child could not have a second, a third, a tenth.[2]

Changing the axis of the globe, Fourier permutates the topography of cities, countries, continents, and stars. He makes Constantinople the capital of the world and digs "navigable canals through Suez and Panama," "child's play for the industrial armies of the Spherical Hierarchy."[3]

The phalanstery, the basic organizational unit of the harmonious society, is both a symbol of and an affair of communication. This "association that cultivates a canton" and exploits a square league of land is a vast common building in which a phalanx lives. Its interior and exterior architecture and its landscaping are conceived in a way that guarantees to the Harmonians the full flowering of their passions by associating the natural environment and the built framework, and by joining the functional and the beautiful.

> The center of this construction should be a place for quiet activity; it should include the dining rooms, the exchange, meeting rooms, library, studies, and so on. This central section includes the temple, the tower, the telegraph, the coops for carrier pigeons, the ceremonial chimes, the observatory, and a winter courtyard adorned with resinous plants. The parade grounds are located just behind the central section.[4]

This center is surrounded by gardens. The parade court is followed by a place for maneuvers, flanked on the left with noisy places (workshops, forges, areas for children) and on the right by space reserved for the caravansary, ballrooms, and halls for meetings with outsiders. Finally come the stables, the granaries, and storehouses, which look out over the land dedicated to "large-scale farming." The "street gallery," modeled on the "passage" and "arcade" of the Paris Palais-Royal, links the different bodies in the phalanstery dwelling.

> The street galleries are a mode of internal communication...The phalanx has no outside streets or open roadways exposed to the elements. All the portions of the central edifice (that consists of three floors) can be crossed by means of a wide gallery that runs along the second floor of the whole building. At each extremity of this spacious corridor there are elevated passages, supported by columns, and also attractive underground passages that connect all the parts of the phalanx and the adjoining buildings. Thus everything is linked by a series of passageways that are sheltered, elegant, and comfortable in winter thanks to heaters and ventilators.[5]

It should be recalled that when Fourier imagined the central plan for the Palace of Harmony, he knew only of the semaphore telegraph, not yet accessible to the French public; pigeons were still used for transmitting news. Notwithstanding, Fourier, in his anticipatory genius, went even farther: he foresaw "miragelike transmission" in a world that, better instructed in the secrets of the atmosphere, would put London into contact with India in less than four hours. The planet Mercury, notified of the arrivals and movements of boats by Asian astronomers, would transmit the list to astronomers in London.[6]

For the Saint-Simonian Michel Chevalier, the means of communication were, so to speak, a social prosthesis: they determined, per se, a new type of social relations. For his elder compatriot Fourier, they were instruments in the service of networks of social relations in multiple combinations, through which the passions of each man and woman were realized.

Of all the nineteenth-century utopians, Fourier was the most radical. He distrusted all power and maintained no link whatsoever with "sacerdotalism" and "administration," avoiding "any research in what pertains to the interests of the throne and the altar."[7] He practiced absolute doubt and distantiation: doubt with respect to "civilization" and all prejudices; distantiation in relation to existing sciences, "distractions of reason" that he judged to be "globally uncertain." He, a simple "shop steward," an unlucky and "illiterate" traveling salesman, "would refute political and moral libraries, the shameful fruit of ancient and modern quackeries." This is the rule of conduct he proclaimed, starting in his first book, *Théorie des quatre mouvements* (*The Harmony of the Four capital Movements*), which appeared in 1808.

Newton and Leibniz had discovered the laws of first movement: the *material*. Fourier himself announced the discovery of three others: the *social*, the *animal*, and the *organic*. The *social* was meant to explain the laws according to which God had determined the ordering and the succession of the diverse social mechanisms on all the inhabited globes. The *animal* accounted for the laws according to which God distributes passions and instincts to all beings that have been or will be created on the diverse planets. The *organic* explained the laws that preside over the distribution of properties, forms, colors, tastes, and so on, to all substances that have been or will be created. From the synthesis of the four movements, Fourier draws the "laws of universal life," the "laws of Destinies," "the mathematical laws of universal movement."

The earth, which is supposed to live eighty thousand years, had up until then lived only five thousand years of pain and misery. This somber period was to terminate with the swallowing up of "Civilization," since the history of "the civilized movement" unfolds according to a scenario in four biographical phases: two phases of "ascending vibration" or gradation (childhood, adolescence); then two phases of "descending vibration" or degradation (decline, decrepitude). Seventy thousand years of happiness and union would come to the earth in its period of apogee, followed by a relapse into evils of all sorts, as a prelude to its death.

The present period corresponds to the phase of the "decline" of "Civilization." "Civilized people are very unhappy": of the three societies that share the earth — Civilization, Barbarism, and Savagery — none is capable of freeing the globe from the infirmity that afflicts it. The latter two, inert by definition, suffer from paralysis; the former from political impotence. The "makers of commercial systems," the "laissez-faire of leeches we call merchants," have precipitated the current age of civilization with all "the vices of the mercantile hydra." The consumer is ceaselessly hoaxed, so variegated are the "crimes of commerce": speculation on the stock exchange engenders falling wages; monopolization, fictitious scarcities; bankruptcy, "societary lesions"; usury, arbitrary estimates; parasitism, legalized duplicity; lack of solidarity, fragmenting currencies. Factories are nothing more than "mitigated penal colonies." Institutions of civilized people such as permanent marriage degrade women. Civilization is therefore a "world upside down" in which the "system of perfectible perfectibility, ideology, have made Egotism or the *self* the basis of all our calculations."[8]

The idea of progress is a mere delusion, a barren idealism, and the followers of the systems of Saint-Simon (and of the Welshman Robert Owen) are its hypocrites [*tartufes*]. Here is how Fourier criticized them in 1831, when the *Globe* was in its heyday:

It [progress] is a fashionable word, like sympathy, association, the human self, eclecticism, rationalism, industrialism. Everyone runs off with these voguish words, each stitches onto them some system of rapid progress and sublime flight toward perfection and perfectibility, and toward "perfectibilization" and perfectible civilization. In response to these illusions, I ask where is the progress of a social state that combines a thousand theories on the richness of nations and then manages, by force of labor, to lead two-thirds of its inhabitants to famine?[9]

The implacable verdict falls: Saint-Simonianism and the Jesuits are two sects, two "theocratic-political" associations that apply themselves to "mastering governments and capturing inheritances."[10]

The only association that will lead to a "societary state," to the society of plenty Fourier calls Harmony, is that which devotes itself to the basic industry, that of cultivation (and most especially of fruit trees, the pear tree foremost), and to cooperative industry, "natural industry, combined, attractive, truthful." To accede to this phase "of compound association," one must follow the "pivotal movement" that is "passionate attraction" and transform into pleasure the labors to which wage earners are now only chained by the necessity of living. To the "civilized pleasures," which are only "unproductive functions," Fourier contrasts the "unknown pleasures of civilization," the variety of pleasures linked to work that has become attractive. His books are that "social compass" that should "guide human policy in the labyrinth of passions" by opening the way to the gratification of human desire.

To play on the keyboard of passions: just as there are twelve musical notes, so there are twelve passions: five *sensory* ones that "tend to the full and direct exercise of the five senses" and that may be united under a single leader, "*luxisme*" or the "desire for luxury"; four *affective* passions that "tend to form the four groups of love, friendship, family, and ambition"; and three *distributive* or "mechanizing" passions that are totally misunderstood by a civilized order that treats them as vices causing disorder. In these three passions, the expression of "serialism" or the "desire for series," lodges the "spring of societary harmony."

The first distributive passion is referrred to as the *cabalist* passion or passion for intrigue; it is the calculating enthusiasm that moves courtiers, ambitious people, leaders, tradesmen, and elegant society. The second one, known as the *composite* passion or blind enthusiasm, is the domain of love par excellence, an enthusiasm that excludes reason, a state of drunkenness that arises from the mixture of two pleasures, one for the senses and one for the soul. The third passion, known as the *alternating* or *butterfly* passion, is the need for periodic change, passing from one task to another, for contrasting situations and piquant incidents, which, if it is not satisfied, engenders indifference and boredom, rendering any pleasure illusory. In the hierarchy of "social mechanics," the butterfly passion holds the highest rank. It is the "agent of universal transition." For this reason, it is the most proscribed by a civilized industry opposed to an organization of work into short and varied sessions lasting from an hour and a half to two hours at the most.

The articulation of all the passions—the passionate stem—gives "unitism" or "harmonism," the tendency to unity, synonym of "unlimited philanthropy," unknown in a civilized order uniformly dominated by "counterpassion" or "egotism." The combination of the twelve passions within individuals gives a maximum of 810 characters or passion types. This is a fetish number since, multiplied by two, it determines the number of members of a normal phalanx of attraction who inhabit a phalanstery. This number of Combined Order is likewise found, according to the organic scheme of Fourierist construction, in the "solids of the human body," with the "muscles of man and woman" amounting to a similar figure, since the "human body is just an abbreviation of the movement of the universe." Through dissection of "the smallest anatomical details," one may admire the "perfect image of the interplay of passions and the social mechanism."[11]

The condition to be fulfilled in order to achieve attractive industry is to form passionate series—from which comes the term "serialism"—of groups subordinate to the interplay of the three mechanizing passions. The first passion sets series in motion, the second competes with them, the third exalts them. Each passionate series is composed of persons unequal in all senses: in ages, fortunes, passions, characters, and tastes; the more the inequalities are graduated and contrasted, the more the series leads its members to work, produces profits, and offers social harmony.

The error of moral visions of fraternity, such as Saint-Simonianism, is to not identify the "geometric mechanism of passions and characters, of passions and tastes." "To mechanize is not to conciliate, but to use discord and antipathies reciprocally; morality wants to change men and their passions; societary mechanics uses them such as they are."[12] Failing to follow this general mechanics, one risks "not establishing the industrial reconciliation of the three classes of rich, middle, and poor," and missing "integral [total] association," Harmony, the union of passions and relationships at work. "Integral" is a nodal term for Fourier: it also serves to designate the ideal of the "integral man," the radiant man, in contrast to the "abstract man"; the integral perfection of a body that is "methodically crippled in the civilized system"; integral perfection of the mind by the union of practice and theory and the linkage of all knowledge, by the combination of work and pleasure, the economic and the ludic. Each individual in turn is only a "particle of the integral soul that requires two thousand (or more) different souls," meaning a world in which each depends in its being on the life of the whole, organized into phalansteries, in which each represents a note in a symphony. The "Seristeries" are the meeting halls of the passion series, where scales and chords are diversified, weaving the most variegated networks.

The metaphor of the machine is combined with that of the organism to produce the image of this new world. This led Walter Benjamin to say that

> the innermost origin [of the Fourierist utopia] lay in the
> appearance of machines... The phalanstery was to lead men back
> into relations in which morality would become superfluous. Its
> highly complicated organization resembled machinery. Through
> the imbrications of the *passions*, the intricate combination of the
> *passions mécanistes* with the *passion cabaliste*, Fourier represented
> collective psychology as a clock mechanism.[13]

Everything in this mode of organization of Harmonian territory calls for communication. The "Exchange" or "negotiation assembly" is the most vibrant example. A critic of stock-exchange mechanisms, source of the vices of the commercial hydra, Fourier parodies and subverts them, just as he diverted the street galleries from their primitively commercial ends by turning them into houses and places of conviviality. Held in the smallest canton, the Exchange deals each day with the "disposition of meals and tasks," with "work and pleasure meetings for the following days, the borrowing of cohorts among various cantons who cooperate in industry and entertainment," and with "gallantry, trips, and other things." To handle the considerable quantity of "intrigues" that the Exchange must untangle each day, Fourier advances the following solution:

> There are functionaries of all kinds, and dispositions by means of which each individual may follow thirty or so intrigues at once; in such a way that the Exchange of the least canton is more animated than those of London or Amsterdam. There one negotiates principally through signals by means of which each director-trader may, from his office, enter into debate with all individuals and deal, through his acolytes, on behalf of twenty groups, twenty series, twenty cantons at once, without racket or confusion. Women and children also trade as well as men in order to fix meetings of all kinds, and the struggles that arise each day on this subject among series, groups, and individuals form the most piquant game, the most complicated intrigue, and the most active that may exist. Thus the Exchange is a great entertainment.[14]

The idea of coded information is a constant in the Fourierist work: "A language of signals will be created, just as languages have been created for maritime exercises, the telegraph, deaf-mutes, etc."[15]

No Harmony without universal unity; no universal unity without means of communication. Fourier enumerates some jobs that the phalanx could perform within its own "domestic and industrial unity" in order to promote "unity in all global relations." In top place he puts "unity in language, measurement, typographical signs, and means of communication." But he concludes:

> By speaking only of this accord, how does the civilized world dare to speak of unity, vaunting its perfection, sublime flight, when it has not even achieved the lowest source of harmony, in means of communication? Two civilized people, a Frenchman and a German, who call themselves perfected by the metaphysics of Kant or Condillac, do not even know how to understand each other, speak to each other; in this branch of relations, they are

well below brutes, since each animal knows right from the start how to establish between itself and its fellow creatures all the communications of which their kind is capable...Hence, if civilization fails over the most urgent unities, that of communication for which it possesses all the seeds, think of the unities over which it is really hindered, like sanitary quarantines and the general extirpation of illness.[16]

In a posthumous book entitled *Le Nouveau Monde amoureux* (The new world of love), discovered much later and only published in 1967, we learn how much the epicurean Fourier stresses food, "the pleasure of taste," "aromal motion," the "passionate mechanism of combined gastronomy" in the construction of this universal bond. This passion even seems, this adept of "gastrosophy," cousin of Anthelme Brillat-Savarin (1755–1826), the author of *The Physiology of Taste* and *Gastronomy as a Fine Art*, more universal than the other primary passion, the "pivotal" passion of sexuality, because it involves people of all ages, including children, who are excluded from sexual love. Moreover, the meals at Harmony are carried on over "intrigues of all sorts" in which the pleasures of the table are joined to those of love. This, according to Fourier, is what explains the value acquired by the Christian symbols of bread and wine, the "veritable mystical communion."[17]

Fourier died in 1837. In 1842, a Fourierist colony was aborted in Brazil, that very land where Thomas More, still under the impact of the "discovery of the Americas" and inspired by *The First Four Voyages* of Amerigo Vespucci, had in 1516 located his ideal republic. In 1843, some American disciples of Fourier, whose doctrine had been introduced into the United States by Albert Brisbane (1809–90), seized on his conceptions of "passionate attraction" and its architectural expression in order to construct their communities. The most well known of these experimental communitarian societies lasted from 1844 to 1847 at Brook Farm Institute of Agriculture and Education in West Roxbury, Massachusetts. In 1855, the North American Phalanx voted for its own dissolution.[18] As for his French disciples of the time, here is the verdict of Simone Debout, a specialist in Fourier's work:

Fourier certainly had disciples but, whether modest or important, whether they were Just Muiron or Victor Considérant, they misunderstood the bizarre genius of their master. From his work they took only what they could comprehend: a doctrine cut to their size. Hostile to the vacillations of this prodigious traveling salesman of God, Fire, and Nature, they lost sight of the most astonishing strokes of inspiration, in which the burlesque and the profound were combined.[19]

Like other Fourierists, the polytechnician Victor Considérant (1808–93) in 1838 reviled the "fascination" and the "mania for railways," veritable example of the "social folly of our time." While five-sixths of the population, he alleged, lived in a state of misery, states spent fabulous sums on building them. In this polemic against railways, Considérant pleaded for the discovery of a "machine that would facilitate locomotion on ordinary roads" and that could "abolish at a stroke, forever, the immense capital they propose to bury in the railways."[20] This attitude breaks not only with that of the Saint-Simonians but also with that of the utopian Étienne Cabet, who became a disciple of Robert Owen (1771–1858) during his brief exile in England.

Étienne Cabet's Journey to the Sources

Here are the great railways in red, the small ones in yellow, the rutted lines in blue, and all the others in black. You also see all the canals, large and small, all the rivers, navigable or canalized. You see as well all the mines and quarries being exploited. On this map of the province you see provincial roads and on the map of the commune, the communal paths. And now tell me if it is possible to find more varied or easier communications! In fact I was astounded, since it is even better than in England.[21]

In this passage, we are being transported to Icaria, that imaginary country of the sage Icarus, to follow the adventures of Lord Carisdall in the "treatise" or "philosophical and social novel" *Voyage en Icarie* published in 1840 by Étienne Cabet (1788–1856), former deputy, former attorney general, and lawyer in the royal court.

Community is marriage and family purified and perfected; it is fraternity, association, unity, democracy, quality, the organization of labor, the triumph of machines, solidarity, mutual assistance, universal insurance, order, economy, administration, intelligence, the triumph of education, and happiness for everybody; the community is the ideal of almost all philosophers; it is Christianity — these are the traits of the ideal community and of "Icarian communism" as sketched by Cabet.[22]

Cabet lays claim to the "primitive purity" of Christianity. He identifies himself as a descendant of a communitarian lineage that he does not hesitate to trace back to Moses, to the Jewish Essenian sects, to the Spartan King Lycurgus, to Socrates and Plato, to Saint John Chrysostome and Pelagius, Thomas More, and, more recently, to Morelly, the author of the *Code de la Nature* (1755), someone who had already become a source of inspiration for all communitarian thought. Since the begin-

ning of the nineteenth century, Robert Owen had been invoking Morelly
to institute his "New Moral World" in the communities of New Lanark,
on the banks of the Clyde in Scotland, and New Harmony (1824–27)
in Indiana. Rousseau, Babeuf, Saint-Simon, and Fourier—without always
concurring with him—had also read Morelly, an author whom posterity
would consider as the "true precursor of the movement of communitarian thought" and "one of the principal sources of modern socialism."[23]

Cabet shares with Morelly, but also with More, a return to the precepts of primitive Christianity, an admiration for the original Christian
assemblies, a belief in a "golden age." Icaria is a "second Promised Land,
an Eden, an Elysian Field, a new terrestrial Paradise."[24] What also brings
Cabet and Morelly together (and radically distances Cabet from Rousseau) is a shared view of the positivity of the sciences and technology:

> Machines are a good in themselves, since they relieve the worker
> by augmenting production; it is social organization that is vicious
> and that taints everything... Of all social systems, the Community
> is that which most facilitates great and powerful machines,
> because it is the one that most concentrates all the intellectual and
> material strength of a great nation... Innumerable machines will
> be invented, and everything will be done by machines; and man,
> emulator and rival of the Creator, will reduce his role to that of
> inventor and commander of machines.[25]

Belief in the blessings of machine concentration as a means to establish perfect equality and a community of goods inspired Cabet's model
for organizing the press in Icaria:

> The national printing houses where machines have become so
> prevalent that they do almost everything, replace, we are told,
> nearly fifty thousand workers; everything is so combined that rags
> are transformed into paper and pass directly under the presses that
> print it on both sides and then deposit it already printed and dried
> in the folding workshop, located alongside other immense and
> parallel buildings for the assembling, stitching, and binding of
> printed sheets, for bookbinding and bookstore deposits.[26]

This concentration of machines in a single place is supposed to recon-
cile production and habitation.

Icaria has only one newspaper at the level of the commune, one at
the provincial level, and one for the nation. There is no need for more
since evil is cut off at the root: no more financial speculation, no more
monopoly, no more personal interest, partiality, calumny, insults, false
information, daily contradictions, uncertainties, and confusion of doc-

trines. The editing of newspapers is entrusted to public servants elected by the people or their representatives, "disinterested, temporary, and revocable." These newspapers are merely "minutes":

> They contain only accounts and facts, without any discussion on the part of journalists. Since any citizen can submit his opinion to his communal Assembly, which discusses it and supports him or refutes him, and each person can publish his opinion by submitting it to his Assembly, why allow him to publish it in another way that would leave dangerous errors to run out of control? Our very own freedom of the press is our right to propose things to our popular assemblies. The opinion of these assemblies—that is our public opinion! And our press, which makes all our proposals known, all discussion and deliberation with voting figures and even the minority opinion, is the expression of our public opinion, with all the force of that phrase.[27]

Icaria predisposes people to trips and migrations. There are no customs officers. The Queen is the Republic and it is she who possesses the carriages, horses, hotels, and steamboats in this territory, which is stitched together by a tight network of great railway lines, roads, and canals. To move about the city, there is a proliferation of "popular cars" or "staragomi," double-decker omnibuses. And for intercity transport, "voyager cars" or "staramoli" combine comfort and security.

To communicate with foreign peoples, the popular assembly of Icaria has approved a project for "composing a new language, perfectly rational and regular, with no exceptions to adopted principles and containing the smallest number of rules possible, and consequently the most simple, the most concise, and the easiest to learn."[28]

Fourier had scarcely preoccupied himself with elaborating a strategy for entering the communitarian age. But as for Cabet, the moral reformer and head of Christian communism, he insists on the means of achieving it: "To the community, the future, by the sole strength of Reason and Truth."[29] One must write, discuss, persuade by convincing the rich and the poor, until everyone—people, electors, legislators, and governors—is converted to the principle of community. "Preach, convert, propagate." Take up the pilgrim's staff of "Jesus Christ, the most intrepid propagandist and the bravest revolutionary who has ever appeared on earth."[30]

Twice, in Texas and in Illinois at Nauvoo, Cabet experimented with communitarian societies. Expelled from the Nauvoo community in September 1856, he died a month later in Saint Louis. The dissolution of the last community—that of Corning, Iowa, founded by the remnants from Nauvoo—took place in 1898.

"In actual truth, the whole history of Icaria," the philosopher Jacques Rancière would write in 1981 at the end of his study of the "archives of the working-class dream,"

> will be this interminable settling of accounts between travelers who did not find the Icaria promised by the writings of its founder, and a founder who, instead of the advertised Icarians, found this strange army of double beings, influenced simultaneously by the vanity of philanthropists and the avidity of the desperate, and caught up in the endless contradiction of discouraged dedication and impatient enjoyment.[31]

It remains true that the decades of the Harmonian and Icarian communitarian dreams are also those when the first "popular papers" and "papers made by the workers themselves" flourished in France, founded by "distributionists," "world menders," or "reds," whether Fourierists, Saint-Simonians, or communists. These were papers of often precarious existence, such as *L'Atelier, La Ruche Populaire, L'Union, La Femme Libre, La Fraternité, L'Humanitaire, La Voix des Femmes,* and *Le Républicain Populaire et Social.* Cabet himself launched three publications (*Le Populaire, Bon Sens, Propagande Républicaine*).[32]

Proudhon, De Paepe, and Communal Emancipation

With respect to the utopias of the first half of the nineteenth century, Marx spoke of the "fantastic pictures of future society" arisen from the "first instinctive yearnings for a general reconstruction of society." Only the rudimentary form of the class antagonism at the time seemed to him to explain the tendency of that "chimerical contestation" to believe itself above the melee and to want to improve the existence of the whole society without distinction. The author of the *Communist Manifesto* thought in 1848 that the importance of doctrines that wanted to set up a "Little Icaria," "these castles in the air," these "duodecimo editions of the New Jerusalem," was "in inverse relation to historical development": the more the proletariat organized itself into a social class, the less "historical action is to yield to [utopians'] personal inventive action." The more scientific socialism advanced, the more the disciples of utopian socialism would be converted into "reactionary sects."[33] In fact, this quest for community would be even more tortuous than Marx foresaw. Communitarian thought would illuminate the first debates about the roles to attribute to the state and to organized civil society in the construction and management of the avenues of communication.

At a time when the resistance to rail was tenacious in many sectors, the theoretician of individualistic anarchism, Pierre-Joseph Proudhon (1809–65), openly stood up against all those who thought that "the creation of rail routes would realize the universal peace dreamed of by Bernardin de Saint-Pierre [a Rousseauist apostle of the return to nature and author of the bucolic novel *Paul et Virginie* (1787)]." Proudhon reproached those who proclaimed that "thanks to this means of transport, all the hatreds and antipathies and prejudices that separate people are finally going to evaporate," and said they were practicing a diversion. He thought that priority should go to the suppression of the "sources of misery, dissension, vices, and crimes found in cities and communes." Before seeking to found "universal understanding, prosperity, and the association of humankind by iron routes," we must "search for a greater understanding among ourselves and for paths of order and prosperity."[34] In this he joins up with the arguments of the Fourierist Victor Considérant. However, Proudhon cannot be called a utopian. He even defends himself against this label with all the more virulence when Marx includes him among the exponents of utopian socialism. Proudhon is ironic about the "sentimental ecstasy" of Fourier, Owen, Cabet, and the Saint-Simonian school. Of Fourier, he goes as far as to write that he is a "joker who counterfeits [Rabelais's] Panurge, [the court jester] Triboulet, and Campanella."[35]

The idea of a national network having entered into the state's ambit, Proudhon once again denounces the railway model by publishing in 1855 *Des réformes à opérer dans l'exploitation des chemins de fer* (Reforms to be adopted in the operation of railways), a principled attack on the star-shaped model adopted by the French state:

> On top of the chessboard network, a federating and egalitarian network of land and water routes, has been superimposed the monarchic and centralizing network of the railways, tending to make departments subaltern to the capital, to turn a great nation, free until now, into a population of servants and serfs, and to give the lie to the most certain laws of economic science in general and the transport industry in particular.[36]

If large and small transport, canals and rivers, ought to belong to the state and be maintained at its expense, then, thought Proudhon, the railway should be subject to other rules. The state should take charge of the construction of the lines and embankments, and conserve eminent domain over the track. Then, taking into account conditions relative to fares especially, it must abandon the operation to private companies, destined to be transformed one day into workers' cooperatives—an idea that he launched in his major book, *Idée générale de la révolution au XIXᵉ siècle* (*General Idea of the Revolution in the Nineteenth Century*) (1851).

Within the framework of his federalist and contractual project for decentralizing to local authorities, he entrusts the exploitation of railways to workers' companies, which would set up contracts with the regional departments. In certain cases, this would be with the commune, the basic social cell, on the basis of which society must be reconstructed from the bottom to the top.[37] The federalist and mutualist solution seemed to him the most consistent with individualist anarchism, which seeks, in his own words, to "construct a world between property and community"—two institutions that he places back-to-back as causes of the threat to individual liberty. Here we have the strict application of the magic formula of the "contract" by which Proudhonian anarchism believed it could dissolve and replace statist organization at the same time as it restores the autonomous will of the individual. Society organizes itself according to a multitude of contracts at all levels, in both the political and economic domains. These contracts engender others, between groups of citizens, communes, cantons, departments, guilds and companies, and so on, in a society that draws its dynamism from the respective autonomy of the economic and the political. This is "positive anarchy," the absence of power and authority. Clearly this doctrine can only be understood as a reaction against the overcentralized model of the state such as that incarnated by the Jacobin state in postrevolutionary France.

The question raised by Proudhon did not cease to haunt the socialist movement until the end of the century. By whom should public services be organized and performed? This debate was launched again in the 1870s by the Belgian César De Paepe (1841–90), representing the anarchist or antiauthoritarian wing of the First International Workingmen's Association (in opposition to its centralizing and authoritarian wing, closer to Marx). Here again, the original site of this new phase of discussions on the idea of public service is by no means neutral. To the tradition of a weak state, Belgium allied a workers' movement that goes hand in hand with a real sociability of associations and cooperatives.

To the Jacobin idea of the omnipotent state and the "subalternized Commune," De Paepe opposed the "emancipated Commune," and to the visceral rejection of the state, he contrasted a new type of state constituted by federated communes. "The state becomes essentially the organ of scientific unity and of the great collective works necessary for society."[38]

The rising international workers' movement that believed the seizure of state power was a necessary precondition for all social change will leave this question unresolved. In 1874, to an audience of the First International, on the eve of the split in the workers' movement, De Paepe sketched the divergence of opinion as follows:

> What touches us most closely is the instinctive repulsion felt for any function entrusted to the state, for any intervention by the state, among Socialists who on other points march side by side with us; between them and us, we believe there exists quite simply a great misunderstanding: perhaps the word "state" is the only point that separates us from them. But in addition to those who reproach us for the role we attribute to the state, there are also those who would refuse the role we attribute to the Commune. For Jacobins of all shades, the state is the be-all and end-all, the god Pan that gives life and motion to everything. For them, the state is not just a particular organ, but the body social itself. These people do not understand that one may be born without a ticket of entry from the state, and depart this world without a state-issued passport.[39]

Kropotkin, Geddes: From Paleotechnics to Neotechnics

With Kropotkin and Geddes, we encounter the first debates over the construction of a geography and a sociology that would place technology at the center of the discussion of the history of civilizations.

There is an instinct of human solidarity and sociability and there is in nature a law of mutual support that is as strong as the law of mutual struggle. So wrote the Russian geographer Peter Kropotkin (1842–1921) in a work published in London in 1902 under the title *Mutual Aid—A Factor of Evolution,* whose chapters were first published in *The Nineteenth Century* as a series of articles between 1890 and 1896.[40] From the sociability among animals to the mutual aid of the medieval city, to "mutual aid among ourselves in the present day," Kropotkin outlines the long history of progressive social institutions: tribes, village communities, guilds, cities, popular revolts, labor unions, strikes, cooperatives, free associations, and "countless societies for combined action."

This great figure of the anarchist movement finds his hypothesis in Darwin, not the Darwin of the "Struggle for Existence," but that of *The Descent of Man* (1871). "Social animals are impelled partly by a wish to aid the members of their community in a general manner," the naturalist had written, "but more commonly to perform certain definite actions. Man is impelled by the same general wish to aid his fellows... Sympathy, though gained as an instinct, is also much strengthened by exercise or habit."[41]

After having analyzed the hegemony of relations of competition and elimination, Darwinian anthropology undertook in effect to think through the "reversive effect of evolution," according to the judicious expression of philosopher Patrick Tort.[42] Natural selection selects certain organic variations, but also variations in instincts. Among the latter are those that have produced social instincts. These are accompanied in their development by an advance in rationality, by a withering away of individual instincts, and an indefinite growth in the sentiment of *sympathy*, that leads to rescuing and rehabilitating the weak instead of eliminating them. Natural selection therefore has progressively selected *its contrary*, by favoring through the hegemony of social instincts the domination of more and more marked *antiselective* behaviors. According to Darwin, it is this selection of the "altruist-assimilative" kind, over a "dissimilative-eliminatory" form that was formerly dominant, that results, without a "jump" or "break," in *civilization*. The selection of civilization and of its fundamental ethical characteristics takes place to the detriment of genetic performance to the extent that it protects infirm beings and allows their reproduction. As regrettable as it may be on the strictly biological plane of the health of the group and of the species, this consequence of civilization should nevertheless be tolerated, according to Darwin, since it is a small price to pay for enjoying an advantage that expresses in supreme form the nature of man, and that is no longer of a biological order, but ethico-cultural.

This "natural law of mutual support" that complements the formula of "struggle for existence" was the guiding thread in the thought of Prince Kropotkin who, wrongly condemned at the trial of anarchists in Lyons in 1883, served three years in prison at Clairvaux, and then moved to England until 1917, when he returned to his native country. This conviction about the force of the sympathy and fraternity felt among "inhabitants of the world commonwealth" also inspired his companion in militancy, the French geographer Élisée Reclus (1830–1905), author of a monumental *Nouvelle Géographie universelle* published between 1876 and 1894:

> Thanks to the incessant crossovers from people to people and from race to race, thanks to the prodigious migrations that take place and to the growing facilities offered by trade and means of communication, the equilibrium of the population will gradually be established in diverse areas, each country will furnish its share of riches to the grand assets of humanity, and on earth what we call civilization will have "its center everywhere, its circumference nowhere."[43]

To realize his great work, Reclus explicitly situated himself "within the standpoint of human solidarity"—a standpoint completely dissonant with that of geographers who, at this century's close, were numerous in lending their support to the strategies of imperial conquest.

Kropotkin, a fervent believer in the idea of science and progress, placed his faith in the decentralizing virtues of new forms of energy for the restoration of communal life. The Fourierist dream of "integral instruction" and "attractive work" seemed to him finally at hand. Electricity had opened a new era; the distribution of its power to homes and to the smallest villages favored a new territorial distribution of industries and made it possible to imagine "an intelligent combination of industrial work with intensive agriculture, as well as of intellectual work with manual work": this is the central thesis he developed in a book that bears the programmatic title *Fields, Factories and Workshops, or Industry Combined with Agriculture and Brain Work with Manual Work,* published in London in 1898. He concluded the work with the following exhortation:

> If you return to the soil, and cooperate with your neighbors instead of erecting high walls to conceal yourself from their looks; if you utilize what experiment has already taught us, and call to your aid science and technical invention, which will never fail to answer to this call—look only at what they have done for warfare—you will be astonished at the facility with which you can bring a rich and varied food out of the soil...Have the factory and the workshop at the gates of your fields and gardens, and work in them...Not those factories in which children lose all the appearance of children in the atmosphere of an industrial hell;...[but] factories and workshops into which men, women and children will not be driven by hunger; but will be attracted by the desire of finding an activity suited to their tastes, and where, aided by the motor and the machine, they will choose the branch of activity which best suits their inclination.[44]

This belief in the liberating character of electrical power had a precedent: in 1888, Edward Bellamy (1850–98), an early New England socialist, had made this invention the symbol of the future social order in *Looking Backward, 2000–1887.* He had even predicted the discovery of radio through the transformation of the telephone—which had existed since 1876—into a mass technology. Through this "collective telephone," the new society organized around the "Industrial Army" would deliver its propaganda to citizens' homes. In this complex system of mutual dependency and support geared to human needs, messages would incite every member of the vast industrial partnership—as large as the nation, as large as humanity itself—to perform the sort of work he or she could do best. The working hours are short, the vacations regular, and all emulative labor ceases at age forty-five, at midlife. Bellamy's utopian romance exercised a great influence on American social thought of the time (over one million copies were sold) and was read the world over, particularly in Russia, where it was translated as early as 1890. According to exegetes of Bellamy's works, his conception of the role of the public service and nationalized industry anticipates the New Deal.

The fundamental questions "What should we produce and how?" and "Produce what for the satisfaction of human needs?" had been left too much in the background by political economy, thought Kropotkin, whereas they ought to be its "real subject."

The critics of industrialism, united by an unlimited confidence in a reoriented technological progress, would have direct effects on a biologist of Scottish origin, Patrick Geddes. He represents an essential link for understanding the distant kinship connecting certain doctrines of communication of the second half of the twentieth century with a way of thinking born at the end of the nineteenth.

Patrick Geddes (1854–1932) divided his professional life between the Universities of Edinburgh and London, the Scottish colleges of Paris and Montpellier, while also spending long working periods in Bombay, New York, and Mexico City. A biologist by training, and a Darwinian like a number of his contemporaries, he nearly went blind from the overtaxing of his eyes from excessive microscope work and had to abandon botanical and marine biological laboratories. But thanks to his long stay in darkened rooms, he devised a project: the classification of knowledge and the graphic expression of thought.[45] His conversion to sociology occurred under the double patronage of Auguste Comte's positivism and the ethnographic work of Frédéric Le Play.[46]

In 1892, he founded in Edinburgh an institute called the "Outlook Tower," installed on Castle Hill in a building that had served as observatory for an optician who was an amateur astronomer. Hailed at the time as "the first sociology laboratory in the world," this watchtower dominating the city and the neighboring region not only housed a center for social science research and teaching but also a "museum index" that gathered and classified local resources — material, intellectual, and spiritual.

This tower is a symbol. It is the architectural and museographic concretization of a pedagogic project for the social sciences. On the highest terrace rose the dome of a camera obscura. On its screen, the visitor (whether student, scholar, or ordinary citizen) could see a panorama of the living scenes of the city, the region, and its inhabitants. This dark chamber, point of departure for the study of the region, taught a way of seeing, looking, and observing.

Then one descended to the "Viewing Terraces," the "Outlooks." Visitors saw their real environment through the eyes of a meteorologist, geologist, botanist, painter, poet, historian, sociologist, geographer, anthropologist, economist, and so forth.

Each floor was devoted to a geographical level of reality. Under the terraces, it was that of Edinburgh with its plans, maps and photographs. Then followed Scotland, the English-speaking countries, and Europe. Edinburgh and its region were always situated in relation to all these levels. On the ground floor, an immense terrestrial globe on a ten to a million scale and a bust of Pallas Athena reminded visitors that all knowledge is born of experience of the world.

From Le Play, author of the first surveys on the working classes, Geddes borrowed a "method of observation": the monograph. However, for the formula "Place-Work-Family," taken as the unit of analysis by the French, who were anchored to a religious and patriarchal tradition, he preferred a slogan that replaced the term family with "folk," which "covers at once the family, a group of families, and the pervasive spirit of social life that molds them into a community (*Place-Work-Folk*)."[47] These monographs or a "mapping" of an ethnographic kind of "social practices" were the result of a triple approach: investigate the facts, ask inhabitants about what escapes direct observation, and learn from members of the locality who have known the folk for a long time or have influenced its existence. Geddes forged the "Regional Survey" tool. For this admirer of the earlier Garden Cities movement launched by Sir Ebenezer Howard, author of *Tomorrow: A Peaceful Path to Real Reform* (1898) and pioneer of the "Town Planning Movement," regional monographs became the essential instruments for rethinking the management of cities and their articulation with the countryside. From this came the close connection between Geddes and the paths of research and reflection developed at the time by Kropotkin and Reclus.

The influence of the Russian geographer exiled in London was felt in Geddes's proposal to distinguish, on the basis of different forms of energy, between two periods within the era of industrialization: the "paleotechnic" under the sway of steam and mechanics, that coincides with the "imperial-financial age," the era of *Kriegspiel* or "wardom"; and the "neotechnic," the age of electricity, of decentralization, of territorial redistribution, of *Friedenspiel* or "peacedom." In his conceptualization of the different stages through which humanity passes, Geddes extends Comte's teaching by incorporating the observations and intuitions of anarchist geographers on the role of the means of communication. Returning to Comte's generalization that human society in every age organizes itself into four groups — *chiefs* (inventors, bankers, captains of industry,

military and political leaders) and *people, emotionals,* and *intellectuals*—
he seeks to correlate them with the main features of the modern town
and the older mechanical-imperial-financial age.

The Scot made himself an ardent propagandist of the concept of neotechnics. A major opportunity came his way with the Universal Exposition in Paris of 1900. With the help of the highest scientific authorities
in France, the United Kingdom, and the United States, he launched an
"International School" with eight hundred lectures on "the arts, applied sciences, industry, social economy, and peace" spread over 120 days,
delivered in four languages by a hundred professors, with an attendance
of between fifty and three hundred auditors, all accompanied by 450
guided tours with teachers from all the sections, pavilions, and palaces
at the Exposition. There Geddes explained his theory of the technical
stages of industrialization and revealed to his listeners the indices of the
neotechnic age by organizing his own commented tour of the Exposition.
In the program guide, Geddes explains:

> It is not just a matter of organizing the most vast of all the
> Summer Meetings held up until now; our project also has a
> synthetic goal. It tries to examine and to present the Exposition in
> its most elevated aspects—the Museum of the Present interpreted
> by the University of the Present...Projects of popular education
> are reproached, not always without reason, for being superficial,
> whereas purely academic studies are susceptible of attracting the
> reproach of being of a narrow intensity or a vague generality. But
> in the presence of the concrete museum of this Exposition and the
> critical and constructive values of the Congresses, we may hope to
> reconcile—if not completely, then at least to some degree—the
> specialist's exactitude with synthetic clarity.[48]

After the closing, Geddes fought in vain to transform the Palace on
the rue des Nations into "museums of sociology." A citizen of the world,
he did not cease professing an unshakable faith in the peaceful virtue of
the circulation of knowledge and of international scientific cooperation.
A quarter of a century later, at the Conference on World Education at
Edinburgh, he presented, along with the Belgian Paul Otlet (1868–1944),
a pioneer of bibliology, ancestor of information sciences, plans for a
veritable "World City," a site including a university with a world vocation, a synthetic museum of human knowledge, various headquarters
for all international associations, and an institute to complete a universal bibliographical index covering all books, articles, anthologies, and images.[49] Geddes's assiduous search for a principle of classification for the
sciences, and most particularly the social sciences, which in his view had
not yet learned to "think and feel internationally," would be recurrent.

In the early 1930s, the ideas of Kropotkin, Howard (founder of the Garden City movement), and Geddes were relayed in the United States by several architects (Daniel Burnham, Louis Sullivan, Frank Lloyd Wright) from Chicago, symbol of the "electrical city," and by Lewis Mumford (1895–1990) who in *Technics and Civilization* (1934) took up the Scotsman's classification and made technological change a central element in the evolution of civilization. This book celebrates the decentralizing virtues of electrical technology, whose potential was still bridled by capitalism and which awaited a socialist project in order to realize the new community.[50]

The messianic vision of technology developed by Mumford, who in 1922 had also written a history of utopias, would be taken up by Marshall McLuhan (1911–80) in his first book, *The Mechanical Bride: Folklore of Industrial Man* (1951), a critique of industrialism.[51] But some ten years later, at a time when the Canadian professor had lapsed into the optimistic determinism of the "global village" made possible by television, Mumford had evolved in a different direction. He now violently repudiated all his former conceptions of the redeeming effect of new technologies.[52]

Samuel Butler and Machine Evolution

In a debate enclosed in a utopian perspective and its instrumental dilemma of good versus bad uses of technology and science, a dissonant note was sounded by the examination of machine reason contained in *Erewhon*, by the Englishman Samuel Butler (1835–1902), originally published at the author's expense in 1872. It is a collection of humorous and satiric essays linked by a novelistic fiction that Valéry Larbaud, translator of the book into French, places in a direct line of descent from Swift's *Gulliver's Travels* and the *Histoires Comiques. Voyages aux États de la Lune et du Soleil* by Cyrano de Bergerac.

Erewhon is the palindrome of *Nowhere*, the Greek *ou-topos*. The adventures are those of the discoverer of a people until then unknown by the rest of the world. In Erewhon, the museum is filled with glass cases in which the largest place is given to broken and rusted machines of all kinds: labeled parts of steam machines, cylinders, and pistons and a broken flywheel, clocks, and watches — in short, the "fragments of a great many of our own most advanced inventions," except for the fact that these objects seem to be several centuries old. Having just entered the country, the hero is put in prison because he is wearing a functioning watch, because in this society watches and all other mechanisms are out of use, just curiosities. To bring in a watch is a crime as serious as having typhoid fever (Swift's Lilliputians had thought Gulliver's watch was his god, since he took it out and looked at it so much).

The reason is that five hundred years before, a devastating war occurred in Erewhon that opposed two parties, the Machinists and the Anti-Machinists. The latter won and suppressed any trace of the mechanical inventions of the past. Since then, no attempt had been made to put them back into use. The expert is an archaeologist who digs up the machine past, just as in England one can dig up arrowheads made of flint.

A book had provoked this radical revolution, "The Book of Machines," whose author develops the alarming idea that it is already possible to discover signs presaging a new phase in animal life: new organisms are being prepared that will be capable in a distant future of serving as receptacles for a new kind of consciousness. "There is no security," wrote Butler,

> against the ultimate development of mechanical consciousness, in the fact of machines possessing little conscience now. A mollusk has not much consciousness. Reflect upon the extraordinary advance which machines have made during the last few hundred years, and note how slowly the animal and vegetable kingdoms are advancing. The more highly organized machines are creatures not so much of yesterday, as of the last five minutes, so to speak, in comparison with past time.[53]

In fact, can we assert that a steam-driven machine has no consciousness? Until now, the locomotive in motion that gives a cry of alarm expresses itself via the ear of the mechanic. The risk is great of seeing machines attain animate or quasi-animate existence. Butler asks: "May we not conceive, then, that a day will come when those ears will be no longer needed, and the hearing will be done by the delicacy of the machine's own construction? — when its language shall have been developed from the cry of animals to a speech as intricate as our own?"[54]

In the same way, one can well imagine that these machines might acquire their own system of reproduction, a machine capable of systematically reproducing other machines. If we allow these machines to become more and more perfected, and to modify themselves from generation to generation, a new master would emerge within the servant, and man's status would be fundamentally called into question. As Butler wrote, "The power of custom is enormous and so gradual will be the change, that man's sense of what is due to himself will be at no time rudely shocked; our bondage will steal upon us noiselessly and by imperceptible approaches."[55] Then if the individual thinks as he thinks, and feels as he feels, it would be "thanks to the changes that machines have made in him." His soul would be "the product of the machine."

Other Erewhon experts had tried in vain to refute this apocalyptic prospect of the moral and intellectual development of the human species, arguing that the whole nature and function of a machine predispose it to be just a "supplementary limb," an "extracorporeal limb" of man, a "machinate mammal." But there was nothing to be done: the first hypothesis had won, unleashing a civil war that had ended in the destruction of all machines.

After Butler's *Erewhon*, there would be another "nowhere," that of William Morris (1834–96), published in London in 1891 in the form of a book but that had appeared previously as a series of articles in the magazine *Commonweal* under the complete title *News from Nowhere, or an Epoch of Rest, Being Some Chapters from a Utopian Romance*. The book was revisited in 1955 thanks to the historian Edward P. Thompson, who reconstructed its genesis and its author's socialist vision, directly inspired by Marx and Engels's writings about the society of communist abundance in a natural world (rediscovered thanks to the revolution) in which reason is sovereign. For Morris, the machine would still be necessary for a long time to come, since the first stage—that of socialism—would be characterized by an unprecedented development of machinism; this would then allow humans to enter into the golden age of communism, the final stage. Faithful to a mechanist interpretation that would become the majority view within the world communist movement in the following century, and that we know was largely responsible for so many misunderstandings of the role of culture (and communication) in social change, Morris postulated that only the prior transformation of the base would open up the era of transforming superstructures. In order to reach this utopian society, Morris—also a theoretician of art, a poet, painter, and one of the founders of the Socialist League—was ready to accept a temporary eclipse of art in order for it to be rediscovered afterward in a world rid of capitalist oppression and corruption, when it would return to the pure and natural sources of beauty. If the machine continued to exist in this world, it would be to relieve the new humanity of any kind of unpleasant and strenuous labor, henceforth handed over to technology.

Zamyatin and Kremniov: Dystopia and Utopia Come in from the Cold

We know that philosophers, on the basis of the closure of the utopian narrative, suggest that it is a "novel of the state," a prosaic account of the conditions of the state's rationality and efficiency. "Utopia," writes Pierre-François Moreau, "thinks in terms of techniques of social management... Nothing can be managed better than a closed space. Closing down time, the country, laws, fortunes, or their symbols — these are so many ways of preventing the initiation of any process that escapes rationality — any 'black market' of life."[56]

Here is an argument to which the Russian naval architect Yevgeny Zamyatin (1884–1937) could have subscribed, from the appearance of his first novel in Saint Petersburg in 1918, following his return from the British Isles, where he had spent nearly two years monitoring the construction of icebreakers commissioned by the czarist government. In his parody of stuffy suburban English bourgeois life entitled *Ostrovityane* (*Islanders*), we already find the themes that obsessed Zamyatin until his death: the programmed, dehumanized universe, the air-conditioned hell:

The face of a well-bred person should be as immutable as... eternity, or as the British constitution. And by the way, have you heard Parliament is introducing a Bill to make all Englishmen have noses of the same length? Yes, it's the only irregularity left, which must of course be eliminated. And then, they will be identical, like buttons, like Ford motor cars, like ten thousand copies of *The Times*. A grand scheme, to say the least.[57]

Zamyatin can be situated at the opposite extreme from utopias of the ideal city and all the organizers of future societies. He speaks of the "rosy colors and mawkishness of utopias"; he feels closer to the "sinister colors of Goya" that he detects in the immense majority of novels of social and science fiction by H. G. Wells, such as *The War of the Worlds, The Time Machine, The First Man in the Moon,* and *The War in the Air* — all books that, according to him, successfully illuminated the faults of existing social organization. Moreover, we owe to Zamyatin two genealogical portraits of Wells, whom he locates in relation to his contemporaries and to other utopian authors:

A frozen well-being, a petrified paradise of social equilibrium are logically linked to the content of a utopia: a static subject and a lack of plot. In novels of social fiction, the subject is always dynamic, constructed around collisions and struggle; the plot is complex and interesting. Wells expresses constantly his social fantasy and his science fiction in the form of the *robinsonnade,* the typical adventure novel with which Anglo-Saxon literature is so taken.[58]

Zamyatin presages the mechanization of life, the engineering of people, and the grip of great machines, whether technology itself or the Great Machine of the State or Religion. He predicts a humanity oiled like a locomotive, carried along "as if on rails." The rails are the "Precepts of Compulsory Salvation" whose author is the Reverend Dewley, the vicar of *Islanders*: "Life must be like a well-run machine and lead us to our goal with mechanical inevitability."[59] Since the wisdom of life lies in figures, timetables worked out according to the "Precepts" are hung on the walls of the Reverend Dewley's library: the schedule for the hours of ingestion, for the days of repentance, for the use of fresh air, for charitable undertakings, and even for performing conjugal duties; as well as rubrics for treating diverse humors (sincere emotion, cold indignation, etc.). For houses, there is a uniform style of construction and interior decoration; for people, a standardized type of dress. In this world that condemns humans to compulsory salvation, the only thing that cannot be brought into the schedules is dreaming; the single fear is to see "the train come off the rails and lying with its wheels in the air above the embankment." This never fails to happen since in Zamyatin's works, unlike the closed island of the *New Atlantis*, there is always a "foreign body" that the author mischievously tosses into the "gears" of the all-powerful machine.

In *My* (*We*), Zamyatin goes much farther in the direction of "One-State" and its absolute ruler, the Benefactor. Written in 1920 and prohibited by the Soviet regime, this book would circulate covertly, arousing the ire of the censors. Some people have read it as a satire of the socialist regime, although it was still too soon to build a story based on this reality. Others have interpreted it more broadly as a portrait of the deep tendencies of the Leviathan State and of the machine everyone helps to deify.[60] In any case, the book has played the role of oracle. A Bolshevik and then a dissident, Zamyatin died in exile in Paris.

Between freedom without happiness and happiness without freedom, the builders of OneState have chosen the second. Life there is mathematically perfect, governed by the "Tables of Hours." Zamyatin's "We" is a body with a thousand heads, none of which has a name, where each individual is represented by a number and enjoys being a molecule, an atom, a phagocyte. The others are other ourselves — whom I perceive through the walls, with my room, my clothes, my movements — repeated a thousand times. In each of Us, there is an invisible metronome, an automaton, with a voice like a phonograph. The grandest of all the ancient literary monuments that have come down to Us is the two thousand-year-old "Railway Timetable." Taylor is celebrated as the "greatest genius of the ancients," despite the limits of the distant time in which he lived:

True, his thought did not reach far enough to extend his system to all of life, to every step, to the twenty-four hours of every day. He was unable to integrate his system from one hour to twenty-four. Still, how could they write whole libraries of books about some Kant, yet scarcely notice Taylor, that prophet who was able to see ten centuries ahead?[61]

Only the Christians, "our only predecessors," knew the grandeur of a church marching as a single flock; they knew that "humility is a virtue, and pride a vice; 'We' is from God, and 'I' from the devil."[62]

Imagination is a sickness. The national Science of OneState has discovered the center of the imagination, and a triple application of X rays will cure you forever. This is the "Great Operation," a kind of lobotomy. Neutralize this center, and "you are perfect, you are machine-like; the road to one hundred per cent happiness is open."[63] The enemies of happiness, harmony, the Numbers who betray reason, are those who refuse happiness and do not want to save themselves.

We opened the way for the Hatchery and Conditioning Centre of Aldous Huxley's sardonic novel Brave New World (1932), a World State guided by the planetary motto "Community, Identity, Stability," and for the Big Brother of George Orwell's 1984 (1949). But before the construction of the Orwellian world, there would be another 1984. In 1920, when Zamyatin wrote We, a short utopian novel managed to slip through the barrier of Soviet censorship and twenty thousand copies were printed by the newly created State Publishing House; the preface is by the publishing house's director, who does not spare his criticism of the book. Its title is My Brother Alexei's Trip to the Country of the Peasant Utopia, and its author, Ivan Kremniov, is the pseudonym for the economist and specialist in agrarian matters Alexander V. Chayanov (1888–1939). It is set in the Russia of 1984!

The division into town and country is no longer valid. The peasant is no longer a potential proletarian, a second-class constituent of a society that recognizes him only if he ceases being a peasant. State socialism has failed, bringing with it the failure of the collectivist model, of urbanization, and of the macrocephalic state. The stimulation of the private economy has been reestablished. Everything began in 1930 with the "great peasant revolution." Convinced of the "danger to a democratic regime represented by the enormous urban concentrations of population," the peasant parties have persuaded the Congress of Soviets to adopt a decree condemning to destruction cities of more than twenty thousand inhabitants. The concept of the city—a self-sufficient place, with the countryside serving as its pedestal—has completely disappeared. Towns and villages are no more than "points of application of a node of social connections," gathering places, the central points of a district, places full of color, culture, theaters, museums, cafeterias, leisure, and public services.[64] Although Moscow still has a hundred thousand inhabitants, there are hotels for four million outside visitors, and lodging for a hundred thousand visitors in each district of ten thousand inhabitants. Factories have moved to the country and fields are run as cooperatives. Technical inventions oriented to the new land management plan have allowed for the installation of "meteophores," a network of 4,500 stations of magnetic flows capable of mastering atmospheric conditions.

The rural habitat is dispersed. But an intelligent policy of communication routes has placed each peasant at one to one and a half hours from his town. And he goes there often. The administration of these routes is, along with justice, one of only two items belonging to a central power, to state control (a state that has become a means and not an end in itself). What is essential to the organization of social life is found elsewhere: not only in the cooperatives, but in different associations, congresses, leagues, newspapers and other organs of public opinion, academies, and clubs.

The birthing of this new mode of organizing society was not without pain. Parallel to the policy of creating communication routes, it was necessary to encourage their use by the population so that people would take advantage of all the elements of culture gathered into these "social nodes." A "special league for organizing public opinion" has even been formed to goad the peasants along. The idea of obligatory trips for young boys and girls, borrowed from medieval corporations, has been revived to put young persons into contact with the whole world and enlarge their horizons. By 1984, these campaigns to put people "under psychic tension" are no longer necessary, since "the culture of a people that has attained a very elevated spiritual level continues to maintain itself automatically and acquires an internal stability."[65]

In real history, however, 1930 would be the year of the collectivization, which would bring Kremniov-Chayanov in front of the firing squad nine years later.

PART III

Geopolitical Space

Chapter 7
The Hierarchization of the World

The world as a single workshop and market; mutually dependent nations divided up according to an international division of labor inscribed in the nature of things; humanity cooperating in the exploitation of the globe — these representations of the planet do not stand up to an analysis of the cartography of communication flows in the era of empires.

Technical networks have a centripetal configuration. Their points of origin are diverse, but their end points converge on a small number of countries. At the center of this system lies the capital of the Victorian Empire. On its periphery, schemes for implanting networks of railways and long-distance communication are congruent with the needs of Britain's new world-economy.

Unequal Exchanges on Universal Time

In 1884 the International Meridian Conference took place in Washington at the invitation of the U.S. government. In the wake of many international agreements of the time, twenty-five countries decided to align themselves on Greenwich to reckon a universal time. Long since, the great majority of navigators had taken the observatory built near the mouth of the Thames as their reference point. French ships were among the few exceptions, orienting themselves by the meridian of Paris.

Mathematically neutral, the Greenwich geographical point was not politically neutral. National susceptibilities led some countries, such as Brazil, France, and Spain, to see in this normalization of the world's time and this partition of the globe into time zones a veritable provocation, the British Empire imposing its rationale on the rest of the world. After having fruitlessly proposed situating zero meridian at the Paris Observatory, whose longitude differed from that of Greenwich by less than two degrees, the French acted on their own for another generation. When in 1891 the French authorities, in concert with the Académie des Sciences, adopted a legal time, it was expressed in relation to the time in the French capital. This Paris Mean Time (PMT) was in fact nothing other than Greenwich Mean Time (GMT), but without the word "Greenwich" and delayed by nine minutes and twenty-one seconds. It was only in 1911 that a global convention agreed to create the International Time Bureau, based in Paris, dividing the earth into twenty-four time zones, one for each fifteen degrees of longitude, with the zero axis passing through the place where the English astronomic observatory was located. Meanwhile, not only did timetable nationalisms die down, but experiments by Guglielmo Marconi (1874–1937) led to a suggestion that each country henceforth align itself according to a time signal transmitted from nine radio stations spread around the globe. While finally rallying to universal time, France would decide to advance its clocks by one hour in relation to those of London.[1]

Beyond this excessively nationalistic reaction, one thing is certain: while the City of Lights shone forth its models of a high culture that it saw as universal, in fact it was from London that the great technical networks of the world-economy radiated.

The late Fernand Braudel defined the concept of "world-economy" on the basis of a triple reality: a given geographical space; the existence of a pole serving as "center of the world"; and intermediate zones around this central pivot, with very large marginal areas, which, in the division of labor, find themselves subordinate to and dependent on the needs of a center that dictates the law. This scheme of relations has a name: unequal exchange. This exchange creates disparities that continue to increase between the core and the periphery of the capitalist system, which led the economist Immanuel Wallerstein to say, in a dialogue with Braudel, that capitalism is a "creation of the inequality of the world" and that it can only be conceived in a vast and "universalist" space.[2]

The fruitfulness of the concept of world-economy, associated with that of exchange as a creator of inequalities, resides in the fact that it offers much more satisfying explanations than does the customary "successive model" of a history cut up into slices, following the biographical law of ages. By insisting on simultaneity and synchronism, it resituates the interdependence of nations in the era of "world-time" within the contradictions ignored by the different variants of evolutionism.

Europe furnished the matrix of a capitalism of world dimensions. In a process of decentering and recentering, Venice developed into the hegemonic city starting in 1380, to be replaced by Antwerp around 1500; hegemony then moved to the Mediterranean, this time to Genoa around 1550, and returned north to Amsterdam around 1590–1610. London, sustained by its national market, did not become the "dominant point" of a new world-economy until between 1780 and 1815, and remained so until 1929. The London Stock Exchange was established in 1773. After the Napoleonic Wars, the Bank of England reconstituted its reserves. The pound sterling imposed itself as the international currency, and London definitively dethroned Amsterdam as the financial and stock market center. With British hegemony, notes Braudel, "for the first time, the European world economy, overthrowing the others, can aspire to dominate the world economy and identify itself with it through a universe in which any obstacle disappears before the English, first of all, but also before other Europeans."[3]

The gap between the industrial world and the rest of the world began to deepen. Using the statistical studies of Paul Bairoch, Braudel tried to measure the evolution of the gap. In 1750, the sum of the gross national products of countries that would be classified two hundred years later as the "developed countries" (Western Europe, the USSR, North America, and Japan) was 35 billion dollars (in 1960 terms), as against 120 billion dollars in the rest of the world; in 1860, it was 115 as against 165. The developed countries did not fully overtake the others until the last twenty years of the nineteenth century: 176 as against 169 in 1880; 290 against 188 in 1900. The difference would be 3,000 to 1,000 at the end of the 1970s.[4]

The expansion of the European states reached its peak between 1884 and 1900. During this period, the British Empire grew by some 6.75 million square kilometers and by some 57 million inhabitants; France grew by 6.3 million square kilometers with a population of 36.5 million, and Germany by 1.8 square kilometers and 14 million people.[5]

The Empire of Cable

What, then, is the configuration of the communicational flows of the Pax Britannica and its division of the world-economy into concentric zones?

The empire properly speaking included a quarter of the earth's population and covered a fifth of its land area. Its hold extended both over and under the seven seas.

The sea, moreover, was a dimension of British national sentiment. "The Englishman," observed Elias Canetti in 1960, sees himself as a captain on board a ship with a small group of people, the sea around and beneath him. He is almost alone; as captain he is in many ways isolated even from his crew. The sea is there to be ruled. This conception is decisive. Ships are as much alone on its vast surface as isolated individuals; and each is personified in its captain. His power of command is absolute and undisputed. The course he steers is a command he gives the sea. The fact that it is carried out through the medium of the crew makes people forget that it is actually the sea which has to obey.[6]

The Victorian Empire controlled the great navigation routes, starting with the Suez Canal, a strategic point par excellence. The Constantinople convention of 1888 had tried to neutralize this canal and shield it from acts of war, but in fact it was England that guaranteed its security. A critical zone, the Mediterranean was subject to tight control on the west, center, and east, and continued by a Red Sea closed at both ends and an Indian Ocean that was little more than an English lake. It is by this route that the greater part of trade with the colonies, the major commercial partners of the metropolis, took place. At the turn of the century, a flagrant imbalance characterized interoceanic commercial flows: English ships, on their own, represented more than 60 percent of the trade and tonnage. Far behind came the German commercial fleet with slightly more than 10 percent and the French with 5 percent. The British navy, which divided the world into nine naval stations, everywhere maintained surveillance of the free flows. The merchant navy and the port of London were also the best in the world. The specialization of docks and warehouses and the division of labor among the various British ports (Liverpool, Cardiff, Hull, Grimsby, Tynemouth, the Firth of Forth, Glasgow, Southampton, etc.) were a living image of the diversity of the trade flows corresponding to the division of labor of the world-economy.

Under the seas, the first link in a network of communication to encircle the globe had begun in 1851 with the laying of the first underwater cable across the English Channel. The final link was achieved in 1902 with the inauguration of the cross-Pacific cable. Demonstrating the convergence of different technical networks during this whole period, this cable linking British Columbia with Australia and New Zealand via the Fiji Islands, began at Vancouver, where the trans-Canadian railway and telegraph ended.

Before the end of the 1870s, cable broke through the threshold of technical obstacles. There were many questions to be solved before the era of underwater communication could really get under way: how to envelop the copper wire (with hemp, gutta-percha, and finally rubber), the organic structure of the wires, the exploration of the topography of the ocean bed, the unwinding of the cable from a boat specialized in this purpose, and so on. For example, it was not until the third attempt that a permanent transatlantic link could be established in 1866, after breaks in the cable in 1858 and 1865. And the first attempt at immersing a cable in 1859 in the direction of the Red Sea and the East Indies had also been a failure.

After the breakthrough in the North Atlantic, the British network was extended to India and Singapore by 1870, to Australia and China in 1871, to South America three years later, and to West Africa in the 1880s. (On land, the telegraph had begun to link European nations between 1850 and 1865. This period culminated in the creation of the International Telegraph Union.)

By 1866, England had equipped herself with a fleet of cable-laying ships, the Eastern Telegraph Company, later renamed the Eastern and Associated Companies. France would not own this type of specialized vessel until the turn of the century. The first cable linking Calais to Dover and the financial center in the City of London had been laid thanks to a concession granted by Napoléon III to a British builder. In the thirty years following, English cablers laid a transatlantic line for the French network, eight lines under the Channel, twelve in the Mediterranean (including the first links with Corsica and Algeria), and several in Asia.

The supremacy of British companies was overwhelming. Their control of the network was either direct, by ownership, or indirect, by means of diplomatic censorship over the messages transmitted via British cables. In 1904, they constituted two-thirds of the world network of underwater cables, and twenty-two of the twenty-five companies that managed international networks were British-affiliated. The great majority of cable companies had their headquarters in London. Only Paris and New York each had three others; Berlin, Copenhagen, and Buenos Aires had one apiece. The six vessels of the French cable fleet paled in comparison to the twenty-five British ships, comprising an armada more than ten times greater in tonnage.[7] The British owed this advantage to the financial power of the City, to the support of the Admiralty and government subsidies, and finally to the privileged position of London in setting the prices of raw materials used in the manufacture of cable. Copper and rubber were products that the empire could monopolize thanks to its hegemony over the mines and plantations in countries as diverse as Chile and Malaya.

The network of the British underwater cable operations was in the hands of private companies—Eastern Telegraph, Eastern Extension Australasian and China Telegraph, Brazilian Submarine Telegraph, and others—unlike the French network, which was publicly controlled. From

a diplomatic and strategic point of view, this regime of private ownership made no difference, so great was the convergence between private
and government interests in the management of this planetary network,
as was confirmed by several events. In 1870, the notification of the declaration of Franco-Prussian war reached the French squadron in the Far
East only after it had been communicated to the enemy German war
vessels, which were anchored in Chinese ports. In 1885, during the Tonkin
expedition, the conflict with the Chinese troops at Langson on the Indochina frontier was telegraphed from London to the British Embassy
in Paris before it became known to the French government. In 1893, an
ultimatum sent from Paris to Admiral Humann to be transmitted to the
King of Siam at Bangkok was in fact communicated to the Foreign Office by the British companies entrusted with telegraphing it. In 1894,
France learned of the death of the Sultan of Morocco in the same way.
In 1898, when French and British plans for colonial expansion confronted
each other at Fashoda, Paris could only communicate with the Sudan
and the commander of the French expeditionary force by using the network of its rival power.

The British news agency Reuters, founded in 1851, later than the
French agency Havas (1835) and the German agency Wolff (1849), took
full advantage of the power networks that sheltered it. In the agreement
dividing the world market signed in 1870 by the cartel of the three great
international agencies, the London firm kept the territories of the empire for itself and made commercial and financial information one of its
specialties.[8]

The British Admiralty would be the first to benefit from experiments
in radio communications undertaken by Marconi (that is, the first wireless linkup across the English Channel in 1897 and the first transmission bridging the North Atlantic four years later). The principal users of
this technology were the naval powers who organized radio links among
ships, and between ships and their bases. Not just England, but also
Germany, France, the United States, and Russia used radio in this way.
As the principal users, these countries brought all their weight to bear
on the formulation of rules for world radio spectrum management. The
International Radiotelegraph Union, founded in Berlin in 1906 by twenty-
eight states, adopted the rule — imperial in nature — of "first come, first
served." A country had only to notify the Union of its intention to use a
particular radio frequency in order to be awarded it; thanks to this doctrine, a half century later, the world's radio spectrum would be practically monopolized by the great industrial countries.[9]

At the turn of the century, the peerless domination by the British Empire of the networks of long-distance communication would become more

and more contested. The following item in *L'Illustration* of 12 May 1900 provides an example:

> It is announced that the Turkish government has just entrusted a German company with the immediate construction of a telegraph line designed to link Syria with Hedjaz, that part of Saudi Arabia that includes Medina and Mecca. It was pointed out in this connection that by asking the Germans to establish this line, instead of accepting the English proposals, the Ottoman government has followed the example given by other European nations trying to break away more and more from British control over their telegraphic communications.[10]

The German Empire tried in this same period to get the better of London by actively participating in the construction of the Baghdad Bahn, or the "3B" railway (Berlin-Byzantium-Baghdad). By this means, the Pan-Germanist government sought to short-circuit the Suez bottleneck, by laying the bases for an overland access route to the Indies and the Far East. Germany had come on to the scene in this region around 1890 when it secured the concession for the Ankara line. It was thus in direct competition with the British Empire, whose engineers and capital had secured, thirty years previously, the concession for the Ottoman Empire's first rail link, which provided the means for Anatolian products to reach the port of Smyrna. The strategic position of Asia Minor for the control of the route to India held by the Great European powers thus did not prevent the Ottoman Empire from having its own policy for implanting a telegraphic network. The electric telegraph and the underwater cable entered the scene during the Crimean War (1854–56), when the Turkish army was allied with British and French forces against Russia, which made a link possible between Constantinople, Paris, London, and the theater of operations. The subsequent extension of networks throughout the Turkish territory went hand in hand with the centralization of power and administrative structures; it also provided the occasion of the first disputes among the mullahs over the nature of Western technology.[11]

In the matter of submarine cable as well, the Reich tried to overcome the preponderance of British firms. In 1894, the British Post Office had refused to authorize a German transatlantic cable project to pass through British territory, out of fear of seeing a rival communication center develop in the future. This refusal was the point of departure for an aggressive industrial and financial strategy sustained by the Reich. The result was that in 1900 the Germans laid their first cable from Emden to New York via the Azores. By securing a foothold on these Portuguese islands, they also reinforced their strategic position in communications links to South America.

The United States, too, found the preeminence of British companies harder and harder to bear. In 1903, it laid its own cable across the Pacific, linking San Francisco and Guam to Manila via Honolulu. Five years earlier, the Philippines entered into their orbit following the Spanish-American War, one of the first modern imperial expeditions.

From the Periphery to the Center

Dependence on foreign technology, engineers, and operators took on a different significance as one moved away from the core of the system. The constraints of subordination to British companies would not prevent France, an intermediate power, from building an international network to correspond with its own economic and political interests. It would be late in happening, but it did occur around 1920.

The relations of domination between center and periphery would be etched into the very networks of national communication within dependent zones. Extroversion and outside-oriented configurations would be the rule. The case of colonial territories where the railway and telegraph were implanted basically according to the pattern of "routes of penetration" no doubt represented an extreme schema. The military rationale of troop transport was at the origin of numerous railway networks. This was especially the case in India—at least until the great revolt of the Bengal native army, the Sepoy Mutiny of 1857–58—which saw its first railway in 1853. But the necessity of establishing liaisons between ports, mines, and other deposits of raw materials accounts for the rest of the cases of extroversion, most often depriving these lands of transversal communication, frequently cutting them off from their close neighbors when they paid allegiance to rival empires.

One can thus hardly speak of a model of communication synonymous with national integration, and still less of social integration. Michel Chevalier's dream of the train as an instrument for bringing classes, ethnic groups, and peoples together was constantly belied in the accounts of European travelers of the day, such as the following report by a Frenchman on the Indian railways in 1865–66:

It is difficult to imagine the luxury of these sleeping carriages of
the Indies . . . The third-class wagons are far from being
comfortable: they are large boxes without compartments, into
which the poor Hindi are pushed and knocked down, and where
they are locked in. Sometimes there are many more of them than
there are seats, but the train leaves without anyone paying

attention to their complaints and cries; they are crammed in, piled on top of each other, and suffocated until their destination.[12]

Within sovereign nations, the model oriented toward the needs of the core system was also at work, with its own modalities. This was notably the case with Latin American countries. Practically none possessed a uniform rail network. The situation was that of multiple networks with different gauges and managed by different private companies.

Argentina is a classic case. The railway era opened in 1861 with the inauguration of the Southern lines. Nearly two-thirds of the tracks were constructed by British engineers and thanks to British capital, the rest being by French companies, who adopted the metric gauge for their portions. As for the English, for the majority of their lines they chose not their own norm, Stephenson's gauge, but a 1.676 meters gauge corresponding to material salvaged from the Crimean War! Stephenson's gauge was used on about 10 percent of the lines. The framework of the central station in Buenos Aires was conceived in Liverpool, and originally it had been destined for Calcutta! As for the fan-shaped design of this very meager network, centered on the port of Buenos Aires, it followed the direct path of exports to the metropolitan countries of meat and cereals.

One better understands the bond that was forged in the nineteenth century between railway concessions and the formation of the economic hegemony of London when one is aware that a part of the construction costs was paid in land situated along the track, covering a width of forty-five kilometers on each side. These lands were duly colonized by a British company, the Central Argentine Land Company.

Supremacy in rail rhymed with monopoly of cable and wire. Between 1882 and 1929, the United River Plate Telephone Company Ltd. would be the center of the Argentine telecommunications apparatus. The U.S. firm International Telegraph and Telephone (ITT) would take it over and, following the pattern of the British during their time of uncontested hegemony, would make Buenos Aires the headquarters of its activities in the whole of South America.[13]

For many Argentineans contemporary with the implanting of these technical networks, the problem of national sovereignty later raised by this servitude was not yet on the agenda. Argentina's official report for the Philadelphia Exposition of 1876, written in French, the diplomatic lingua franca of the time, by Ricardo Napp, espoused the prevailing common sense concerning these events:

Like the railway, the telegraph wire has rendered immense service to our country. It formerly took several weeks to get news from distant provinces. This disadvantage was most felt when a revolt broke out in a province far from the capital. According to the federal constitution, neighboring states could not intervene in a quarrel without authorization from the central government, so the insurrection had time to develop before any measure could be taken against it. Telegraphic communications have thus powerfully contributed to strengthening the tranquillity the Republic now enjoys... Besides the inland network, we are in direct telegraphic communication with several countries. The first international telegraphic line was set up by an English company between Buenos Aires and Montevideo; these two cities were linked by a cable underneath the River Plate. This venture has obtained excellent results. Another company was formed soon afterward to link Buenos Aires with Valparaiso and other Pacific ports over the Cordilleras. A third line, putting us in contact with Europe, has been open for several months.[14]

Let us note in passing the undeniable role played by the telegraph and railway in the movement of troops fighting local caudillos of the interior, but also fighting those of neighboring countries. For example, the first Brazilian telegraph line was constructed to resolve communication problems during the war waged from 1865 to 1870 by Paraguayan dictator Marshal Solano López against Brazil, Argentina, and Uruguay.[15]

The communication system of Brazil—the first country in the Latin American subcontinent to be linked by submarine cable to Europe (1874)—is another exemplary case. The railway began there in the 1850s, in the absence of any overall plan. A half century later, the result was the coexistence of five independent networks (Pernambuco, Bahia, Minas Gerais, São Paulo, and Rio Grande do Sul), each centered on a port and fanning out to a hinterland. The best-equipped states and the only ones joined together were those with concentrations of natural riches (São Paulo and Minas Gerais). No less than forty-seven companies managed the railways of these regions in the 1940s when the state bought up the concessions one after another: São Paulo Railway Company, Leopoldina Railway, Great Western of Brazil Railway, and so on.

This disjointed rail landscape resembled the situation prevailing in other communication technologies: telegraph, telephone, radio, and later television, at least until the coming of satellites in the 1960s. The decision to adopt the "Brazilian telecommunications code" of 1962 would be the first step taken by authorities to establish an integrated national communication system.[16] Up until that date, Brazilian Traction, a Canadian company, kept for itself more than 60 percent of the country's telephones, the rest being administered by roughly a thousand concessionaires.

The American Mediterranean, New Regional Configuration

Distortion was also the rule in the relations the United States established with the periphery, well before becoming the leading power of the world economy.

From 1867 on, cable and telegraph linked the emerging U.S. monopolies of tropical products to the sugar zones of the Caribbean. When the use of railways became generalized, they were placed at the service of large sugar-refining plants, as in Cuba in 1873.[17] Between 1884 and 1899, the contracts granted by the Liberals of Costa Rica to railway and telegraph companies, which were also banana companies, dominated after 1899 by United Fruit, would serve as models for all contracts signed by other governments in the region at the time. They played a key role in the concept of the "banana republic." Nor can this concept be understood outside the context of the geopolitics of the communications ensemble of this area, designated by Washington as the "American Mediterranean." The Panama Canal episode was merely one of the manifestations of this geopolitical situation.

The failure of Ferdinand de Lesseps and the liquidation of his Compagnie Universelle du Canal Interocéanique (1888) would leave the field free for the United States to take over the canal project, after supporting the secession of Panama, until then a province of Colombia, in 1903. The second Compagnie de Panama, represented by the French engineer Philippe Bunau-Varilla, who with Washington's help had organized the insurrection in Panama that resulted in its independence, sold its concession to the United States for forty million dollars. In August 1914, the canal and its locks were opened for navigation, allowing the maritime traffic between New York and California to gain about 60 percent in transit time. The act that ceded the occupation and control of the canal zone in perpetuity was signed in 1903 in Washington, in the absence of any representative of the new Panamanian Republic.

And thus one more Saint-Simonian utopia crumbled. In 1844, Michel Chevalier had invited French capitalists to ally themselves with the English to dig this interoceanic route. He had justified this major construction in the following way:

> Europe is now in an expansionist movement, by which she and
> her laws are ranging over the entire planet. She wants to be
> sovereign in the world but she intends to be so with magnanimity,
> so as to raise other men to the level of her own children. Nothing
> is more natural than to overturn the barriers that arrest her in her
> dominating thrust, in her great civilizing enterprise. What could be
> strange about the two most powerful and advanced nations

getting together to tear down the wall that bars the way to the Great Ocean and its infinite shores? The way to make people love peace and preserve its reign is to show it to be not only fruitful, but also full of majesty and even audacity. Europe should possess the gift of astonishing men, of making them passionate if possible, at the same time as it has the gift of enriching them. Woe to her, or rather woe to us, if she appears condemned to be coldly egotistical in her sentiments, mean-spirited in her conceptions, pusillanimous in her enterprises![18]

These few historical examples of the functional definition of systems of communication should not, however, let us forget another history: that of the erratic paths taken by each nation in the installation and use of its networks, beyond or in spite of dependence. The first train inaugurated in Mexico in 1850 linked Veracruz to one of its suburbs. Seven years later, the second one transported pilgrims to the basilica of the Virgin of Guadalupe, patroness of the Republic, several kilometers from Mexico City. Some European journalists at the time were stunned to see rail, one of the symbols of work, being assigned a mission of "amusement" (sic).[19] But this assessment did not take into account the weight of the church's temporal power over Mexican society at the time. In the 1860s, the port of Veracruz, the terminus of the shipping lines with Europe, was still not linked to Mexico City. This would happen only in 1872, with the help of British engineers—and nearly eight years after Chevalier's geopolitical statement, aimed at carrying Napoléon III's expeditionary force to the capital.

It was not until the 1880s, that is, with a delay of from fifteen to twenty-five years with respect to the countries of the Southern Cone and Europe, that large-scale railroad construction began in Mexico—with a push from the authoritarian regime of Porfirio Díaz, inspired by the philosophy of Comtean positivism introduced in 1867 by Gabino Barreda on his return from France. U.S. companies would be the builders of these lines—which used different gauges, were scarcely linked among each other, but were joined to major U.S. lines. A first network ran from California along the Pacific commercial coast to Acapulco, and a second, along the Atlantic industrial coast, put Monterrey and Veracruz in touch with Texas.

In 1882, a U.S. network first reached El Paso. The great neighbor to the north was then on the second phase of construction of its railways, that is, the phase following territorial implantation and whose aim was to build "systems" by means of interterritorial connections, so as to unite trade centers with sources of natural wealth.[20] In Mexico, however, intraterritorial communication was not on the agenda, since the economy, on the eve of the 1911 Revolution, concentrated nearly 80 percent of the investments of U.S. private firms in Latin America. From the conflictual relations between Mexico and the United States, the filmic imaginary would capture the train in its connections with foreign military expeditions, but also with revolution, as illustrated by the screening of John Reed's *Insurgent Mexico* (1914).

Imperialism: Tensions around a Concept

The new world order established after the 1880s with the carving up of Africa called for fresh analytical tools.

In 1902, the English economist John Atkinson Hobson (1858–1940) published *Imperialism* in London and New York, and the term was launched. Previously, colonization had given birth, within power circles, to the notion of "empire"; Benjamin Disraeli had first designated the set of English possessions by this word, and urged Queen Victoria to accept the title "Empress of India" in 1876.

In 1910, the Austrian author Rudolf Hilferding (1877–1941) published in Vienna *Das Finanzkapital* (Finance capital) with the subtitle "the latest phase of capitalist development." In 1912, both the congress of the German Social Democratic Party, held in Chemnitz, and the *Basel Manifesto* on war published by the Second International took a position against "imperialist policy." In 1913, *Die Akkumulation des Kapitals* (The accumulation of capital) by the German Rosa Luxemburg (1870–1919) appeared in Berlin. Finally, in 1917, a few months before the Revolution, Lenin (1870–1924) published in Russia *Imperialism, the Highest Stage of Capitalism,* relying largely on the analyses of Hobson and Hilferding, though at times refuting the latter.

Hobson offered an analysis of the economic mainsprings that were motors of imperialism, as well as discussing certain of its political effects. Going so far as to address themes like the "pleasure of the spectacle," present in the forms of the dramatization of war and the grand deployments of universal expositions, this convinced pacifist was concerned about the penetration into the popular masses of the doctrine of "national mission," then taking on the crude aspect of "jingoism" or chauvinism.[21] For Hobson, there could be no imperial ideology that was not associated with nationalist ideology. This idea was manifestly in disagreement with the doctrine of the primacy of class over national struggle defended by the entire communist movement, and by Lenin in particular.

Hilferding's analysis was that of an economic theoretician and sympathizer with German social democracy. Lenin's book, too, intended to treat "the economic nature of imperialism," and his critique of Hilferding and social democracy in general was situated on this terrain, as the following quote illustrates: "We shall try to show briefly, and as simply as possible, the connection and relationships between the *principal* economic features of imperialism. We shall not be able to deal with noneconomic aspects of the question, however much they deserve to be dealt with."[22] He set forth a definition of imperialism that encompassed five basic characteristics: (1) concentration of production and capital that gives rise to monopolies, whose role is decisive in economic life; (2) the fusion between bank capital and industrial capital, and the emergence on the basis of this "financial capital" of a financial oligarchy; (3) the particular importance of the export of capital with respect to the export of commodities; (4) the formation of monopolist combines, cartels, syndicates, trusts, and the carving up of the world among them; (5) the division of all the territories of the world among a handful of rival empires.

At the center of the analysis of the interpenetration of capitals and the division of the world into cartels, trusts, and other forms of alliances, Lenin placed his close examination of the structure of economic power in the electrical and railway industries. According to him, "railways combine within themselves the basic capitalist industries: coal, iron and steel; and they are the most striking index of the development of international trade and of bourgeois-democratic civilisation."[23]

This book, whose explicit objective was limited to examining the "economic nature" of imperial relations, would quickly gain acceptance in the workers' movement. At the founding of the Communist International in 1921, it would provide the basis of a global theory of domination across borders, eclipsing the contradictory genesis of the concept and legitimating an economistic conception of the relations among nations, and of the role of communications technologies and networks in these relations.

Within the international communist movement, Rosa Luxemburg had tried to make another voice heard, insisting on the political structure of imperialism. Her central thesis was that "capitalism is the first economic mode equipped with the weapon of propaganda, a mode that intends to swallow up the entire globe and to sweep away all other economies, tolerating no others alongside it."[24] Unlike the other great economic modes that were always distinguished by a lack of dynamism, the process of accumulation of capital was, for Rosa Luxemburg, a growth process that could not be conceived in static fashion. It transformed the history of humanity into an uninterrupted process of the destruction of old civilizations. This new economic mode was also the first that could not exist by itself. It relied on the existence of noncapitalist social strata, regions, countries, and a whole noncapitalist world-space. In a word, imperialism is the "political expression of capital accumulation in its race to take possession of the remains of the noncapitalist world." Precapitalist societies represent both a means and a terrain. As long as there is something to be conquered and integrated into its own economic sphere, capitalism will find the means to continue to exist and to grow. Capitalism can only live surrounded by other modes and to their detriment; it implies, above all, a hierarchy. Braudel and Wallerstein were later to build their history of "world-time" on similar hypotheses regarding the coexistence of modes of production.

The central problem in Rosa Luxemburg's work was indeed the march of accumulation over the whole earth. It was too much for Lenin, who, obsessed by the problem of surplus value and the course taken by capitalism in Russia, would see in her approach a relentlessness to describe the ferocious process of penetration of the great colonial powers into newly acquired territories. He would reproach her for making it a "moral question" and thus turning militants' attention away from the effects of imperialism in their own country and seeing only effects on faraway peoples. Lenin would go as far as to write: "The description of the torture of Negroes in South Africa is full of sounds and colors without meaning. And above all it is un-Marxist."[25]

Nevertheless, the whole problem lay here, as Hannah Arendt would note in 1951: South Africa was the "cradle of imperialism," and the Boers the "first people to be unequivocally converted to the tribal philosophy of racism." Was it not one of its founders, Cecil Rhodes, who proclaimed: "Expansion is everything... these vast worlds which we can never reach. I would annex the planets if I could"?[26] Luxemburg, then, was simply recalling the link that would form during the Boer War between imperialist ideology and racial thinking, that is, dividing humanity into a race of masters and a race of slaves, into whites and people of color. These phenomena were so manifestly in contradiction with the Marxist belief in the primacy of the division into classes and of the struggle of class against class, that race and the racial cleavage went completely unnoticed by Lenin. "Even the breakdown of international solidarity," wrote Hannah Arendt, "at the outbreak of the first World War, did not disturb the complacency of the socialists and their faith in the proletariat as such. Socialists were still probing the economic laws of imperialism when imperialists had long since stopped obeying them, when in overseas countries these laws had been sacrificed to the 'imperial factor' or to the 'race factor.' "[27]

It was in this Africa, conditioned by racist ideologies, that the propagandist documentary film made its first appearance. Its mission was to promote the colonial adventure and it was financed by private and pub-

lic pressure groups in Germany, Belgium, France, and the United Kingdom, with companies such as the Société Générale, the Union Minière,
and Tanganyika Concessions Ltd. in the forefront. This experience is
little known among specialists in film study, as noted by Guido Convents in 1988, after a study of the rare archives that have survived:

> It seems that World War I caused the memory of documentaries
> made in the early days to fade away. Hardly anything in fact is
> known of images shot, for example, in tropical Africa before
> 1914 . . . For most film historians, the frequent use of film in
> propaganda campaigns arises in the World War I. [But] It can be
> asserted that the 'convincing' effect of photographic documents,
> and above all moving pictures, was almost immediately
> recognized, with the first images taken by a camera. In these years
> the colonial pressure group in Europe played an important role in
> using film intentionally as the tool for propagandizing its
> opinion.[28]

Chapter 8
Symbolic Propagation

Ecclesiastical language has left to posterity the term "propaganda." Its rise in the seventeenth century was linked to the strategy of re-Christianization at the time of the Counter-Reformation. Two centuries later, the communication networks of the missionaries were at the forefront of European expansion.

Michel Chevalier made the church's networks a model for propagating the industrialist faith, and turned communication into a secular religion. The struggles for linguistic hegemony that intensified across the planet in the last quarter of the nineteenth century also borrowed from the language of propagation, inherent in the ideology of cultural influence.

Propaganda, the Church's Prerogative

It was in 1622 that Pope Gregory XV, taking up a plan Gregory XIII had conceived around 1580, instituted the Sacred Congregation for the Propagation of the Faith, De Propaganda Fide, flanked by a homonymous college. Endowed with a great library, rich in books and manuscripts on the "Orient" and Oriental issues, this college trained future missionaries and maintained a printing works with very diverse typefaces, making it possible to publish in many languages the books necessary for their apostolate. In 1616, the same Gregory XV had prohibited Galileo from divulging his ideas on the Copernican system.

"To amplify the faith in all corners of the world"; "To bring the flock back to the fold of the church": this was the double mandate assigned to the Congregation by the papal bull that created it. The second goal was quite as important as the first, since this same church had to face up to "heretics" or "lost sheep" in the countries of early evangelization. The pace at which new beachheads of Roman Catholicism were implanted in different parts of the world stands as proof of this priority. The kingdom of France was the first to execute the pontifical instructions — within two years of the papal bull. The creation of an apostolic college for the propagation of the faith outside Europe would have to wait until 1683, when one was established in Mexico.

The French bishops proposed turning this new institution into a tool of re-Christianization in a country where a quarter of a century earlier the Edict of Nantes handed down by Henry IV had authorized the exercise of the Calvinist faith, except at the Court in Paris. François Véron, "His Majesty's advocate in controversies and doctor of theology," was charged with drawing up the "rules of the French chapter of the Roman Congregation for the Propagation of the Faith." The articles of this document set forth the marching orders for future missionaries who would be responsible for carrying out "work so important for the good of Religion and the State."[1] In each province "infected with heresy," a particular congregational office would be established. The missionaries would be recruited from among the faculties of theology at all the universities in France, in particular the one in Paris, and among all religious orders. Their "exercises" consisted of "combating and demonstrating the errors of Calvinist ministers in regular confrontations, refuting before the people in public squares what they might have heard from these ministers in their preaching"; "instructing the heretics under their covered markets or going to find them in their dwellings"; "gaining access to the houses of the Huguenot nobility in order to disabuse it." Covering the provinces in pairs, one combating heresy and the other catechizing and administering the sacraments, the missionaries received credentials from the king to carry out this mission "so necessary for the conversion of heretics, and therefore for the peace of the State." Each year, they were to give an account of their work in a letter to the secretariat of the national chapter of the Congregation.

By the end of the eighteenth century, the Congregation of Rome will have become the head of a network of a vast apparatus of communication of international dimensions. Napoléon Bonaparte and his expeditionary army in Egypt understood this so well that in 1798, in order to equip the twenty-odd printers who accompanied the auxiliary corps of scholars and engineers, they brought to Alexandria type taken from the Vatican, in order to be able to print their bulletins and proclamations in Arabic, Greek, and Turkish.

The Missionary Press of a Predestined Nation

"To envelop the earth in a network of missions": this was the objective fixed for the Roman Catholic Church by Gregory XVI, who presided over the destinies of the Vatican from 1830 to 1846.[2]

Merchant, military officer, and missionary: the classic trilogy of agents of colonial conquest. The latter occupies a strategic place in the area of international communication. Napoléon foresaw this new foreign policy configuration even before becoming emperor, at which time he decided to bend the religious orders to his designs for conquest. In 1802, the future emperor asked one of the editors of the civil code, the jurisconsult J. E. Portalis, future Minister for the Empire's Cults, for a report on the missions. For Napoléon, it was a matter of not letting himself be outdistanced on the religious terrain by an England that had long understood how much proselytism could serve the "interests and glory of the nation."

Napoléon tried to separate the apostolic vicars from the Roman Congregation for Propagation in order to make them dependent on the archbishop of Paris—that is, on himself. Faced with the Vatican's refusal, the Congregation was relinquished, and the direction of religious establishments in the colonies was entrusted to a head chaplain. He restored the Foreign Missionary Society of Paris and that of the Holy Ghost, two religious orders that had been suppressed on 1798 at the height of the campaign to despoil the clergy of its properties. During the whole Napoleonic period, this question was the subject of a standoff between the imperial state and the Vatican. The Holy Father succeeded in restoring the authority of the Congregation for Propagation in 1808. The emperor once again proceeded in 1809 to dissolve the Foreign Missionary Society of Paris; it would be reconstituted in 1814 at the same time as was the Order of Jesuits, originally founded in 1540.

Napoléon's declaration at the meeting of the Council of State on 22 May 1804 gives an insight into his relations with the Catholic missionary networks:

My intention is that the Foreign Missionary Society of Paris [created in 1663] be reestablished; these secular priests will be very useful to me in Asia, Africa, and in America; I will send them to gather information on the state of countries. Their robes protect them and serve to conceal political and commercial designs. Their superior will no longer reside in Rome, but in Paris . . . We know of what utility the missionaries of the Congregation of Saint Lazarus [founded in 1625] were as secret agents of diplomacy in China, Japan, and throughout Asia. There are some in Africa and Syria; they cost little, are respected by the barbarians, and having no official status, they cannot compromise the government, nor cause it to be snubbed; the religious zeal that animates the priests makes them undertake works and brave perils that would be beyond the strength of civil agents. Missionaries could serve my plans for the colonization of Egypt and the African coasts. I foresee that France will be forced to renounce its colonies in Oceania. Within fifty years, all those of America will become the domain of the United States; it is this consideration that has determined the sale of Louisiana: therefore we must find the means to form similar establishments elsewhere.[3]

After the emperor's defeat, France, whose various sovereign pontiffs would not cease recalling the country's apostolic vocation as the "first-born of the church, a predestined nation, a chosen vessel," would furnish missionary Catholicism with its first modern press: the *Annales de la Propagation de la Foi* (Annals of the propagation of the faith). This bimonthly publication was created in 1822 in Lyons, seat of the "Primate of the Gauls," and included from sixty to eighty pages, in octavo, bound in blue, the Virgin's color. Very quickly the periodical underwent several printings in foreign languages and circulated throughout Catholic Europe. As a bonus, reading it brought one five days of indulgences.

These *Annales* were the organ of expression of the Institute for the Propagation of the Faith in Infidel Countries that was founded, with the help of the Holy See, by two devotees from Lyons, Mesdames Petit and Jaricot, also in 1822. The aim was to "aid by prayer and alms Catholic missionaries who go in peril of their lives to carry the faith and civilization to the infidel nations."[4] The bulk of the content of *Annales* consisted of the publication of letters written from different parts of the world by Catholic missionaries. To each issue of the month of May, the Virgin's month, was added a statement of the payments made to the central treasury of the Institute by various benefactors, individual and collective. In each parish in France, the Institute had a chapter that served as a conduit for offerings collected.

In the years when the Institute and the *Annales* appeared, the missionary movement took on new vigor: new religious orders were founded and the Order of Jesuits was reborn. The persecutions and prohibitions of which it had been the object in the eighteenth century — it was abolished in France by Louis XV in 1764 and the pope dissolved it nine years later — had deprived evangelization of about three thousand missionaries in America, Africa, and Asia.[5]

In the history of the Catholic missionary press, the *Annales* are not the first periodical publication with an international scope. There was a precedent, again French, in the eighteenth century from which it took inspiration: the *Lettres Édifiantes et Curieuses* (Edifying and curious letters) published from 1701 to 1781 under the editorship of the Jesuit fathers Le Gobien, Maréchal, and Patouillet.

The Institute for the Propagation would serve as model elsewhere. Other societies sustaining the missionary apostolate arose in Austria in 1829 (Leopoldverein), in Aachen in 1832 (Saint Francis-Xavier Society), and in Bavaria in 1843 (Ludwigverein). Also in 1843 was born the Organization of the Holy Childhood for the redemption and baptism of abandoned Chinese babies, which was later extended to the children of all infidel countries.[6]

In 1859, the Institute for the Propagation of the Faith—in accord with the Roman Congregation of the same name—would share collected donations among 198 Catholic dioceses or missions in Europe, Asia, Oceania, America, and Africa. From the height of his pulpit of truth, the bishop of Orléans, Félix Dupanloup, devoting a pastoral letter "to call for the benedictions of God on the success of our expedition and our negotiations in the Far East (China, Japan, Cochin China) and to recommend the Institute for the Propagation of the Faith," exclaimed:

Trade will do its business and it will do ours, that is, God's, the business of Religion and Souls. Merchant vessels will carry missionaries; and the missionaries will preach charity first to the traders, and aboard warships it will preach humanity to soldiers . . . The capitalists make a railway without thinking of God, but this route will carry the men of God. The cannon opens a continent, and through this opening we will see God pass . . . Moreover, let us not disparage the motives that propel the governments and nations of Europe. Alongside the legitimate interests of trade, public opinion, in France especially, gives pride of place, loudly and clearly, to the interests of Christian civilization: each nation, in dealing for itself, gives generous example to the others; and if religion owes something to trade, trade—let it not forget this—also owes even more to Religion, whose sacred cause has moved all nations.[7]

In 1868, a weekly illustrated publication, *Les Missions Catholiques,* took the place of the *Annales.* Its program:

Devoted to making known the daily progress of Christ's reign, it will record new events relating to the glorious march of the Apostolate. Thereby, a mass of documents that the character or the format of the *Annales* would have condemned to an unfortunate oblivion, will henceforth have their place in a more varied and wide-ranging publication: voyages, natural history, necrology, statistics, bibliography, and so forth.[8]

In 1872, fifty years after the creation of the Institute for the Propagation, the offerings received during the week for the missions were published for the first time. England, Italy, Poland, Germany, Spain, the United States, and other countries had their own bulletins. After World War I, a German Jesuit counted throughout the world more than four hundred Catholic missionary magazines in different languages, quite apart from directories, almanacs, and annual reports.[9] The missionary press was then enjoying its heyday and *Les Missions Catholiques*, still marked by the language of the great wartime conflagration, reiterated the call to the faithful to "maintain contact between the Front and the Rear, in this secular and worldwide struggle to which the Catholic church must devote her energies to ensure the triumph of the Truth."[10]

Shortly after the Armistice, the triumphal assessments of the missionary Catholic church coincided with those of the Allied forces. "Day by day a little more," noted the editor of *Les Missions Catholiques* in the first issue of 1919,

we see the forces of evil fall before the European conquests and the development of missions. The railways and the telegraph wires cross deserts, steppes, forests, and plateaus previously unknown by the white man, and from one ocean to another, the Christian traveler can on his various stopovers now pray before the altar of the true God . . . Islam is struck down and weakened in the person of the "Grand Turk." What the Crusades did not succeed in doing, the War has done. The Byzantine schism is borne away along with the rampart of the czars. Lutheran Protestantism, source of so many later revolts, is overcome by the criminal ambitions with which it had poisoned Prussia and, through Prussia, all of Germany . . . What would have become of Christian life and of civilization itself if Prussian and Lutheran *Kultur* had been able to dominate Europe and the world and to organize it to its own profit?[11]

If the pontificate of Gregory XVI represented a turning point in propagating the "evangelical light," it also consecrated the enclosure within obscurantism with regard to communication. Under this pope, the encyclical "Mirari vos" (1832) appeared—quite simply a violent plea against the notion of "freedom of the press"—"freedom to spread whatever kind of writings, this detestable freedom that will never be sufficiently execrated and that some dare to demand and promote with so much noise."[12] Behind this reaction there lies the pope's anger at the reading of articles on "modern freedoms" issuing from the "principles of 1789" published in the newspaper *L'Avenir,* created in 1830 by the liberal French Catholic Lamennais and to which Lacordaire and Montalembert also contributed. The Vatican's doctrine remained faithful to the first encyclical on the subject, put forth by Clement XIII in 1766, at the time of the *Encyclopédie,* which railed against the "insolent and dreadful license in books produced each day in greater number"!

This painstaking vigilance of the "sentinels of the faith" had at that time led Diderot to be very prudent in his treatment of themes pertaining to the church. Favoring purely orthodox articles on Adam, Councils, Christianity, Hell, and Theology, he had carefully avoided tackling the history of the Roman Congregation for Propaganda. The article "Propaganda," written in 1765, had sought its examples elsewhere: a "Society established in England for the propagation of the Christian religion," chartered in 1643 and revised in 1701 with a view to "carrying the good word to Indians and to the colonists of New England." The author of this article retraced in great detail the history of this society, composed of laypersons and clergy, even to the point of noting the frequency of its meetings in Westminster or Saint Paul's. Only a brief mention in the article titled "Propagation of the Gospel" hints that there existed in the French kingdom some "establishments of this kind," "worthy imitators of the apostles," which *in cauda venenum* had the fault of demanding of the "peoples to whom they preach" a "spirit of tolerance" that they did not practice in turn.

Nor, clearly, could the *Encyclopédie* refer to that other aspect of "religious propaganda" — the communication that took place among Errants [people persecuted for their religious beliefs], characterized by an organization of clandestine networks for the distribution of books and an intense exchange of correspondence, indissociable from the prehistory of the postal service. This network was established throughout Europe despite the pitiless public notices forbidding any contact with seditious individuals, following the emigration of the reformed populations of the Catholic Low Countries to Holland, England, and northern Germany, as well as the flow into other countries of German and English Catholics chased from their homes by the Reformation.[13]

One of the few islands of toleration on the church's part mentioned in the *Encyclopédie* was its doctrine favorable to the "image," as contrasted with the negative position of other religions such as Islam, Judaism, or even Calvinism. The article devoted to this term recalls, in great detail, that in 787 the Nicean Council had condemned the heresy of "image-breakers," the iconoclasts, thus putting an end to this form of anti-iconic sectarianism and casting a positive light on these "artificial, man-made representations." We know how much the later evolution of this vector of communication owes to this historic moment.

The Alliance Française and the Darwinian Struggle for the Survival of the Language

The language of propagation and, beyond this, the religious model of propaganda impregnated the modes of speaking of and practicing communication. This was true from the moment that the first socialist activists began their campaigns. It is equally true among circles of the established powers.

Propagation was part of the discourse of those who made the "struggle of languages" a stake at once political, economic, and cultural. Should there be one or several languages? The question was raised by the new character taken by the expansion of European nations in the two last decades of the nineteenth century. Many were convinced that there was now a mighty combat for world hegemony and that there was no place for linguistic plurality.

In 1878, the geographer Onésime Reclus (1837–1916) coined the term "francophony" to designate all the "French-speaking" peoples, above and beyond "colonial and imperialist cleavages." But no official initiative with a view to meeting the linguistic challenge would lay claim to this term, which is only a marker in the growing of awareness. It was not until the end of the 1970s that the term "francophony" proposed by O. Reclus, the brother of Elisée, would become the very spearhead of a state strategy of mobilization against Anglo-Saxon "cultural hegemonism."[14] The reason for this is that the initiatives made in the last two decades of the nineteenth century went in another direction.

In 1883, the Alliance Française, a "national association for the propagation of the French language in the colonies and abroad," was created. Its secretary-general Pierre Foncin (1841–1916), geographer and inspector of public education, laid out its objectives: "One of the means of warding off the crisis that threatens both French industry and trade is to propagate the French language; as I repeat, wherever one speaks French, one will buy French goods. Every French word that resonates in the world is equivalent to the purchase of a French product."[15]

"Trade follows the flag," goes an English proverb. But the French in the last quarter of the nineteenth century seemed to prefer "Trade follows the language." As the economist and theoretician of the cooperative movement Charles Gide (1847–1932) exclaimed in 1885, at the end of his lecture on the "struggle of languages over the surface of the globe" before an audience of Alliance members: "Wherever the French language resonates, there lies the French homeland!"[16]

The Alliance Française was born in Paris at a symbolic site: the rue Saint-Simon, in the Saint-Simon circle, headquarters of the Historical Society. Among its founders, besides the secretary-general already mentioned, were a plenipotentiary minister and representative of France in Tunis; the director of public education in Tunisia; a bureau chief at the Ministry of Foreign Affairs; a former minister of education who had also been resident general (a diplomatic post) in Annam and Tonkin; and representatives of three faiths (a Protestant, a Jew, and an apostolic missionary, director of Catholic Organization of Oriental Schools). The honorary presidents were General Faidherbe, former governor of Senegal and creator of the port of Dakar; the admiral Jurien de la Gravière, former commander in chief of French expeditionary forces in Mexico; Cardinal Lavigerie, founder in 1878 of the Society of African Missionaries (the White Fathers); and Ferdinand de Lesseps. Finally, among its honorary members were numerous scientists, either specialists in the human sciences or men of letters like Renan, Maspéro, Taine, Duruy, and Pasteur.

The Alliance was a private association, but it was created with the knowledge and approval of ministries of public education and foreign affairs, and more generally with the cooperation of the government. This character allowed it to accomplish "what the state could not always undertake without other states' taking umbrage." As such, it promoted itself as "an example of a positive initiative in this country where not enough is known about moving outside conventional circles of power."[17] Its networks were especially reliant on the influential circles its adherents wove (and continue to weave): French public schools abroad, Protestant and Catholic mission schools, and the schools of the Jewish Alliance opened in all corners of the world. The support committees of what could be called "friendship networks," as much in France as abroad, included military people, the liberal professions, bankers, teachers, diplomats. The association's means of communication were its own bulletins and those published by various local branches. Its relays were numerous French language publications in the countries where members were present (in 1919, the apparatus would be completed by the creation in Paris of an International School of French Language and Civilization).

At the origin of this initiative was an assessment of the balance of linguistic power in the world. The positive side of the evaluation was that the French language had a long history of hegemony and remained the "universal language of well-educated people, of polite society," the complement of any good education.[18] It continued to occupy the place of honor in education establishments abroad. As proof, the Italian Ministry of Public Education decided in the 1880s to make French obligatory in that whole kingdom. It was again French that was adopted as the scientific language in international congresses. Finally, it was the diplomatic language, since it reigned in courts and chancelleries and was used for treaties. The cabinets of Vienna and Petersburg used it as the vehicle for their dispatches addressed not only to foreign governments but also to their own agents.

The French language had acquired all these positions because of what Gide called its "proverbial virtues of clarity." Only these could explain why "the language of the nation that has become the most democratic in Europe has preserved this privilege of remaining the most aristocratic language."[19] But there is something that must be changed: one must hasten the day when French will finally be spoken by the "ragged little Kabyles or by the piccaninnies of Niger who go naked," because these "barbarians," from the day they learn French, will be won to the influence of France, and will become its "clients" and its "friends." This, added Charles Gide, had not been the case with the Prussian officers who expressed themselves perfectly in French but had nevertheless invaded and humiliated France in 1870.

This economist recalled that Europe had twice failed to adopt the French language as a "universal language." Even around 1785, the Academy of Berlin put this matter up for discussion: "What has made the French language universal? Is it to be presumed that it will preserve this prerogative?"

A hundred years later, some have started to doubt it. For various reasons, its geographic space was threatening to shrink. The country's trade and industry were more and more threatened by foreign competition on the world market. Inside its frontiers, the weak rate of demographic growth was not helping matters. As Pierre Foncin wrote:

> What above all made for the grandeur of France in the seventeenth century was its numerical force. We were twenty-five million Frenchmen as against eight, ten, twelve million English, Spanish, Germans. Today see how much the figures are reversed. Formerly France was the first power in the world, and today other nations have become as great, as strong, or even stronger than she. It is time that she defend herself. It would surely be better if the number of Frenchmen grew, and that the high rate of emigration, creating gaps in our population, stimulated its growth, but such a result can only be produced in the long run, and while waiting, to teach French is still to make Frenchmen.[20]

"Woe to the weak!" Among languages, the struggle takes the form of a Darwinian confrontation. A language is born, grows, gets old, and dies. This was a thesis that had been at the center of the linguistic debates since 1863, when the German August Schleicher (1821–68) published a book on the unbending nature of phonetic laws that inserted the determinism of nature into the realm of language, considered as a living organism.[21] Linguistics becomes one of the "sites of the flowering of the universal language of the organism."[22] In using this metaphor, Schleicher had an illustrious predecessor in Wilhelm von Humboldt (1767–1835).

In the front rank of conquering languages was the already victorious English language. Even if one struck England off the map, wrote Foncin, "more than twenty peoples, issuing from its blood and speaking its language, would perpetuate into the most distant ages the name, the ideas, the religious and political customs, the practice of *self-government*, the hereditary pride, and, to put it in a nutshell, the very genius of the mother country!"[23] The second language that "pretends to world empire" is Russian, which little by little is winning all of central Asia and threatens to fill almost the whole Northern Hemisphere. The third is the language of Cervantes, and the fourth, that of Camões, Portuguese. Apart from these four reigning languages whose entry into the future is assured, there is German—but the poetical phrase may be applied to it: "It came too late into a world too old." As for the Arabic language that still extends from the mouths of Senegal to those of the Ganges and from Constantinople to Zanzibar, it was, in Foncin's view, not "well enough armed for the struggle for existence." It would be one of the vanquished, and other languages would gather up its heritage—probably French, Italian, and Greek.

Another essential trait of this vision inspired by the historic law of the struggle for linguistic existence is that the propagation of new conquering languages is a natural, spontaneous, and irresistible fact. This was not the case with the French language. Its spread was and would be artificial. "And this," declared Foncin, "is precisely why the Alliance Française was founded."[24] It could only be the expression of a voluntarist strategy, since it involved "accomplishing an operation of grafting onto an indigenous race." This graft would take time, work, and money, and success would never be guaranteed. To support this conviction, he took the example of the slow acculturation within the national territory itself, still marked, he wrote, with "black spots" where French was not the native language (Flemish toward the north, Breton in Brittany, Basque and Catalan at the borders of Spain, and offshoots of the ancient Oc language throughout the southern regions).

All this took place in a republican France in which the laws of Jules Ferry (passed in 1881–82) had recently made schooling mandatory. Many among the agents of this public education system made constant connections between two contexts: that of "teaching the indigenous," most particularly in colonial Algeria, and that of literacy teaching among those sectors of the French people who still lived in the "recesses" of their own languages and cultures. Thus they transposed to Algeria the methods and the project for teaching the people of France. They compared the aptitudes and performances of pupils in these two areas, on opposite sides of the Mediterranean, which functioned as veritable mission lands for the school system. The young hill folk of the Auvergne or the Jura had their counterparts in the Kabylian Mountains. The resistance of "Breton brains" to the French language or to mental calculation helped to understand that of "Arab brains."[25]

Historians such as Furet and Ozouf, Le Bras and Todd would show in the 1970s how in the history of the French nation this republican expression of its unity, embodied in juridical, administrative, or political models, was able to create an illusion and obliterate the concrete situation of peoples among whom cultural and ethnic diversity survived. In 1920, the linguistic cartography of non-French speech would still make it widely apparent that more than a third of the population had as its mother tongue something other than the language of "republican citizenship."[26]

H. G. Wells: Linguistic Hegemonies in the Year 2000

Which language will prevail tomorrow in Europe and in the world? If this question did not especially interest the Victorian Empire, which was living its expansion metabolically, it did impassion one of her subjects, Herbert George Wells. In *Anticipations,* published in 1902, the writer dealt at great length with the "conflict of languages," at the same time as he speculated on the effects that the evolution of the means of locomotion and communication would have on ways of living and thinking, urban organization, war, and democracy toward the year 2000.

All the forces in the world were moving against the maintenance of local social systems, in Wells's view. The hour belonged to the development of "Pan-this-and-that movements." However, unity certainly did not imply homogeneity. "The greater the social organism," wrote Wells, "the more complex and varied its parts, the more intricate and varied the interplay of culture and breed and character within it."[27] This did not mean that in the year 2000 there would not be two or three "aggregating tongues." Contacts, voyages, and transportation would plunge the world into "a bilingual compromise," in which each community would use one of these languages of worldwide appeal along with its own, which would be limited to the sphere of its particular community.

French and English would surely be the languages that would impose themselves, according to Wells, along, possibly, with German. But Chinese and Japanese remained the great unknowns. What gave French a strong chance of winning out, particularly in Europe where the third millennium would begin with the realization of the old dream of the European confederation, was that it had the advantage of having a public of readers that spilled far beyond the borders of its political system. Moreover, the French published more books, and especially more serious ones. English could not hope to take the lead unless there was a veritable "cultural renaissance," since, while the books published in French achieved a high scientific, philosophical, and literary level, the literature circulating in English was dominated by "novels adapted to the minds of women, or of boys and superannuated business men, stories designed rather to allay than stimulate thought—they are the only books, indeed, that are profitable to publisher and author alike."[28]

The major problem in Great Britain's future could be summed up as follows:

The small class that monopolized the direction of British affairs, and probably, will monopolize it yet for several decades, has never displayed any great zeal to propagate its use. Of the few ideas possessed by the British governing class, the destruction and discouragement of schools and colleges is, unfortunately, one of the chief, and there is an absolute incapacity to understand the political significance of the language question.[29]

Absorbed by futurology, Wells skipped lightly over the past of a linguistic policy that was still within the memory of colonized peoples, such as the time when Thomas Babington Macaulay, appointed president of the Committee of Public Education in India, tried in 1835 to impose English rapidly via the school system. Let us recall the violence with which this liberal historian spoke of the culture of India:

The question now before us is simply whether, when it is in our power to teach this language, we shall teach languages in which, by universal confession, there are no books on any subject which deserve to be compared to our own; whether, when we can teach European science, we shall teach systems which, by universal confession, whenever they differ from those of Europe, differ for the worse; and whether, when we can patronise sound philosophy and true history, we shall countenance, at the public expense,

medical doctrines which would disgrace an English farrier—
astronomy, which would move laughter in the girls at an English
boarding-school—history, abounding with kings thirty feet high,
and reigns thirty thousand years long—and geography made up
of seas of treacle and seas of butter.[30]

Wells also made light of an earlier event that had projected the question of the linguistic domination into the modern history of relations of
force: the anglicization of the first colony of the future British world-
economy, Gaelic Ireland. It was a country that, still in the seventeenth
century, and despite military defeat, boasted a strong language, owing
to the number of its native speakers, and a cosmopolitan culture oriented to the Continent, supported and maintained thanks to a network
of Irish colleges built by the order of Franciscan Friars in most of the
great university cities. As Tadgh O'Hifearnain remarks:

> The anglicization of Ireland seems as much a cultural and
> socioeconomic process as a linguistic one. As Ireland in the
> eighteenth century became more and more anglophone, its
> political class and especially its businessmen became more and
> more tied to English markets and to those of the anglophone
> world. When the English empire extended its power as well as its
> language to the entire world at the end of the eighteenth century,
> the economic and cultural ties between Ireland and continental
> Europe became looser and looser, inversely proportional to the
> progress of English in the country. Paradoxically, it is therefore
> possible to say that the horizon was restricted to the "parochial
> anglophone area." The anglophone world is so widespread that it
> is possible to practice there all the socioeconomic trade necessary
> in a multinational but monolingual world.[31]

The question of language as an instrument of world unification may
be found as well in other texts by Wells such as his novel *The World Set
Free,* written on the eve of World War I and dedicated to Frederick A.
Soddy, future Nobel Prize winner in chemistry (1922) for his discovery
of the isotope and the theory of the disintegration of radioactivity, but
also one of the first partisans of atomic energy for peacetime uses. In
Wells's novel, after a planetary conflict in which atomic bombs leave
only ruins, liquidating the old civilization, humankind builds a new one.
This construction is undertaken by a worldwide Congress, sole organ of
world leadership and elected by universal suffrage. This instance of world
unity gradually effaces itself and proclaims a free order, one without
need of power, in which "the complete freedom of questioning, of criticism, and of movement" are guaranteed—but not without having previously developed a single universal language and a single monetary unit.

Then an "Age of Efflorescence" occurs in which the majority of the population devotes itself to art.[32]

The Backlash of a Saint-Simonian Strategy

The Alliance Française was the product of a society in which, since Turgot's first sketches of the role of language and languages in his "political geography," a propensity to speak of communication by privileging the level of discourse, meaning, and the speech act was always clearly asserted. This approach was already inscribed in the *Encyclopédie* when Diderot defined "the science of communicating" as "rhetoric" or "the science of instrument, method, and the ornament of discourse." In the course of history, this focus has often been to the detriment of technical forms of communication; it is part of those "silences" peculiar to French society, of which the historian Bertrand Gille spoke.

The program of the Alliance Française expresses above all a conception of culture and its relation to the economy. With it, a model of an international cultural relations policy proper to France undertakes its trajectory.

This conception would inspire many other cultural activities. One of the most revealing examples is the interuniversity cooperation with the sovereign nations of Latin America, at a time when in France a specific interest in this continent first manifested itself—a cultural interest, of course, but also political, commercial, and financial. This exchange began at the turn of the twentieth century, but was already emerging when Brazil became a republic in 1889. It was inspired by Saint-Simonian principles and took as its pivot the local elites in their role as organizers and modernizers.

Its ambassador was Georges Dumas (1866–1946), one of the best experts on Comtean thought—and not by chance. Sent to Brazil as spokesman for the "Groupement des Universités et Grandes Écoles de France pour les Relations avec l'Amérique Latine," founded in 1908, this Sorbonne philosopher and psychologist was particularly well placed to lay the basis for cooperation with the centers of higher education in a country where the positivist graft had taken well. The following year a Franco-American committee was created, which in addition to promoting cultural exchanges also included a commission for industry and trade. French lycées (high schools) were founded and university teaching missions set up.

But the real interest of this classical experiment, faithful to a "social Saint-Simonianism" that did not doubt the "organizing role of the industrial elite in the perspective of a triumphant modernity," lay elsewhere, in the interaction between the senders and receivers of these exchanges.

The university missions took on a new significance after World War I
with the sending of young social scientists like economist François Perroux, historian Fernand Braudel, geographer Pierre Monbeig, and anthropologists Claude Lévi-Strauss and Roger Bastide, who contributed
to founding the faculty of philosophy, arts, and sciences at the University of São Paulo.[33]

In the interwar period, François Perroux clearly expresses the goal of
this strategy of French cultural expansion as an integral part of economic
expansion:

> What political effort it would take for "French cultural
> dissemination" to spring from clear bases, or more simply, for
> "French propaganda" to have something to propagate! The best
> thing would be to postulate that our nation remains capable of
> engendering creators of all kinds. Then one could say that the
> strategy of cultural independence, too, is defined in a movement of
> expansion. It is not within our borders that it takes the measure of
> its reality, but in the entire world.[34]

This was not to count on the backlash against any attempt at cultural
transplanting: the fact that the Other and its reality help one to better
understand oneself.

Fernand Braudel would return from Brazil with the conviction that
Latin America does not exist but rather "Latin Americas—in the plural,"
a "complex continent of histories of races and destinies mixed and distinct, divergent and convergent; another America, as *one* and as *diverse*
as Europe itself."[35] This had been the impasse for the pan-Latinism of
Michel Chevalier, conceived from the operating concept of a Jacobin
Latinity. From Latin America, the *Annales* school of history would learn
to develop a cross-fertilizing perspective on the history of the formation
of Europe and the world—starting with its first studies in 1929. Lucien
Febvre recalled this in a special anthology issue of the journal of *Annales* of 1948 that he and Fernand Braudel devoted precisely to "the
Latin Americas":

> They [historians of the Americas] need us—as we need them, and
> their countries, and the lessons they teach us ... Are we going to
> forget that we, historians of the Old World, face the Atlantic? And
> that for a long time our side was of the two the more enlightened,
> if not the only one? ... This is recognized, still today, in the quality
> and the considerable importance for us of a history that is as
> much European, as fully European, as it is powerfully South
> American. A history that is an integral part of our national
> histories, but still more of our cultural history. A history of back-
> and-forth movement, of loans and repayments, of borrowings and

refused borrowings, of adventurous comings and goings with composite interest. It is already one of the first and most important chapters in this history of exchanges of worlds that each of us begins in his dreams to develop for the near future.[36]

Twenty years earlier, Lucien Febvre had titled his first contribution to *Annales* "Un champ privilégié d'histoire: l'Amérique du Sud" (A privileged historical field: South America). In questioning the North from the vantage point of the South, in convoking around the theme of reciprocal exchanges the two continents' historians, philosophers, and anthropologists, *Annales* in 1948 already represented a first stage in a reversal of perspectives. In this exemplary issue, a review of a book by the young Mexican philosopher, Leopoldo Zea, on "positivism in Mexico" written by the Brazilian João Cruz Costa, clearly summarized where this history of loans and repayments was leading: "Philosophy in Latin America, let us say forcefully, comes from abroad, from the wide world; in the nineteenth century it was a traveling cultural good and should be treated as such. The current originality is perhaps to consider the addressee more than the baggage itself, the port that receives the ship rather than ship that sails toward it."[37]

As for the economic advantages of the strategy of propagating language, teaching, and culture to the "creators," adopted by France in the interwar period, they were far from clear. This was the opinion of its competitors who had never concealed their annoyance at this manner of viewing the conquest of market shares. Here is the assessment, written in 1942, by one of the pioneers of geopolitics in the United States, Nicholas Spykman (1893–1943):

> France, as a matter of fact, was more pursued than pursuing. France was the intellectual and artistic inspiration for the educated classes of both Spanish and Portuguese America, and it required very little effort to keep this favored position. Paris fashions and French luxury goods have met little competition in their appeal to the preferences of the Latin American buyers. With the "Alliance Française" operating in most of the capitals and a limited number of visiting professors lecturing before Latin American audiences, the cultural situation has been kept in hand, but the results outside of the luxury trades have been economically unimportant and politically without consequence.[38]

In the interwar period, French diplomacy's view of the cultural field was the opposite of Great Britain's. In 1926, the British government created the Empire Marketing Board, whose mission was to foster sales of products of the empire (the "Buy British" campaign). Within it, film production occupied a subsection of the service of "Publicity and Education."[39] Its key agent was the Scot John Grierson (1898–1972), who, after spending World War I on a minesweeper, spent three years in the United States studying public relations on a Rockefeller Research Fellowship in Social Science and observing the emergence of mass communications, and there became aware of the first films of Robert Flaherty. On Grierson's return in 1927 he joined the staff of the Empire Marketing Board and founded, along with directors who had also taken part in the first mass war, a group that would become the core of a British school of documentary film and of the new board. It included foreign filmmakers such as the Brazilian Alberto Cavalcanti, one of the pioneers of documentary in his country and on the international scene. Cavalcanti collaborated with Bertolt Brecht, Anna Seghers, and Joris Ivens, another founding figure of the documentary, who was Dutch in origin and French by adoption.[40] This same Grierson, in proposing a vast plan of action for "projecting England" in which film propaganda occupied the prime place, hastened the formation of the British Council and its international network of cultural branches.

Spykman's negative verdict on the mercantile efficacy of the French cultural strategy did not prevent the scheme from continuing for a while longer. More than thirty-five years after this uncompromising diagnosis, one would read in an official report on "external cultural relations" commissioned by the French Foreign Ministry: "Too commercial for their cultural attributes and too cultural for their commercial attributes." The report's author, Jacques Rigaud, stigmatized the "angelic" naïveté of those who "do not dare speak of cultural trade" and deplore the overly discreet presence of French cultural industries abroad.[41]

In any case, when the Alliance Française began to weave its networks, the contrast was great between this cultural strategy of market penetration and the commercial policy adopted, for example, by the German Empire. This makes the study published in 1915 by the French economic historian Henri Hauser (1866–1946) on the "German methods of economic expansion" especially interesting. The author—who, incidentally, was also one of the major proponents of interuniversity cooperation with Brazil—reviewed the international apparatus of a Reich that had demonstrated keen awareness of the necessity of forging a culture of business intelligence, "approaching the conquest of a market like a military headquarters, like a war academy studying a strategic operation."[42] This culture of intelligence was symbolized by the Schimmelpfeng agency of Berlin, which boasted having files on most of the world's firms and already prospered from the sale of its data. The multiplication of the Hamburg export companies, the systematic study of outlets and clienteles, the restructuring of consular corps and commercial attachés, agencies of commercial espionage, the organization of press offices, the use made of communities of national immigrants, the teaching of export techniques — all of this was inventoried by Hauser, even the way in which Imperial Germany had redefined the function of a medieval spectacle, the Leipzig fair, at a time when the world only had eyes for the formula of the universal exposition.

Chapter 9

Strategic Thought

The development of road, rail, and telegraphic networks changes the rules of conduct of war and the strategic ways of preparing for it. The mobility of troops becomes the surest guarantee of success. A new branch of military science appears: logistics or "the practical art of moving armies."

Following the invention of the train, Germany, seeking to construct a "national economic system" even before achieving its political unification, made the installation of the "railway system" a basic element, both of its economic setup and of its national defense. It was a German geographer who formulated the premises of geopolitics, the science of space and its control.

At the end of the nineteenth century, the United States emerged as a power of planetary scope, and from its first imperial expeditions, it made plain the role of press information in this endeavor. At the approach of World War I, the international community tried to fill the juridical void it faced with the advent of new weapons and new devices for long-distance communication.

Lines and Troops of Communication

"We are so convinced of the advantage of having the initiative in war operations that we prefer the building of railways to that of fortresses. One more railway crossing the country means two days' difference in gathering an army, and it advances operations just as much."[1] This statement by Field Marshal Helmuth von Moltke (1800–1891) is often quoted as indicating the Prussian general staff's early awareness of the new strategic situation constituted by this new means of movement. Back in 1842, another officer in the high command, the writer Karl Pönitz (1795–1858), proposed in his book *Railways and Their Utility from the Viewpoint of Lines of Military Operations* to cover Germany with a network of lines designed to facilitate war on two fronts, French and Russian. At that time, at the highest level of the French government, there were still doubts about the strategic utility of this means of transport, which was suspected of making soldiers effeminate. This provoked von Moltke to reflect in 1844 that "while the French Chamber debates railways, Germany builds them." The architecture of the system proposed by Pönitz was groups of lines running directly toward the borders, interlinked by other transversal lines. Unlike the star-shaped network adopted by the French authorities, the German system played on the combination of tracks radiating in all directions from Berlin as well as concentric lines circling the empire, so as to maintain communication between big cities in case tracks were destroyed.

The railways were henceforth considered as "military operations lines." Since the end of the eighteenth century, this concept had been at the center of the strategic debate over the new ways of making war. As Napoléon put it: "In war, time is the great element between weight and force," or again, "The force of an army, like the quantity of movement in mechanics, is evaluated by the mass multiplied by the speed" — a law he put into practice in his "war of total movement" by making judicious use of the road network as a means of assuring the greatest speed of transportation and the "*réunion*" of troops, a means that, apart from and despite inevitable detours, spared troops the most fatigue. Napoléon created the "artillery train" (1800), the "engineering train" (1806), and the "baggage train" (1807).[2] He also sought ways to depend less on sheltered magazine stores: war should nourish war; an army in a campaign must try to live off what is available in the country. Thus the risk of seeing the supply lines of food and munitions cut off was diminished thanks to "lines of communication" that linked an army in the field to a "base" and which the Prussian Heinrich Dietrich von Bülow in 1799 compared to "muscles whose rupture paralyses the human body."[3] Napoléon was especially innovative in organizing his army in such a way that it allowed decentralization under a single command, thanks to the separation of the army into largely self-sufficient commands: it was divided into various army corps, in turn grouping together two or three divisions of tens of thousands of men. Two battalions made a regiment, two regiments made a brigade, two brigades made a division.[4] This model would eventually be used by all European armed forces.

The war of movement, a transformation in military strategy toward the idea of a "maneuvering" army, "easier to shift and lead," had been imagined back in 1770 by the philosopher and strategist Count Jacques de Guibert (1743–90). In a prophetic text, he advocated mobility and concentration and endorsed the divisionary system. Instead of troops formed in rectangles and a compact organization of a troop in depth, he proposed linear formations, a firing line, and mobile columns, which, when troops are on the offensive, form a converging network:

> Let us begin by destroying the old prejudice that one increases the strength of a troop by augmenting its depth. All physical laws about movement and the shock of colliding bodies become chimeras when one tries to adapt them to tactics. In the first place, a troop cannot be compared to a mass, since it is not a compact body without interstices. Second, in a troop approaching the enemy, only the men in the rank who join it have the shock force... The more the total quantity of movement, the greater the product of mass and speed, the greater the shock. Shock presupposes that the speed, once imposed on the moving body by the motor cause, continues until the encounter with the body being hit... It is by dividing a large troop into several parts that one can succeed in moving with facility. These are the divisions that have always been known in tactics, that we call regiments, battalions, squadrons, companies, divisions, etc.[5]

No longer a single mass forming an unbroken front, but articulated wholes, with detachable and autonomously maneuverable members: Napoléon put the finishing touches to this kinetic transformation. Encirclement took the place of breaching and the army of speed took the place of the "army of time, nailed down to its positions," in Guibert's phrase. The Swiss Henri de Jomini (1779–1869), former aide-de-camp to Napoleonic Marshal Ney and after Waterloo in the czar's service, would theorize and define "logistics": "The art of moving armies, the material detail of marches and formations, the provisioning of unentrenched camps and billets—in a word, the execution of combinations of strategy and tactics."[6] Strategy decides where one ought to act; logistics brings one there and positions the troops; tactics decides their use and the mode of execution. The lines of operations designate that part of the general theater of war that the army encompasses in its undertakings; the strategic lines are the important lines that link the different decisive points of the theater of war, either among each other or with the operations front of the army. As for communications lines, they are defined as the practicable routes that link the different fractions of an army spread out over the zone of operations. The most important problem of strategy, and the most difficult to resolve, is how to combine the relationships of the operational lines with the bases and with the army's march in such a way as to cut off the enemy's communications without exposing one's own to loss.

The advent of the railway confirmed the introduction into the art of war of two operations that were first conceptualized by Prussian strategists: mobilization and concentration (what Napoléon called "gathering" [*réunion*]). *Mobil machen,* to make mobile; *Mobilmachung* translates as "mobilization."

Many years would pass between Pönitz's recommendations and their realization. The treaties of Westphalia in 1648, concluded between the Germanic emperor, France, and Sweden to put an end to the Thirty Years' War, had sealed the failure of the Hapsburg attempt to unify the whole of its territory. The Germany of Pönitz and von Moltke was a set of tangled and overlapping territories, a mosaic of kingdoms, principalities, bishoprics, and margravates, jealous of their prerogatives and reticent about a project for a single network. In addition, the public sector was far from being the exclusive project manager for rail lines. The interests of industrial and commercial development, and its profit-making logic, entered into conflict with the layout required by the needs of national defense. To set up such a network of a strategic nature would require approving interregional agreements and, especially, procedures for the state's buying up of numerous private companies, and meanwhile building the missing links in the chain.

This program would not really commence until after the founding of the German Empire, under the rule of Chancellor Otto von Bismarck and his adviser von Moltke. In 1880, private companies still possessed a third of the lines, and the marshal was more impatient than ever to finish with this mixed regime:

> There is no doubt that it is absolutely desirable, from the standpoint of military interests, to take under state administration the most important railway lines. Railways have become in our era one of the most effective means of war; the transportation of great masses of troops to certain points is an extremely vast and complicated operation that should be the object of constant preparation. Any new line of communication brings changes in our plans. Even if we do not travel on all the lines, we should lay claim to all their means of exploitation, and it is evident that operations would be considerably simplified if, instead of negotiating on this with forty-nine administrations, we had only to do so with a single one.[7]

The purchase of the last major private network would be concluded in January 1909. But as of 1898, that is to say, at the moment when Bismarck left power shortly after the coronation of Wilhelm II, the imperial network was already largely operational for the purposes of national defense.

The slowness of the construction of the strategic network did not prevent Prussia from carrying out in 1846 the first experiment in the mass transport of troops: twelve thousand men with horses, cannons, and munitions were brought to Krakow. After that, general staffs would continue developing increasingly effective plans for mobilization and concentration. In 1859, they foresaw that it would take thirty-five to forty-two days to concentrate their troops. In 1870, the Prussian army was ready on the nineteenth day of the war with France. The speed of movement was one of the causes for the French defeat. "The great simplicity of transportation [of Prussia]," General Colin (1864–1917) would write in 1911,

> largely made for its success in 1870; the French, on the contrary, first gathered regular troops in Lorraine and Alsace, and only then began to send them the reservists, victuals, munitions, equipment, and vehicles necessary to get them onto a war footing. These transports, executed without preparation, would result in unimaginable disorder. Entire trains of victuals and munitions were sent to Metz without personnel to unload them. Stations and tracks were soon covered with packages and trains to such a point that circulation became impossible.[8]

Prussia had already taken advantage of information derived from the first war of the modern age: the American Civil War (1861–65). In 1861, the Northern General George B. McClellan (1826–85) had created a corps specialized in the construction, repair, destruction, and operation of railways. The Americans had also tested the role of the telegraph in tactical deployments. They made intensive use of it, bringing about technical improvements and discovering the art of wiretapping that made it more adept at responding to the needs of an army in the field. As an indication of the importance that they attached to this tool of transmission, in November 1861 the general superintendent of Western Union Telegraph Company, Anson Stager, was named superintendent of all Union military telegraphs (land, field, and submarine lines) and promoted to the rank of general. When this fratricidal war broke out, the United States had just inaugurated in 1861 a first transcontinental telegraph that consisted of a single wire passing through the cordon of forts alongside the Pony Express line, and where there were not yet tracks alongside roads on which animal-drawn stagecoaches ran. During the Civil War, the telegraph network gained some fifteen thousand miles of wires and conveyed around 6.5 million dispatches, a new level of utilization that the civil telegraph services would not again attain until the beginning of the 1910s.

In 1866, the Prussian army had demonstrated its capacity for maneuver in the war against the Austrians, whom they beat at Sadowa. It was on the occasion of this conflict that a "Campaign Railways Section" was created, under the orders of general headquarters, the first "bureau of communication lines." Drawing the lessons from this precedent, a royal decree made this wartime organization permanent. Only in 1876, five years after its defeat in the Franco-Prussian War, would France begin to organize its own military administration of railways.

In 1899, Prussia would decide on the fusion of all technical units with its railway, telegraphic, and aerial services, under the name "communication troops" (*Verkehrstruppen*), and place them under the authority of a division general. At this date in France, it was the chief of the general staff who directed the military railway service, which was under the control of the minister of war, unlike in Germany, where, since 1883 with von Moltke, the general staff enjoyed quasi-autonomy in relation to the war ministry.

By the end of the century, the railway had completely transformed the concept of "base" and obliterated the age-old dependence on marching and horses for conveying men and matériel. Long-range weapons would be the rule. Smokeless powder and magazine-fed rifles that shot ten times farther than in the Napoléon period, portable 80 mm, and later 65 mm "mountain guns" and the "Maxim" gun, the weapon par excellence of the colonial conquests that appeared in 1883, would all change the givens of mobility and tactical defense. The dynamite invented by the Swede Alfred Nobel in 1867, followed by gelatinous dynamite seven years later, would considerably increase firepower. The Anglo-Boer War provided the first test in which the new panoply of field artillery was used on both sides.

Friedrich List, Rail and Economic Nationalism

The strategic doctrine of the Prussian officers was close to that of Friedrich List (1789–1846). Before the general staff even became aware of the upheavals that the train had brought to the conception of war, this economist had laid the foundations for a project of national union in which the rail network was the backbone.

In 1819, he founded a German Company of Industry and Commerce, of which it would later be said that it was the cradle of the idea of a customs union. At the end of the Napoleonic Wars, the Germanic Confederation included no less then thirty-eight interior customs barriers, not counting numerous tolls and tariffs that put a strain on the circulation of goods in each of the states. This locking up of interior trade contrasted with the liberalization then in force in the import of products from abroad, exempt from any customs duty. So, with the end of the continental blockade, an influx of English merchandise loomed. In 1818, Prussia organized a customs union among its different territories and set a tax of 10 percent on manufactured objects at its borders while allowing the free circulation of raw materials. In 1834, this experiment resulted in the opening of the German Customs Union, the Deutscher Zollverein, which most of the German states joined, but not Austria, nor entities such as the free cities of the Hansa, Hannover, and Brunswick.

A native of Württemberg, List was obliged in 1825 to abandon his chair of politics in Tübingen and choose exile under pressure from authorities of a state that did not view the unitarian cause very favorably. He left for the United States, where he lived until 1832. As a naturalized citizen and member of the U.S. consular service by Andrew Jackson's appointment, he then returned to Germany, profiting from his solid experience in railway affairs acquired in the Reading, Pennsylvania, area. During his residence in America, he established a rail link from the coal mine he owned (the Schuylkill Navigation, Railroad and Coal Company) to a canal, and in passing he made the businesses and mines of the area profitable, at a time when only England dared wager on the railway.

List became a propagandist for rail, and never stopped repeating: "A German railway system and the Zollverein are Siamese twins." In 1833, he addressed a document to the government of Saxony, *Über ein Sächsisches Eisenbahnsystem als Grundlage eines Allgemeinen Deutschen Eisenbahnsystems* (On a Saxon railway system as the basis for a general German railway system). In 1837, a line from Leipzig to Dresden was opened for traffic; it was the first major line built in Germany and the one on which Gauss and Weber performed their first experiments in signal automation. In 1835 and 1836, List was editor of *Das Eisenbahn Journal,* the railway journal. His articles were considered too liberal by Austria, which forbade distribution of the publication within its borders.

Starting from his Saxon plan, List proposed the layout of a future German network from which nine years later the military would draw inspiration. The strategic objectives he assigned to it were explicit:

> Every mile of railway which a neighboring nation finishes sooner
> than we, each mile more of railway it possesses, gives it an
> advantage over us ... [Hence] it is left just as little in our hands to
> determine whether we shall make use of the new defensive
> weapons given us by the march of progress, as it was left to our
> forefathers to determine whether they would shoulder the rifle
> instead of the bow and arrow.[9]

The strategist-economist was not content with just the national perimeter. More than sixty years before Turkey and the Near East became political and economic stakes for Imperial Germany, he anticipated the need to build the Constantinople-Baghdad-Basra-Bombay railway. He also visualized a transcontinental line from Moscow to China. Each time, he coupled his plans for establishing railways lines with telegraph lines, and he combined rail routes with projects for steam navigation routes.

Long after his death, List would continue to be invoked as an authoritative argument to convince resisters to national and international networks. The paradox was that this scattered Germany that the economist tried to assemble by rail would turn out to be one of the most active artisans of the construction of a Europe of communication without frontiers, at least until the end of the nineteenth century. Before the end of the century, Berlin, which was already the center of the great international line parallel to the European axis (that is, the line from southwest to northeast, linking Lisbon, Paris, Berlin, and Saint Petersburg), became the undisputed seat of the Association of Railway Administrations, an organization that managed to group together the networks of Belgium, Holland, Germany, Austro-Hungary, Romania, Italy, Switzerland, and France. In another German city, Munich, the first international conference on railway timetables took place in 1871.

Germany was also a forerunner when it came to the postal service. List dreamed not only of a national system of railways but also of a national postal system. The first document developing the principles of a Universal Postal Union was written by an economist from Frankfurt-am-Main, J. von Herrsfeld, and dates from 1841, that is, about thirty-five years before this institution actually came into being. In both cases, the intraregional organization of its fragmented territory was an excellent training ground for negotiations. And it is certainly not by chance that in 1849 the first six important telegraph lines constructed in Europe linked Berlin to six large German cities.

What relations existed between Friedrich List—a contemporary of Michel Chevalier—and the Saint-Simonians? The short answer is conveyed by Eugène d'Eichtal, himself a Saint-Simonian: "List denies 'any suspicion of Saint-Simonianism,' from the standpoint of a community of property (which, moreover, was never a Saint-Simonian doctrine)."[10] During a stay in Paris in 1831, List published an article in La Revue Encyclopédique, where he writes: "They cry in the streets of Paris—'Work! Bread!'—To give employment to the poor, we propose building without delay a rail-road from Le Havre to Paris and from Paris to Strasbourg."[11] Besides this prophetic fascination with the train, the German economist shared with the Saint-Simonian school the essential idea that public authorities have a determining role to play in the functioning of the national economy. On the other hand, what the strategist of the German nation did not agree with were, above all, the ideas of universal association and the conversion of armies to peacetime tasks professed by the Saint-Simonians.

List's doctrine is formulated in an important book, published under the title *Das Nationale System der Politischen Ökonomie* (translated into English as *The National System of Political Economy*) in 1841,[12] a year when the debates on the reform of the Zollverein divided the partisans of free trade and those who thought it was urgent to set up protectionist laws so as to allow the Confederation to develop an industrial policy. The latter was the position of List, who made his book a manifesto for a "national economy" and brought it forward with the slogan "Country as well as humanity!"

His bête noire was the political economy of Adam Smith, the "Smithianism" that legitimated the English model. He reproached the initiator of the classical school for his cosmopolitan hypothesis in particular. Smith's vision of the world as a workshop and "universal union of perpetual peace" presupposed an international community already realized and preserved from the menace of wars. But reality was quite different. The Global Republic was not going to happen tomorrow, even if it remained a goal to be pursued. By limiting his analysis to the interface between individuals and the world market, Smith and the free-trade movement neglected the mediations, but it was these that gave meaning to the actions of concrete individuals living within a given territory. The famous idea of individualism as organizing principle was just a delusion. The defense of self-interest alone could only produce disorganization. The most important mediation was that of the nation and nationality. By taking account of it one could not help but arrive at the following assessment: in trade, different nations do not meet on equal footing.

Political union should precede commercial union, and it was within the framework of the nation that the former could be realized: the nation as site of "human capital." For to the nation individuals owe their security, their culture, their language, their source of work, the guarantee of their property. "Between each individual and entire humanity," he noted,

> stands *The Nation*, with its special language and literature, with its peculiar origin and history, with its special manners and customs, laws and institutions, with the claims of all these for existence, independence, perfection, and continuance for the future, and with its separate territory; a society united by a thousand ties of mind and of interests that combines itself into one independent whole.[13]

The suppression of hindrances to freedom of trade can only be gradual, as would a universal entente. The "economic development" of nations passes through successive phases: the "savage" stage, the pastoral
stage, the purely agricultural stage, finally the stage both agricultural-
manufacturing and commercial (this viewpoint would be the point of
departure for the historical school of German political economy mentioned earlier). A nation is "normal" only when it reaches the last stage.
There can be no national independence and power unless the nation
possesses an apparatus to produce wealth, "productive power"—contrary to Smith's doctrine, which only took account of the "quantity of
wealth" and "exchange values." This "productive power" is the key to
national security. To proceed along the successive stages of development,
the state must apply a system of progressive regulations faced with foreign competition. Hence the necessity of establishing a "protective system," an "educating protectionism," a veritable "industrial education."
    Protective duties are not the same for all products. While it was nec-
essary to protect the establishment of a manufacturing base by reserving the national market for national producers, one might, on the other
hand, allow free trade in agricultural goods. For manufactured products
themselves, the scale of protection could be modulated as a function of
the degree of autonomy attained in each type of economic activity. If
autarky is indeed difficult to conceive, the adherence to a policy that relies exclusively on the international division of labor risks ending up in
the nation's rapid loss of employment and sources of innovation. What
is certain is that free trade cannot be profitable for a nation and the individuals who inhabit it unless the nation assures its industrial superiority as a precondition. Moreover, says List, this is the major lesson to
be drawn from England's development. Protectionism has no meaning
unless the "national forces"—a conjunction of natural, financial, and
instrumental forces—are understood in both a defensive and a construc-
tive way. All the preceding arguments were to haunt the debates 150 years
later over the construction of a single Europe and the free-trade agreement at the heart of GATT (General Agreement on Tariffs and Trade).
    Critical of the hegemony exercised by London, List delineated the pos-
sible contours of another hegemony, that of a Greater Germany having
succeeded in its national union and consolidated its foreign expansion.
Under the pretext of completing the grand project of the Zollverein and
allowing Germany to "round out" and find its "natural boundaries," he
incorporates the *hinterland*, encompassing the space necessary for the
nation's existence—the future "life space" or Lebensraum—and the territory of small states such as Holland, Denmark, and Belgium (an idea

that had been brewing in his mind since the early 1830s, when he personally intervened with the government in Brussels to advocate laying tracks linking the Belgian ports to Germany, thereby weakening the Dutch monopoly on navigation). It was within the context of this plan for expansion, legitimated in the name of "security and order," that he relocated his projects for maritime, rail, and telegraph communication routes to Turkey, the Near East, and Russia.

With the passage of time, more than one commentator would discern in List's book the grand outlines of the Pan-Germanic scheme. Here is one French economist's commentary, formulated at the end of World War I:

> One is struck upon reading this book to see to what degree he had already, in 1841, traced a program of expansion that Germany has since tried to realize, and prepared arguments that she has not stopped invoking right up until the present day... This book has for eighty years been for Germany like a "testament" from Richelieu or Peter the Great.[14]

In any case, belief in the unifying virtues of the railroad would never weaken. The Third Reich would offer ultimate proof of this by proposing to make Berlin the center of a new international network. Here is how in 1941, a hundred years after the publication of List's *National System*, the magazine *Signal*, published in Berlin and translated into several languages, explained to readers of its French edition, with the aid of maps, the coming of the new networks of a "Europe without borders":

> When Friedrich List had the premature idea of a German network of railways, they laughed in his face, and treated him like a dangerous revolutionary, and drove the disappointed man to his death... Today, the Reich is at the heart of Europe; it is the crossroads of East and West, North and South. After the current war, we can envisage European traffic on a new basis... New Europe, conscious of itself, will absorb first of all the great spaces to the East, which will have to be initiated into European culture and civilization. The Southeast will be joined to the East; the Balkan states, with their inexhaustible agricultural riches, oil deposits, and mineral production, will rejoin the European network. There is only one step from the Balkans to the countries of the Levant, and Asia Minor will be nearer to the young Europe. The Mediterranean, under the domination of European powers and no longer the exclusive appendage of the English government, will be part of the new Europe; and the Mediterranean is the door of Africa.[15]

Friedrich Ratzel and the Science of Territory

"Friedrich List was the first among the economists to clearly distinguish the economic and political meaning of the national territory of a people."[16] It was in these terms that Friedrich Ratzel (1844–1904), in his *Politische Geographie* of 1897, described the influence of the theoretician of the Zollverein.

"The state is an organism anchored in the soil" and political geography should study the organic relations they have with each other. Ratzel, a zoologist by training converted to Darwinism under the influence of Ernst Haeckel, the inventor of the term "ecology" (1859), reckoned that only an evolutionist and biologistic conception of the state could put an end to the wild imaginings of "certain political scientists and sociologists" for whom "the state floats in the air"—provided that this biological approach really had the "value of a hypothesis," and was not just an "illuminating analogy," as was the case for many of the disciples of Darwin and Spencer (Ratzel elsewhere criticized the founder of English positivism for the imprecision of his concepts); and, provided as well that it be admitted that the more a society develops, the more it distances itself from the model of simple organic growth. "The more a state develops, the more its whole evolution is manifest as a surpassing of the organic foundation; also, the direct comparison between the state and an organism is better suited to primitive states than to evolved ones."[17]

Unlike the animal or vegetable kingdom, where the organism appears in its most advanced form, since the members of a species are the most completely tributary to the whole, the state, as an "association of individuals," "expression of a communitarian sentiment felt by the inhabitants toward the soil, oriented to a common goal," is an extremely imperfect organism, because it is endowed with a spirit and a moral sense. This "spiritual link that compensates for the lack of material cohesion cannot be accounted for by any biological comparison."[18] After these reservations, biogeography recovered its legitimacy. And on this point the science of the animal territory for which Ratzel laid the foundations is consistent with a tradition that Hannah Arendt characterizes in the following manner: "Organic naturalistic definitions of peoples are an outstanding characteristic of German ideologies and German historicism."[19]

Growth, evolution, development, body, soul, spirit, organs, function, energy, performances, division of labor, and so on, are the terms that endlessly recur in Ratzel's writings to express the living dynamic of the state as an organism. He expresses the phenomenon of communication, its networks and circuits, with the polysemic term *Verkehr,* which in

English signifies sometimes "trade," sometimes "traffic," "intercourse," "circulation," or "transport." Commerce, that "movement of people, goods, information from one place to another," is the "mastery of space." Its essence is "displacement in space of people and goods toward determined places, and having as its object the exchange of natural and human resources; the mail, the telegraph, and the telephone that transport data certainly do not exclude commerce, even when their role is reduced in so many situations to an exchange of ideas."[20] Exchange, interaction, and mobility are expressions of life energy.

Traffic and the routes of circulation are, for Ratzel, a "preliminary condition for the growth of the state, which follows close behind."[21] Certain parts of an organism are more tightly tied than others to the life of the whole. "These are the *vital parts of states,*" he writes, "which are above all else those through which pass the major flows of circulation."[22] They hierarchize spaces and order the differentiation between center and periphery. By this concentric differentiation, the center, site of the "intensification of life" and the "acceleration of a circuit," attracts into its sphere of influence more and more extended spaces. This line of argument takes account of the propagation and spreading of the city in the direction of the country. It is also valid for explaining the tendency toward concentration developed by major states with respect to those of smaller size.

Paraphrasing and extending List, the biogeographer writes: "The more simple and direct the nexus of a state with its soil, the more healthy its life and growth. It is equally imperative that at least the great mass of its population conserves a tie with the soil of the state that makes it also its own soil: here lies the importance of the economy for the state."[23] Ratzel's scientific project is bound up with politics: to produce a useful knowledge, a technology for the spatial management of the state's power.[24] "Think in terms of space": the aim is to develop a "geographical sense" comparable to "historical sense," such that it becomes a habit.

This preoccupation of German theoreticians with the interface between space and the state goes back to the end of the eighteenth century. One of the first to tackle the political importance of the spatial factor in strategic thought was von Bülow in *Der Geist des neuern Kriegssystems* (*The Spirit of the Modern System of War*). Published in 1799, this book was soon translated into English and French. The notion of "natural borders" is central to it: it defines the natural limits of the state's action and the conditions for an international equilibrium that makes peace possible. Here we see a prospective outlining of the natural areas reserved for the different European countries, areas beyond which they should not venture under risk of endangering the balance of forces. As analysts of military thought have noticed, Heinrich Dietrich von Bülow's speculations in 1799 as to the future of the European map are not far from what it would effectively become in 1870.[25]

Moreover, when German theory speaks of the state, it is not just any state. Ratzel could not ignore a tradition with a very particular genesis. In the slow intellectual and material edification of the future Germanic state, space and patriotism converge. In contrast to what happened in France and in England, which did not launch themselves into patriotism and revolutionary—or imperialist—war until after the juridical constitution of the state, the Germans became nationalist in order to establish their state. "They are inventing the state-nation," according to the political philosopher Blandine Barret-Kriegel.[26]

The very title of the famous *Reden an die Deutsche Nation* (*Addresses to the German Nation*) by Johann Fichte (1762–1814), spoken from his chair in Berlin in 1807–8—more than sixty years before state unification—is highly significant from this point of view. "The country and the people," proclaims the philosopher, "as representatives and stakes of terrestrial eternity, as that which here below may be eternal, greatly surpass the notion of state. This is why patriotism rightly should dominate the state itself as its supreme instance."[27] Or again: "In directing the state, it is patriotism that should assign it higher goals than those of maintaining domestic peace, defending property, personal freedom, the life and well-being of all. This higher goal is the only one that incites the state to gather an armed force."[28] This triple displacement, with the state, the law, and peace each relegated in turn to a subaltern position, does not result in the objectification of power but the inverse: the subjectification of society. The German state "must generate depths, a patriotic memory that in a rough way its philosophers, military men, and musicians are awakening."[29]

For this geographer steeped in nineteenth-century naturalism and scientism, everything happens as if "rootedness in the soil" were a battle of the "lived" against the "conceived." This "subjectification of society" is closely related to the inclination to organicist representations of the individual and of the social whole.[30]

In this general context, another more specific factor came into play in the genesis of the spatial theory of power, still referring to its German modality: the American experience. His confrontation with this nation had been decisive for List in the conception of his *National System*, which owes in fact much to his experience in the United States, which at the time had opted for customs protection—the so-called American system—with a view to constructing its growth. Moreover, List knew very well of the protectionist and nationalist views of economic policy developed by Alexander Hamilton, who had inspired the succession of tariff acts since the beginning of the nineteenth century. Like Hamilton, List linked his economic system with national unification and development of natural power as guarantees of national security. For his part, Ratzel drew on the example of the United States, where he stayed in 1873, for his paradigm for theorizing the spatial dimension of power and developing a "continental thought," in the phrase of the geographer Michel Korinman.[31] On the basis of this model of the dynamic North American continent, Ratzel laid the premises for a planetary vision of international relations. His *Political Geography* was preceded, moreover, by another book more specifically about the young nation. In it he spoke of a "giant space that is taking on importance in our eyes with the forces developing there — forces that await with a cold tranquillity the dawn of the Pacific Age, successor to the Atlantic Age." This vision incited him to forge conceptual tools such as "world power" (*Weltmacht*), "spatial representation" (*Raumvorstellung*), and "life space" (*Lebensraum*) or "propagation space." We know now how ambiguous was the fortune of this latter concept, "mobile in essence," once it was mobilized by Pan-Germanism and National Socialism.

Precursor of what will become the German school of geopolitics, Ratzel is not the inventor of the word, however. This distinction belongs to the Swedish political scientist Rudolph Kjellèn (1864–1922), who in 1905 published *Geopolitische Betrachtungen über Skandinavien* (Geopolitical considerations on Scandinavia), a relatively unknown book (and author) until the publication in 1916 of a second work, this time a classic entitled *Staten som Lifsform* (The state as life-form). The term "geopolitics" would be definitively ratified in the 1920s when, under the impetus of geographers Otto Maull and Erich Obst and of General Karl Haushofer — the "Munich School" — the journal *Zeitschrift für Geopolitik* was created.[32] The origins of the word explain why, long after World War II, the British and American war academies would continue to banish "geopolitics" from their conceptual matrix.

Maritime Space and "Manifest Destiny"

The United States that Ratzel elevated to a model of power of planetary scope indeed entered, in those years, a phase of asserting its geostrategic pretensions.

This first took the form in the 1880s of a diplomatic offensive on its Latin American neighbors. The White House tried a Pan-American strategy to counter the European powers, which basically meant, on the one hand, a hegemonic Victorian Empire whose investments south of the

Rio Grande largely exceeded those of United States firms, and on the other a Pan-Latinist France that had not yet failed in its project of digging the Panama Canal, a strategic route if ever there was one from the U.S. government's standpoint. In order to justify this new continental solidarity, Washington dusted off two historical precedents for offers of cooperation: the 1823 doctrine of President Monroe according to which the United States undertook — in the name of its own security — to prevent European powers from intervening on the continent; and the Panama Congress of 1826, a first attempt at creating a permanent assembly of representatives of all the American states, renewing an idea launched from Jamaica by the *Libertador* Simón Bolívar in 1815. What the White House neglected to recall was the despoliation of which Mexico had been the victim, with California, Texas, and New Mexico amputated in 1848.

In 1889, the State Department invited the southern nations to Washington to attend a first inter-American conference to discuss the means of promoting peace on the continent, to arbitrate conflicts and territorial disputes, to lift customs barriers and standardize weights and measures. The Commercial Bureau of American Republics in which this meeting resulted would soon prove ineffective; a Pan-American Union would see the light of day in 1910 during the fourth conference of this type, held in Buenos Aires. In the event, the spectacular World's Columbian Exposition in Chicago, celebrating the fourth centennial of the "Discovery," offered another opportunity for the United States to reaffirm its right to be master of its own house, to provide its own interpretation of universality, and to commemorate Christopher Columbus's deed. The Chicago Exposition spread over an area five times larger than the one organized in Paris in honor of the centennial of the Revolution. The first Universal Exposition on U.S. soil, which took place in Philadelphia in the year of the centennial of the War of Independence, had already been the opportunity for a first U.S.-Latin American rapprochement. The emperor of Brazil in person had been a guest of honor.

In the 1890s, signs of growing U.S. power increased on the military front. The Naval Act of 1890 had marked the advent of the new navy. In 1898, the marines landed in Cuba on the pretext of helping the natives rise up against and drive out the troops of the Spanish Empire. The same year, the United States occupied two other Spanish possessions, Puerto Rico and the Philippine Islands. In the Pacific, it took possession of Guam, which was annexed to Hawaii, already under U.S. control since 1893, after American residents in Honolulu had overthrown Queen Liliuokalani and established a republic. And soon they would make off with the Panama Canal Zone. Geopolitically speaking, the Spanish-

American War and the struggle for supremacy in the American Mediterranean represented a turning point in the relations between U.S. and British sea power: the hegemonic position of the former on the American continent was henceforth accepted.

This show of strength had its ideologues and theoreticians. In 1886, the Reverend Josiah Strong published *Our Country*, a plea for an Anglo-Saxon and Christian empire. The concept of Manifest Destiny, launched in 1845 by John L. O'Sullivan and taken up the following year by President James K. Polk to justify his expansionist policy with regard to Mexico, found its preacher in Strong. In 1890, Alfred Thayer Mahan published *The Influence of Sea Power upon History, 1660–1783*, followed two years later by *The Influence of Sea Power upon the French Revolution and Empire, 1793–1812*. These two books by a pioneer of the navy and future admiral profoundly influenced the conception of maritime strength held by Ratzel, a militant for a great German navy.

Mahan (1840–1914) outlined for his country a naval strategy, and more generally developed a geopolitics of sea power, in which oceanic commerce, foreign markets, and "maritime expeditions in remote waters" were combined.

The *amount of trade* that passes enters into the question [the strategic value of a position] as well as *the nearness of the port* to that route. Whatever affects either affects the value of a position . . . Sea power primarily depends upon commerce, which follows the most advantageous roads; military control follows upon trade for its furtherance and protection. Except as a system of highways joining country to country, the sea is an unfruitful possession. The sea, or water, is the great medium of circulation established by nature, just as money has been evolved by man for the exchange of products. Change the flow of either in direction or amount, and you modify the political and industrial relations of mankind.[33]

Mahan, a professor at the Naval War College, studied the implications of the new mobility made possible by steam and telegraphy for the notion of communication lines, the most "important of strategic lines," since directly related to provisioning of fuel, munitions, and food supplies. He defined "communications" more broadly as a "general term, designating the lines of movement by which a military body . . . is kept in living connection with the national power." Mahan designed the map of strategic positions that a power such as the United States ought to occupy to assure its mastery of the seas. The Caribbean thus became quite naturally the "American Mediterranean," whose control proved indispensable for the very security of the United States, designating Cuba as a strategic point of the first order for the Gulf of Mexico. As for Hawaii, it is defined as an incomparable station midway between America and Asia, a "stepping-stone" to China, Southeast Asia, and Japan.

Mahan, the evangelist of sea power, saw annexation as the will of God, the hand of "Providence," as did a good number of his contemporaries, as witnessed by this extract from a speech by Senator Albert J. Beveridge, which would make the Bishop of Orléans, quoted earlier, green with envy:

> We will not renounce our part in the mission of our race, trustees under God, of the civilization of the world. And we will move forward to our work, not howling out regrets like slaves whipped to their burdens, but with gratitude for a task worthy of our strength and thanksgiving to Almighty God that He has marked us as His chosen people, henceforth to lead in the regeneration of the world.[34]

The homily in question, titled "The March of the Flag," was pronounced by the legislator in 1900 on his return from a trip to the Philippines. His speech recalls those of the then encumbent President McKinley, who did not fear asserting that this policy was the fruit of a divine revelation, or of predestination.

In the mouth of William Howard Taft, future president of the United States who was in 1900 asked to set up a civil regime on these islands, this idealism took the following form: "One of our great hopes in elevating those peoples is to give them a common language and that language English, because through the English language certainly, by reading its literature, by becoming aware of the history of the English race, they will breathe in the spirit of Anglo-Saxon individualism."[35]

The military expeditions opened the way to North American Protestant missions, those "Agencies of God," as Beveridge named them, acting in concert with political power. Their numerous magazines and schools relayed the "gospel of regeneration"—what the analysts who came from the countries subject to this new evangelization called more bluntly "Americanization."[36] As of 1899, for example, taking advantage of the very unpopular character of the Catholic church under Spain, different religious groups—Baptist, Presbyterian, and Methodist—agreed to divide up this proselytizing work in Puerto Rico.[37] One sign of the project of acculturation was that this former colony saw itself dispossessed in official publications of its Spanish name and renamed "Porto Rico," which suggests an Italian or Corsican island; it was not until 1932 that the U.S. Congress restored the use of the original Spanish "Puerto Rico." The French language had the bad idea of keeping the bastard form.

Landing in Cuba: The First War in Images

The U.S. intervention in Cuba opened above all a new era of information in wartime. Correspondents had full access to the telegraph and cable for transmitting their stories. Agents of Edison and Vitagraph filmed, for the first time on the spot, the operations of an expeditionary force. The intervention itself was preceded by a gigantic opinion campaign in favor of the war directed at the public and legislators, in which the sensationalist press of William Randolph Hearst played a leading role. To justify their interference in a country that was on the verge of freeing itself from a collapsing empire, the Hearst press invoked the suffering in the *reconcentrados,* the camps in which Spanish General Valeriano Weyler had confined civilian populations so as to deprive the insurgents of the support and sympathies of the noncombatants.

The *New York Journal* story "Famine in Cuba" published numerous photographs of emaciated women and children and a close-up of a very young man, even more dreadful in appearance, with legs swollen by elephantiasis. These photos, whose purpose was to stir up public outrage, went round the world. The French *Illustration* printed them, but not without a note of skepticism.[38] This magazine took a dim view of the anti-French movement reflected in the calls for a boycott launched in demonstrations by the Women's Patriotic League in Washington and Philadelphia and taken up by Hearst's newspapers. In turn, his dailies and weeklies accused the French press pell-mell of being hostile to America, the Bank of Paris of having made a loan to Spain, and the French government of having allowed the enemy fleet to take coal in Martinique and — the height of treachery — of having sent munitions to Havana aboard the French steamer *La Fayette.*[39] *L'Illustration,* for its part, emphasized the historic ambiguity of the Monroe Doctrine, which sanctioned a unilateral right to intervention.[40]

Military strategists in many countries took note of the role played by the press in the Spanish-American War and invoked this precedent — to their minds, regrettable — for legitimating censorship and news embargoes in wartime. This was notably the case with the French military command during the Great War.[41]

The history of the cinema owes to these dramatic episodes not only the first current events newsreels on military operations — thirty minutes of ambushes, skirmishes, and the taking of a hill — but also the faked scenes that were to become a part of modern cinema. Under the glass roof of his small studio in Montreuil on the outskirts of Paris, Georges Méliès filmed, with the artisanal means at his disposal, two outstanding moments in the United States' intervention. At the outbreak of hostilities, this filmmaker and magician went to work with his team to portray events as faithfully as possible. They successively reconstituted the explosion of the battleship *Maine* in the port of Havana (the sabotage that served as pretext for the armed intervention), a visit to the wreck of this ship, and the naval combat off the coast of Manila in the course of which the Spanish fleet was annihilated by the U.S. navy.[42]

In a trompe l'oeil set consisting of an immense canvas representing the ocean floor, a diver appears to be walking through the wreck of the *Maine* (in fact, a cardboard model) in the foreground. In front of the camera lens, Méliès placed a tank full of goldfish, giving the spectator the impression of being at the bottom of the sea. Then Méliès used the trick of superimposition, capturing on the same strip of film the diver examining the wreck. The spectator is under the illusion that he is moving in the midst of giant fish, as filmed in the first shot. *L'Explosion du Cuirassé Maine* was presented at the Robert-Houdin Theater on 26 April 1898, six days after the sabotage of the ship and the day after President McKinley's declaration of war on Spain. The film was immediately sent to the United States. An American cinema company was inspired by it to shoot, in a newsreel faked in New York, *Naval Combat at Santiago de Cuba*.[43]

In this war unfolding in the Caribbean, an underwater cable was severed by one of the belligerents, the United States. The inability to transmit instructions facilitated the destruction of the Spanish fleet under Admiral Cervera. This deliberate act relaunched the juridical debate on the status of means of the transmission of information in wartime, in which the great powers had been mired for several years already.

Information as Intelligence, the Journalist as Spy

"All those who take this route to break through our lines without authorization or to maintain contacts to the detriment of our troops will be liable, if they fall into our hands, to the same treatment as those who would make similar attempts by ordinary routes."[44] Balloonists (or aeronauts) were to be considered as spies because they could "make use of information that they gathered by breaking through German outposts."[45] So read a decree by Chancellor Bismarck in 1870, just as the Franco-Prussian War was raging.

The decree was referring to the siege of Paris (1870–71) by the armies of von Moltke. More than sixty French balloons loaded with dispatches and letters managed to fly, and one even carried the minister of war, Léon Gambetta. But five fell into enemy hands. Should their passengers become prisoners of war or be liable to court-martial? The Iron Chancellor preferred the second option. It was not the first time that an army made use of flying machines. Practically since its birth, the balloon, just like the modern semaphore telegraph, had had a military use. And it is significant for the present history to learn that Nicolas Jacques Conté, who was one of the first to use the balloon on the battlefield, in Fleurus in 1792, would be asked by Bonaparte, during the Egyptian expedition, to establish an optical telegraph network there. The balloon had already performed precious service in Antwerp (1815), Algeria (1830), at the siege of Venice (1849), during the U.S. Civil War, and the Paraguayan War. During the latter two conflicts in particular, the army had even succeeded in establishing telegraphic communications by balloon. But it was in Paris that the flying devices definitively proved their merit. This war experiment would launch the first air bases.

In 1874, the Brussels International Conference, convoked at the request of Russia, invalidated Bismarck's definition of the military spy as a person whose action is characterized by "secrecy and disguise." This was not the case with aerononauts or balloonists. In the same conference it was pointed out that the carriers of messages could not be classed as spies.

The texts that comprised contemporary jurisprudence on the subject are the *Traité du droit des gens* (Treatise on the law of nations) by the German publicist Emmerich de Vattel (1714–67), and the *Instructions of 1863*, written for the use of U.S. armies in the field by the jurist Francis Liebers and ratified by President Lincoln. Vattel defines spies as those who "find means to insinuate themselves among the enemy, in order to discover the state of its affairs, to pry into its designs, and then give intelligence to their employer." The American document representing the first codification of the laws of war contains nothing on balloons, whose use was still too rare at the time. But four of its articles treat in a novel fashion the notions of "spy," "dispatch-bearers" or "messengers," and "ruse." The definition of a spy is unambiguous: "To be considered as a spy is the individual who secretly in disguise or under false pretenses seeks to procure information that he proposes to communicate to the enemy. The spy may be hanged—whether or not he has succeeded in obtaining the information that he sought or in sending it to the enemy."[46] This article, like the others, would be taken up almost word for word by the international declaration concerning the laws and customs of war—formulated and adopted, but not ratified, at the Brussels Conference. Balloon ascensions were assimilated to military reconnaissance. The Institute of International Law gathered at Oxford in 1880 would follow the same philosophy in its *Manual on the Laws of War on Land*, on the eve of the launching of the first dirigible, which occurred in 1884 and would culminate with the zeppelin in 1900.

The first peace conference, which took place in 1899 in the Hague, followed in the steps of the jurisprudence established in Brussels. Germany signed the declaration on spies. Only Great Britain refused to approve a text "produced by a bastard compromise between divergent positions." The affair (1894–99) of the Jewish army captain Dreyfus, a French officer unjustly convicted of handing military secrets to the Germans, weighed on people's minds when espionage was discussed.

The second Hague peace conference organized in 1907 contributed, according to an observer, only "in very restricted terms to developing regulation of war in the air. It renounced the idea of laying down fundamental principles to follow, and as for what was decreed, manifold details of precision and clarity were still lacking."[47]

This was all the more understandable since war in the air was becoming more complex each day. Aerostats proved an increasingly effective means of reconnaissance from the moment they managed to photograph from an altitude of fifteen hundred meters. (At the Paris Exposition of 1900, the hall of precision instruments contained a specimen of the views taken during the Civil War, alongside the first aerial photographic view by Nadar in 1858.) The principal danger was that aerostats would be converted into new means of attack, with dynamite thrown from up high. This threat had been pressed since 1868, when the declaration of Saint Petersburg had tried to limit recourse to explosive bullets. The 1907 declaration is an admission of powerlessness: "The contracting Powers consent, for a period running until the end of the third conference on peace, to the prohibition of launching projectiles and explosives from the height of balloons or by other analogous new methods."

There would not be a third peace conference. The different attempts to codify the laws of war and to guarantee the respect for the law of nations would have no follow-up. In 1902, the historical research section of the German general staff sent its officers a manual on the laws of war on land, which reads, in part:

> As the moral tendencies of the nineteenth century were essentially guided by humanitarian considerations that have often enough degenerated into sentiment, if not into sentimentality, there has been no lack of attempts to develop the uses of war in a direction absolutely opposed to its nature and goals, and the future certainly holds still more efforts of the same kind for us, all the more so since they have already received moral recognition in the Geneva Conference and the conventions of The Hague and Brussels.[48]

At the time when the second peace conference was taking place, reality had already shaken up the rules promulgated by the provisional assembly of the international community. Krupp manufactured cannons and mortars designed to hit attacking balloons. The "flying dragons" had already been tested during the U.S. intervention in Cuba, the Boer War, and the Russo-Japanese War. The first airplanes were ready to fly. In 1908, Wilbur Wright managed to cover sixty kilometers in an hour at a height of one hundred meters. The following year, the French pilot Louis Blériot crossed the English Channel. In 1910, the first radiotelegraphic contact was established with an airplane. In the campaign for the pacification of Morocco, which in 1912 resulted in the establishment of a French protectorate, the airplane was equipped with this technology, in addition to its cameras.

Since Marconi's pathbreaking experiments, the wireless telegraph had been reserved for the armed forces. His first applications of the device for which an English company had bought the patents took place during British naval maneuvers held in the same year as the first peace conference. Messages were sent from one battleship to another at distances of more then thirty nautical miles. The French squadron in the Mediterranean, for its part, with devices perfected by Octave Rochefort, had reached a range of thirty-five miles during the 1901 maneuvers. Ten years later, the exchange of radio messages between land-based stations and warships had become common.

The 1907 conference nevertheless had time to touch on another matter that had arisen during the Russo-Japanese War, after the formal protest lodged by the czarist government against the special envoy of the *Times* in the Far East. "Should a newspaper correspondent who transmits information to his employer via a ship equipped with a wireless telegraph installation be considered as a spy or not?"[49] This was a question whose answer did not appear evident to many, who remembered that in the eighteenth century certain British newspapers still classified their coverage of topical events abroad under the rubric "Foreign Intelligence." The Russo-Japanese War (1904–5), marking the first modern victory of the "nonwhite" world and consecrating Japan as a power, was in fact the first conflict in which radiotelegraphy was used for tactical ends as well as for the transmission of news. The international legal community's response to this case of a possible amalgamation of functions was to refer the plaintiff to the second chapter of the "regulation concerning the laws and customs of war with respect to espionage," left intact in the form agreed upon in 1899. Certain nations for their part drew lessons from this first radiotelegraphic war for the benefit of their national security. England, for example, made the wireless telegraph a state monopoly, assigning it to the post office, with oversight granted to the Admiralty.

Over these years preceding the Great War, the military use of flying machines brought a cruel awakening to people such as Léon Bourgeois, president of the French Chamber of Deputies and future promoter of the League of Nations, who still believed in the possibility of establishing an "international community of space," "paths of peaceful exchange and just *rapprochements.*"[50] The airplane would first prove itself an effective means of combat—which it indeed became in 1918, the last year of the war. The first English commercial air route would be opened less than ten months after the signing of the armistice on 11 November. As with the first underwater cable, the two planes in service connected London to Paris.

The First World War represented a quantitative and qualitative leap in the techniques of transmission. The Crimean War, as we mentioned earlier, had been a terrain of experimentation for the underwater cable and telegraph that connected outposts to the high command of the armies in the field, and the latter with the governments in Constantinople, London, and Paris; the Civil War had signified for the electrical telegraph a decisive step in the construction of networks; and now World War I was a war of wireless communication. In 1901, Marconi had demonstrated the utility of radiotelegraphy by making the letter "s" cover the distance from Cornwall to Saint John, Newfoundland. In 1906, the physicist Reginald Aubrey Fessenden opened the way to radiotelephony by linking Brant Rock, Massachusetts, to ships in the Atlantic Ocean. In 1915, American Telegraph and Telephone (ATT) performed the first transatlantic connection by radiotelephony between the naval base at Arlington, Virginia, and the Eiffel Tower. Radiocommunication was already practiced from ship to ship, from ship to shore. Henceforth it would be possible from air to ground, for in 1916, English technicians succeeded in sending a radiotelephone message to a plane. There was the same leap with the telephone, as David Landes stresses: "The development of telephone technology was much advanced by the need to handle a large flow of messages in battle; so much so that the French saw fit as late as 1936 to build central switching stations based on techniques developed by the American Expeditionary Force."[51] World War I was also the first war of modern ciphering and cryptography: the teleprinters transmitted and decoded the hidden meaning of messages, telegrams, radios, and secret orders, opening new avenues for intelligence.

Finally, it was a conflict in which the "logistics of military perception," in Paul Virilio's phrase, took shape. The U.S. Expeditionary Force in France included a section for Operations of Aerial Photographic Reconnaissance. Led by Edward Steichen (1879–1973), painter-photographer and one of the masters of pictorialism, fifty-five officers and 1,111 enlisted men

> organized the production of aerial intelligence "like a factory," thanks to the division of labor (assembly lines for automobiles were operational in 1914!). In fact, aerial observation had ceased being episodic since the start of the war; more than images, it was a matter of image flow, that is, millions of pictures trying to track, day after day, the statistical tendencies of this first great military-industrial conflict. At first neglected by the military command, aerial photography after the Battle of the Marne [September 1914] was to make a claim to scientific objectivity comparable to that of medical or police photography.[52]

After the Peace Treaty of Versailles, the U.S. navy took belated stock of the country's radiocommunications industry in comparison to that of the British Empire. In 1919, at the navy's instigation and in the name of national security, the White House brought together into a national strategy for developing this sector the major firms of the American electrical industry (RCA, ATT, General Electric, and, a little later, Westinghouse), thus laying the foundations for a future military-industrial complex and for the future world hegemony of the United States in electronic communications.

In 1932, epitomizing the progressive integration of the technologies of long-distance communication, the International Radiotelegraph Union and the International Telegraph Union merged into the International Telecommunications Union (ITU). One of its first acts was to officially ratify the term "telecommunications," invented by the French engineer Edouard Estaunié at the beginning of the century. In 1927, the term "information" ceased to belong exclusively to the language of the press. In a memorandum presented to the Washington conference that prepared the merger of the two regulating bodies, Ralph V. L. Hartley proposed a precise measure of information associated with the transmission of symbols. These were the first steps toward the statistical measure of the physical amount of information, the "bit," or the binary digit, as well as a theory of the signal, a statistical theory that sought above all to facilitate the optimal use of a channel employed to transmit information. In 1936, the British mathematician Alan Turing (1912–54) conceived a scheme for a machine capable of processing information.

In the 1930s, the first writings on systems theory appeared, revealing the new theoretical concern with relationships rather than entities or objects. Biologist Ludwig von Bertalanffy published his *Modern Theories of Development: Introduction to Theoretical Biology* (1933), an early outline of his general systems theory. With World War II, the objectives of the systems-informational-cybernetic approach became operational. Problems of military strategy had to be resolved by scientific task forces. During the hostilities, the mathematician and electrical engineer Claude Shannon (born in 1916) worked for Bell Telephone Laboratories on cryptography and wrote a confidential report titled *Communication Theory of Secrecy Systems.* The early information processors were invented to crack the codes of the German "Enigma machines." Alan Turing served the British government as a researcher in electronics investigating the logical possibilities of an intelligent machine. The mathematician Norbert Wiener (1894–1964) performed research on predictors and wave filters in collaboration with the war research group composed of engineers, physiologists, and mathematicians led by Warren Weaver. The construction of computing machines proved essential for the war effort, and more especially for the improvement of antiaircraft fire.

At the end of the conflict, the world entered the era of automatic data processing. In 1949, Shannon and Weaver formulated the mathematical theory of communication, and Norbert Wiener laid the bases of cybernetics in 1948. "We have decided," wrote Wiener,

> to call the entire field of control and communication theory, whether in the machine or in the animal, by the name *Cybernetics,* which we form from a Greek word that means *steerman.* In choosing this term, we wish to recognize that the first significant paper on feedback mechanisms is an article on governors, which was published by [Scottish physicist James] Clerk Maxwell in 1868, and that *governor* is derived from a Latin corruption of the Greek word. We also wish to refer to the fact that the steering engines of a ship are indeed one of the earliest and best-developed forms of feedback mechanisms.[53]

PART IV

The Measure of the Individual

Chapter 10
The Portrayal of Crowds

Since the 1830s, exponents of moral statistics have tried to show that mathematical rules preside over the occurrence and distribution of social pathologies. With them, probability theory becomes a new mode of organizing society.

Half a century later, the criminological sciences of human measurement make their appearance. Nomenclatures and indices serve police officers, judges, and forensic surgeons in their hygienic mission of surveillance and normalization.

How can multitudes in movement be characterized? Should one rely on the determinism of numbers or instead recognize individual free will? In a society that has scarcely freed itself from the legislative shackles that had weighed on freedom of expression and assembly, debates on the nature of collective opinion and its supposed effects on public life are inscribed in a direct line of descent from the theses of the schools of criminal anthropology and crowd psychology. Prefiguring behaviorism, the predominant conception of the receiver is that of an individual functioning like an automaton within a society viewed as manipulative. But the polemic over the relationship between the hypnotized and the hypnotist (the analogy used to characterize the relationship between the individual and the collective) also gave birth to an ethnographic approach to publics as constituents of a new type of society.

Adolphe Quételet, the Average Man, and the Society of Risk

In 1835, the Belgian astronomer and mathematician Adolphe Quételet published *Sur l'homme et le développement de ses facultés, ou Essai de physique sociale* (*A Treatise on Man and the Development of His Faculties*). "The average man is to a nation," he wrote, "what the center of gravity is to a body; it is to him that an appreciation of all the phenomena of equilibrium and its movements refers."[1] This "pivotal value" he makes the axis of a science conceived on the model of physical laws. It is this "fictive being," "the mean around which the social elements oscillate," who must be considered "without stopping over particular cases or at anomalies and without questioning whether such an individual might not have a greater or lesser development of one of his faculties."[2]

In a society moved by "forces," the average man is elevated to the status of basic unit of a new science of social measurement: "social physics." A methodological axiom guides Quételet's approach: "One will judge the degree of perfection a science has achieved by the greater or lesser facility with which it allows itself to be approached through calculation."[3] For him, numbers decide the question of determinism: "Man's free will is effaced and remains without perceptible effect when observations are extended to a large number of individuals."[4]

Quételet demanded of social physics that it answer three questions: (1) By which laws does man reproduce himself, grow in weight, physical size, and intellectual force, develop his greater or lesser penchant for good or evil, his passions and tastes, in accordance with which he produces and consumes and dies? (2) What effect does nature exert on man, and how does one measure its influence? What are the disruptive forces and which social elements are affected by them? (3) Finally, can human force compromise the stability of the social system?[5]

In 1825, Quételet made himself known by publishing a *Mémoire sur les lois des naissances et de la mortalité à Bruxelles* (Report on birth and mortality laws in Brussels). This first demographic study was early evidence of his desire to establish a moral statistics and to deduce "useful consequences" from it. Quételet was a pioneer of both statistics on demographic changes and judicial data. From mortality tables he turned to drawing up "criminality tables." He observes what he called a "penchant for crime," that is, the greater or lesser probability that an individual will commit a crime, according to the influence of the seasons, gender, age, social condition, and geographical area. Measuring and classifying, he draws out general laws of a probabilistic type and makes maps representing delinquency rates and associating them with a series of other indices of social instability. His criminality tables indicate, for different age groups, the degrees of propensity to crime in different European countries. He also worked on the "propensity to suicide."

His work on the ecology of crime created a school of followers, as witnessed, among other things, by the numerous references to his work in studies undertaken by British statisticians starting in the 1840s on juvenile delinquents, beggars, thieves, prostitutes, cheats, and swindlers in the great metropolises of industrial England.[6] His pioneering role in the formation of an international community of statisticians sharing the same analytic framework goes hand in hand with the dissemination of his ideas.

In identifying the "constant" and the "variable causes" that "dominate the social system," Quételet tried to provide the legislator with necessary tools for regulating change faced with "disruptive forces," that is to say, every perturbation "that influences man morally and determines that he act in one way rather than another," the cumulative effect of which imperils the stability of society. In another of his books published in 1848 and titled *Du système social et des lois qui le régissent* (On the social system and the laws that govern it), in which he expounds on his "criminality tables" and shows their utility as an instrument of government, he specifies: "In considering things from this point of view, one better understands the high mission of the legislator who somehow holds in his hands the 'budget' of crimes and may diminish or augment their number by measures that are combined with more or less prudence."[7]

The *Essay on Social Physics* was published in the same year as the appearance in French of the word "normality." Georges Canguilhem dates its birth to 1834, while the *Oxford English Dictionary* marks its first appearance in English as 1849.[8]

In the epigraph to his *Essay,* Quételet quoted the following sentence from the *Essai philosophique sur les probabilités* (Philosophical essay on probability) (1814) by the mathematician and astronomer, former interior minister under Bonaparte, Pierre-Simon de Laplace: "Let us apply to the political and moral sciences the method founded on observation and calculations, the method that has served us so well in the natural sciences." Quételet is in fact beholden to a sum of work and experiments that had begun with Pascal's "geometry of chance" and that continued with research by actuaries to calculate insurance rates, the first analyses of political arithmetic, and the first applications of games theory to the evaluation of trial juries or different election methods.

François Ewald, disciple and friend of Michel Foucault, in his treatise *L'État Providence* (The welfare state), clearly defined the impact of Quételet's social physics on the emergence of a new art of governing: "Quételet's importance is to have been a crossroads, a place of intersection, a point of precipitation. Things still isolated, dispersed, and separated were, thanks to him, placed in contact with each other and took on a new form, new developments, a new future. Quételet was the man who universalized probability calculus — which is the universal converter."[9]

Of the two great attempts at the objectification of society that arose in the course of the nineteenth century (the other being Auguste Comte's positive sociology), the theory of the average man and of means is the one that makes us "suddenly strangers to ourselves" because it confers on us "a new identity." Whereas Comtean sociology is situated within the categories in which human history was already being thought, the same is not true of Quételet: in postulating that only by considering individuals as a mass can we have a real understanding of the individual, his method reveals the "effects of decentering of the subject," linked to objectification, on the way of treating men, things, and the relations between them.[10]

With the application of "probabilistic reason" to the calculated management of society, a new mode of social regulation, which François Ewald calls "insurance society," began. Insurance, the mechanism based on the compensatory model of risk protection, is transformed from a simple "risk technology" into a "political technology." This radical change can be summed up as the shift from a framework of responsibility to one of solidarity, and from civil law to social law. In this trajectory toward calculated solidarity and interdependence can be perceived the emergence of the welfare state that socializes responsibilities; there is not only a proliferation of insurance institutions, but also the progression of a new kind of rationality associated with them. By transposing the philosophy and proven techniques of private insurance to the plane of the whole society, the latter is considered as a "universal mutual insurance company." Insurance is called upon to ground a new social justice within societies as well as among states.

In any case this was how it was understood in 1852 by the journalist and newspaper owner Émile de Girardin (1806–81), exiled in Brussels. In his book *La Politique universelle* (The universal politics), he makes insurance the overall principle of social reorganization. Referring all social problems to questions of risk, he attributes the solutions to all of them to that mechanism:

> Calculation of probabilities, applied to human morality, to maritime risks, to cases of fire or flood, has given birth to a new science that is still in its infancy: that of *insurance*. The calculation of probabilities, applied to the life of nations, to cases of war and revolution, is the foundation of all high policy. According to whether this calculation is rigorous or false, profound or disdained, so policy is glorious or disastrous, grand or petty. To govern means to foresee.[11]

The philosophy of risk and cost-risk calculus abolishes the theological or moral distinction between good and evil: it belongs to the pure materiality of facts:

I asked myself if it were possible to conceive and found a society that, reducing everything mathematically to risks judiciously foreseen and to probabilities exactly calculated, would have as its single pivot universal *insurance.* I asked myself if a society founded on this hypothesis, whether it be true or false, and turning on this pivot like the earth on its axis, would be worth less than the society that rests on the arbitrary distinction between good and evil—an arbitrary distinction since it has always varied and still varies according to different times and places, religions and laws.[12]

The social contract is redefined as an insurance contract. It allows one to face the risk of unemployment and the insufficiency of salaries among workers. For its application, de Girardin goes as far as to imagine a system of identification: everyone should possess a booklet or "life register" into which his "individual evaluation" and a "national evaluation" were written, the latter being a set of statistical information on state expenditures and revenues and on the situation of industry. Thanks to this measure aimed at openness, each person would know in what kind of society he was participating as a part of the whole. In the nation conceived as a great mutual insurance company, this "life register" is like an account opened for each child at birth and credited or debited until his or her death. It is equivalent to a generalized insurance policy. Each year, in each unit of the national territory organized according to a federalist model, an account statement is delivered by the tax collector in exchange for the payment of a "premium tax." This policy would thus replace the birth certificate, the passport, the voting card, and the family booklet.

The new contract also guaranteed against the risk of war: "To remove it and abolish it, there is something simple to be done, which is to propose to all nations sagging under the weight of a peacetime army to contract among themselves a special insurance policy against this prospect. The more states taking part as contracting parties, the lower the risk, and consequently the premium will diminish."

The institutionalization of this new political and juridical rationality in France would take thirty years, from 1880 to 1910, from the beginning of the debate on work accidents to the law on retirement. The congresses on social insurance that were held during the great universal expositions would be one of the important places for the dissemination of this philosophy. As for the incorporation of the notion of risk into a project for a new international sphere, not until the end of World War I would it occur, through the League of Nations. This was the role assigned more particularly to the International Labor Organization (ILO), which would aim to enforce the provision in the Versailles Treaty that "physical, moral, and intellectual welfare is of essential importance from the international standpoint." "Persuaded as they are that labor should not be considered simply as an article of commerce," as an official French report on the treaty read, the contracting parties had also subscribed to the idea that "there are methods and principles for the regulation of the conditions of labor that all the industrial communities should endeavor to apply."[13]

At the turn of the century, the partisans of a system of social insurance against all risks argued that "if there is a risk against which one must insure, it is that of invalidity, since here the risk of the individual is truly the risk of the invalidity of the nation."[14] The questions of "social welfare" and "social defense" were consistent at a national level with those of internal security and "national defense." All the more so in that on the other side of the Rhine, Chancellor Bismarck's "social program," which aimed to diminish the pressure exerted by the workers' trade unions and the Social Democratic Party, had placed the German Empire in the vanguard of social rights: health insurance in 1883; accident insurance the following year; disablement insurance in 1889. Although several French theoreticians were its precursors—for example, Louis Blanc (1811–82), who was one of the first to recommend mandatory social risk insurance—the French government did not rally to the principle until 1898. The first step was the law of 9 April of that year, which instituted workplace accident insurance. But, unlike the German system, the French one did not make employer insurance mandatory, it applied only to enterprises using machines, and it excluded illnesses contracted at work (it was not until 1928 that French law on social insurance took a definitive form).

After World War I, the imperative of mutual security among states became the basis for the "universal insurance" dreamed of by de Girardin. It is scarcely by chance that French promoters of the social insurance policy and of "solidarism" as a political doctrine such as Léon Bourgeois (1851–1925) and Alfred Croiset (1845–1923) found themselves among the major architects of the League of Nations. In the preface to their *Essai d'une philosophie de la solidarité* (Essay on a philosophy of solidarity) published in 1902, one finds the following matter-of-fact definition of the central notion of "solidarity":

> If individuals in one sense are no more than the cells of society, the term by which biologists express the interdependence of cells is the very one that ought henceforth to express the interdependence of individuals. The terms justice, charity, fraternity have seemed insufficient... Fraternity, so dear to sentimental democracy in

1848, has precisely the fault of being just a sentiment, and our modern generations, avid for positive and objective science, have need of a term that expresses the scientific character of moral law. The word "solidarity" borrowed from biology responds marvelously to this obscure and profound need.[15]

Charity was optional; solidarity as a binding contract is compulsory. In 1920, Léon Bourgeois would receive the Nobel Peace Prize.

The biomorphic notion of interdependence would henceforth be the keystone in the successive arrangements and rearrangements of the world order, and the world communication order.

Alphonse Bertillon and Anthropometry

Quételet's last book, published in 1871, three years before his death, was entitled *Anthropométrie, ou Mesure des différentes facultés de l'homme* (Anthropometry, or the measurement of the different faculties of man). His work staked out the methodological terrain on which a project for "anthropometric indexing" would flourish in the 1880s. Alphonse Bertillon (1853–1914), a medical doctor and inventor of scientific police methods, did not mince words in 1892: "It is infinitely probable that without the work of this good and ingenious man, I would never had thought of using human measurements for recognizing identity."[16] But the genesis of the issue of identification and indexing goes back much farther than Bertillon.

Toward 1833, police authorities in France inaugurated use of individual cards or sheets for locating and identifying criminals. The area of criminality was beginning to function, in the words of Michel Foucault, "as a political observatory." Through the observation of criminals, a whole apparatus for controlling the entire social field was constituted. Delinquency, police, and prison are three terms that, as Foucault observed, "support one another and form a circuit that is never interrupted. Police surveillance provides the prison with offenders whom the prison transforms into delinquents, the targets and auxiliaries of police supervisions, which regularly send back a certain number of them to prison."[17] The same year, André Michel Guerry de Champneuf (1802–66) published *Essai sur la statistique morale de la France* (Essay on the moral statistics of France), without displaying any theoretical ambition and without benefiting from the same international renown as Quételet. Director of criminal affairs in the Ministry of Justice, Guerry studied the frequency and distribution of suicides and of crimes against persons and property, using the first statistical series on Paris and the Seine Department, published by the *préfet* between 1821 and 1829.[18]

In 1863, the French penitentiary authorities proposed the use of photography inside prisons. The minister of the interior was opposed to it, arguing that such a measure "would be for the detainees an unforeseen aggravation of their punishment by the law and one more means of preventing any return to the good."

Among the rare scientific references of the time to the issue of individual identification were four texts that circulated in medical and judicial circles.

The first was written by a French ecclesiastic, Abbot Jacques Pernetti (1690–1777), author of *Lettres Philosophiques sur les physionomies* (Philosophical letters on physiognomy), published in 1748, to which La Mettrie and the Encyclopedists had already referred. The second was the work of a Protestant theologian from Zurich, Johann Kaspar Lavater (1741–1801), a devotee of occultism and author of a work published in several volumes starting in 1775 entitled *Physiognomonische Fragmente,* in which he claimed to found a science establishing the relation between exterior and interior, the visible surface and what is invisible underneath it, especially between the face and the personality. Very quickly, Lavater's theory attracted defenders as well as outspoken adversaries. Honoré de Balzac (1799–1850), for example, drew on it for his description of the characters in his series of novels *La Comédie Humaine.* In contrast, Swiss artist and novelist Rodolphe Töpffer (1799–1846), who is credited as one of the precursors of "picture stories" or cartoon strips, in 1845 wrote *Essai de Physiognomonie* in which he rejected the project of physiological localization of human faculties. In 1807, Hegel had taken the trouble to refute in his *Phenomenology of the Spirit* the "false sciences" symbolized for him by "physiognomony" as well as phrenology.

Phrenology itself was the subject of the third reference work. The creator of this science was the German Franz Joseph Gall (1758–1828), who thought it possible to "recognize the instincts, penchants, and talents, the intellectual and moral dispositions of man and animals by the configuration of their brains and their heads"; all the foregoing terms figured in the titles of the ten volumes he devoted to the subject between 1810 and 1825. The fourth text is the work of a specialist on the brain and its language functions, Paul Broca (1824–80), entitled *Instructions Générales pour les recherches anthropologiques à faire sur le vivant* (General instructions for anthropological research on the living), published in 1864, in which this founder of the school of medical anthropology assumes that the brain has something to do with race and that measuring the shape of the cranium is the best method of evaluating its content.

In 1871, the minister for the navy and colonies put out a circular stipulating that anyone condemned irrevocably to more than six months in prison would henceforth be photographed. The following year, the penitentiary administration took the same measure, decreeing that all "civil prisoners," and in particular individuals condemned for crimes of insurrection, would be photographed. Hundreds of men and women condemned for activities during the 1870 Commune were recorded in this way.

In 1882, Bertillon was charged with setting up the scientific system for identifying criminals that he had proposed three years earlier to the *préfet de police*. Two ministerial circulars generalized the use of his method to the rest of France between 1885 and 1888.

The ordinary and banal particulars of detainees, inscribed in the prison register, were replaced by a summary of anthropometric measurements. In addition to body measurements—notably of the head and limbs, the bases of the anthropometric method properly speaking—the index card included the color of the iris of the left eye, a description of individual distinguishing features, deformities, scars, and tattoos. To all this information were added data on civil status, previous convictions, the place of the most recent detention, and the reasons for the current one. The index card was completed by two juxtaposed portraits of the subject, face-on and (right) profile. To facilitate the filling out of the card, Bertillon issued very precise instructions and came up with special measuring instruments: a compass for determining length and breadth of the head, and a sliding ruler for feet, fingers, and arms. His book *La Photographie Judiciaire,* published in 1890, rounded out this method. He also invented the "spoken portrait," a kind of identikit picture, profiting from his statistical studies of the distribution of measurements and frequencies. This description of the individual, made up of conventional and abbreviated symbols, was presented as having the advantage of "being telegraphed in an instant in all directions, to police in major towns and embarkation ports, and thus able to deal with the flight and escape of criminals."[19] The index cards were centralized in the Ministry of the Interior—in duplicate, with one classified by order of measurements and the other in alphabetical order.

In 1885, Bertillon presented his method to the participants in the second international penitentiary congress and at the first congress on criminal anthropology, both held simultaneously in Rome. Before the end of the century, "Bertillonnage" and the "Parisian index card" would have become synonymous in the new era of scientific police work around the world.

From the rostrum of the penitentiary congress, Bertillon took up the question of the international exchange of judicial information and expressed his wish to contribute to its advent via the spread of a method that had already proven itself—his own. To convince his foreign colleagues, he went so far as to argue that the nonuniversality of the metric system was not an obstacle to its adoption: it would suffice to consider the numbers on his measuring instruments not as measures of length, but as "benchmark figures" or orders of magnitude. At the same meeting, his superior in the hierarchy, François-Louis Herbette, director of the prison administration, became bolder and spoke of the advantages there would be, in the interests of both citizens and the state, in generalizing the availability of the data on the cards by including anthropometric particulars on each certificate of civil status, each passport, and each life insurance policy.[20]

Galton, Vucetich, and the Fingerprint

To these procedures for identification, which were seen as unsurpassable, were added in the 1890s another, not of French origin and which even represented a serious challenge to Bertillon's: fingerprinting, a method with a multiple paternity.

Old civilizations like those of China and Japan had already discovered mysteries in the patterns in the palm of the hand. But it is to the seventeenth-century anatomists Ruysch, Albinus, and Malpighi that we owe the first scientific descriptions of the extreme diversity of the papillary spirals and whorls that cover the finger pads. These doctors did not, however, seek the key to this graphic variety by classifying and grouping the curves, arcs, and concentric circles. This innovation fell to Jan Evangelista Purkinje (1787–1869), a Czech anatomist who in 1823 published a book, conceived as purely scientific, on the cutaneous system. Bringing order to the infinite combinations of papillary lines, he discerned nine principal patterns. In the following decades, this discovery of the disposition of papillary lines was confirmed by two or three studies undertaken independently in other European countries, including those of the French physiologists Alix and Gratiolet toward 1865.

But the life-size laboratory that would launch the judicial use of these discoveries was situated outside Europe, in the imperial periphery. In the middle of the nineteenth century, the British civil servant J. W. Herschell imposed on the illiterate of Bengal a systematic use of the thumbprint as a seal to authenticate public acts—a practice that evidently had many precedents. From this administrative experiment devoid of scientific pretensions, undertaken over a period of forty years, would result considerable data records that would be used by a London scientist, Francis Galton (1822–1911).

Toward 1888, Galton, a cousin of Darwin, discovered the work of Purkinje at the library of the Royal College of Surgeons. Taking up the methodical study of digital patterns, he published three years later a first method of indexing fingerprints.[21] He arranged the dactylograms, or figures showing the papillary lines, those of the thumb, for example, into forty-one types that were further divided into subtypes.

Galton's purpose had nothing to do with forensic medicine, and the identification of the individual was only secondary for him, for he was essentially an anthropologist—though of a very particular sort. Galton is above all remembered as the initiator of eugenics, that is, breeding for selective inheritance, which supposedly could produce "hereditary genius"—a phrase that provided the very title of his 1869 book. In this work he presented the aristocracy as the natural fruit of natural selection, of pure lineage. In the course of his research, Galton made his contribution to statistical methods—in particular, to correlational calculation based on the "family records" of "eminent men," with the aim of confirming his aristocratic prejudices about other races and classes!

In 1891 Juan Vucetich (1850–1925), head of police statistics in the city of La Plata, Argentina, simplified Purkinje's and Galton's classification by reducing the fundamental types to four. Five years later, his method, already tested, was extended throughout the province of Buenos Aires. It distinguished among the governing lines four categories of shapes— arch, internal loop, external loop, whorl (in Spanish, *verticilo*)—designated, respectively, by the letters A I E V when dealing with the thumb, and by the letters 1 2 3 4 when dealing with the other fingers, so that the formula A.2431, for example, meant there was an arch on the thumb, an internal loop on the index finger, a whorl on the middle one, an external loop on the ring finger, and an arch on the little one. With the two hands, this notation allowed for a considerable number of possible combinations. Vucetich thus succeeded in creating a repertory of more than a million different types.

The Argentinean functionary's system had the advantages of simplicity and operational ease over that of the British scientist; he even conceived a filing cabinet, an "organ," to classify fingerprinting cards, whereas Galton was not even interested in record keeping. Scotland Yard, which at first expressed an interest in his research, would in the end find his system too difficult to apply in large numbers and would choose another system—that of Henry—in 1901. Vucetich had the support of his country's authorities, who were among the first to rally to Bertillonnage, but also the first to criticize it for being too complex to manage. The Argentinean police did not foresee the adoption of his method except within the judicial framework of administrative reforms they were working to promote among legislators. Their identification method, which originally registered only the criminal population, would be successively extended to immigrants, civil servants, conscripts, and finally the whole population. The inauguration of the mandatory identification card for all citizens in the second half of the 1910s presented the opportunity for generalizing fingerprint identification.

The system invented by Vucetich, a recent immigrant from central Europe, would be adopted by a number of countries in South America. He gathered together police chiefs from Argentina, Brazil, Chile, and Uruguay in 1905 to discuss the need to generalize the use of the identity card (featuring fingerprints).[22] The principle was unanimously accepted. Before the end of the 1930s, the majority of Latin American countries would make an institution of the identity card. The fingerprint would thus become the sole means of individual identification.

Indeed, Latin America was precocious in this area. By contrast, in France, after a first fruitless plan in 1939, the identity card would not become mandatory until after World War II (in 1941, the Vichy regime imposed the INSEE [Institut National de la Statistique et des Études Économiques] identification number, which would later become the basis of individual classification for Social Security purposes). The contrast is all the more great with Great Britain and the United States, which, three-quarters of a century after Argentina's adoption of the identity card, have not yet adopted this practice.

The control of the immigration flow seems to have been one of the original major explanations for Latin American alacrity. It was, in any case, one of the principal legitimating arguments for this measure, as one may judge from the following quote from a proposal, dating from 1909, by L. Reyna Almandos, one of Vucetich's most faithful collaborators:

> Our countries were shaped by immigration . . . All the pernicious social elements of the Old World rush toward the American peoples, especially in Brazil and Argentina, because the ports are open to those who want or solicit entry. This liberalization leads to increased offenses of all kinds—from the smallest, in the form of acts of bad faith, right up to inconceivable terrorist attacks by the ferocious anarchist who, carried away by an idea of equality as lofty as it is impossible to achieve, finds no other means of establishing the social order of his dreams than destroying by violence and crime . . . Social prophylaxis would be successfully achieved by establishing fingerprint identification of each individual who lands in an American port.[23]

Three years later, Argentina created an "immigrant register," the first application of the fingerprint index to a category of the population apart from prison inmates.

In 1907, the French minister of justice invited the Academy of Sciences "to make known its sentiment about the credibility of anthropometric methods as compared to fingerprints in determining the identity of an individual, and about the means of control to be established for preventing inexact deductions in their application." Five academic experts were charged with writing this report; after having reviewed the different fingerprint systems in use in the world and designating the Argentinean system as the most operational, they concluded:

> In all the countries that have adopted it, this system has shown its superiority over the anthropometric system. At first subordinated to the latter, then employed concurrently, it soon dethroned it... It is not subject to the objections made to the anthropometric system; it applies to all ages. It is less costly. Its functioning demands no large personnel difficult to train... It can be recommended for the establishment of an international index that police in all civilized states would use for the joint search for criminals.[24]

At the time when the Academy of Sciences issued its report, no less than ten fingerprinting methods were being applied throughout the world, most having been perfected by those in charge of scientific police work; for example, the Henry method, which, first tried out in India before being adopted in the British metropole, was also used in Saxony, Denmark, and Sweden; or the Pottecher method, used in French Indochina, which was different from that of the French metropolitan police, who chose in 1902 to introduce alongside Bertillon's anthropometry a fingerprint method that closely resembled Vucetich's. In fact, the "South American" variety—as it was named by the forensic scientist Edmond Locard and the whole so-called Lyons school of medicine directed by Dr. Jean Lacassagne (1843–1924), holder of the chair in forensic medicine in the Lyons faculty, who was a supporter of it—was already the most widespread method on the international scene, along with that of London Chief Constable Edward R. Henry.[25]

The "Delinquent Man" of Criminal Anthropology

In affinity with anthropometry a new science was born: criminal anthropology. Its founding group was Italian; at its head was Cesare Lombroso (1835–1909), former military doctor, professor of forensic medicine at the University of Turin and author in 1876 of a key work entitled *L'uomo delinquente in rapporto all antropologia, alla giurisprudenza ed alla discipline economiche* (*Criminal Man*).[26] Among the best-known members of the group were a public prosecutor, Raffaele Garofalo, and a jurisconsult and deputy, Enrico Ferri, professor of penal law at the University of Siena. Although their common characteristic was their claim to positive science, they were still differentiated by their positions in the political spectrum. Lombroso was frankly conservative, while Ferri (1856–1929), founder of the newspaper *Avanti!*, is classified by the *Encyclopedia Italiana* as a "man of the extreme left." This Italian school presented itself as the "school of positive criminology" and had a journal, *Archivio di psichiatria e antropologia criminale*.

The group had an impact beyond the Italian borders, and even launched congresses that, every four years until the eve of World War I, assembled the world's criminologists in the great cities of Europe. Lombroso and Ferri presided over the first such congress held in Rome in 1885. The decade was decisive for setting up networks of international exchanges on judicial questions, as, for example, with the first penitentiary congress held in London in 1882, and the second in Rome three years later, at which Bertillon gave his lecture. In 1889, the International Union on Penal Law gathered in Brussels for the first time, while criminal anthropology had its second congress on the grounds of the Universal Exposition in Paris.

In 1906, Lombroso gave the opening address at the sixth congress of criminal anthropology in Brussels; it would be his last. For more than twenty years, the theses of Italian criminologists had been at the center of debates and polemics at scholarly gatherings.

From the start, the Rome congress had set the tone. A parallel exhibition illustrated the objects of various participants' research. Professor Angelucci showed seventeen craniums, of which sixteen were from epileptics and one a kleptomaniac, and thirty-one photographs of criminals. Professor Lombroso showed seventy skulls of Italian criminals and thirty of epileptics, illustrated in *L'uomo delinquente*, a thief's skeleton, a pitcher covered with graffiti from a prison, some tattered skin with criminals' tattoos, and their handwriting specimens. With his colleague R. Laschi, he showed four panels with portraits of political criminals, geographical maps of the distribution of political crimes (such as revolutions) in Europe and in other parts of the world, and graphs claiming to show the influence of temperature on this type of crime. In other display windows appeared prostitutes' brains, pimps' craniums, photograph albums of prostitutes, pictures (both drawings and photographs) representing the insane and the delinquent, the head of a "nihilist affiliated with the police, condemned to death, and strangled in prison by his comrades," pieces sculpted by a paranoiac and a pederast that suggested primitive sculptures, and other items in this vein.

This museum of horrors was a visual condensation of the hypotheses sustained by the exponents of the new positivistic penal school. Between crime and madness, between the criminal and the insane person, the difference was not great: they were simply two forms of cerebral and mental decay. Three years before his death, Lombroso still repeated the observation that had oriented his research on the "born criminal":

> Ever since time immemorial, one has noticed that vicious men and criminals have abnormal wrinkles, asymmetry of the face and body, clumsiness and squints... In 1870, I pursued research for several months in the prisons and asylums of Pavia on cadavers and living persons to determine the substantial differences between madmen and criminals, without being really successful. Suddenly, one sad December morning, I found on the skull of a brigand a whole series of atavistic anomalies, especially an enormous occipital depression and a hypertrophy of a part of the cerebellum analogous to those found in inferior vertebrates. Seeing these strange anomalies, the problem of the nature and origin of the criminal appeared to me to be resolved: the characteristics of primitive men and inferior animals seemed to be reproduced in our era. And many facts seemed to me later to confirm this hypothesis, especially from criminal psychology: the frequency of tattooing and slang, of passions as fleeting as they are violent, especially that of vengeance; an improvidence that resembles courage and a courage that alternates with cowardice, and a laziness that alternates with agility and the passion for gambling."[27]

In fact, in his search for palpable testimony about somatic anomalies, Lombroso borrowed from phrenology the idea that "the true criminal is one inhabited by an innate penchant for crime, linked to a hypertrophied cerebral organ," and the cranioscopic technique of examination.[28]

A criminal type thus *did* exist, in Lombroso's view, and this criminal was assimilated to the primitive savage, by his traits, his constitution, and his organism. This, in any case, was clearly the thesis that the head of the positivistic school defended in the first edition of his classic book, though he would try to reorient it after being criticized for relying too heavily on biology. In the critics' lead was the Frenchman Gabriel Tarde, who objected that it was not atavism but the social milieu that made the criminal. "Societies have the criminals that they deserve," added Lacassagne.

Lombroso showed himself to be particularly sectarian with respect to "political crime" and "political delinquents," whom he classified as impassioned political criminals and on occasion as born political criminals (Marat), or insane political criminals (Ravaillac). In collaboration with R. Laschi, in 1890 he devoted two volumes to this subject, combining, in this enterprise of dissection, a discussion of the individual political delinquent and of the collective type—the "criminal crowd." Of mass demonstrations, he wrote:

> Research on the criminal crowd has shown us the grave peril that the sole fact of meeting and contact among a large number of people constitutes for the state; consequently, all the currents and traditions that have arisen in our time concerning the great advantages of the absolute freedom of assembly and the guarantees that "meetings" bring to the freedom of a people are perfectly contrary to the truth and cannot be explained except by the desire to ape the British people, for whom the climate, the historical habits, and phlegmatic character permit these political orgies without there resulting grave consequences.[29]

During the international congresses, the issue of "political crime" enflamed passions: anarchism, revolution, social agitation, strike movements, and demonstrations aroused extreme reactions, such as that of Dr. Magitot, for example, at the 1889 congress in Paris. Applauding Laschi's report on the characterization of "political crime," he offered as damning evidence a photographic album containing portraits of several women of the Paris Commune, with the following commentary: "These photographs represent most types of physical and moral degeneration: some display the traits of virility, some the traits of physical inferiority or of bestiality. Others manifestly show signs of hysteria, exaltation, and fanaticism."[30]

Scipio Sighele, Initiator of Crowd Psychology

From individual crime to collective crime, from individual psychology to collective psychology—the path was traced toward "crowd psychology" and the first debates over the relations between society and the new means of dissemination. Three people disputed the claim to be first: the Italian sociologist Scipio Sighele (1868–1913), and the French doctors Henry Fournial (1866–1932) and Gustave Le Bon (1841–1931). In 1891,

Sighele, professor at the University of Brussels, published *La Folla delin-quente* (The criminal crowd), which was rapidly translated into French and includes many references to Gabriel Tarde's work. Fournial's book, *Essai sur la psychologie des foules* (Essay on the psychology of crowds) appeared in 1892, and that of Gustave Le Bon, *Psychologie des foules* (*The Crowd: A Study of the Popular Mind*), three years later. Fournial, a military doctor and former student of Lacassagne in Lyons, had read the Italian book, but cites it seldom; on the other hand, he quotes Tarde many times.[31]

As for Le Bon, in the first edition of his book he ignores his prede-cessors. However, there exists a strange resemblance between his argu-ments and concepts and those of Sighele—which the latter quickly de-nounced, followed by the journal of the Italian positivistic school.[32] For the second French edition of his book (published in 1901), Sighele wrote in the foreword:

> My acknowledgments are great, not only to all those who, like Gabriel Tarde and Victor Cherbulliez, have loyally and lengthily discussed my theory, but also to those who, like M. Gustave Le Bon, have utilized my observations on the psychology of crowds without citing me. And there is no irony in my writing this; I think that when someone adopts your ideas without mentioning you, it is the least suspect kind of praise that can be addressed to you![33]

Le Bon joined in the polemic and added a jarring footnote to his in-troduction:

> The rare authors who have concerned themselves with the psychological study of crowds have examined them, as I said above, solely from the criminal viewpoint. Having devoted to this subject only a short chapter, I refer the reader to the studies by M. Tarde and the opuscule by M. Sighele, *Les Foules criminelles* [*sic*]. This last book does not contain a single idea that is personal to its author, but is a compilation of facts precious to psychologists. My conclusions on criminality and the morality of crowds are, in addition, totally contrary to those of both authors I have just mentioned.[34]

Sighele had wasted his time pinpointing the pirated passages and complaining about breach of copyright before the Society of Authors in France and in Italy, since *Psychologie des foules* was soon to be given promotion through the affair of Captain Dreyfus, against whose cause Le Bon took a public stand. Some years later, during World War I, the role assigned to the propaganda weapon would further benefit the book, which would thereafter be among the obligatory references for under-standing leaders and followers in the era of crowds. The second, com-pletely revised French edition of Sighele's book was the last. As for Le Bon's book, it enjoyed multiple translations into different languages and more than a century later would still be on bookstore shelves. Fournial, for his part, paid no attention to the polemic: the great colonial explo-rations of Africa required his services, and his publisher heard no more from him.[35]

Sighele's project was rooted in the teaching of Enrico Ferri. In 1884, in a book on the "new horizons of law and penal procedure," reissued under the title *Sociologie criminelle* (Criminal sociology), this represen-tative of the Italian school had distinguished three types of psychology: individual psychology or the study of man in isolation; social psychol-ogy (or sociology), the study of people in their normal and constant re-lations; and collective psychology, the study of abnormal or transitory relations among people, that is to say, meetings or groupings that, due to occasion or chance, are not stable and organic but inorganic and ephem-eral, such as juries, agricultural shows, theater audiences, assemblies, or crowds.[36]

Sighele's intention was to stake out this new field of collective psychol-ogy by studying the criminal manifestations of that "psychological poly-hedron that is the crowd." Under the concept of "crimes of the crowd" he placed all the "collective violence of the plebes" that appeared at the close of the century, "from workers' strikes to popular uprisings," "a kind of organ of elimination by which people think they can relieve all the resentment that the injustices from which they suffer have accumu-lated inside them."[37] The author published two other books in Italy in 1892 and 1897, which were translated into French under the titles *Le Crime à deux* (Crime with two authors) and *Psychologie des sectes* (Psy-chology of sects) and are important works for understanding his whole approach.

"Collective crime" in fact has several levels. Its simplest form is that born of the association of two delinquents. Then one moves to the as-sociation of malefactors and that of the criminal sect. And from the sect to the crowd the distance is very short, since the sect itself may also be defined as the chronic form of the crowd, which may then be seen merely as the acute form of the sect.

The key to almost all the mechanisms of collective psychology in its diverse stages is the "phenomenon of suggestion." There are always "sug-gestors" and "suggestees," the leaders and the followers. In a sect, for ex-ample, the followers form a single soul out of all the souls that compose it, creating a uniformity or a unison that is the ideal of any association.

All the sect members tend to realize their ideal of fusion with the precision of human machines, in the same way that all the members of a crowd shout and act in the fashion of automata set into motion by an unexpected shout or act by one of them. And when a sect (a band of anarchists, for example) produces an individual who is going to kill a king or a president of the republic, one might well say of this person that he has been influenced by suggestion, like the individual who in a crowd strikes and kills, not by his free will, but through the tumultuous interlocking of a thousand suggestions that have turned him into a simple automaton.[38]

The distinction between suggestion-maker and suggestion-receiver that is at work in all couples can be extrapolated to the level of the crowd. But it becomes complicated, since the suggestion touches here its highest degree of potency. However numerous a crowd may be, it is a "sort of couple in which sometimes one is influenced by a suggestion from all the others—collective suggestion-making—including the dominant leader, and sometimes the entire group is influenced by the latter."[39] This hypothesis of a continuity between the couple and the crowd, both being subject to the principal laws of individual psychology, is the grounding for an epistemology: sociology is reduced to "psychology writ large."[40]

The second edition of *The Criminal Crowd*, unlike the first, included numerous analyses of public opinion and of the new "form of suggestion" represented by the press. The schema of suggestion transforms the journalist into a leader of his audience. "Created by the latter, he is able to lead it well beyond the point it would itself want to go,"[41] since the public most of the time is only "like the wet plaster on which the hand of the journalist makes his imprint." Any public is conditioned by "strange psychological fermentations," "impulses," "violent, criminal, or insane acts," "mysterious psychic reactions." Sighele even goes so far as to ask whether behind each public there are not "journalists who influence it by suggestion and provoke it, in the same way as behind each crowd there is always a sect that is, so to speak, its leaven."[42]

In his last book, published in 1908 under the title of *Letteratùra e Criminalità* (Literature and criminality), Sighele attempted a response by examining "literary suggestion." Taking as his corpus the novels of D'Annunzio, Zola, and Eugène Sue and analyzing the status they accorded to crime and its characters, he looked at the influence that literature might have on latent crime. He drew the following verdict: "It is beyond dispute that certain novels, plays, and phrases have an incendiary power with respect to that dry straw known as the public, especially the modern public, which is so nervous and excitable."[43] It remained for him only to incite writers to prove their responsibility in an era he described as being "as weak as it is cowardly," where "contemporary literature is nothing other than a clinic."

However, one should not be mistaken: in this examination of literature, novelists are not his real target. In fact, he celebrates Zola's courage and endorses the causes he defended. Unlike Le Bon and Bertillon, appointed in 1894 to report on the handwriting evidence in the Dreyfus Affair, Sighele took the side of the accused. In Eugène Sue he sees a social reformer and recognizes in him a "precursor of criminal anthropology," quoting the opening statement of Sue's popular novel *Les Mystères de Paris*:

> I want to try to put before the eyes of the reader some episodes in the life of other barbarians, as far outside our civilization as are the savage populations described by [James Fenimore] Cooper... These men have their own manners, their own women, their own language: a mysterious language, full of bizarre images and metaphors dripping with blood. Like the savages, these people call each other by nicknames borrowed from their cruelty, energy, certain good traits, and certain physical deformities.[44]

If Sue's approach converges with that of criminal anthropology, it is because he had an intuition of the cause of differences among people: "an arrested development" maintains the delinquent in a stage of savage brutality.

So in fact Sighele's target lay elsewhere: it was "trial literature," dramas that were resolved in criminal court, with coverage by journalists and authors who "search the most secret depths of the criminal life with the cold and lucid impassivity of the surgeon's knife," those dramas that enflame the reader more than imaginary stories do, and in which you find "not only the satisfaction of your curiosity, but a strange egoistic and feline emotion."[45] A behaviorist before his time, Sighele stigmatized the "effects" that this "apotheosis of crime" had on newspaper readers:

> Trial literature... reaches excesses to which it is pushed by the never-satisfied curiosity of the crowd... It is beyond doubt that the press intensifies this orgy by describing it and spreading its details everywhere. But it intensifies it unconsciously. It is the obscure artisan of crimes that are carried out by suggestion... I would say "journalistically." The example is contagious: the idea takes possession of a weak soul and becomes a sort of inevitability against which any struggle is impossible.[46]

Gustave Le Bon: From the Soul of the Race to the Soul of the Crowd

The invasion of foreigners is still more to be feared in that they are, naturally, inferior elements, those who do not manage to be self-sufficient in their own country, and so most of them emigrate. Our humanitarian principles condemn us to undergo an increasing invasion of foreigners ... If these invasions do not stop, it will not be long before in France a third of the population is German and a third Italian. What will become of the unity (or simply the existence) of a people in such circumstances? ... At the nexus of all historical and social questions is always the inevitable problem of races; it dominates all others.[47]

This passage figures in a book by Gustave Le Bon on the psychological laws of the evolution of peoples that appeared in 1894, one year before *The Crowd*, since before conceiving the latter, he had first thought through the psychology of whole peoples — and the two topics are imbricated.

Le Bon's judgments on the coexistence of races are extremely abrupt. The notion of "soul of the race," or, "in other words, the national soul," the "ancestral soul," is at the heart of his analysis. Any mixing of races is necessarily disastrous.

The union of whites with blacks, Hindus with Redskins, has no other result than to disaggregate among the products of these unions all the elements of stability of the ancestral soul without creating new such elements. People of mixed blood, such as those of Mexico and the Spanish republics of America, remain ungovernable for the sole reason that they are crossbreeds.[48]

The cause of all the evils in our societies is the "chimerical notion of the equality of men." The "modern egalitarian dream" pursued by education, which pretends to "reform the unjust laws of nature," is unrealizable.

No doubt education does allow us, thanks to the memory possessed by even the most inferior beings and that is in no way the privilege of man, to give an individual placed rather low on the human scale all the notions possessed by a European. One can easily make a secondary school graduate or a lawyer out of a Negro; but one gives him only a simple and superficial varnish without any effect on his mental constitution. What no education can give him, because heredity alone creates them, are the forms of thought, logic, and especially the character of Westerners.[49]

For Le Bon there are clearly superior and inferior peoples and races, and even within superior peoples there exist inferior beings. Le Bon draws on the anatomical and mathematical research done by Broca's team and on his own work on the variations in brain volume and its relation to variations in intelligence:

> Among inferior peoples or in the lower strata of superior peoples, men and women are intellectually very close. To the extent that a people become civilized or not, the sexes tend more and more to be differentiated. The volume of the skulls of men and women, even when one compares only—as I have done—subjects of the same age, height, and weight, present differences that very rapidly increase with the degree of civilization. Minor in the inferior races, these differences become immense in the superior races, where feminine skulls are often scarcely more developed than those of women of very inferior races. While the average male Parisian skull situates them among the largest known skulls, the average female Parisian skull classifies them among the smallest observed skulls, more or less at the level of those of the Chinese, scarcely larger than the feminine skulls of New Caledonia.[50]

The egalitarian ideal—same rights, same education—brandished by the modern woman is thus a dangerous chimera that, if triumphant, would end up "turning the European into a nomad without country or family."[51]

The slide from race to gender takes place naturally in *The Crowd*: "Crowds are everywhere distinguished by feminine characteristics, but Latin crowds are the most feminine of all."[52]

The inferior individual gains his strength by joining a group, whereas the superior man loses strength thereby. The analogy between the crowd and beings belonging to these "inferior forms of evolution such as the savage and the woman" (to whom Le Bon adds the child) is the last term of an equation developed in the shadow of a theory of race.[53] Impulsive, irritable, incapable of reasoning, exaggerated in sentiments, lacking in judgment and the critical spirit, the crowd commits acts much more under the influence of the spinal cord than under that of the brain. Or, in the terminology employed by Fournial: like the inferior individual, whose frontal lobe is less developed than the occipital lobe, the crowd is never a frontal being; it is scarcely "occipital" at all, but "spinal."

The crowd is a being unto itself. An agglomeration of individuals differs as much from the individuals who compose it as a living being differs from the cells that constitute it. There exists a "psychological law of the mental unity of crowds." A collective soul is formed, the "soul of the crowd," which combines with the invariant and dominant soul of the race. Moreover, it is for this reason that Anglo-Saxon crowds are very different from Latin crowds. Lombroso and Laschi had already said as much.

Different causes explain the appearance of the special characteristics of crowds. First of all, number alone gives a feeling of power inversely proportional to the feeling of responsibility. Then, a phenomenon of mental contagion or hypnotic order takes place. This contagion of ideas and emotions can occur because the individuals in the crowd become highly "suggestible." The individual plunged into a crowd falls into a state of fascination like the hypnotized subject in the hands of the hypnotist. His brain is paralyzed, his conscious personality evaporates. The individual is no longer "himself, but an automaton whom his will has become powerless to guide."[54] The leader or hypnotist—who in turn is hypnotized by the idea of which he has become the apostle—is recruited among "morbidly nervous, excitable, the half-deranged people who are bordering on madness."

Automatism, hypnosis, suggestion, hallucination, magnetism, somnambulism, collective hysteria—all the key words of crowd psychology belong to the register of the Parisian school of psychopathology, the school at the Salpêtrière Hospital where Jean-Martin Charcot (1825–93) taught. Its success is demonstrated by the fact that among the scientific congresses organized as part of the Universal Exposition in Paris in 1889, not just the criminal anthropology one but three others as well dealt with these subjects: one with magnetism, another with hypnotism, and the third with physiological psychology. In 1888, Charcot had even coined the term "ambulatory automaton"; he displayed vagabonds at his "Tuesday lectures" to illustrate the figure of the wanderer whom he considered as a regressive being, savage and degenerate. In 1894, one of his disciples published a book on the "dromomania of degenerates." At the Salpêtrière the mentally ill were treated by hypnosis. The ambulatory automaton was a living machine who wandered off anywhere, anytime, and acted in a sleepwalking manner until exhausted.[55] Here, too, photography was used to "stare" at subjects; at a time when Bertillon used it to record identifying marks and Marey used it to observe the mechanisms of movement, the portraits taken by Albert Londe (1857–1917) traced the symptoms of mental illness.[56]

Le Bon did not deal with the ambulatory vagabond, of course, but with the multitude in motion that he observed by the light of psychopathology, which focused on individuals who fell outside the normal order of things. The problem was that the conception he developed of the crowd, with all that it connoted of degeneration and regression, was not a phenomenon of the past. It constituted the horizon on which could already be discerned the present and a future era of crowds and their "collective logics": "The divine right of the masses is about to re-place the divine rights of kings," he wrote. The opinion and voice of crowds were becoming preponderant. One could not mistake the signs of the taking of power by these collective logics—in associations like trade unions, whose legal existence was recognized in France by a 1884 law, in labor bureaus and parliamentary assemblies. "Today the claims of the masses are becoming more and more sharply defined," wrote Le Bon,

> and amount to nothing less than a determination to utterly destroy society as it now exists, with a view to bringing it back to primitive communism, which was the normal condition of all human groups before the dawn of civilization. Limitation of the hours of labor, the nationalization of mines, railways, factories and the land, the equal distribution of all products, the elimination of all the upper classes for the benefit of the popular classes, etc. — these are the demands.[57]

In a word, society had entered an "era of universal disintegration."

As for the press, "which formerly directed opinion, it has had, like governments, to humble itself before the power of crowds."[58] "Today the writers have lost all influence and the newspapers only reflect opin-ion."[59] What is ironic about this apocalyptic diagnosis is that barely three years after the publication of The Crowd, the Dreyfus Affair and Zola's "J'accuse" clearly indicated the rising to power of intellectuals, and not their eclipse!

In 1921, Sigmund Freud (1856–1939) would take Le Bon to task for his "painting of the soul of crowds." Admitting having kept his distance from this polemic for thirty years, he refuted the notion of "tyranny of suggestion" (as he called it) among individuals and the contagion and prestige of leaders as psychological explanations of the psychic trans-formation of the individual in the crowd. He detected the same thesis in The Group Mind, published in 1920 by the head of the psychology of instincts school, William McDougall (1871–1938).

Suggestion is only a screen, Freud asserted, behind which is hidden another and deeper motivation. One must tear down the screen to escape from the impasse crowd psychology created by making the aptitude for suggestibility an originating phenomenon, a fundamental fact of psychic life. Relying on the concept of libido he had used in the study of psy-choneurosis, Freud ventured the following hypothesis: "Love relation-ships (or, to use a more neutral expression, emotional ties) also constitute the essence of the group mind." What characterizes the crowd are libid-inal ties. Each isolated individual is tied libidinally on the one hand to the leader, and on the other to other individuals in the crowd. In the first instance, the crowd owes its cohesion to the power of Eros. In the second instance, if the individual abandons his singularity in the crowd and lets himself be influenced by the suggestion of the others, he does so "because he feels the need of being in harmony with them rather than in opposition to them—so that perhaps after all he does it '*ihnen zu Liebe*' [for their sake]." It was for having neglected this libidinal claim and the mechanisms of the individual's emotional ties, the so-called identifications, that Prussian militarism, for example, "which was just as unpsychological as German science," proved incapable of countering the neurotic fear or anxiety that afflicted the German army and that rendered it so receptive to the fantastic promises of enemy propaganda during the First World War.[60] The army, along with the church, are the two "artificial crowds" on which Freud tested his hypothesis of the "libidinal investments" of the members of any crowd.

Gabriel Tarde: The Era of Publics

The fourth major figure in the history of crowd psychology is Gabriel Tarde (1843–1904). The same year as the publication of *The Criminal Crowd,* this precursor of social psychology shared his own reflections on the topic "The Crimes of Crowds" with participants at the third international congress on criminal anthropology in Brussels.[61] From the moment he expressed his points of agreement and divergences with Sighele, he became the omnipresent arbiter of the debates on the nature of the crowd. At this time, in 1892, he was still a magistrate in Sarlat in his native Dordogne. Two years later, at age fifty-one, he turned up in Paris, at the request of the minister of justice, who had asked him to reorganize criminal statistics (which his rival, the founder of sociology Émile Durkheim [1858–1917], would use to carry out his famous study of suicide!). In 1900, he was named to the chair of contemporary philosophy at the Collège de France.

Tarde was opposed to the narrow conception of collective action defended by crowd psychology, in particular by Le Bon. The crowd, in Tarde's view, was a social group of the past. The group of the future was the public—or publics. Printing, the railway, the telegraph, and the press had made possible the formation of a public whose main characteristic was to be indefinitely extensible. These changes were preceded by a long history of the development of the post, roads, permanent armies (which allowed soldiers from all provinces to get to know each other and fraternize on the battlefield), and earlier, the development of royal courts.

The "sensation of the new" is henceforth a given of civilized life. Binding together and condensing the habitual readers of the same newspaper into a kind of association (too little noticed yet one of the most important), this sensation "progresses along with sociability."[62] We know about the "force conveyed at a distance"—yet it is nothing compared to this "thought conveyed at a distance."[63]

Unlike the crowd, which is a concert of psychic contagions produced essentially by physical contact, the public is a purely spiritual grouping among individuals who are physically separated and whose cohesion is wholly mental. The substitution of publics for crowds takes place gradually:

> The formation of a public presupposes a mental and social
> evolution much more advanced than the formation of a crowd.
> The purely ideal suggestibility, the contagion without contact that
> is the condition for this purely abstract and nevertheless real
> grouping, this spiritualized crowd, elevated so to speak to a
> second degree of power, could only arise after many centuries of a
> coarser and more elementary kind of social life.[64]

Invisible contagion, suggestion at a distance, communion of suggested ideas—the language of psychopathology is of course still present with Tarde (and Freud would criticize him for it—without, however, discerning the gap that separated the psychology of crowds from that of publics). But these references do not make up the basis of an intellectual system.

Crowd and public are two polar opposites in a social evolution that began with the family and the horde, which was a crude band of pillagers and a crowd on the march. Regarding the public, "the imprint of race is much less profound than it is on the crowd."[65] The transformation of the crowd into a public is accompanied by progress in tolerance—or else an increase in skepticism. One belongs to only one crowd at a time, but one may simultaneously belong to several publics. Society is divided more and more into publics that are superimposed on religious, economic, aesthetic, and political divisions—into corporations, sects, schools, parties. This transformation of all groups into publics was, in Tarde's view, inevitable, and it reflected the necessity of a "regular communication of those associated by a continual flow of common information and enthusiasms."

Le Bon, in his nostalgia for a yesteryear before the spread of the "popular crowd," took refuge in apocalypse. By contrast, Tarde thought that what mattered most was to define the consequences of publics for the destinies of various types of groups—political parties, religious groupings, professional bodies, parliaments—from the standpoint of "their duration, their solidity, their strength, their struggles, and their alliances."[66] These groups and publics would become more and more complex as they were increasingly confronted by internationalization:

> The winged words of the papers easily cross borders which were never crossed by the voice of the famous orator, or the party leader. Certain large newspapers, the *Times*, the *Figaro*, and certain journals have their public spread throughout the entire world. The religious, scientific, economic, and aesthetic *publics* are essentially and *constantly* international; religious, scientific, etc. *crowds* are so only rarely, in the form of a congress. And the congresses could only become international because they were preceded in this direction by their respective publics.[67]

Journalism is a "suction pump of information," which then propagates it to all points on earth. This information constitutes a more and more irresistible force.

However, Tarde conceded that the line of demarcation between the crowd and the public is sometimes difficult to trace. The public is always a "virtual crowd" and the collapse of a public into a crowd is always possible:

> The public is a much less blind and much more durable crowd, whose most perspicacious rage is amassed and sustained over months and years. One may also be surprised that after having talked so much about the crimes of the crowd, we have said nothing about the crimes of the public. For assuredly there are criminal and ferocious publics, thirsty for blood, as there are criminal crowds.[68]

Much emphasis was put on the fact that the public might be the victim of a veritable crime by the press. But did it follow that the public could itself be the criminal?

Tarde's writings on the constitution of publics swarm with observations and hypotheses that convey a great intellectual curiosity about the daily phenomena of communication in his time. In an article titled "Opinion and Conversation," he ponders the future of private letters:

> The utilitarian terseness of telegrams and telephone conversations, which are trespassing on the domains of correspondence, has repercussions on the style of the most intimate letters. Invaded by the press from one side, by the telegraph and the telephone from the other, preyed upon on both sides at once, if correspondence still lives and even, according to postal statistics, gives illusory signs of prospering, it can only be because of the increase in business letters.[69]

From conversation to correspondence, from personal opinions to local opinions, from the latter to national opinion and "worldwide" opinion, Tarde considers the long secular process that results in what he calls "the unification of the public mind" or "rational internationalism."

But we still lack a concept for fully grasping Tarde's line of thought on crowds and publics. In his first lecture on the topic "The Crimes of Crowds," he introduced his subject by asking: "How is a crowd formed?" His answer: "By virtue of sympathy, source of imitation, and the vital principle of social bodies."[70]

He had begun to work on the notion of imitation in the 1880s, publishing articles that were edited in augmented form in 1890 in *Les Lois de l'imitation* (*The Laws of Imitation*), the first book in which he ventured into a domain other than criminal studies. It would be followed in 1895 by a sequel, *La Logique sociale*.

The idea of imitation was not new. It belonged to a long, mostly British, tradition illustrated by sociologists such as Spencer and economists such as Smith, Malthus, Stuart Mill, or even Walter Bagehot (1826–77), one of the founders of modern political liberalism.[71] In 1869 Bagehot had published a book in which he makes imitation an essential element in nation-building. The British film historian Michael Chanan points out that two years earlier Bagehot had published *The English Constitution,* in which he stresses the importance of "theatrical elements" in inducing "reverence on the part of the 'ruder sorts of men' towards the 'plain, palpable ends of government.' "[72] This proposition seemed to him the useful complement of a strategy aiming to produce the adherence of recalcitrants to a national idea by virtue of imitation. The individual fashions himself or herself through imitation.

Imitation, for Tarde, precursor of social psychology, had a very precise meaning, which flowed from the axiom that the psychological is explained by the social precisely because the social is born from the psychological. It implied "an action at a distance of one mind upon another, consisting of the almost photographic reproduction of a cerebral image onto the sensitive plate of another brain."[73] The imitation of another person is the imprint of interspiritual photography, willed or not, passive or active, out of almost machinelike habit or thoughtful will. Along with heredity and invention (or creation), imitation is one of the three forms of universal repetition.

Imitation is a social bond; any social relation, any social fact, is a relation of imitation. It is what makes a society into a "group of people who present among themselves many similarities produced by imitation or counterimitation."[74] There are many varieties of imitation: imitation by custom, by fashion, by sympathy or obedience, through training or upbringing; it can be naive or thoughtful. Imitation cannot be conceived without invention and individual initiative. The most imitative individual is an innovator in some respect, even if he or she is unaware of it. Imitation, opposition (or counterimitation), and invention are the three tendencies that combine to produce a society in which both "the purest and most powerful individualism and consummate sociability" flourish.

One of the fundamental laws of imitation is that it functions from top to bottom, from the center to the periphery. This is the case, for example, with the dissemination of values from the capital to the provinces:

> Paris rules royally, orientally, over the provinces, more than the court ever securely ruled over the city. Each day, by telegraph and train, it sends throughout France its ideas, its will, its conversations, its ready-made revolutions, clothing, and furnishings. The suggestive fascination, the imperative that it exercises instantly over a vast territory, is so profound, so complete, and so continuous that almost nobody is struck by it. This magnetization has become chronic. It is called quality and freedom. In vain does the worker in the city think himself egalitarian and work to destroy the bourgeoisie by becoming bourgeois—he is no less himself an aristocrat, very admired and envied by the peasant. The peasant is to the worker what the worker is to the boss—hence emigration from the countryside.[75]

This vision of imitation as the spreading of a model emanating from the center is further extrapolated by Tarde to the relations among nations.

On the basis of analyses of this type, some have counted Tarde among the proponents of "diffusionism," the evolutionist conception of the diffusion of innovations that, as we have seen, divided cultural anthropology in the last quarter of the nineteenth century, and would be taken up in the following century by the functionalist sociology of development/modernization, in which imitation of the models of core countries would be elevated to a general rule for overcoming economic and cultural backwardness. However, Tarde never took the view of intercultural relations held by this school of thought, and to reduce him to this current would be to deform the history of ideas. Testimony from 1937 by Robert Löwie is pertinent here:

> Where Tarde sees more clearly than the contemporary evolutionist anthropologists is in his objective attitude toward the civilization of his period. Here there is no trace of smugness, no suggestion that in 1885 man had reached a peak from which he might look down pityingly, if not scornfully, upon his predecessors. Tarde does not accept the traditional fetishes of modern life ... This sane position reacts on the judgment of savagery. Unlike Lubbock, who

minimizes moral sentiments among primitive peoples, Tarde convincingly shows that they are identical on their and our level, being simply more narrowly applied at the earlier stage.[76]

This position clearly breaks with the xenophobic basis on which Le Bon developed his theory of race and the crowd; moreover, it helped Tarde to exercise a certain influence over the cultural anthropology of his time. He left his mark, for example, on the young German-American ethnographer Franz Boas (1858–1942), one of the pioneers of functional theory in its American version and one of the first social scientists in the United States to criticize theories that explained intellectual and mental differences by membership in a race. But Tarde's influence went beyond anthropology and extended to North American sociology in its period of early development.

The Chicago School and the Psychosociology of Interaction

Attentive to the ordinary aspects of social life, Tarde never stopped contesting in his many writings the one-sided approaches of the social sciences of his day. He criticized political economy for its tendency to economism, for its resistance to treating the three aspects that seemed to him essential for understanding economic life at the daily level: *repetition,* or the propagation of habits of consumption called *needs,* and the corresponding habits of work; *opposition,* or the struggles among producers and among consumers and between the two; and finally *adaptation,* or the totality of successful inventions. Above all, he reproached political economists for not taking into account "currents of modes or passions," and for not "examining the caprices that are born and that extend by interpsychic means to the formation of desires and influence the conditions of exchange and value."[77]

To scientific sociology and its founder Émile Durkheim—who considered that one should not explain social phenomena only by other social phenomena, and that social facts exist outside the particular cases where they are realized—Tarde objected that one must be able to "take account of the subjective nature of social interactions," or else risk reifying social facts and letting them be swallowed up by physical phenomena in the purest Comtean tradition. For him, sociology should be the "solar microscope of psychology."[78] Reduced to a Manichaean dilemma between sociologism and psychologism, the debate between "schools" would be too quickly truncated.

Still, in France after Tarde's death there would be a long silence in French social science concerning the means of communication and formation of public opinion. A paradox would appear: Tarde's studies would contribute to the formation of the bases of North American sociology with its psychosociological orientation, and more precisely the nascent sociology of the media, whereas in France the institutional hegemony of positivist sociology, later nurtured by official Marxism, would indefinitely postpone the analysis of the stakes of this new era of publics foreseen by the founder of social psychology.

Tarde's influence would be felt more particularly on the Chicago School, that is, the department of sociology and anthropology at the University of Chicago, founded in 1892, which would become in the 1910s the foremost center of sociological teaching and research in the United States and would remain so for more than two decades. Tarde's studies would serve to define the complex phenomena related to immigration and ethnicity in the urban neighborhoods of the United States; the seminal work on the Polish peasant transplanted to the United States by William I. Thomas (1863–1947) and Florian Znaniecki (1882–1958) was based on research undertaken in 1908 and published ten years later.[79] And, above all, Tarde's work would guide the representative of this current, Robert Ezra Park (1864–1944), in formulating his first hypotheses on the relation between the media and the organization of democratic life in the framework of his "human ecology."[80] Park, author of a doctoral dissertation on the crowd and the public (1903) and one of the leaders of the school for forty years, would cross-fertilize these hypotheses with those of the German sociologist Georg Simmel (1858–1918), whose courses he had taken.

The encounter between the epistemological concerns of the Chicago School and the work of Simmel and Tarde influenced the study of the "small objects" of collective life and prefigured a sociology of everyday life, of commonplace activities and "experienced culture."[81] If the approaches of the two Europeans found an echo in the United States, it was because within the geographical and theoretical perspective that predominated in Europe at the time, Tarde and Simmel were the exceptions who broke with the dominant speculative vision that constructed and interpreted the facts on the basis of a corpus of conceptual abstractions. Their way of conceiving social science is nearer to that of nascent American psychosociology than to the academic sociology that was then taking shape in the majority of European universities.

The formation of the department of sociology and anthropology at Chicago at the close of the nineteenth century was in fact a sign among others of the birth of a tradition in social sciences that distinguished itself from the European one. The two traditions tended to be systematically opposed, with empiricism on one side, theoreticism on the other. The former privileged the inductive approach to a kind of research that sought immediate social applications, a science useful to a "philosophy of action." The latter opted for a hypothetical-deductive approach and constructed its body of knowledge of social reality on the basis of a system of postulates.

North American sociology took nourishment from the philosophy of pragmatism inaugurated by Charles Sanders Peirce (1839–1914) and William James (1842–1910). In the years 1867–68, Peirce had begun to develop a theory of signs that he called "semeiotic" or "semiotic," an intellectual enterprise that occupied him his entire life. In Europe, the Swiss Ferdinand de Saussure (1857–1913) developed the bases of what he called semiology. Unlike the latter, which was reduced to the sole linguistic model, the semiotic method was not primarily linguistic; it treated all human creations, all signs, not just linguistic ones; it did not aim to decode meaning, but to elucidate the relation between a sign and its object, and in this respect it was faithful to the philosophy of pragmatism. This philosophy was conjugated in fact with a radical empiricism and a theory of language: ideas are mere propositions whose application constitutes the only test of their meaning. As summed up by Peirce, a sign or *representamen* is constituted by three elements: the ground, the object, and the interpretant. "A sign, or *representamen*," he wrote,

> is something which stands to somebody for something in some respect or capacity. It addresses somebody, that is, it creates in the mind of that person an equivalent sign, or perhaps a more developed sign. That sign which it creates I call the *interpretant* of the first sign. The sign stands for something, its *object*. It stands for that object, not in all respects, but in reference to a sort of idea, which I have sometimes called the *ground* of the representamen.[82]

Pragmatism is defined as a "social philosophy of democracy," and as such it orients a conception of social-science field research, linked to social work and to reforms; one discerns in it the strong presence of the ideals of Christian charity in its Protestant version. John Dewey (1859–1952) found in pragmatism the principles of a philosophy of education and a practical pedagogy. The psychosociologist George Herbert Mead (1863–1931) developed "symbolic interactionism," a theory that broke with Durkheim's view of actors, seen as too subjective to express the social world. It stressed the symbolic nature of life in society and viewed social meanings as "produced by the interacting activities of actors"; it postulated that knowledge of the world and of our action in it can depend only on them. In its initial formulation, it gave rise to an ethnographic kind of methodology, seen as being the only one capable of accounting for these interactions and for those of the individual and his environment: case studies, monographs on neighborhoods, life histories, and participant observation.[83] These were the protocols of investigation that the engineer and economist Frédéric Le Play, motivated by a religiously tinted (this time Catholic) viewpoint, tried to realize in France; he failed to do so for lack of institutional support within the academic world. Meanwhile, the Scot Patrick Geddes, in symbiosis with American researchers, openly shared these methods in the first two decades of the century.

One Chicago-allied sociologist, a former student of Dewey and Mead and a faculty member at the University of Michigan, assured the transfer of the interactionist schema to the study of communication processes: Charles Horton Cooley (1864–1929). He is also the author of one of the first works of sociology to explicitly tackle American society from the communications angle, *The Theory of Transportation* (1894). Still very influenced in this book by Spencer's organicist model of the social whole, he would gradually shift, under the influence of interactionism, toward the study of "psychic mechanisms," without ceasing to confront the impossible task of articulating the mobility of individual psychologies with the weight of society, free will with determinisms.[84]

Nearly a century after the publication of *The Laws of Imitation* and *Social Logic*, the crisis of structural-functionalist sociology, which had been hegemonic for decades, would confer a new legitimacy on the question of the "subjective nature of social interactions" and of "interpsychics," the major concern of Gabriel Tarde. The return, however ambiguous, to daily life, the shift to culture and to the contemporary ethnographic perspective, and the crumbling of utopias and systematic, totalizing discourses about the perfectibility of societies—all those developments would oblige people to recognize the need for an approach to the social bond that would both restore individuality to actors and be attentive to causes, structures, and determinations.[85]

In his attack on the restrictive character of academic disciplines, Tarde had written: "Historic evolution always spends its energy resolving the rigorously insoluble problems, reconciling the irreconcilable, squaring the circle."[86]

Chapter 11

The Pace of the Human Motor

In the last two decades of the nineteenth century, a need was felt in the factory, stadium, and barracks for an expertise in kinematics in order to master bodies in movement and improve performance and productivity. The invention of the motor, whose purpose is to set in motion a series of organs for an infinite range of functions, brought life back to the analogy between the animal and the machine.

In France, physiologists perfected for their experiments certain instruments to record the work of the muscles. The successive improvements in these devices for measuring movement thanks to new photographic technologies were a decisive step toward the invention of the motion picture. In the United States, the decomposition of time and motion and the disciplining of the workers' gestures were the business of mechanical engineers, who were converted into economists to formulate a new scientific organization of labor based on the maximization of output. This was the end result of a "managerial revolution" that began with the construction and operation of rail networks.

The Recording Devices of the Physiologist Étienne-Jules Marey

In March 1883, experiments began at the Physiological Station recently built on the grounds of the future Parc des Princes stadium in Paris, thanks to subsidies from the municipal council and the Ministry of Education. The following problems were on the agenda: (1) to determine the series of movements that occur in human locomotion of various kinds, such as walking, running, leaping; (2) to find the external conditions that influence these movements—those, for example, that increase the rapidity of pace or the length of the step, and thus exercise a positive or negative influence on human locomotion; (3) to measure the energy expended each instant in various locomotive actions, in order to find the most favorable conditions for the efficient use of this energy.[1]

The site consisted of a huge chalet containing a circular and perfectly level track, formed of two concentric lanes; the inside one, four meters wide, was designed for experiments with horses, while the outside one was for humans. Along these lanes was strung a telegraph wire whose posts were spaced fifty meters apart. Each time an animal or person passed a post, a telegraphic signal thereby produced was automatically registered in a room of the main building. One could thus at any moment know the speed, the degree of acceleration or deceleration, and the frequency of the subject's steps. The subject could be carrying a burden or not, according to the hypothesis to be verified.

At the center of the track was a tower with a mechanical drum to regulate the subject's pace. This drum was operated by an electromagnetic switch located in the main building and connected to the track by a telegraph wire. From the center of the track there also ran a railway spur on which a small wagon containing a photographic chamber rolled: inside this chamber instantaneous shots were taken of persons whose successive paces were to be analyzed. These photographs were taken each time the moving person, dressed in white, passed in front of a black screen, in the form of a canopy, situated alongside the outside lane, three meters wide, fifteen meters long, and four meters high.

The director of this laboratory station was Étienne-Jules Marey (1830–1904), holder of the chair of Natural History of Organized Bodies at the Collège de France. This physiologist explained the practical interest of his team's experiments on the mechanisms of different walking and running movements as analogous to

> those having for their object the determination of the product of machines, and the most favorable conditions for this production . . . They [physiologists] will teach us, doubtless, how best to utilize the muscular work of man and of the domestic animals; they will lay down rules which shall control the physical exercises of the young people, the work of the artisan, the drill of the soldier.[2]

Marey was a theoretician of movement, which he defined as "the relation of time to space," or "the most apparent of the characteristics of life, manifest in all its functions and the very essence of many of them."[3] These functions belonged to various categories: some corresponded to "actions of organic life"; they were carried out inside organs and independently of will, as was the case with blood circulation and respiration. With others, conscious control regulated speed, energy, and duration; these were "acts of relational life," such as muscular actions of locomotion on the ground, in the air, or in the water, but also phonation or the movements of speech organs and associated air movements (tonality of sounds and constitution of vowels).

In order to observe these movements and to trace this relation between space and time, Marey used registering devices or "graphic inscriptors" that he either invented or refined; these devices translated into graphs the external signs of the life functions—heartbeats and artery pulses, respiratory movements and muscle contraction. He began with the chronostylograph, an instrument in which a clocklike motion of a uniform speed guided a sheet of paper under a stylus that traced the curve of a phenomenon; the myograph measured muscle tremors; the sphygmograph recorded pulse rates, while the pneumograph recorded respiration, and the cardiograph registered heartbeats.

The principle of the registering or recording device goes back to the eighteenth century and was the creation of meteorologists. The first anemometer, whose function is to detect the speed and direction of the wind, was invented in 1734 by the Frenchman Louis-Léon d'Ons-en-Bray (1678–1754). Measuring instruments for temperature variations, barometric pressure, the speed and direction of the wind, and levels of precipitation had continued to improve since then.

The name "Station" taken by the center for physiological experimentation testified, therefore, to a thread running from meteorology to this branch of medical science. "Like meteorologists," explained Marey,

> physiologists have felt that the senses are not sufficient for observing simultaneously all the phenomena of which the organism is the theater. Temperature, pressure and speed of blood circulation, the force and rapidity of muscular action—everything had to be measured, and noted with precision, while taking into account the various perturbing influences that the physiologist is used to studying.[4]

But the kinship stops here. Meteorologists' inscribing devices are called "passive": over periods of years, they trace the fluctuations of atmospheric conditions. What remained to be invented were "subtle" devices, capable of recording hypersensitive phenomena, their frequency and rapidity in a fraction of a second. It was here that a major invention by Thomas Young (1773–1829) came into play: the chronograph. In 1807 this English physician registered graphically on the smoked surface of a rotating cylinder the vibrations of solids and cords. The stylus brushing against the rotating paper cylinder showed how many oscillations per second the cord performed. According to the number of recorded vibrations, one knew the time that a certain length of paper took to run through. This first graphic measure of time was then perfected by researchers like Léon Foucault (1819–68) and Hermann von Helmholtz (1821–94) who standardized the cylinder's movement. Young's invention is to be situated in the early history of electroacoustics that would take off much later, in December 1877, when Thomas Edison patented the phonograph, a device that included a cylinder. The recording of vibrations took the form of indentations pressed into a sheet of tinfoil by a vibrating recording stylus; this tinfoil was wrapped around a cylinder that rotated as the sounds were being recorded.

The use of automatic recording instruments in physiology began relatively late, around 1850. Previously, the inscribing device had begun its career in another realm, that of mechanics. James Watt's apparatus, designed to assure the graphic measurement of the energy generated by steam in a pump, had already produced several more or less direct offshoots. The Scottish mechanic traced the movements of his pressure gauge on a cylinder that turned thanks to the action of the pump's piston. The next step was the dynamometer, whose purpose was to measure the intensity of power generated by machines and motors.

The first application of registering devices to physiology took place in Germany in 1847, when Karl Ludwig (1816–95) conceived for the study of blood pressure an inscribing manometer that he called the *kymographion* or kymograph. He was not able to apply it to human beings, however, since it required direct insertion into the artery. Certain of his compatriots refined devices for studying circulation, respiration, and muscular action. This "graphic method" had not yet arrived in France in 1857, the year when Marey undertook to create his own version of the sphygmograph.

From the Chronophotograph to the Cinematograph

The second generation of recording devices opened with what Marey first called "photochronography," a term that would later be replaced by chronophotography or the "application of instantaneous photography to the study of movement."[5] In brief, the purpose of chronophotography was to determine the "trajectory" of any moving object, the different places in space that it crossed. More explicitly, it is the "method that *analyzes* movements by means of a series of images collected at very short and equal intervals of time; a method that, by thus representing the successive attitudes and positions of an animal, for example, allows us to follow all the phases of its gaits and even to translate them into veritable geometric graphs."[6]

In 1873, the French astronomer and physician Jules Janssen (1824–1907) came up with the idea of taking photographic images automatically of the successive phases of a phenomenon, in particular, the passage of the planet Venus across the face of the sun. With his own invention, the "astronomical revolver," he took the first chronophotograph on a single glass plate. In front of a telescope pointed at the sun he fixed a photographic chamber whose light-sensitive plate, in the shape of a circle, turned around its center in jerking movements like the barrel of a Colt so as to present, every seventy seconds, a different point of its circumference to the lens. In this series of images arranged into an arc, one sees the planet enter the solar disc, cross it, and finally leave. Knowing the interval of the images, one can measure the speed of this phenomenon. Janssen sensed the possibility of photographing the variations of a very quick movement in a series of images taken at much closer intervals. But a major technical obstacle remained: plates for instantaneous impression had not yet appeared, since photography was still in the wet collodion stage.

Success was finally achieved in 1878 by an English photographer established in San Francisco, Eadweard Muybridge (1830–1904; curiously the very same dates as Marey), in collaboration with the railroad engineer John D. Isaacs. He was able to capture the phases of a horse's gait, even at its fastest gallop. In order to do this along the horse's track, he stationed twenty-four lenses whose shutters were kept closed by electromagnets. Across the track he stretched twenty-four electric trip wires. As it ran, the animal broke the wires one by one, tripping the shutters.

At the origin of Muybridge's experiment, as Marey would recount it later in a lecture in 1899, lay Marey's own chronographic study, which had succeeded in 1872 in showing that a galloping horse rests first on one hoof, then on three, then on two, and again on one—by placing in the horseshoe a rubber bulb connected by a long tube to a stylus moved by compressed air and tracing its line on the cylinder held by the rider. Marey had then asked a certain Colonel Duhousset, who was both an equestrian specialist and a draftsman, to draw figures representing the postures of the horse as they could be deduced from this abstract chronography. These images of the quadruped would reach the hands of the former governor of California and railroad magnate Leland Stanford, who, incredulous, financed Muybridge's experiment. The photos only confirmed the hand drawings.

The same year in which Muybridge performed his experiments, George Eastman, future founder of Kodak, developed an alternative dry-plate process using gelatin-silver-bromide (an emulsion invented in 1871 by the Briton Richard Leach Maddox, who substituted it for collodium), thus opening up new perspectives in scientific experimentation.

With its black screen, its scaffolding to facilitate downward plunging views, and its black darkroom mounted on rails, the Physiological Station became the center of development for the applications of chronophotography. In 1882, Marey took up Janssen's idea and built a "photographic rifle" that seized images eight hundred times faster. This time his goal was to analyze birds in free flight. In the barrel of the gun he placed a long-range lens; in the breech, a circular plate that turned and presented before the lens different points on its circumference. A trigger similar to that of an ordinary rifle put the gear into motion. A cartridge belt of sorts collected the exposed plates.

Marey had special devices built for shooting. He worked with chronophotography on fixed plates that gave him proof of the movements of a white body moving in front of a black background. In 1887, he tried another procedure, chronophotography on mobile film, after the appearance of Kodak's roll film known as "paper stripping film," that is, long bands of paper covered with gelatin-silver-bromide, which would soon be followed by celluloid-base roll film. In 1899, Marey made a new rifle, electrically operated and loaded with a film strip twenty meters long in 35 mm format. The first arm yielded only twelve images. The same year, he adapted the chronophotograph for the study of movements that took place in the field of a microscope.

In the complementary area of reproduction of analyzed movement, or "synthesis," Marey experimented in 1893 with the chronophotographic projector. But it had not been perfected: the images jumped due to the unevenness of their intervals. The previous year in the United States, Thomas Edison had opened to the public the first "kinetoscope parlor" and succeeded in selling his device to the organizer of the Chicago Exposition. In 1894, a first demonstration of the kinetoscope took place in Paris. Edison had the advantage of having found a solution to the problem of giving images regular intervals, by perforating the filmstrip with a series of equidistant holes and causing it to be driven by a pegged cylinder. But one problem remained: this machine offered only a brief peep show for the pleasure of a single viewer.

In 1895, Auguste and Louis Lumière solved the problem with their cinématographe. The band of the kinetoscope stayed in constant motion and the clearness of the images was obtained by the brevity of the exposure, lasting only a tiny fraction of a second (1/7,000). They borrowed from Edison the sprocket holes by which the film was driven and managed to control the speed of the teeth that seized the film so as to avoid tearing. To govern this movement, the two brothers manufactured an essential piece, the "excentric cam," adapting the model of the mechanism on a sewing machine that presses the cloth against the feed. Finally, for the projection of the positive image on the screen, the Lumières reduced the rate of exposure from Edison's forty-eight images per second to sixteen per second, the theoretical standard that would be used in silent pictures, and had recourse to a powerful lamp to illuminate the film. The first public exhibition of moving images projected by their cinématographe took place in Paris in December 1895. The illusion of movement created by this device was perfect.

In 1896, projectors were launched on the market. The commercialization of film began in fairs and traveling shows, a situation that lasted roughly until 1903 in the United States and 1907 in Europe. The first permanent movie theater was founded in Los Angeles in 1902. Soon large production companies arose: Pathé and Gaumont in France; Edison, Biograph, and Vitagraph in the United States; and Messter in Germany.[7] Between 1907 and 1913, various independent companies founded the Hollywood studios and gave rise to the star system, when Carl Laemmle and R. H. Cochrane, founders of the Independent Picture Company, made the experiment of indicating the name of an actress in the film's credit titles.

At the Paris Exposition of 1889, which also celebrated the fiftieth anniversary of the invention of photography, Marey had a long discussion with Edison, the future inventor of the kinetoscope. Ten years later, he wrote: "I had the occasion to show him, at the exhibit of Fontaine the electrician, an electrophotographic zootrope. The kinetoscope, with which he better produced a synthesis of the same kind, is not without resemblance to my device with rollers, and yet the American inventor working on his own was in no way inspired by it."[8]

At the 1900 Exposition, Marey presided over the photography commission. In a great wood-framed window with a floral decoration, he exhibited the instruments and images of the short history of chronophotography: a set of eighteen devices, from Janssen's revolver to his own electric rifle. It was the first historical retrospective of image in movement.

When all is said and done, what did this learned physiologist think was cinema's function? Two passages in his writings shed some light on this. In 1899, in the conclusion to his book on chronophotography, he notes:

> The merits of chronophotographic analysis do not exclude those of synthesis. The appeal of spectacles that the latter method gives us in the form of animated photography has been a powerful stimulus for the perfecting of these devices; the clearness of the images and the greatness of their dimensions are important

conditions to be achieved in any case. Moreover, it has allowed us to understand what our eye can see; animated photography opens a vast new field for scientific study. It can, in effect, popularize knowledge of a large number of phenomena now known only to fervent observers of nature.[9]

But some months later, he confessed in his report on the Paris Exposition: "The animated projections, of such lively interest to the public, have few advantages from a scientific standpoint; they give us nothing in fact that our eye cannot see with more clarity. At most we might ask projection to slow down a movement if it is too quick and to accelerate it if it escapes observation by its excessive slowness."[10] From the standpoint of research on movement, only chronophotography on fixed plates, he stressed, "has furnished experimental solutions to a great number of problems in geometry, mechanics, physics, and physiology that no other method could have offered as easily."[11]

Having come to cinematography propelled by the methodological needs of his experimentation, Marey would be motivated by the latter throughout his career.

A New *Discourse on Method*

Cinematography was chronologically the last of the experimental tools that Marey was led to study. Prior to it he worked with recorders or inscriptors. And before that, there had been the "graphic representation of phenomena," a question that had already captured the attention of Descartes in his *Discourse on Method*. Marey, following d'Ons-en-Bray, proclaimed Descartes to be his guiding reference.

In 1878 he published *La Méthode graphique dans les sciences expérimentales et principalement en physiologie et en médecine* (The graphic method in the experimental sciences). This is the missing link we need to reconstruct the genealogy of the central focus of his research. Marey devoted the entire first part of the book to "graphic representation." In the introductory note, he wrote: "Everything the mind can conceive and measure with exactitude can be expressed graphically clearly and precisely: numbers, lengths, durations, and forces find in the use of graphic figures their most concise and striking expression."[12]

In approaching the subject, he forgot about the second part of his book's title. Abandoning his usual disciplinary area, he turned into a theoretician of the mode of representation of volume, time, and space, taking his examples from a broad array of phenomena: demographic movements, curves of agricultural production, circulation flows by land, rail, and water routes, figurative maps of commercial flows, and statistical maps on education, criminality, and the occurrence of diseases. Medical and meteorological curves, magnetic variations, and many other aspects of social and economic life could be translated into figures and graphs. Nor did he neglect military concerns; the "figurative map," for example, seemed for him self-evidently suitable for "portraying the sphere of action of forts, whose range of fire extends to variable distances in different directions, depending on the caliber of its cannons and the level of the terrain."[13]

Conciseness, clarity, and precision were the terms he customarily used to describe the project underlying this kind of graphic method. He sensed the relative novelty of this new technique for the public when he recalled that it was only in 1789 that the first statistical graphs appeared in political economy, in a work by William Playfair (1759–1823) on the "linear arithmetical tables of commerce, finances, and debt." This British economist had invented the idea of translating into graphs the yearly variations of the kingdom's debt in the preceding century, but he ran up against the difficulty of making his eighteenth-century public understand how the dimension of a line could express a sum of money.

The rest of Marey's book goes on naturally to treat other modes of graphic method for the experimental sciences, including recording devices and, in the second, revised edition, chronophotography.

The context of Marey's experimental project was a society in which, in his own words, "scientific questions are intimately linked to economic problems, or rather, are dominated by them."[14] In his own lifetime, his utilitarian research produced effects well beyond his own field. Chronophotography was applied to falling bodies, the resistance of air to differently inclined surfaces, hydrodynamics, wave movements of liquids, currents, and eddies, oscillations and vibrations, the rocking movement of ships, vibrations in metal bridges, cord vibrations, and of course ballistic experiments, where the notion of trajectory took on its full meaning. The study of bird flight, which began in the 1860s by installing in the Collège de France a kind of turntable pulled by a bird held in a corset and linked to inscriptors by rubber tubes, was of great interest to aviation in its nascent stage. Marey was designated in 1898 to present a report to the Academy of Sciences on the first flight worthy of the name, accomplished in the preceding year by Clément Ader in the "Avion III."

Gymnastic activities occupied the choice place in studies of locomotion: the high jump and the pole vault, fencing, foot and bicycle races. Georges Demenÿ, his assistant, author of an essential book on training in physical movements, taught applied physiology at the military school of gymnastics in Joinville and was professor for the city of Paris in the same discipline, at a time when the Baron de Coubertin was waging a campaign to rehabilitate physical education.[15] Other researchers at the Station, such as Charles Comte and Félix Regnault, at the army's request, compared the "flexing" technique of marching and running with the ordinary one. This led them to recommend this technique, very close to that of Sinhalese and Japanese soldiers, for the French troops. Similar concerns for bettering performances motivated studies of the movements of the horse, which was still essential to military strategy, and experiments on the training of dogs. Later, during World War I, Marey's disciples would place their "ergonomics" in the service of the armed forces by testing on the battlefield the aptitude and reaction times to visual and auditory stimuli of machine gunners, and by calculating their "index of fatigability."

In 1874, in the first edition of *La Machine animale*, Marey had written about "animated motors": "We must accept as a way of expressing work, effort multiplied by space covered."[16] He took as examples a horse pulling a boat, a man planing a board, and a bird flapping its wings. The same year, Marey presented to the Academy of Sciences a memorandum titled "Du moyen d'économiser le travail moteur de l'homme et des animaux" (Ways of economizing the motor efforts of men and animals). He included in this report the results of his experiments measuring the muscular effort of men or animals harnessed to a carriage, and their implications for productivity. He concluded: "The economy of labor and the reduction of fatigue obtained with the aid of elastic traction seem to us to constitute an important application of physiology to the betterment of the fate of man and animals."[17]

Twenty years later, the engineer Charles Frémont undertook in Marey's laboratory the first chronophotographic studies of the economy of movement in the workplace. Deconstructing the whole work cycle of a blacksmith wielding his hammer, he concluded that, in Diderot's and d'Alembert's *Encyclopédie,* "the representation of all movements was erroneous."[18]

La Machine animale opens as follows:

> Quite often and in all epochs, people have compared living beings to machines, but it is only these days that one can understand the implications and accuracy of this comparison . . . Modern ingenuity has created machines much more legitimately comparable to animated motors, which in effect, in return for the little fuel they burn, unleash the force necessary to set in motion a series of organs . . . Thus, we often borrow from pure mechanics the synthetic demonstrations of a phenomenon of animal life.[19]

Taylor and the Scientific Organization of Labor

The experiments of Frederick Winslow Taylor (1856–1915) are contemporary with those of the Physiological Station. According to the American engineer, it was natural laziness or "loafing" and systematic "soldiering" that prevented the realization of maximum productivity in factories. The former was engendered by natural instinct, that is, the tendency of the "average man" to take it easy and work slowly; the latter resulted "from more intricate second thoughts and reasoning caused by their relations with other men" and stimulated "mutual suspicion" and "discord" between employers and workers.[20]

Hired as an ordinary worker by the Midvale Steel Company in 1878, Taylor climbed up the ladder in eight years to the position of chief engineer. His biographers recount that the young Taylor, crowned doubles tennis champion of the United States in 1881, investigated the shape of the rackets and invented for his own use a grip better adapted to high performance; much later, at the time of his retirement, he endeavored to determine the ideal chemical composition of the soil so that grass would offer the least possible resistance to the rolling of a tennis or golf ball. In 1882, as factory manager, he began to develop the principles of *scientific management,* a notion that would not be enunciated explicitly until thirty years later. Prior to this, the Taylor method, as defined in his publications, would successively take the names of *piece-rate system, shop management,* and *task system.*

Taylor presented many of his writings before members of the recently founded American Society of Mechanical Engineers (ASME), which he joined in 1885 and of which he would later be president. This professional association played an important role in the ongoing debate over methods of industrial organization—a debate that began well before Taylor arrived on the scene.

At its May 1886 assembly, ASME's president, Henry R. Towne, gave a speech with the eloquent title "The Engineer as an Economist":

> The questions to be considered ... group themselves under two
> principal heads, namely *shop management* and *shop
> accounting* ... Under the head of Shop Management falls the
> question of organization, responsibility, reports, systems of
> contract and piecework ... Under the head of Shop Accounting
> fall the questions of time and wage systems, determination of costs
> whether by piecework or daywork, the distribution of the various
> expense accounts, the ascertainment of profits, methods of
> bookkeeping, and all that enters into the system of accounts which
> relates to the manufacturing department of a business and to the
> determination and record of its results.[21]

It was not until 1895 that Taylor presented to his peers his differential salary scheme. His considerations on factory management would not appear until 1903. These two contributions did not meet with unanimous approval. He had earlier defended a voluminous monograph titled "On the Art of Cutting Metals," a method he had demonstrated at the 1900 Exposition and that was to have great repercussions on the automobile industry. He thus returned to a type of work on the machine that had already earned him attention in 1893 when he produced his first text, "Notes on Belting." Citing figures on profits and losses, he demonstrated how engineers and they alone could avoid the loss of time and energy occasioned by the accidental breakdown of the conveyor belt.[22]

Even in the opinion of his preface writers, Taylor's written work is to be classed in the category of occasional papers.[23] Aimed at a very precise audience, his memoranda and books are the fruit of a particular set of circumstances. His intention was never to produce a treatise on these questions, even if the title of his last book, *The Principles of Scientific Management* (1911), gives that impression.

This book came off the presses at a time when the concept of "scientific management" was widely condemned in trade-union circles. This period was particularly agitated, since strikes had broken out against this new production method. In 1912, the U.S. government would forbid state-owned firms, particularly the national arsenals, from using the Taylor method. (This prohibition would be lifted only in 1949, on the eve of the Cold War.) In 1910, public hearings took place before the Interstate Commerce Commission, which had been created at the end of the 1880s and was charged with regulating the liberal principles of free enterprise and acting as their watchdog inside and outside the factory walls. In these hearings, for the first time, the concept of scientific management was discussed.[24] The commission inquired into the relations between workers and owners in certain firms accused of applying this new form of scientific organization of labor in an abusive fashion.

In the winter of 1911–12, Taylor was called in person before a special committee of the House of Representatives investigating the "Taylor's system and other systems of shop management." *Principles* appeared at the beginning of 1911 and was conceived as a plea *pro domo,* aimed to convince his questioners and a wider public than his colleagues in the ASME. To those inclined to think that his system was far too disciplinary and totalizing, Taylor offered his "philosophy of human labor." "Scientific Management is not a theory," he stated to the congressmen, "but is the practical result of a long evolution."[25]

There is no better way of understanding this system, he went on, than through the metaphor of a major-league baseball team. Just like players in the stadium, there is no way for employees and employers to "win" without intimate cooperation, the sharing of tasks and rigorously separated roles, the precise regulation of movement accepted by everyone. Such was the basis of scientific management. It was not a preestablished formula, according to Taylor, but demanded "an immense change in minds." It required a "complete mental revolution" on both sides. Peace should be substituted for war, and mutual confidence for distrust.

When invited to list the advantages of his method, Taylor referred to the experiments of Frank B. Gilbreth (1868–1924), who in 1911 published *Motion Study*.[26] This specialist of micromotions had broken down the gestures and postures of bricklaying, his former trade. By analyzing the worker's trips to the cement mixer and to the brick pile, the lifting of the bricks up the scaffolding, and so on throughout the whole operation, he managed to reduce his movements from eighteen to between two and five per brick.

Although Taylor's system is not a "theory," it does claim to be a science: each element of a person's work should be scientifically developed. Worker selection and training should be scientific. Although one finds scant reference to phrenology (or cranioscopy) in his writings, Taylor was immersed in a culture that, during the greater part of the nineteenth century, had consecrated it as the "prototype of scientific knowledge of man."[27] According to the historian of phrenology Georges Lanteri-Laura, the United States was the first country to have adopted this medical discipline, in the period 1840–50, for the purpose of "rational utilization of individuals." "Phrenology underwent a major expansion there," writes Lanteri-Laura,

> and quite a durable one, since the *American Phrenological Journal* did not cease publication until 1911. But study of the anatomy of the brain itself played no role in this and did not progress; permanent reference to the brain was more and more gratuitous and founded only on a general hypothesis. American phrenology had nothing theoretical about it, and its originality lay in its wide applications, in particular in professional recruitment, and in the basic optimism that underlay it along with its cerebral determinism . . . The idea was not to speculate on free will, but to recruit with certainty the type of worker one needed. The enterprise owes its success to how well it responded to the exigencies of American society, and to the fact that no other system resulted in such applications.[28]

One thing is certain: psychological factors remained largely absent from Taylor's system, which relied excessively on individual coercion and rejected out of hand the subjective and intersubjective experience of the worker.

The Taylorist division of labor is intended to relieve workers in the shop of any intellectual work, which is to be centralized in a planning department that prepares everyone's work and systematically plans and directs the factory. The managing center sets up circuits and emits messages that fix the paths each piece must follow from one machine to another on the shop floor.

From 1882 on, Taylor recorded, classified, cross-referenced, and worked into tables a quantity of information collected on the interaction between man and machine, and converted it into "laws" in an effort to formulate the "standard" conditions and applications that assured the best "work flow" for each operation, each of its constituent "units," each series of operations. He set up procedures to measure "time units" by chronometer. One of his collaborators had even invented a *watch-book*, which he described as follows in his book on shop management:

> It consists of a framework, containing concealed in it one, two or three watches, whose stop and start movements can be operated by pressing with the fingers of the left hand upon the proper portion of the cover of the notebook without the knowledge of the workman who is being observed. The frame is bound in a leather case resembling a pocket notebook, and has a place for the note sheets described.[29]

To bring his own time and motion studies to fruition with workers in industry, Gilbreth, meanwhile, would invent the "Gilbreth chronometer," a moving picture camera connected to a clock. Twenty years after the experiments of Marey's team, Gilbreth would use the cyclograph for the same purpose.

Because it was supposedly scientific, the system could be generalized. Before the investigating committee, Taylor demonstrated its universal scope by boasting of his links with the management of a French automobile company:

> I had a recent visit from the owner of the Renaud [*sic*, for Renault] Automobile Works, the largest automobile works in France, together with Monsieur de Ram, the young French engineer who personally became interested in the art of cutting metals some years ago, and in our system of management, and who put this system into one of Renaud's departments. These two men ... assured me that in those departments in which they had introduced the art of cutting metals and our system of management that they had much more than doubled their former input ... The warning I gave them before they left me was this. I said, "You have been at it three years. Do not expect to get

through with it for five years, because you will not. It will take you more than five years before you will get through the entire process of putting our system in."[30]

In March 1913, the workers at the Renault complex at Billancourt, on the outskirts of Paris, would undertake a strike against the presence of these time-motion experts, the first major social conflict over Taylorism.

One of the sharpest criticisms of the Taylor system came on the eve of World War I from the physiologist and psychologist Jean-Marie Lahy, who combined laboratory studies and investigations in the workplace. He reproached Taylor for having passed off as scientific a method whose conditions of development did not respect the necessary distance from vested interests. Yet, without taking up this question of scientificity, it is hardly possible to think through the new link between science and industry.[31]

After the hiatus of war mobilization, the quarrel over the scientific foundations of Taylorism would be enriched by another debate, over the question of "Americanism." At the end of the 1920s, the propagation of methods of rationalizing and modernizing production and labor in Europe would appear intimately linked to the rise in the hegemonic power of the United States, center of the new world-economy. The Italian Antonio Gramsci (1891–1937) would show for the first time that the model of scientific organization of the firm could only be understood as a component of a new way of life, a "new human type," a culture different from that of the Old World, which was in crisis and in search of new landmarks.

Reviewing the cultural networks of Americanism in his day, Gramsci noted that "America has the Young Men's Christian Association (YMCA)."[32] This institution of young Protestants founded in London in 1844 and that had come to the United States in 1851 was, according to Gramsci, the best incarnation of the idea of the American "muscular Christianity."

U.S. Railroads and Their Managers

Taylorism would have been impossible if it had not been preceded by a managerial revolution, as Alfred Chandler demonstrated in a book on managerial capitalism that has become a classic in business history.

In his correspondence, Taylor referred to accounting practices of the railroads and noted that he had drawn inspiration from them in devising his own methods of statistical control.

In fact, the railroad companies—but also, to a certain extent, the telegraph companies—represented the first modern business enterprises in the United States. This is Chandler's central thesis. Guaranteeing both the construction and operation of their own tracks and the management of the traffic of transport firms and the mail services that used their lines, these "multidivisional" or "divisionalized" companies, in which a separation of production operations from strategic decision making is made systematic, were the first to employ a large number of full-time managers to coordinate, watch over, and evaluate the activities of competing operating divisions. They were also the first to create administrative hierarchies and invent management functions (such as finance, sales, and commercial development). In short, they were the first to feel a need to make innovations in their organizational form so as to be able to manage continuous flows of goods, services, and information on a large scale — while keeping an eye on the future.

The new modes of administrative procedure, accounting, statistical control, and organizational charts that would inspire experts in scientific organization at the end of the century began to take shape in the 1850s. However, according to Chandler, modern methods did not really appear in the railroad sector until the beginning of the Civil War. "This need for accurate information," he notes,

led to the devising of improved methods for collecting, collating and analyzing a wide variety of data generated by the day-to-day operations of the enterprise. Of even more importance, it brought a revolution in accounting; more precisely, it contributed substantially to the emergence of accounting out of bookkeeping. The techniques of Italian double-entry bookkeeping generated the data needed, but these data, required in far larger quantities and in more systematic form, were then subjected to types of analysis that were new. In sum, to meet the needs of managing the first modern business enterprise, managers of large American railroads during the 1850s and 1860s invented nearly all of the basic techniques of modern accounting.[33]

A premonitory sign of this vanguard position was the fact that the first business publication to appear in the United States was the *Rail-Road Journal,* in January 1832 — even before any steam railroad was in operation![34] (It was also shortly before the founding of banking publications in the 1830s.) In the course of the expansion of the rail networks, journals on this subject continued to occupy an important place in the constitution of the U.S. business press.

The first modern corporations, moreover, had a multiplier effect, helping other sectors, starting with banking, to become structured. As the first private enterprises to call on transregional capital, the railroad companies contributed to the centralization of the U.S. capital market in New

York and to the development of investment banks. They also helped launch major construction firms.

To build its own railroad networks, Germany in the era of the Zollverein was guided by a strategic vision arising from the needs of the army. By contrast, and contrary to what one might expect from the Civil War experience, the military model in the United States had very little influence on the development of modern management of business — except possibly in the beginning, when the United States Military Academy offered the best training in civil engineering.

The case of George B. McClellan is the exception that proves the rule: he is the only military figure among the pioneers of modern management. This Union general had a double career, as an officer from West Point and as a railroad engineer. McClellan served in the Mexican campaign, which was a decisive one not only for the formation of the interventionist ideology of Manifest Destiny, but more concretely as the first testing ground for the use of the train and the electric telegraph, both for coordinating expeditionary troops and for transmitting news in wartime. McClellan was then sent as an observer to the battlefields of Crimea, where the telegraph, train, and underwater cable also occupied strategic places in the military operations of the Franco-Turkish-British coalition. Next he performed a secret mission in the Dominican Republic to investigate the possibility of establishing a naval base. In 1857, he returned to civilian life, first as chief engineer and then president of a railroad company. He took up active service again when the Civil War broke out.

All the pioneers of management via railroads have the common characteristic of having received training as civil engineers and working for a salary.

What escapes Chandler's historical perspective is the political aspect of managerial capitalism, which Canadian historian Gabriel Kolko helped to reveal. In June and July 1857 a strike broke out among railroad workers threatened with a major cut in their wages. It was the United States' first industrial conflict. It ended with an intervention by the federal government and later the adoption of the first railroad legislation, which in fact protected the interests of the "robber barons," who until then were not united, and were thus endangered by collective ruin because of cutthroat competition. According to Kolko, this intervention from Washington inaugurated the era of "political capitalism," which became a defining characteristic of the economic system of the United States, henceforth "protected from the attacks of a virtually democratic society."[35]

Chapter 12

The Market of Target Groups

The idea of the targeting strategy, the last part of the triptych that makes up the measure of the individual, caught on slowly. Between the appearance of the popular readership for the first serialized novels and the segmented audiences of mass culture, almost a century passed. The route that led to targeting audiences followed the twists and turns of a culture more and more oriented to entertainment, addressing the wide majority and manufactured according to industrial norms. Marketing and advertising are its matrix, and American democracy is the site where it takes shape as the mode of cementing the "general will" and constructing the nation's social bond.

Neither high culture nor the project to enlighten the popular classes nor the idea of public service prepared the societies and mentalities of the Old World to grasp the nature of these new manners of organizing leisure as a mass phenomenon that are emanating from the New World. On the contrary, a historical accumulation of misunderstandings prevents the perception of these new ways of using free time as representing not only a way of being entertained, but a new model of society.

The Serial Novel: A Popular Genre and Audience

In 1836, the first serial novels (*feuilletons*) appeared in Paris newspapers. The true inventor of this formula was Émile de Girardin, who had just founded *La Presse*. The same year, Armand Dutacq founded *Le Siècle*. These were the first papers in France to rely systematically on advertising revenue. In August, *Le Siècle* brought out the first serial, a Spanish novel of manners entitled *Lazarillo de Tormès*. In the autumn, the rival paper responded by beginning publication of a Balzac novel, *La Vieille*

Fille, Scènes de la vie de province, in twelve installments. The formula increased the sales of both dailies, and so it spread.

From 19 June to 15 October 1843, the public was in suspense over the appearance of *Les Mystères de Paris* (*The Mysteries of Paris*) in *Le Journal des Débats*; its 147 chapters achieved unprecedented success and created a stir. Its author, Eugène Sue (1804–57), received a huge number of readers' letters. The interaction between the writer and his public led him to make modifications in plot developments and to incorporate current events, each time further blurring the boundary between reality and fiction. As Hubert Juin explains:

> He had begun a serial. He wanted to draw on his knowledge of slang and describe those outside the law, the lower classes, the underworld of a city that had grown too fast and that nurtured the chancre of crime with superb arrogance. But he modified his plan, as the novel's changing course shows, and it is no longer the sinister bandit who occupies the foreground, but the unhappy proletariat.[1]

The poor found in the novel a portrait of their suffering, while the rich saw themselves promoted to the rank of grand philanthropists and reformers, invested with the evangelical mission of helping their neighbors.

Sue, a former navy surgeon, assumed the role of "rhetorician of the people's mysteries." In his books, he suggested reforms and put them into practice in his imaginary society: schools and apprentice shops, a model farm, a bank for the poor that comes to the aid of unemployed workers and gives them interest-free loans. He denounced the penitentiary system and capital punishment, proposing to replace the latter with "cell isolation." In the thousands of letters he received, people asked him for help and protection, thanked him for having supported the creation of orphanages and schools for the children of needy proletarians.[2]

It was in fact the imaginary advent of the Universal Republic and Association of Saint-Simonian doctrine. Antonio Gramsci was not mistaken about this when he wrote in the 1930s that the novels of Eugène Sue had done much more for the penetration of Saint-Simonianism into Italy than all the works of social theory of the master and his disciples.[3]

But the rise and triumph of this form of literature aimed at the people, whom it thrilled in France in the 1840s and 1850s, occurred to the detriment of an older form of "popular culture," the literature of chapbooks, which became a target of government repression. This type of booklet was denounced as "subversive" and "immoral."

In a legislative circular on the press of 27 July 1849, a little more than a year after the defeat of the republican and socialist movements in 1848, the French minister of the interior wrote to the prefects:

The most common characteristic of the writings being
disseminated at this time and which are offered in the most
popular form, is to divide society into two classes, the rich and the
poor, to represent the former as tyrants and the latter as victims,
and to excite the envy and hatred of one group against the other
and to thus prepare in our society, which has such need of unity
and fraternity, all the elements of a civil war.[4]

Hence the creation by the minister of police in 1852, the year of the inauguration of the empire, of an "Examining Commission of Chapbooks."
It no longer sufficed to keep an eye on those who hawked them; one
had to control the content of disseminated works by verifying that they
were not contrary "to order, morality, and religion."

This important episode in the history of the status of the "popular" as
seen from the perspective of the agencies of power has been well studied by Michel de Certeau, Dominique Julia, and Jacques Revel in a work
called "La beauté du mort" (The beauty of the dead man). As they explain the title, "popular culture" had to be censored in order to be studied, and only became an object of interest when its danger had been eliminated. "The birth of studies devoted to chapbook literature is linked,"
they write, "to the social censorship of their object." And it is significant
that the first *Histoire des livres populaires et de la littérature de col-
portage* (History of popular books and chapbook literature), published
in 1854, was the work of Charles Nisard, secretary of this censorship
commission.

In the preface to its first edition, the writer-censor did not conceal his
preconceptions about the childlike people, who had to be preserved from
bad reading habits:

> I estimated that although, in the interest of people who are easy to
> seduce, as are the workers and the inhabitants of the countryside,
> the commission should not fail to prohibit the hawking of three-
> quarters of these books, this prohibition would not concern
> people capable of resisting such habits, that is to say, the erudite,
> bibliophiles, collectors, and even those simply curious about
> eccentric literature. I therefore thought I was doing something that
> would be agreeable to both groups by gathering together all those
> booklets in a single binding, and saving them en masse from the
> wreck in which they would have perished in isolation.[5]

This is one of the numerous vicissitudes in the modern history of the
notion of "popular culture," which is sometimes confiscated or traves-
tied, but at other times tries to give an account of the expression of
those deprived of a voice.

The Sue-Marx Controversy and the Ideology of Content

In 1845, Marx spoke out against the author of *The Mysteries of Paris*. What bothered him about the serial novel was the utopia of harmony, which was presented as having already come to pass thanks to the good-will of the rich, and of the character Rodolphe in particular: the means by which this character accomplishes "all his redemptions and miracle cures is not his fine words but his *ready money*...You must be a millionaire to be able to imitate their [the moralists'] heroes."[6] The model farm and the bank for the poor founded by Rodolphe, wrote Marx, are illusions; the exploits he carries out with "his *fixed, Christian* ideas, by which he measures the world, with his 'charity,' 'devotion,' 'abnegation,' 'repentance,' the 'good' and the 'bad,' 'reward' and 'punishment,' 'terrible chastisement,' 'isolation,' 'salvation of the soul,' etc.," are mere "buffooneries" and would not be possible without the fabulous wealth the hero possesses.[7] Marx goes so far as to criticize in the name of socialist realism the accounting of the Bank for the Poor, where "the worker loses his interest and the Bank its capital," a formula that appeared to him to fall short of what savings banks already offered.

Nevertheless, it is via these contradictory paths that the serial novel, emblematic of the first serial fiction, played a role in the democratization of daily life, as Michael Palmer has shown:

> The journalism of the imagination plays a role as important as news journalism. *Le Petit Journal* (founded in 1863 by Moïse Polydore Millaud, and one of the first to reach a circulation of a million copies) looked for categories of information and news capable of pleasing the mass public, and a style of presentation that suited them. It used the writing techniques of the serial novel and of the human interest story [*fait divers*] that least disconcerted the popular reader; their components were both universal and outside of time...In fact, the serial novel is itself a rubric of current events. It expresses the imaginary of an era.[8]

In the building up of a popular readership for the daily press, the feuilleton played in France a role that in the United States would fall to comic strips, starting in the 1880s.[9] This means of expression that combines pictures and literary language met — just as the first films did — the need of a population of recent immigrants who did not speak English or were still illiterate. In these years, the pressure on communication to play an integrating role was felt to such an extent that Taylor proposed the idea of jumping over language barriers and illiteracy in the factories by recommending that managers and "route clerks" issue daily "orders of work" for workers on graphically coded instruction cards.

The genesis of the comics genre, the first product of U.S. mass culture and the first as well to become internationalized (in the 1910s, with the foundation of the syndicate Internews [a Hearst operation] and King Features Syndicate), was already indicative of the importance the image was to assume in this country's industrial culture.

As for Palmer's observations on the role of the serial in the rise of the popular newspaper, it would be a long time before the serial would be taken for granted in France. This kind of literature, noted the critic Hubert Juin as recently as 1976, "remains little known, and it must be admitted, to our shame, misunderstood, except when it comes to Dumas or Sand, or even Balzac, and even in those cases people pretend to ignore totally that the needs of the serial dominated the progression of part of their works."[10]

Paradoxically, it was from abroad that the genre acquired its intellectual legitimacy in France. One of the rare authoritative studies of the serial was by an Englishwoman, Nora Atkinson, a graduate of Liverpool University, who presented a doctoral thesis on the subject in 1929 before a jury at the Sorbonne.[11] In the same period, Antonio Gramsci rediscovered this literature and forged, to account for it, the concept of the "national-popular," analyzing the place it occupied in the formation of a "way of feeling" proper to a people — an "aggregate of sentiment" — and of the organic link uniting them to its intellectuals. This rediscovery was undertaken by the Italian Marxist in parallel with a questioning of the reinforcement of the mechanisms of rationalization of social relations — their Taylorization — between the two world wars: "The question is this: there has always been a large part of humanity whose activity was Taylorized and disciplined, and it has tried to evade the strict limits of the existing organization that crushed it by turning to fantasy and dreams."[12] Gramsci did not leave the matter there, but asked to what extent this literature, beyond its populist tendencies, "expresses the background of democratic aspirations" that are reflected in it. This is precisely what Marx, who saw in Sue above all the expression of "false consciousness," did not do: Sue moved in the sphere of the heart and of pathos; Marx, as a critic of utopian socialism, invoked reason and "true discourse," referring to scientific socialism.

The controversy between Sue and Marx was the first in which the revolutionary project expressed an incomprehension of the mechanisms assuring the success of a culture of entertainment aimed at the wide majority. In the course of time, the misunderstanding would only get deeper. More than a century later, Jean Baudrillard could criticize this instrumentalist conception of the media and say of the left (and of its parties) that it understood nothing about media phenomena because it persisted in seeing them as "purely and simply means of distribution...the relay of ideology," whereas "it is not as vehicles of content, but in their form and very operation, that media induce a social relation."[13]

As the Gutenberg galaxy gradually receded and the electronic era gradually drew closer, this ideology of content would in fact become the ideology of a whole society: it would preside over the definition of public service, with its vocation for "cultural pedagogy." Thus, of the three functions assigned to it by its public mandate or charter—to inform, educate, and entertain—public-service broadcasting would grant a clear priority to the first two, in the name of an idea of the democratization of culture as a way of placing into the hands of citizens of all classes the expressions of a nation's cultural patrimony. This idea of cultural democratization implies a social philosophy, according to which cultural forms occupy different levels of legitimacy, and the definition of culture is marked by a hierarchy of high (or legitimate) culture over low culture. It implies, moreover, the implicit recognition of a certain hierarchy in the access to culture thus defined, hence the idea of an inequality in the face of cultural goods that has to be remedied. The progressive development of commercial logic, inseparable in turn from the logics of internationalization of the whole media field, would precipitate a crisis in the tutelary conception of public service. The largely educational and cultural vocation of broadcasting would be put into competition with another conception of its use determined essentially by the "entertainment" function.[14]

But underneath this ideology of content hides something else: distrust of "amusement," which also has deep roots and would work, too, to delay awareness of what was at stake in the slow but no less irresistible ascension of the new industrial methods of production of mass culture.

The Regime of Laziness, the Negative Side of Leisure

At the very moment when Taylor undertook in the United States his first attempts at shop scientific management, Paul Lafargue (1842–1911) published in France *Le Droit à la paresse* (literally, "the right to be lazy" but translated as *The Right to Leisure* in the 1893 Glasgow edition). "A strange folly," he wrote, "possesses the working classes of nations where capitalist civilization reigns. This folly brings with it the individual and social misery that for two centuries has tortured sad humanity. This folly is the love of work, the moribund passion for work, pushed right to the exhaustion of the vital forces of the individual and his offspring."[15]

The author of this 1880 pamphlet, who had the blood of three eth-
nicities (black, Jewish, and Caribbean) in his veins, was a future French
legislator and the son-in-law of Marx. He took up the cause against
"Christian hypocrisy" and "capitalist utilitarianism," which had made
work "sacrosanct." He also attacked the apologias of numerous theoreticians of the First International who had broken, in the name of scientific socialism, with utopian thinkers who favored pleasure and celebrations. He also shared with these latter an unbounded confidence in
the promises of technical progress:

> Our fire-breathing machines, with limbs of steel, tireless, of a
> marvelous fecundity, inexhaustible, docilely carry out their sacred
> work all by themselves, yet nevertheless the genius of the great
> philosophers of capitalism remains dominated by the prejudice of
> wage labor, the worst kind of slavery. They still do not understand
> that the machine is the redeemer of humanity, the God that will
> redeem man from the *sordidae artes* of salaried labor, the God
> that will give them leisure and freedom.[16]

The question of liberation from work is a component of all utopian
visions. But laziness is often, despite everything, treated as a vice. In his
Utopia, Thomas More had reduced the workday to six hours—around
half of what it was in his day for a worker or farmer—but meanwhile
he took up his cudgel against the "lazy." His satire on this category of
individuals would often be repeated by other utopians. Campanella had
limited daily work to four hours, which seemed sufficient to him to procure abundance for all. Morelly had allowed in his Code of Nature
for short work sessions, rest every five days, and four occasions in the
year for collective celebrations that could last up to six days. Cabet had
his Icarians work seven hours in summer and six in winter, refusing to
speak of "laziness," since in Icaria work was no longer a punishment.
In Fourier's proposals for "attractive work," "the Harmonians do not
know about vacations and do not want them," as Walter Benjamin remarked. For Lafargue, the norm did not exceed three hours. Ten years
after the publication of the pamphlet, Kropotkin followed suit, while
substituting the "right to ease" for the "right to laziness."[17] At the end
of the century the eight-hour day was a working-class demand, but a
day of ten or twelve hours was the reality.

The Enlightenment had attacked "idleness," a privilege reserved for
unproductive people. Voltaire in his *Candide* had gone so far as to feel
sorry for the "man overcome with the weight of his leisure." This representation was reiterated countless times in the articles of the *Encyclopédie,* confirming a philosophical and literary tradition that had seen

"leisure" and its organization as a weapon invented by tyrants in antiquity to anesthetize their people and make them stupid.

In his pioneering text called *Le Discours sur la servitude volontaire* (*Discourse of Voluntary Servitude*) (1574), Étienne de La Boétie (1530–63) spoke of "pastimes" being transformed into "drugs," and whose purpose was to "soften and make free men effeminate by pleasures, games, spectacles, so as to render them more docile for the yoke."[18] This friend of Montaigne, who died in the flower of his youth after having confided his manuscript to him, reminds us about the first etymology of the word *ludique* ("ludic"), from the Latin *ludi*. The term is a deformation of *Lydi* or the Lydians, inhabitants of Lydia whom Cyrus, to complete his conquest, had corrupted with games, the new "lure into servitude." La Boétie adds that "to entertain an entire people in idleness, amuse it, satisfy its vices" has become in the course of time quite a feeble aid to "governments that only have the means to take care of the pleasures of the moneyed classes."[19]

La Boétie's text was still a beacon in the nineteenth century. Militant readings of this book contributed to perpetuate the idea that "amusement in leisure" rhymed with "turning people into morons" and was a "compensation for a ravished freedom" (all of these are his expressions). Some went as far as to apply it mechanically to contemporary "amusements" and to throw into the same net parades and revues, greased poles and balloons, jousts and free shows, illuminations and fireworks, horse races, expositions, museums and the "great bazaars of industry," as well as "games on the stock exchange still more nefarious than all those, and certainly unknown to the ancients."[20]

These interpretations draw on an instrumental view of power and hence evade La Boétie's central questioning of the pathways of voluntary servitude: How does it happen that individuals fight for their servitude as if for their salvation? How does it happen that they obey one person among them? Instead of this subtle question about the internalization of the mechanisms of servitude, one finds in later commentaries an inventory of the means of subjection, supposedly applied to an inert and passive people, with the tyrant envisaged as an autonomous subject, omniscient and omnipresent, pulling the strings in a marionette show. The political corollary of this is a conception of change in society: in order to overturn the order of things, it suffices to dislodge the tyrant or the occupant of the sites of power and then make other uses of these sites.[21]

From the rejection of the idea of a precise type of amusements and pleasures to the evasion of the very idea of amusement and pleasure there was only one step. The mobilizing paradigm of progress helped people to take that step, and the ascetic road of access to its grand values would metamorphose the "regime of laziness" into a kingdom of vices.

The Theory of the Leisure Class published in 1899 by the American Thorstein Veblen (1857–1929), whom we are accustomed to see as a precursor of the sociology of leisure, does nothing to dissipate the misunderstanding. The book reinforces the idea that leisure, a domain reserved for a "rich and idle" class smitten with hedonism, is a defense technique, embodied in institutions cut to measure for, if not manipulated by, an economic power designed to maintain people in silence and to prevent them from thinking about their exploited condition. The *gentlemen of leisure* induce a model of "conspicuous consumption"; the consumption of valuable goods, including entertainment, is a sign of social prestige and status, a "means of reputability"; it is a lifestyle, a behavior to be imitated, that is diffused throughout society.[22]

To have an idea of the disarray in which editors of the socialist press like Jean Jaurès were plunged when it came to deciding on a policy about the publication of serials in their own papers, one need only refer to Anne-Marie Thiesse's study, published in 1984, of popular readers and readings in the Belle Epoque.[23]

Within the working-class movement the tension would be permanent between the increasingly forceful logic of entertainment in a culture destined for the masses, on the one hand, and the goal of enlightening the popular classes that it had originally given to its own press and propaganda, on the other. This was all the more true as the question of propaganda became more and more associated with the problem of which concrete form to give to workers' organizations. This correlation was accentuated in the last two decades of the nineteenth century. This is borne out by the handful of texts on the role and forms of propaganda in the socialist movement that were published at the time, including, for example, a lecture by Piotr Lavrov (1823–1900), a militant of the Russian populist party and veteran of the Paris Commune, given in Paris before the Society of Russian Workers in 1887.[24] This was still a significant moment, since the Leninist model of agitation and propaganda—with the hierarchies it established between a vanguard composed of the most self-conscious elements, depositories of truth, and the other strata of the people—had not yet cut off other alternatives. With the model invented by Lenin, which appeared at the turn of the century, the instrumental function of the working-class paper as a tool of organization, and nothing else, would be pushed to an extreme.[25]

In the course of time, the voluntarism of schemes for propagandistic communication would appear more and more ineffectual in comparison with another institutional model of communication, one that was rooted in daily interests and contributed to reproducing, in metabolic fashion, the conditions and values of a mode of living and a social system. Here we must return to the genealogy of this institutionalization, in which the advertising complex is called upon to occupy a central place.

The Distant Origins of the Advertisement

Starting in the 1830s, and more or less at the same time in France, England, and the United States, the activity of the press took on the structure of a commercial enterprise. The great trusts in this sector were constituted around 1875 (for example, Hearst in the United States and Northcliffe in England). Between these two dates there arose high-circulation newspapers; the mechanism of advertising from this point on became an essential ingredient in the functioning and survival of the press.

But the invention of the institution of advertising is much older, having begun with the creation of the "agency" formula around 1630, at the instigation of the French doctor Théophraste Renaudot, better known as promoter of the *Gazette de France* (it is a striking coincidence that in the preceding decade the Vatican created its Congregation for the Propagation of the Faith!). Renaudot established in Paris a "bureau of encounters and addresses," an idea advanced by Montaigne in one of his essays. In the essay "D'un défaut de nos polices" (On a failing of our policy), Montaigne indicates, in fact, how profitable it would be for the "regulation of the poor" to have a "designated site" to which "those who need something could go and register the matter with an officer created for this purpose": someone who wants to "sell pearls" and someone else who wants to buy them; one to find a master, another a servant, worker, or a companion for a trip to Paris, and so forth. "This way of alerting each other [*entr'advertir*] would bring no slight convenience to public commerce," reckoned Montaigne, "since at all times there are situations looking for each other, and for want of hearing of each other, men left in dire necessity."[26]

In Montaigne's view, the "advertisement," an announcement inserted into a medium such as a newspaper, might fill a social role and be counted as an extension of charitable works. Taking its inspiration both from religious and patronage institutions, advertising would be a kind of public service. In the context of this period, Renaudot's bureau, where the supplies of some and the demands of others converged, did not serve only as a clearinghouse for the publication of "advertisements." It was also a site for the propagation of useful medical knowledge, a particularly important activity at a time when quacks and their remedies abounded. Finally, it was a center of dissemination for ideas close to those of Cardinal Richelieu, who supported the doctor's plans to ease the fate of the poor.

The functional schema of the advertising agency in its still rudimentary form emigrated to London in the seventeenth century, where it would be adapted in the guise of "Offices of Intelligence." In crossing the Channel, it changed its nature: whereas in France the advertising agency and its printed medium would remain separate until the end of the Old Regime, each relying on its own royal privilege, in England the two functions were one. At the end of the eighteenth century, the mixed print medium that combined the news and opinions with commercial messages was symbolized by the *Times,* founded in 1785. In the British capital, Renaudot's invention was thus significantly alienated from its initial project for social assistance and public benefaction and became a mercantile instrument. In the transition from the harmonious regime of advertising advocated by the humanist to the conflictual model of advertising, there had been a drift toward a competitive model in which commercial intention and exchanges predominated. This shift has been well examined by the historian of advertising institutions, Gérard Lagneau, who summarizes the trajectory as follows:

> At the end of the classical age, we are still under the Old Regime of advertising, in which the commercial purpose is overdetermined by public service, in this case by what we today call Social Security. It is English political economy that will consummate this rupture: with Adam Smith, the goal is displaced from "regulation of the poor" to the "wealth of nations"; with T. R. Malthus, the extinction of pauperism by social progress becomes a mere utopia.[27]

From London, the practice of the mixed print medium will reach the future United States in 1729, with the founding of the *Pennsylvania Gazette* by Benjamin Franklin (1706–90), who had brought the idea back with him after his stay in the colonial metropole. The first relatively stable daily paper after Independence, the *Pennsylvania Packet & Advertiser* (created in 1784), included ten columns of ads (for auction sales, ship sailings, and real-estate availabilities) out of a total of sixteen.[28]

This long genesis of "conflictual advertising" in England was concomitant with the construction of a public sphere that assumed political functions — a public sphere whose realization was facilitated by the suppression in 1694 and 1695 of the institution of prior censorship, allowing the press to play its role as mediator and to disseminate political decisions to the public. The results are analyzed in detail by Habermas:

Thus raised to the status of an institution, the ongoing commentary on and criticism of the Crown's actions and Parliament's decisions transformed a public authority now being called before the forum of the public. This authority thereby became "public" in a double sense. From now on, the degree of the public sphere's development was measured by the state of the confrontation between government and press, as it drew out over the entire century.[29]

This period coincides with the increase in gathering places such as ale-houses and coffeehouses.

The ironic aspect of this genesis is that the Anglo-Saxon notion of commercial advertising—the word comes from the old French *adver-tissement*—was born under a parliamentary regime, whereas advertising in a spirit of public service, known then as "publicity" and later as "public relations," was developed under absolutism.

The last institutional obstacles to the full development of advertising and the press in England would not be overcome until the years 1853–61, with the abrogation of "knowledge taxes," which hurt newspapers, particularly those on advertisements instituted by a law of 1712. The United States had first shaken off this yoke by refusing the application of the Stamp Act in 1765, and then after Independence by renouncing any taxation on the press. The Second Congress instituted in 1792 the practice of subsidizing the Post Office, whose cheap rates were an important factor in the development of the U.S. press. In France, the law on freedom of the press of July 1881—adopted some fifteen years after the invention of the rotary printing machine and five years before the linotype—suppressed the last juridical obstacles to the rise of the mass press. But the persistence of the harmonious model of advertising via Saint-Simonian views on the social mission of ads would be, as we have seen, a major reason for the French "backwardness" in the development of a national advertising market when contrasted with the English-speaking mercantile model.

Born of a Franco-British intersection, then, the formula of the modern advertising agency found its most favorable climate in the United States, the first country in which modern corporations emerged, along with their problems of managing mass production and distribution. "Advertising draws a straight line from the manufacturer to the consumer," was the dictum of J. Walter Thompson, whose agency was the prototype of the American-based multinational advertising network. In 1899 it set up a subsidiary in London—the first step toward its internationalization.[30]

The Internationalization of the First Advertising Networks

The history of the formation of networks of advertising agencies merges with the advent of media-age modernity. Indeed, it is via these networks and their flows of messages on a transnational scale that the first confrontation took place between a public culture circumscribed to the particular territories of the nation-state and the market culture with its parameters and ambitions of mercantile universality. It was through the connection with this vanguard of the media complex that the first tensions appeared between the dispersion of popular cultures and the centralizing project of industrialized culture, between the local and the transnational at the level of everyday life.

The first authentic advertising agency in U.S. history was created in Philadelphia in 1841, but it was not until the Civil War that the sector really became organized. It was in this period that J. Walter Thompson founded his agency.

Around 1870, the religious press in the United States still had an important share of the advertising market: four hundred periodicals with a circulation of some five million copies. In 1887, J. Walter Thompson has already changed course: his catalog of proposals to advertisers included a list of twenty-five magazines, among which women's magazines stand out. The *Ladies' Home Journal,* launched only four years earlier, soared to a million copies by the turn of the century. *Cosmopolitan* had first come out in 1886. The appearance of this genre was the occasion for the first speculative thinking about targeting markets. In 1909, J. Walter Thompson summed up his own totally empirical experience of the previous forty years:

> The women spend the money, and to reach the women, one must
> enter the family. And to reach the family hearth, the young
> advertising agent turned to the magazines. He noticed that these
> publications were bought at the news stands to be carried home,
> or subscribed to directly from the family circle. There the
> publications lived for thirty days. The young man was amazed
> that the business and publishing world hitherto had failed to grasp
> the possibilities of such a medium in the advertising business.[31]

In 1900, advertising billings in the United States were estimated ten times greater than on the eve of the Civil War, and for some time already, the professional order of the day had been better organization. In 1873, the advertising agents held their first congress. By 1888, the advertising industry had its first trade journal, *Printers' Ink,* founded by an advertising agent, George Presbury Rowell. From 1900 to 1917, the

National Federation of Advertising Clubs of America sought to incorporate the whole profession at the national level and to define professionalism by formulating codes, in order to establish the legitimacy of an activity whose image was still tarnished by deceptive and fraudulent practices, and particularly by the sale of fake pharmaceutical products.[32] In 1914, the "Standards of Practice," prelude to the first ethical code adopted by the clubs, relied on the highly symbolic idea of advertising as a "public service," entrusted with the defense of the "interests of the consumer." The stakes of this semantic game were all the higher since federal authorities in 1906 had taken the first regulatory measures to protect consumers by promulgating the Pure Food and Drug Act. In 1917, there were no less than three hundred accredited agencies, which formed the American Association of Advertising Agencies (AAAA) to replace the federation of clubs. In 1914, agencies, advertisers, and press publishers created an Audit Bureau of Circulation, a nonprofit body inspired by the idea of self-regulation, which collected all useful data about media outlets and published a verified volume of sales.[33] In the same year, the government established a new agency, the Federal Trade Commission (FTC), to identify unfair business practices and to help avoid them.

In 1924, organic links were forged between the U.S. ad organization and its British counterpart through the creation of the Associated Advertising Clubs of the World. English firms shared with the North American ones not only the drive to internationalization but also the pioneering project of organizing the profession around the idea of self-regulation, inspired by economic liberalism, as opposed to the idea of a control exercised by public authorities. The profession declared its intention to fix its own rules for the use of the public sphere for advertising purposes. In 1938, this embryo of an international corporatist organization, with its headquarters in New York, gave birth to a worldwide interprofessional association, the International Advertising Association (IAA), which assumed the defense of the interests of media, advertisers, and agencies. One year earlier, the International Chamber of Commerce—a distant ancestor of the GATT (General Agreement on Tariffs and Trade), which has been recently converted into the World Trade Organization (WTO)— founded by the private sector in 1920 with the purpose of regulating the new world order of trade after World War I, had developed the first ethical code for advertising activities. Thus the idea of "free commercial speech," closely tied to the doctrine of self-regulation, took its first step across national boundaries[34]—long before the famous doctrine of the "Free Flow of Information" was formulated at the beginning of the Cold War, under the auspices of the U.S. State Department.

At the time, the idea of self-regulation was completely foreign to the tradition of state regulation in France, which in the 1920s was absent from international advertising markets, and so the French went to the United States to learn the techniques of competitive advertising. As Marcel Bleustein-Blanchet, founder in 1926 of the Publicis agency, recalled in his memoirs:

> At age 18, without knowing a word of English, I left for America, the one place I knew I would learn what advertising really was. I was like a Muslim going to Mecca. What I learned was very simple: you can't have good advertising for a bad product. My admiration for the United States comes from two things: democracy in communication and respect for public opinion. I returned with one desire, to make advertising a respected, responsible profession, something more than shrill claims and slogans.[35]

In 1927, the top two U.S. agency networks, from their New York headquarters, began to encircle the globe with foreign affiliates, meeting the demand of their country's industrial and commercial firms who were setting up branches in the four corners of the world, from London to Calcutta, from Madrid to Rio de Janeiro, and from Paris to Sydney.[36] The Great Depression propelled them outside the mother country, where between 1929 and 1933 advertising expenditures collapsed. Only the coming of World War II would halt this first generation of advertising networks, but their expansion would continue at a faster pace than ever in the 1950s, thereby eroding national agencies that in most countries were incapable of adapting to the new know-how of Madison Avenue networks.

The Birth of Marketing and "Mass Culture"

Advertising is an integral part of the marketing process. This means, according to its professional leaders (who are fond of pithy formulas), that there is no way of "developing a good message" if you don't respond to "T(arget)-Square": "What are we selling? Where are we selling it? When are we selling it? To whom are we selling it? How are we selling it?"[37] Identify the market, get to know it pragmatically, divide it up, segment it in order to meet it better—such is the goal of marketing, born in the wake of modern enterprise with its techniques of analytical accounting.

In their studies of the origins of market research, North American historians generally go back to 1879, when the Ayer and Son advertising agency, founded ten years earlier, carried out, on behalf of a manufacturer of agricultural machinery, a nationwide survey asking state officers and publishers about grain production and media circulation by county. In 1895, a professor at the University of Minnesota, Harlow Gale, used mailed questionnaires to obtain public opinions on advertising. Six years later, Walter Dill Scott, later longtime president of Northwestern University and author of the first book for a large audience on the subject, *Psychology of Advertising,* launched an experimental research program for an advertising club of Chicago. Around 1910, the first research bureaus were created; in 1911, a pivotal year, the former editor of *Printers' Ink* set up his own research company with the symbolic name Business Bourse. Meanwhile, the Kellogg Company undertook a mail survey of magazine readership; Curtis Publishing, publisher of the *Ladies' Home Journal,* launched a commercial research division; and the Harvard Graduate School of Business established its own Bureau of Business Research.[38]

The notion of "marketing," having appeared at the end of the nineteenth century in economic literature and present in the texts of Frederick Winslow Taylor and his disciples (who at the beginning of the 1920s referred to it under the general heading "Merchandising and Selling"),[39] would not have an official definition conferred on it until 1931. In that year, the American Association of Marketing and Advertising Professors characterized it as including "all the business activities implicated in the flow of goods and services from producer to consumer, with the sole exception of activities that imply a change in form."[40] Under the effect of managerial logic, which was gradually imposing itself in all forms of communication in society, the American Marketing Association would swap this first definition for the following one: "Marketing is the process of planning and executing the conception, pricing, promotion and distribution of ideas, goods and services to create exchanges that satisfy individual and organizational objectives."[41] Convince and persuade are the keywords: "Anything employed to influence people favorably is advertising. The mission of advertising is to persuade men and women to act in a way that will be of advantage to the advertiser."[42] This is how a textbook for students defined the objectives of advertising in 1921. Starting in the first decade of the century, advertising courses were offered in several American universities, such as New York University, the University of Missouri, Northwestern. By 1930, more than thirty centers of higher education had included this subject in their curricula.

The task marketing assumed for itself was to guarantee the conditions of communication and information that allow demand to be met, and this aim would make a qualitative leap in the 1920s. Managers perceived that it was just as important to organize the demand as the supply. To make mass production profitable, since it had already been proven that this was possible, industrialists tried to enlarge their markets, geographically and socially. Advertisers reshaped the family target, assigning new roles to the mother ("entrepreneur" of the home, the arena of consumption), to the father (a fallen symbol of patriarchal authority, reduced to his money-earning capacity), and to "youth" (symbol of a mass culture in which nothing becomes old-fashioned as quickly as fashion).

The quantifying and classifying of consumers' behavior assumed strategic proportions. By the 1920s, a new type of firm specializing in opinions and attitudes was created; its pioneers were Daniel Starch, George Gallup, and Claude Robinson, developers of the first quantitative measure of the relationships between media, product, and consumer (the recognition method and the "impact" method of evaluating advertising). Arthur C. Nielsen invented the concept of *share-of-market* and organized the first panels to measure it, auditing the flow of selected merchandise through a representative sample of all the nation's stores of the relevant category. At the end of the 1920s, the foremost U.S. advertiser, the detergent maker Procter & Gamble, created the first market study department. The following decade, in synergy with the Ayer Agency, this company, which dated back to 1837, invented the soap opera genre on radio, and would transpose it to television in the 1950s. Publishing companies scrambled to study the purchasing power of the readerships of their various publications (in 1928, the International Magazine Company issued the first *Study of All American Markets,* in which it reviewed the household budgets of the inhabitants of the circulation areas of newspapers in towns with more than one hundred thousand people).

Behaviorism and behavioral sciences were mobilized by advertisers to measure the "impact" or "effect" of the message on the consumer. The quest for motivations drove the founding fathers of the "public relations" industry who, along with Ivy Lee and Edward Bernays (1892–1995), developed "publicity techniques on a policy-making level" and christened their project "the engineering of consent." This occurred in a world context in which, abroad, totalitarian regimes and ideologies had placed propaganda onto their agenda of domination.

The Great Depression provoked a sharpening of the objectives in seeking effective instruments for analyzing the consumer-citizen. In the 1930s, the search for ways of measuring behavior resulted in the first surveys and barometers of public opinion, under the impetus of the pollster George Horace Gallup (1901–84). Its first application was electoral marketing, in fact during the 1936 campaign to reelect Franklin D. Roosevelt—a victory that Gallup managed to predict. The New Deal strategy applied by the president since his first election had relied on techniques of communication to mobilize citizens around his policies for dealing with the crisis, as, for instance, with his radio "fireside chats." The consolidation of commercial radio networks deepened this interest in the consumer: Nielsen operated the first mechanical measure of audience ratings, a meter system devised by the Massachusetts Institute of Technology; surveys carried out with the methods of empiricist sociology lent themselves to evaluating these same audiences.

The 1920s thus witnessed the launching of a new regime of communication. In this decade, Fordism, initiated in 1910 by the automobile manufacturer on his assembly lines, arose both as a form of labor management and a mode of social regulation. If consumers, their purchasing power, and their behavior were the object of all this carving up and dissection, if the observatories of their movements were multiplying, it was because the "captain of industry" was being transformed into a "captain of consciousness," in the expression of U.S. historian Stuart Ewen. This transformation contributed to "displacing the center of gravity of social control" from work toward entertainment, from effort toward pleasure, from the fact to the dream, from the rational to desire. An equivalence was conceived between the idea of access to consumer goods via the market and the idea of democracy and the democratic ideal. All these structural transformations have been authoritatively analyzed by Ewen in a key study of the social genesis of advertising and "consumer culture."[43]

The critique of this fundamental movement was reduced, generally speaking, to the simple dilemma of lying or telling the truth in advertising. This instrumental and, frankly, moralistic conception of the function of advertising prevented a real understanding of the successive shifts that would change it from a simple tool to the cornerstone of a mode of communication, particularly in countries where the culture of communication adhered to a logic of public service. So, whether or not it was "clean," and whether or not it was aggressive, advertising already appeared as a way of combining the realm of commodities with the realm of spectacle, of producing commodities *as* a spectacle and the spectacle *as* commodity. As a laboratory for the production of culture and the imaginary of "the event," advertising was converted little by little into the basis of a commercial logic that, in the course of time and in the wake of technological advances, would become more and more determining, less as an incitement to buy than as a key component in the configuration of the media complex, to the point where it swallowed up the latter in its own complex.

This is how historian Daniel J. Boorstin expresses the phenomenon of advertising modernity as the emanation of a certain model of society:

In other cultures outside the United States, it is the *high* culture that has generally been an area of centralized, organized control...In the United States, the expressions of our peculiar folk culture, the *low* culture, come from advertising agencies, from networks of newspapers, radio, and television, from outdoor advertising agencies, from the copywriters for ads in the largest-circulation magazines, and so on...Advertising has taken the lead in promising and exploiting the new...The problems of advertising are, of course, not peculiar to advertising, for they are just one aspect of the problems of democracy. They reflect the rise of what I have called Consumption Communities and Statistical Communities, and many of the special problems of advertising have arisen from our continuously energetic effort to give everybody everything.[44]

The early grip of a culture produced industrially and organized centrally over the production of the social bond in the United States has blurred the conceptual register and opened the way to ambiguity. There, the notion of "popular culture" merged with that of "mass culture." *Popular culture*, conceived as one of the basic elements of adherence to consensual values, has acquired a theoretical status radically different from that in force within other intellectual traditions, in which the "popular" and "popular cultures" (the plural is important) continue to be perceived as forms of reaction to symbolic domination. This remains true even if, as Jean-Claude Passeron observed as late as 1989, this definition of the term is not exhaustive: "If popular cultures are obviously not frozen in an attitude of perpetual deference to cultural legitimacy, this is no reason to assume that they are mobilized night and day in an attitude of confrontation. They can also function while at rest."[45]

Toward Functional Analysis

The rise of a Fordist culture of leisure and work engenders a demand by corporations and governmental institutions for studies carried out by academics.

Some university figures passed completely over into the private sector. The inventor of behavioral science, John B. Watson (1878–1958), author in 1924 of *Behaviorism*, left his chair at Johns Hopkins University in 1922 to join J. Walter Thompson's agency as a research executive. In 1924, Daniel Starch, professor and Ph.D. in psychology at the University of Iowa, became director of research for the American Association of Advertising Agencies. His colleague George Gallup, author of a psychology thesis on the memorization of various newspaper items, joined the large Young and Rubicam Agency in 1932, there to develop tests of memorization of advertising messages, before creating his own institute for research on public opinion. Meanwhile, other university researchers went into the business of selling their expertise while keeping their chairs.

In 1937 appeared the first academic journal on mass communication not confined to the study of journalism (the *Journalism Quarterly* had been created in 1930). This new journal was called the *Public Opinion Quarterly* and was the organ of the American Association for Public Opinion Research (AAPOR). The first issue's editorial clearly revealed the thrust of its approach and its guiding alliances:

The editorial staff of the *Public Opinion Quarterly* undertakes to serve that need by creating a convenient medium for regularly bringing together from all the sources indicated above— scholarship, government, business, advertising, public relations, press, radio, motion pictures—the latest available information on the phenomena and problems of public opinion and the developing thought in connection with those phenomena and problems, of scholars, governmental officials, business men, public relations, counsel, and the rest.[46]

Backing up words with deeds, the inaugural issue of January 1937 included contributions from social scientists like Floyd H. Allport ("Toward a Science of Public Opinion") and professionals in counseling firms like Edward L. Bernays, who contributed a portrait of public-relations activities, or the pollster Archibald M. Crossley.

Historians of this current trace "mass communication research" back to the publication in 1927 of a book by the political scientist Harold Lasswell (1902–78), *Propaganda Techniques in the World War.* He draws lessons from World War I, the first conflict of propaganda in history, in which the modern art of managing opinion was tested in a real-life situation, amid a confrontation referred to as "total."[47] Faithful to the behaviorist perspective and representative of the spirit of the times, this book outlines the features of a target audience blindly obedient to the stimulus-response schema. Mass communication appears endowed with the absolute power to make and unmake events. Belief in the "effect" of the media as divorced from society would last for a very long time.

Within the very field of research staked out by empiricism, the difference was great at the time between, on the one hand, researchers like R. E. Park and other members of the Chicago School, exponents of a sociology that was certainly empirical but also qualitative, and, on the other hand, the increasingly quantitative approaches of "mass communication research." Between the wars, there was a sharp contrast between these two tendencies in the chosen fields of study growing up on U.S. soil. Park, a former journalist and an early advocate of the civil rights cause, which he embraced even before being invited in 1914 by William I. Thomas to teach in Chicago, devoted himself almost entirely, along with most of his colleagues, to the question of immigration and the integration of immigrants into American society. Park investigated the formation of ethnic ghettoes. In his first article, published in 1914, he expressed his faith in a multicultural and multiethnic society. It was in Chicago that the first sociologists from the black community would be trained; later they would devote themselves to research on ethnic interactions and on the racial tensions that the United States discovered as a result of the first violent demonstrations, which took place in Chicago itself in the summer of 1919.

In the histories of research that the epigones of quantitative sociology would write once their hegemony over the field was consolidated, "mass communication research" would become synonymous with "American mass media sociology." Tailoring the story to suit their own vision, they would canonize four founding fathers: Lasswell, of course; Paul F. Lazarsfeld, whom we will encounter shortly; and two social psychologists, Kurt Lewin (1890–1947) and Carl I. Hovland (1912–61). Thus at least two elements were left out of the account: the decisive contribution of an original perspective from a conflictual America on the mechanisms of intercultural communication and communication in general, and second, the context of social commitment in which it arose. And with good reason, since what best characterized quantitative empiricism—what the Russian émigré sociologist Pitirim Sorokin called "quantophrenia"— is precisely its tendency to decontextualize both its objects of study and its explanations of how conceptual frames of reference are formulated.

In contrast to the work of Park and his colleagues, this quantitative sociology would be built on a close relationship to the needs of industrial and commercial corporations. It was tied not only to media firms but to other types of firms as well. This connection opened the factory doors to researchers and led to the birth of industrial psychosociology. At its origin stands Elton Mayo (1880–1949), a psychiatrist by training who taught at the Harvard Business School, whose first significant study was commissioned by Western Electric, a subsidiary of American Telephone and Telegraph. Carried out between 1924 and 1932 in the company's shop in Hawthorne, Massachusetts, its original objective was to study the relationship between factory lighting and productivity. When Mayo and his team discovered that isolating the lighting variable did not provide an answer, they evolved toward more general research into human relations within the firm, and more direct involvement of employees in the investigation. Obliged to go beyond the narrow initial framework of the analysis of the "manifest functions" of an industrial organization, Mayo was led to reorient his study toward the "latent functions" of primary groups, the social contacts that were formed between the members of a firm but were not limited to the principal goals of the organization. The result was one of the first psychosociological reflections on the role of "human relations" and communication in the factory (via newsletters, bulletins, suggestion boxes, etc.).[48]

As the 1940s began, the quantitative trend was consummated by another of the "fathers" of empiricist sociology, Paul F. Lazarsfeld (1901–76), a mathematician of Austrian origin who also had experience in applied psychology. Culminating a process launched by Adolphe Quételet, validation of conclusions by figures became the criterion of scientific worthiness. The split that was to affect mass media sociology and sociology in general after the war already began to manifest itself. Lazarsfeld, who belonged to socialist circles in Vienna in the 1920s before emigrating to the United States to stay in 1935, broke with his past and became a leader and symbol of an applied sociology that defined itself as apolitical and was incapable of distancing itself from its objects of study. At the opposite pole, the exponent of the Frankfurt School, Theodor Adorno (1903–69), who had been similarly linked to European socialism and had emigrated to the United States to escape Nazism, would never cease pursuing his project of a critical and engaged but speculative sociology, denouncing the effects of the industrialization of culture.[49]

A symbol of Lazarsfeld's operational goal in his first studies of radio was the *program analyzer* or *profile machine,* known as the *Lazarsfeld-Stanton Analyzer,* which Lazarsfeld developed along with Frank Stanton, at the time director of research at the CBS radio network and future president of that company. The analyzer was a device to record the reactions of the listener in terms of like, dislike, or indifference. The listener expressed satisfaction by pressing a green button in the right hand and rejection by a red button in the other hand, throughout the duration of a sequence; pushing neither button signified indifference. The buttons were linked to a graphic recorder—as in Marey's experiments—in which a stylus traced the reaction curve on a paper cylinder. Here applied to radio, it would later be used to measure the reactions of filmgoers.

This generation of administrative researchers would carry out numerous elaborate studies of the media and the attitudes of voters and consumers. Lazarsfeld coined the term "administrative research" for them (others would call it "social engineering"), legitimating his partisan approach in the name of the usefulness of the results for those who commissioned these studies. At first intuitive, the theoretical framework of functional analysis was not formalized until the immediate postwar period, under the decisive impetus of Robert K. Merton (born in 1910), Lazarsfeld's colleague at Columbia University. This theoretical codification of empirical research would become an umbrella paradigm just as ample and all-encompassing as that of French structuralism in the 1960s. It would confuse things more than clarify them, with Merton asserting loudly and clearly in 1949 that "This motley company [Albert Einstein, Frank Lloyd Wright, A. N. Whitehead, etc.] suggests anew that agreement on the functional outlook need not imply identity of political or social philosophy."[50]

And yet this kind of functionalism was strongly conditioned by the postulates of a certain Anglo-American anthropology, developed for the most part in the 1920s and the first half of the 1930s (but whose roots go back much farther, of course, in the history of nineteenth-century social sciences, particularly to classical ethnology). The major referents are the models offered by British anthropologists A. R. Radcliffe-Brown (1881–1955) and Bronislaw Malinowski (1884–1942) based on their respective field research among Australian tribes and in the Trobriand archipelago in New Guinea. The concept of "social function" was shaped in the language of the biological sciences, where functions are "vital or organic processes to the extent that they contribute to the maintenance of the organism."[51]

Thus, for Radcliffe-Brown, who claimed his own free interpretation of Durkheim, any particular culture is "normally a systematic or integrated unity in which every element has a distinct function."[52] The functional unity of society is defined as a "state of cohesion or harmonious cooperation among all the elements of the social system, that removes from it all persistent conflicts that are impossible to regulate."[53] Transferred to the realm of the media, this model of functional analysis would articulate a triple social function: "surveillance of the environment, correlation of the parts of society in response to that environment, and transmission of the social heritage from one generation to the next."[54] To this original trilogy formulated by Lasswell would be later added the function of "entertainment." A further distinction would be introduced between manifest and latent functions, according to whether the function is admitted, willed, and recognized or not in its social and psychological consequences. The idea that "dysfunctions" might exist would also be admitted.[55] However elementary this last proposition might seem, it went unnoticed by Lasswell, obsessed as he was by a system's instruments of regulation and the maintenance of a social and productive order, and hence little inclined to theorize dissonances, which he classified, moreover, under the heading of psychopathology.

The emergence of mass communication systems between the two world wars started to shake the established idea of culture and cultural democratization. The ratification of New York as the center of the new world-economy accentuated the contrast between a culture tied to the market, industry, and technology, bearer of a new cosmopolitanism, and a culture inherited from the Enlightenment project of pedagogical universality, which had developed in the context of the nation-state and the welfare state. There was a reversal of the tide. The United States, which had been built upon European philosophies, doctrines, and peoples, had begun to disseminate its own model of society, lifestyle, and legitimacy. But that is the beginning of another history.

Epilogue

New Organic Totalities?

Traversing the successive ages and discoveries of the life sciences, the biological analogy has been established as the natural matrix, the great unifying paradigm, for accounting for the functioning of systems of communication and the link that binds them to society as an organic whole. We may even ask whether it is not in this realm of knowledge and of the social sciences that it has most held sway, so much has the give-and-take between the life sciences and the representations of communication increased since the enthronement of the notion of "information" in its mathematical sense.

When, in 1948, Claude Shannon formulated the first mathematical theory of information and communication while in the service of Bell Telephone Laboratories, he borrowed heavily from biology's discoveries about the nervous system. Six years earlier, in a famous book titled *What Is Life?*, Erwin Schrödinger (1887–1961) had introduced into this branch of the life sciences the vocabulary of information and coding in order to explain the models of individual development contained in the chromosomes. The landmark discovery of DNA, the molecules present in the nucleus of each living cell, led to a further progression in the analogy: in 1944, Oswald Avery, a researcher at the Rockefeller Institute in New York, showed that the basis of heredity is DNA; nine years later, the Englishman Francis Crick and the American James Watson elucidated its double helix structure. To account for biological specificity, that is, what makes each individual unique, specialists in molecular biology used the communication model developed by Shannon. François Jacob, author of *The Logic of Life* (1970) and holder of a Nobel Prize in medicine and physiology (1965) obtained jointly with François Lwoff and Jacques Monod for their work on genetics, described heredity in terms of programs, information, messages, and codes. In the architecture of the cell, the transmission of information was in a certain way that of the "orders of life." By the 1960s, people referred to the cell as being a veritable self-regulating cybernetic system.

From its beginnings, the mathematical theory of information was the gatekeeper of many disciplines, and thanks to its powers of organization, nourished fields of knowledge as diverse as economics and physics, sociology, psychology, and linguistics. With Roman Jakobson (1896–1982) in the 1960s, structural linguistics, the leading discipline of the then triumphant structuralism, not only borrowed this mechanicist model of communication formulated by Shannon but proposed to share with molecular biology a common framework of metaphoric interpretation, via concepts such as code, message, and information. This analogical alliance even seemed essential to Jakobson for giving the "soft sciences" of humankind and society the status of respectability only the "hard sciences" could claim until then. Out of this question came a first generation of semantics that thought of communication as a linear process and believed it could flush out meaning by remaining enclosed within media texts, abstracting from both the sender and the receiver.[1]

Of course, the history of this reciprocal borrowing had begun long before, and it did not stop there. It has continued since, and we may wager that it can only continue and become increasingly sophisticated. The problem resides in the uses prescribed for this *analogon* and the role it is made to play in the economy and ideologies of the regulation of human societies—sometimes even unbeknownst to, or on the margins of, disciplines that appeal to it, and sometimes with their complicity. It must be acknowledged that the organic metaphor has been mobilized, all too often, in visions of communication derived from a neo-Darwinist framework for the organization of society, particularly in its worldwide dimension.

In the nineteenth century, the biological discourse erected on the basis of an identification between evolution and progress had accompanied a partition of the world according to the principle of the international division of labor, under the hegemony of European investments. This partition deepened a process begun at the end of the sixteenth century with the expansion of the important Dutch East India Company at a time when the world-economy was centered in Amsterdam. Thanks to its avenues and networks of transport, communication was promoted quite naturally as the agent of civilization.

At the end of the millennium, the process of financial globalization begun in the 1980s and the historic turning point of the deregulation of communication networks, whether material or immaterial, as important as the opening up to free trade in the preceding century, have precipitated the move to worldwide economic integration. A new era has opened: a market moving toward planetary unification, involving actors for whom the sphere of conception, production, and distribution of goods and services extends worldwide. The framework of international relations that is emerging relies heavily on technologies of information and is organized according to a reticular logic. The space of globalization is woven together by enterprises structured into corporate networks, "global firms" that interconnect all the sites of their implantation and manage their operations in real time. The principle of contiguity that Diderot held as one of the characteristics of "communication" recedes to the background, to the advantage of "connectedness."

The end of our millennium is also witnessing the consummation of the crisis of the positivist idea of a "necessary and continuous" progress, without deviations, detours, or retreats. The bankruptcy of this ideology of progress has radically changed the status of communication and its technological systems: it has propelled them to the rank of a symbol of evolution. Originally considered as one of the principal agents of civilization and progress, communication has been gradually converted into the outstanding metaphoric image of society. "Modern forms of social exchange," writes Alain Mons in *La Métaphore sociale* (The social metaphor),

> indicate a marked tendency toward the *metaphorization* of reference points. In a context of generalized "communication," fluidity of systems, and the rapid circulation of goods, bodies, and objects, now reference games, connections, and telescoping may be deployed via images and displacements of meaning. The analogical game becomes a paradigm of our contemporaneity, characterized by the globalization of economies, the mass-mediatization of society, the postmodernity of forms (artistic, architectural, design).[2]

This process of metaphorization is occurring in a society that recognizes more and more the limits of the perfectibility of the world, and where the defense of what exists has taken the lead over the search for what ought to be. The paradigm of communication replaces that of progress and social change. From particles to man, from family organization to modern state, from ethnic group to coalition of nations, from the international to the global: in the history of forms of integration, "social and cultural integrons," as François Jacob called them, the means of communication are expected to furnish to evolution all its meaning. Jacques Ruffié, author of a book with the suggestive title *De la biologie à la culture* (From biology to culture), has written:

> Almost all animals communicate among themselves. Communication thus appears as a very general phenomenon of the living world. It forms the "cement" of the social bond: the more the means of communication are precise and rigorous, the better society will perform ... Without an adequate means of integration, the human type of society would have disappeared long ago ... Today, it is the audiovisual means of communication that, via the mass media, spread knowledge throughout the world. These constantly expanding means of communication are indispensable for the maintenance of equilibrium and harmony in the human group. They ensure the cultural unity of humankind.[3]

Communication as a mode of organization of a finite world once more encounters the natural philosophy of history. Evolution, measured in terms of performance, is evaluated by the extent to which peoples are equipped with communicating machines. The struggle for existence takes over from the quest for the lost community, and the Malthusian prediction overwhelms Condorcet's hypothesis about the infinitude of progress.

At the end of the nineteenth century, communication implied universal solidarity and biological interdependence in a world that was certainly menaced by war, but in which people believed in the potentialities of social redistribution and compensation for inequalities by means of the national and international mechanisms of the welfare state. For decades, hopes and energies were directed toward the horizon of a development that would necessarily come about if the peoples who aspired to it rigorously followed the historic stages through which the great elder nations had passed. In the years following World War II, with the rise of anticolonial revolts, some social scientists even forged the notion of a "revolution of rising expectations"; by offering its audiences models of aspirations and behavior labeled modern, the media were conceived as a spur to social change.

The crisis of the idea of linear progress is contemporary with the crisis of the idea of social equality. The egalitarian representation of a "global village" that aggregates television viewers around the planet in a common participation in the symbols of modernity is in constant discrepancy with the reality of the standards of living of the immense majority of humankind. The dynamic of the economic model of globalization now unfolding risks leading to a "ghettoized" world organized around a few megacities and regions usually in the North, but occasionally in the South, called on to serve as the nerve centers of worldwide markets and flows.

Inegalitarian logics threaten to lead to what Riccardo Petrella calls the "new Hanseatic phase of the world economy," and to "global techno-apartheid."[4] The integration of everyone into the material benefits of modernity reserved up to now for a few has become more and more problematic. The very idea of struggle against inequalities, which at the world level have never stopped growing since the end of the nineteenth century, has been called into question.

The "global village," which is on its way to becoming a "true virtual planet coexisting with the real world village," the space of a "viral circulation of symbols and programs" (in the words of Philippe Quéau, a specialist of virtual worlds), is also a world of security-oriented logics. Apparatuses of electronic communication have another function, that of protecting individuals from the violence of others, those left by the wayside of the Hanseatic model with its exclusive and excluding networks. The more the hindrances to the free flow of commodities and the free circulation of its agents continue to tumble, the more the major multimedia and multinational groups try to outbid each other in their transborder vocation, and the greater the use of electronic passports against the "excommunicated," in the eloquent term of the Encyclopédistes.

In this decade of the centenary of fingerprinting, what better parable is there than the schema governing the system of formalities for entry into the United States, inaugurated in 1993 at Kennedy airport in New York? This mechanism, christened INSPASS (Immigration and Naturalization Service Passenger Accelerated Service System), uses a biometric technology that identifies the traveler by his or her hand and fingerprints. Information concerning each person is transcribed on a personal magnetic card issued by the immigration service after an interview. It thus suffices, upon arrival in New York, to introduce one's card into a scanner, place one's hand over a metal plate, and enter one's flight number. The system identifies the traveler and automatically furnishes an immigration form while unlocking the entry door. This procedure, which takes only twenty seconds, is offered, however, only to the citizens of twenty-four countries. Moreover, it is reserved to passengers having entered the United States at least three times in the preceding twelve months. Not so long ago, only strategic places under high surveillance, such as military intelligence agencies, were guarded by such a mechanism.

The criterion of fitness and performance in the globalized market inaugurates a new cycle in the paradigm of the organism, as witnessed by its growing penetration into the discourse of the new form of organic totalities known as the enterprise, or better still the "enterprise-as-system," or the world-society as enterprise—to paraphrase Saint-Simon—and particularly its penetration into the discourse of managerial communication. We are told that the "Balkanized" or "vertical" model, divided between an "up" and a "down," and allergic to the circulation of information, is giving way to a horizontal schema characterized by multidirectional flows of information and communication. From the perspective of its systems approach, this new form of organization is explained by analogy with the functioning of living organisms. Its structures constitute its anatomy. Its systems or modes of functioning are the equivalent of cardiovascular, respiratory, digestive, and nervous systems. Its representations, or the internal and external "mental images" associated with the existence of this new being, its corporate image as a capital, are the "psyche" of the organization. Others speak of the new "polycellular" enterprise.[5]

Activating its borrowings from the broadest range of disciplines and ways of thought, and mobilizing knowledge and skills every which way without establishing their epistemological grounding, administrative research blurs its own reference points. "With the intellectual legitimacy conferred by innumerable references to Jacques Derrida, Michel Foucault, and Jean-François Lyotard," as I originally wrote in *Mapping World Communication,*

> such works claim to explain to us the birth of "postmodern enterprise." The enterprise of the 1980s becomes an immaterial entity, an abstract figure, a universe of forms, symbols, and communication flows, in which the problems posed by the restructuring of the world economy and the redistribution of the dependencies and hierarchies on the planet become diluted . . . [into] a vaporous world of flows, fluids, and communicating vessels evolving into "dissipative structures."[6]

The enterprise is an organism, and the sphere of globalization a macroorganism. Vital competition takes the form of technological, economic, linguistic, cultural, and media battles. Let us listen once more to a biologist, Guy Béney, who in this case is more circumspect regarding the new paradigm: "The recent calls to 'get on-line' to information technologies evoke old slogans ('get rich,' etc.) and resonate like a thinly veiled justification of the form of a *social Darwinism* that has become predominant: selection by aptitude for following technical trends, whether it involves individuals, peoples, states, or corporations."[7]

In its mode of organization and management of the planetary market, the global corporation portrays itself as a self-regulating cybernetic system. This idea of self-regulation, which goes along with that of the self-discipline and the self-equilibrium of the market, legitimates all sorts of conceptual convolutions. The idea of freedom is reduced to the freedom of enterprise and trade; "Free Thinking, Free Trade, Freedom of Information for a Free World," says the promotional blurb of the *Economist*. "Freedom of commercial speech as a new human right" is the demand formulated within the major international bodies by the opponents of any form of regulation to control the growing commodification of the public sphere, whether exercised by the state or by organized civil society.[8]

In *Le Mythe de l'entreprise*, Jean-Pierre Le Goff writes: "[There exists] a more pernicious mode for spreading managerial ideology: the dissemination and massive taking up of its vocabulary and its ways of thinking in all social activities and in everyday life."[9] The essential problem becomes each time the internalization of the new form, its assimilation by the individual, the formation of a personality type, of a "veritable sociomental system," that is the only force capable of lowering the threshold of the intolerable and rendering it natural.[10] Discourse about self-regulation and the freedom of commercial speech and, more generally, the neoliberal ideology of communication, are part and parcel of the strange mixture that at this century's end plays the role of a veritable Trojan horse in the privatization of the public sphere.

In his astonishing *Erewhon*, Samuel Butler combined a critical reflection begun in the late nineteenth century with a frame of reference that strikes us as contemporary.[11] At 120 years' distance, the late Félix Guattari's appeal that the machinelike dimensions of the production of subjectivity be taken into account resonates like an echo of Butler. In what was to be his last book, *Chaosmose*, the philosopher and psychiatrist wrote in 1992:

Like the social machines that one may put under the general heading of collective equipment, technological machines of information and communication (from computing to robotics to the media) operate at the heart of human subjectivity, not only at the core of its memories and its intelligence, but also on its sensibility, its affects and unconscious fantasies... One cannot judge this machinelike evolution either positively or negatively; everything depends on its articulation with the collective agencies of enunciation. The best outcome is creation, the invention of new universes of references; the worst is the unchecked mass-mediatization to which billions of individuals are condemned today. Technological evolutions combined with social experimentation of these new domains are perhaps capable of surmounting the current oppressive period and causing us to enter a postmedia era characterized by a reappropriation of the media, notably by the individual.[12]

The reappropriation of this machinelike world is all the more crucial in that "communication" is on the verge of becoming in our societies a fetishistic object, and an object of speculation for demagogues and demiurges. Here is yet another reason to enable communication to escape this amnesiac universe by breathing into it a dose of history, so as to imagine it differently.

Notes

1. The Paths of Reason

1. P. Virilio, "L'Empire de l'emprise," *Traverses*, no. 13 (December 1978).

2. J. Cassou, "Cervantes," *Encyclopaedia Universalis*. See also his introduction to the work of the Spanish writer in *Cervantes, Don Quichotte, Nouvelles Exemplaires* (Paris: La Pléiade, 1949).

3. M. Cervantes, *The Ingenious Gentleman Quixote of La Mancha*, trans. C. Jarvis, ed. E. C. Riley (Oxford and New York: Oxford University Press, 1992), Part II, chapter 62, "Which treats of the adventure of the enchanted head with other trifles that must not be omitted," 977–78.

4. M. Malthête-Méliès, *Méliès l'enchanteur* (Paris: Hachette, 1973).

5. S. de Vauban, *Oisivetés de M. de Vauban* (Paris: J. Corréard, 1843), 139. On Vauban's initiatives with respect to canals, see J. Mesqui, *Vauban et le projet de transport fluvial* (Paris: Association Vauban, 1983).

6. J.-L. Marfaing et al., *Canal royal de Languedoc. Le partage des eaux* (Éditions Loubatière, published by the Conseil d'Architecture, d'Urbanisme et de l'Environnement [CAVE] de la Haute-Garonne, 1992).

7. R. von Kaufmann, *La Politique française en matière de chemins de fer* (Paris: Librairie Polytechnique, C. Béranger, 1900), 803.

8. *Oisivetés de M. de Vauban*, 45.

9. M. Gautier (architect, engineer, and inspector of the kingdom's routes, bridges, and roadways), *Traité de la construction des chemins* (Paris: Chez Laporte, 1778).

10. Quoted in G. Reverdy, *Atlas historique des routes de France* (Paris: Presses de l'École des Ponts et Chaussées, 1986), 89.

11. See J. Langins, "La préhistoire de l'École polytechnique," *Revue d'histoire des sciences*, vol. 44 (1991).

12. Y. Chicoteau and A. Picon, "Forme, technique et ideologie, les ingénieurs des Ponts et Chaussées à la fin du XVIIIᵉ," *Culture technique*, no. 7 (March 1982): 193–94.

13. F. Braudel, *Civilisation and Capitalism: 15th–18th Century*, trans. revised by Sian Reynolds (London: Collins, 1981–84), vol. 3, *The Perspective of the World*, 322.

14. Ibid., 367.

15. R. Taton, ed., *Histoire générale des sciences* (Paris: PUF, 1958), vol. 2, 430.

16. S. de Vauban, *Le Directeur général des fortifications* (The Hague: Chez Henri Van Bulderen, 1685), 20–21.

17. Ibid., 62–63.

18. Ibid. On this matter, see also D. L'Aisné, *L'expérience de l'architecture militaire où l'on apprendra à fonds la méthode de faire travailler dans les Places* (Paris: Chez Maurice Villery, 1687).

19. *Oisivetés de M. de Vauban,* 82.

20. De Vauban, *La dîme royale* (Paris: Guillaumin, 1889), 175–76.

21. Ibid., 191.

22. D. S. Landes, *Revolution in Time: Clocks and the Making of the Modern World* (Cambridge: Belknap Press of Harvard University Press, 1983), 110–11.

23. M. Grmek, *La première révolution biologique* (Paris: Payot, 1990).

24. J. Kepler, *The Secret of the Universe,* trans. A. M. Duncan (New York: Abaris Books, 1981). On this evolution, see A. Koyré, *The Astronomical Revolution: Copernicus, Kepler, Borelli,* trans. R. E. W. Madison (Ithaca, N.Y.: Cornell University Press, 1973).

25. R. Sasso, "Système et discours philosophique," in *Recherches sur le XVIIᵉ siècle* (Paris: CNRS, 1978).

26. J. Schlanger, *Les Métaphores de l'organisme* (Paris: Vrin, 1971), 89.

27. W. Petty, *The Economic Writings of Sir Willliam Petty,* ed. Charles Henry Hull (Cambridge, England: Cambridge University Press, 1899), 128–29; 113.

28. Quoted in P. Vilar, *Or et monnaie dans l'histoire* (Paris: Flammarion, 1974), 277.

29. Quoted in P. Harsin, *Les doctrines monétaires et financières en France* (Paris: F. Alcan, 1928), 146.

30. Petty, *The Economic Writings,* 244.

31. A. Desrosières, *La Politique des grands nombres* (Paris: La Découverte, 1993).

32. See Desrosières, *La Politique des grands nombres*; A. Landry et al., *Traité de démographie* (Paris: Payot, 1945); R. Gonnard, *Histoire des doctrines de population* (Paris: Nouvelle Librairie Nationale, 1923); J. Dupâquier, *Histoire de la démographie* (Paris: Perrin, 1985). For the view of a historian of insurance creation, see J. Delumeau, *Rassurer et protéger: le sentiment de sécurité dans l'Occident chrétien* (Paris: Fayard, 1989).

33. See Vilar, *Or et monnaie dans l'histoire.*

34. Desrosières, *La Politique des grands nombres,* 36.

35. Schlanger, *Les Métaphores de l'organisme,* 35.

36. Ibid., 30.

37. Ibid., 59.

38. Landes, *Revolution in Time.*

39. *The Encyclopédie: Selections,* trans. Stephen Gendzier (New York: Harper and Row, 1967), 239.

40. La Mettrie, *L'Homme machine* (written in 1747 and published in 1748), translated as *Man a Machine* by Gertrude C. Bussey (La Salle, Ill.: Open Court, 1961), 135.

41. Ibid., 141.

42. P.-L. Assoun, Introduction, *L'Homme-Machine* (Paris: Gonthier/Denoël, 1981), 40–41.

43. La Mettrie, *Man a Machine,* 109.

44. M. Foucault, *Discipline and Punish: The Birth of the Prison,* trans. A. Sheridan (London: Penguin Books, 1977), 136.

45. Ibid., 171.

46. Assoun, Introduction to La Mettrie, *L'Homme-Machine,* 69.

47. J. Perriault, "Le concept de machine et de système chez Ledoux, Sade et Vaucanson," *Culture technique,* no. 7 (March 1982).

48. R. Barthes, *Sade, Fourier, Loyola*, trans. Richard Miller (New York: Hill and Wang, 1976), 152–53.

49. Perriault, "Le concept de machine."

2. The Economy of Circulation

1. R. Gonnard, *Histoire des doctrines économiques* (Paris: Librairie générale de droit et de jurisprudence, 1941), new edition (original edition 1921), 14. On "consumption-ism," see S. Ewen, *Captains of Consciousness: Advertising and the Social Roots of the Consumer Culture* (New York: McGraw-Hill, 1976).

2. F. Quesnay, "Maximes générales du gouvernement économique d'un royaume agricole," in *Œuvres économiques et philosophiques de F. Quesnay*, ed. A. Oncken (Paris: Jules Peelman and Company, 1888), 336.

3. F. Quesnay, "Despotisme de la Chine," in ibid., 602–56.

4. Ibid., translated as "Despotism in China" in Lewis Maveric, *China: A Model for Europe* (San Antonio, Texas: Paul Anderson and Company, 1946), 209.

5. F. Quesnay, *Observations sur les effets de la saignée* (Paris: Chez Charles Ormont, 1730), 1–3.

6. F. Quesnay, "Mémoires de l'Académie royale de chirurgie," in *Œuvres*, 735.

7. See the monograph issue devoted to Quesnay and Physiocracy in *Population* (Paris: INED, November 1975).

8. "Éloge de F. Quesnay par G. H. Romance, marquis de Mesmon," in *Œuvres*, 85.

9. F. Quesnay, *Essai physique sur l'œconomie animale* (Paris: Chez Guillaume Cavelier, 1736).

10. Quesnay, "Despotisme de la Chine," 640–41.

11. Ibid., 598.

12. Ibid., 660.

13. J. Habermas, *The Structural Transformation of the Public Sphere: An Inquiry into a Category of Bourgeois Society*, trans. T. Burger and F. Lawrence (Cambridge: MIT Press, 1992), 4th printing, 95.

14. Ibid., 96.

15. A. Farge, *Dire et mal dire: L'opinion publique au XVIIIᵉ siècle* (Paris: Seuil, 1992), 16–17. The quotation from Condorcet is taken from this book.

16. A. de Tocqueville, *The Old Regime and the French Revolution*, trans. John Bonner (New York: Harper and Brothers, 1856), 178.

17. B. Lepetit, *Chemins de terre et voies d'eau, Réseaux de transports, Organisation de l'espace* (Paris: Éditions de l'École des hautes études en sciences sociales, 1984).

18. M. Gautier, *Traité de la construction des chemins* (Paris: Chez Laporte, 1778), 118–19.

19. A. Young, *Travels in France* (1792) (Paris: A. Colin, 1931), vol. 1, 98.

20. "Actes du ministère de Turgot: Observations et contre-observations de Turgot sur la suppression de la corvée," in *Œuvres de Turgot*, ed. E. Daire (Paris: Guillaumin, 1844), vol. 2, 256.

21. Ibid., 297.

22. Ibid., 287.

23. Ibid., 466.

24. See R. Finzi, "The History of Historical Stages in Turgot and Quesnay," *Economic Review*, vol. 33, no. 2 (1988). Turgot's youthful writings (notably his *Discours en Sorbonne*) are published in a book edited by E. Daire (see note 20).

25. F. Braudel, *Civilisation and Capitalism: 15th–18th Century*, trans. revised by Sian Reynolds (London: Collins, 1981–84), vol. 3, "The Perspective of the World," 581.

26. "Rapport de Grégoire (session of 4 June 1794)," in *Orateurs politiques, Tribune française*, ed. A. Amic and E. Mouttet (Paris: Société du Panthéon littéraire, 1844), 575–86.

27. See J. Langins, "La préhistoire de l'École polytechnique," *Revue d'histoire des sciences*, vol. 44 (1991).

28. F. Quesnay, "Questions intéressantes sur la population, l'agriculture et le commerce," *Œuvres*, 285.

29. W. Kula, *Measures and Men*, trans. R. Szreter (Princeton, N.J.: Princeton University Press, 1986), 3, 8. The Polish edition of 1970, translated into French on the initiative of *Annales* historians, constitutes one of the most complete studies of the question. See also A. Macharey, *La Métrologie dans les musées de province et sa contribution à l'histoire des poids et mesures en France depuis le XIIIᵉ siècle* (Paris: CNRS, 1959) (doctoral thesis).

30. G. Ardant, *Histoire financière de l'Antiquité à nos jours* (Paris: Idées/Gallimard, 1976), 265.

31. Kula, *Measures and Men*, 287–88.

32. G. Canguilhem, *Le Normal et le Pathologique* (Paris: PUF, 1966), 181.

33. See S. Bianchi, *La Révolution culturelle de l'an II* (Paris: Aubier, 1982); A. Magoudi, *Quand l'homme civilise le temps* (Paris: La Découverte, 1992).

34. M. J. A. de Condorcet, *Sketch for a Historical Picture of the Progress of the Human Mind*, trans. Jane Barraclough (Westport, Conn.: Hyperion Press, 1955), 8.

35. Ibid., 198.

36. H. Le Bras, "Reproduction démographique, reproduction familiale, reproduction sociale," in *Information et communication: Séminaire interdisciplinaire du Collège de France*, ed. A. Lichnerowicz et al. (Paris: Maloine, 1983), 205.

37. See R. Gonnard, *Histoire des doctrines de population* (Paris: Nouvelle Librairie Nationale, 1923).

38. A. Desrosières, *La Politique des grands nombres* (Paris: La Découverte, 1993), 47–48.

39. P. Flichy, "The Birth of Long Distance Communication," *Réseaux: French Journal of Communication*, vol. 1, no. 1 (1993). See also the same author's *Une Histoire de la communication moderne* (Paris: La Découverte, 1991).

40. Y. Stourdzé, *Pour une poignée d'électrons: Pouvoir et communication* (Paris: Fayard, 1987), 82–83.

41. A. Belloc, *La Télégraphie historique depuis les temps les plus reculés jusqu'à nos jours* (Paris: Firmin-Didot, 1888). By the same author: *Les Postes françaises* (Paris: Firmin-Didot, 1886).

42. C. Bertho, *Télégraphes et téléphones: De Valmy au microprocesseur* (Paris: Livre de Poche, 1981).

43. H. G. Wells, *Anticipations of the Reaction of Mechanical and Scientific Progress upon Human Life and Thought* (London: Chapman and Hall, 1902).

44. Braudel, *Civilisation and Capitalism*, 543. For a history of the railways, see H. Peyret, *Histoire des chemins de fer en France et dans le monde* (Paris: SEFI, 1949).

45. P. Virilio, "L'Empire de l'emprise," *Traverses*, no. 13 (December 1978): 24.

46. G. E. Rothenberg, "Maurice de Nassau, Gustavus Adolphus, Raïmondo Montecuccoli, and the 'Military Revolution' of the Seventeenth Century," in *Makers of Modern Strategy, from Machiavelli to the Nuclear Age*, ed. P. Paret (Princeton, N.J.: Princeton University Press, 1986).

47. Virilio, "L'Empire de l'emprise," 21. By the same author, *Speed and Politics* (New York: Semiotext[e], 1986).

48. Ministère des Postes et Télégraphes, *Exposition internationale d'électricité, Rapport administratif* (Paris, 1881), vol. 1, 330.

49. Ibid., 341.

50. J. R. Beniger, *The Control Revolution: Technological and Economic Origins of the Information Society* (Cambridge: Harvard University Press, 1986). See also the studies assembled in J. Prades, ed., *La technoscience: Les fractures du discours* (Paris: L'Harmattan, 1992).

51. D. S. Landes, *Revolution in Time: Clocks and the Making of the Modern World* (Cambridge: Belknap Press of Harvard University Press, 1983), 286–87.

52. *Dictionnaire (Robert) historique de la langue française*, ed. A Rey (Paris: Dictionnaires Le Robert, 1992), vol. 2.

53. P. Larousse, *Grand dictionnaire universel du XIXᵉ siècle* (Paris: Administration du Grand dictionnaire universel), vol. 4, 751.

54. P. Leroy-Beaulieu, *L'État moderne et ses fonctions* (Paris: Guillaumin, 1890).

55. A. Guillerme, *Genèse du concept de réseau: Territoire et génie en Europe de l'Ouest (1760–1815)* (Paris: Université de Paris VIII, Institut français d'urbanisme, 1988); G. Dupuy, "Réseaux (Philosophie de l'organisation)," *Encyclopaedia Universalis* (Paris, 1989), Corpus 19, 875–82.

3. The Crossroads of Evolution

1. A. Smith, *An Inquiry into the Nature and Causes of the Wealth of Nations* (London: Methuen, 1930), vol. 1, 5.

2. Ibid., 14.

3. "Épingle," *Encyclopédie*, vol. 5 (1755), 804.

4. The plates appear in *Recueil de planches sur les sciences, les arts libéraux et les arts mécaniques avec leur explication* (Paris: Chez Briasson, David Le Breton, 1755), vol. 4.

5. "Épingle," 807.

6. See E. Cannan, Introduction, Smith, *An Inquiry into the Nature and Causes of the Wealth of Nations*, 6 and 9.

7. Ibid., 15.

8. Ibid., 20–21.

9. J. S. Mill, *Principles of Political Economy with Some of Their Applications to Social Philosophy* (1848), ed. W. J. Ashley (Toronto and New York: University of Toronto Press, Routledge and Kegan Paul, 1965), 102–3. The subsequent quotations from book 4 and book 5 come from the seventh edition (1871) (published by Oxford University Press, 1994), 121, 233–34.

10. J. R. Beniger, "Comparison, Yes But—The Case of Technological and Cultural Change," in *Comparatively Speaking: Communication and Culture across Space and Time*, ed. J. G. Blumler et al. (Newbury Park-London: Sage, 1992), 39.

11. Mill, *Principles of Political Economy*, 121.

12. C. Babbage, *On the Economy of Machinery and Manufactures* (1832) (New York: A. M. Kelley, 1963).

13. This anecdote also appears in *Note sur la publication proposée par le gouvernement anglais, des grandes Tables logarithmiques et trigonométriques de M. de Prony* (Paris: F. Didot, 1830).

14. M. Palyi, "The Introduction of Adam Smith on the Continent," in *Adam Smith 1776–1926. Lectures to Commemorate the Sesquicentennial of the Publication of "The Wealth of Nations,"* ed. J. M. Clarke et al. (Chicago: University of Chicago Press, 1928), 229.

15. T. R. Malthus, *An Essay on the Principle of Population, or a View of Its Past and Present Effects on Human Happiness with an Inquiry into Our Prospects Respecting the*

Future Removal or Mitigation of the Evils Which It Occasions, selected and introduced by D. Winch using the text of the 1803 edition as prepared by P. James, showing the additions and corrections made in the 1806, 1807, and 1826 editions (Cambridge, England: Cambridge University Press, 1992), 249.

16. Ibid., 329.

17. Ibid., 244.

18. Ibid., 322.

19. Ibid., 330.

20. Ibid., 277, 250.

21. T. Parsons, *The Structure of Social Action* (Glencoe, Ill.: Free Press, 1964), 102–7.

22. G. Deleuze, *Foucault,* trans. Sean Hand (Minneapolis: University of Minnesota Press, 1988), 92.

23. See H. Le Bras, "Reproduction démographique, reproduction familiale, reproduction sociale," in *Information et communication: Séminaire interdisciplinaire du Collège de France,* ed. A. Lichnerowicz et al. (Paris: Maloine, 1983), 205.

24. G. Canguilhem et al., *Du développement à l'évolution au XIXᵉ siècle* (Paris: PUF, 1985), a special issue of the journal *Thalès,* anthology of work by the Institut d'histoire des sciences et techniques of the University of Paris (vol. 11, 1960). It is on this collective work that I have relied to trace the genealogy of the concept of evolution.

25. F. Jacob, *The Logic of Life: A History of Heredity,* trans. B. E. Spillman (New York: Pantheon Books, 1982), 127.

26. A. Comte, *Cours de philosophie positive* (Paris: Sleicher Frères, 1908), vol. 4, 203.

27. A. Comte, *The Positive Philosophy,* freely translated and condensed by Harriet Martineau (New York: C. Blanchard, 1855), reprinted by AMS Press (New York, 1974), book 5, Biology, chapter 6, 367.

28. Ibid., 444.

29. Ibid., 398.

30. H. Spencer, *Autobiography,* 2 vols. (London: Watts and Co., 1926), vol. 1, 337.

31. A. Comte, *Système de politique positive* (1822), quoted in M. G. Hubbard, *Saint-Simon: Sa vie et ses travaux* (Paris: Guillaumin, 1857), 98.

32. A. Comte, Introduction, *République occidentale Ordre et Progrès, Rapport à la Société positiviste par la Commission chargée d'examiner la nature et le plan du nouveau gouvernement révolutionnaire de la République française* (Paris: Librairie scientifique et industrielle de L. Mathias, 1848), 3.

33. B. Gille, "Pour un musée de la science et la technique," *Culture technique,* no. 7 (May 1982): 210–11. By the same author: *Histoire des techniques* (Paris: La Pléiade, 1978).

34. For example, see M. De Fleur, *Theories of Mass Communication* (New York: D. McKay, 1966).

35. H. Spencer, *The Study of Sociology,* intro. T. Parsons (Ann Arbor: University of Michigan Press, 1966), 300–301.

36. On this polemic, see T. Huxley, "Administrative Nihilism," *Fortnightly Review,* no. 16 (1871): 525–43.

37. H. Spencer, *First Principles* (London: Williams and Norgate, 1911), 6th ed., 321.

38. Quoted in M. Barthélémy-Madaule, "L'évolution darwinienne investie par la durée bergsonienne," in *De Darwin au darwinisme. Science et idéologie,* ed. Y. Conry (Paris: Vrin, 1983), 216ff.

39. H. Spencer, *The Evolution of Society: Selections from Herbert Spencer's Principles of Sociology,* ed. Robert Carneiro (Chicago: University of Chicago Press, 1967), 24.

40. Ibid., 215.

41. Ibid., 43.

42. J. Needham, *The Sceptical Biologist* (London: Chatto and Windus, 1929), 50. Quoted by Carneiro, *The Evolution of Society*, xiii.

43. C. Darwin, *The Origin of Species by Means of Natural Selection*, 6th ed. (London and Toronto: J. M. Dent and Sons, 1936), 116.

44. C. Guillaumin, preface to Darwin, *De l'origine des espèces au moyen de la sélection naturelle ou la lutte pour l'existence dans la nature* (Paris: F. Maspero, 1980).

45. C. Darwin, *The Voyage of the Beagle* (London: Penguin Classics, 1990).

46. Darwin, *The Origin of Species*, 461–62.

47. Ibid., 19.

48. S. S. Schweber, "The Origin of the *Origin* Revisited," *Journal of History of Biology*, no. 10 (1977): 229.

49. Darwin, *The Voyage of the Beagle*, 376.

50. See Y. Conry, *L'Introduction du darwinisme en France au XIXᵉ siècle* (Paris: Vrin, 1974).

51. M. Foucault, "Vérité et pouvoir," interview with M. Fontana, *L'Arc*, no. 70 (1977): 24.

52. M. Fallex and A. Mairey, *Les Principales Puissances du monde (moins la France) au début du XXᵉ siècle* (Paris: Delagrave, 1906), 586.

53. K. Marx, "Speech on the Question of Free Trade" (9 January 1848), in *Marx and Engels: Collected Works* (New York: International Publishers, 1976), vol. 6, 464–65.

54. E. Hobsbawm, *The Age of Capital 1848–1875* (New York: New American Library, 1979), 285.

55. R. Löwie, *History of Ethnological Theory* (New York: Holt, Rinehart and Winston, 1937), 23.

56. See R. Gonnard, *Histoire des doctrines économiques* (Paris: Librairie générale de droit et de jurisprudence, 1941), chapter 4.

57. I. L. Claude, *Swords into Plowshares: The Problems and Progress of International Organization* (New York: Random House, 1964), 3d ed., "Appendix I: The Covenant of the League of Nations," 415.

58. Canguilhem et al., Foreword, *Du développement à l'évolution au XIXᵉ siècle*, 2.

59. W. W. Rostow, *The Stages of Economic Growth* (Cambridge, England: Cambridge University Press, 1960).

60. I have devoted a chapter to this topic in my book *Mapping World Communication: War, Progress, Culture*, trans. S. Emanuel and J. Cohen (Minneapolis: University of Minnesota Press, 1994), chapter 7, "The Revolution of Rising Expectations."

4. The Cult of the Network

1. P. Musso, "Métaphores du réseau et de l'organisme: la transition saint-simonienne," in *Technologies et symboliques de la communication*, ed. L. Sfez, G. Coutlée, and P. Musso (Grenoble: Presses Universitaires de Grenoble, 1990), 206.

2. C. H. de Saint-Simon, "De la physiologie appliquée à l'amélioration des institutions sociales," in *Œuvres de Saint-Simon et Enfantin*, vol. 39, 177–78. The preceding quotation comes from the same text. These *Works* consist of no less than forty-seven volumes and were published between 1865 and 1878 by the members of the council set up by Enfantin to execute his last wishes. There is a reprint published in 1966 by Anthropos Editions of fifteen of the volumes collected into six books.

3. F. Jacob, *The Logic of Life: A History of Heredity*, trans. B. E. Spillman (New York: Pantheon Books, 1982), 3.

4. G. Canguilhem and M. Caullery, "La physiologie animale," in *Histoire générale des sciences*, ed. R. Taton (Paris: PUF, 1958), vol. 3, Part I.

5. Saint-Simon, "De la physiologie appliquée à l'amélioration des institutions sociales," 189–90.

6. C. H. de Saint-Simon, Préface, *Du système industriel* (1821), in *The Political Thought of Saint-Simon,* ed. Ghita Ionescu (Oxford: Oxford University Press, 1976), 153.

7. Ibid., 158 n. 2.

8. J. Schlanger, *Les Métaphores de l'organisme* (Paris: Vrin, 1971), 104.

9. C. H. de Saint-Simon, *Du système industriel* (Paris: A. A. Renouard, 1821), 245.

10. Ibid., 247.

11. C. H. de Saint-Simon, *Industrie* (1817), *Œuvres,* vol. 19, 47.

12. C. H. de Saint-Simon, "De la réorganisation de la société européenne. De la nécessité et des moyens de rassembler les peuples d'Europe en un seul corps politique en conservant à chacun son indépendance nationale," in *Œuvres,* vol. 15, partially translated as "The Reorganization of the European Community, or the Necessity and the Means of Uniting the Peoples of Europe in a Single Body Politic while Preserving for Each Their National Independence," in F. M. H. Markham, *Henri Comte de Saint-Simon: Selected Writings* (Westport, Conn.: Hyperion Press, 1952), 49.

13. "Conception d'un Parlement industriel," *L'Organisateur* (1819), reproduced as an appendix in M. G. Hubbard, *Saint-Simon, sa vie et ses œuvres* (Paris: Guillaumin, 1857), 226–37 (this text also appears in his *Œuvres,* vol. 20, 52 ff.). The parable is reproduced in Ionescu, ed., *The Political Thought of Saint-Simon,* 138–39.

14. C. H. de Saint-Simon, *Lettre au bureau des longitudes* (1808), Préface, *Œuvres,* vol. 15, 64.

15. B. P. Enfantin, "À tous, Parole du Père," *Le Globe,* 20 April 1832.

16. "Religion saint-simonienne. Instruction pour la propagation. Degré des industriels," *Fonds des Archives Enfantin* (Paris: Bibliothèque de l'Arsenal, 1831, MS 7815).

17. "1831: Extraits de la correspondance sur Missions en Province à Paris," in ibid.

18. "Rapport à Messieurs les actionnaires du *Producteur* par le Père Enfantin, 1826," in ibid.

19. "Circulaires relatives à l'envoi du *Globe* par Michel Chevalier, 1831," in ibid.

20. "Lettre du 29 janvier 1862: M. Soulard au Père Enfantin," in ibid., MS 7784.

21. *Fonds des Archives Enfantin,* MS 7803.

22. Quoted in S. Charlety, *Histoire du saint-simonisme* (Paris: Gonthier, 1931), 188–89.

23. *Fonds des Archives Enfantin,* MS 7834.

24. *L'Isthme du Suez,* no. 1 (25 June 1856): 3.

25. *Daily National Intelligencer,* Washington, D.C., vol. 31, no. 9421 (28 April 1843). Note, however, that as for the attitude of the French press, this assertion is partially false. Papers such as *Le Rhône, L'Indicateur,* and *Le Moniteur industriel,* among others, published extracts or commentaries.

26. M. Chevalier, "Système de la Méditerranée," *Le Globe,* 12 February 1832. In fact, this is the last of four articles that began publication on 20 January of the same year. These articles have been collected in an anthology published by the same magazine. The quotation is from the latter publication (34).

27. See M. Barbance, *Histoire de la Compagnie Générale Transatlantique* (Paris: Arts et métiers graphiques, 1955), 39.

28. Société Générale, *SG Centenaire 1864–1964* (Paris: Imprimerie Chaix, 1964), 18. See also the classic book by B. Gille, *La Banque en France au XIXe siècle* (Paris: PUF, 1970).

29. K. Marx, "Letter to Danielson" (10 April 1879), in *Marx and Engels on the Means of Communication: A Selection of Texts by Y. de la Haye* (New York: International General, 1980), 151.

30. J. M. Goger, "Le temps de la route exclusive en France 1780–1850," *Histoire, Économie et Sociétés*, no. 4 (4th trimester, 1992): 609–10. For a history of railways in France, see Y. Leclercq, *Le Réseau impossible* (Paris-Geneva, Droz, 1989).

31. Quoted in ibid., 597.

32. P. Larousse, *Grand dictionnaire universel du XIXᵉ siècle* (Paris: Administration du Grand dictionnaire universel), article titled "Chemins de fer," 1147.

33. M. Roulleaux, "À propos des chemins de fer aujourd'hui et dans 100 ans chez tous les peuples," *La Presse*, 13 January 1859.

34. Ibid.

35. M. Chevalier, "Chemins de fer," *Dictionnaire de l'économie politique* (Paris, 1852), 20.

36. Chevalier, "Système de la Méditerranée," 34.

37. "M. Chevalier, apôtre," *Le Globe*, 20 April 1832, 96.

38. Chevalier, "Système de la Méditerranée," 38.

39. "M. Chevalier, apôtre," 89.

40. Chevalier, "Système de la Méditerranée," 50.

41. M. Chevalier, *Lettres sur l'Amérique du Nord* (Paris: Librairie C. Gosselin, 1836), vol. 1, 3. In English: *Society, Manners and Politics in the United States* (Boston: Weeks and Jordan, 1839), reprinted (New York: Augustus M. Kelley, 1966).

42. P.-J. Proudhon, *Des réformes à opérer dans l'exploitation des chemins de fer* (Paris: Garnier Frères, 1855).

43. H. Peyret, *Histoire des chemins de fer en France et dans le monde* (Paris: SEFI, 1949), 19.

44. Larousse, *Grand dictionnaire universel du XIXᵉ siècle*, article titled "Chemins de fer," 1150.

45. "Revue des affaires," *Journal des travaux publics*, 8 August 1858.

46. J. Chesneaux, "Jules Verne et la tradition utopique," *L'Homme et la Société*, no. 4, (April–June 1967): 232.

47. "M. Chevalier, apôtre," 88.

48. See M. Martin, *Trois siècles de publicité en France* (Paris: Éditions Odile Jacob, 1992).

49. See T. R. Nevett, *Advertising in Britain: A History* (London: Heinemann, 1982).

50. See Peyret, *Histoire des chemins de fer.*

51. On the history of Saint-Simonianism in French advertising, see Martin, *Trois siècles de publicité*, as well as the doctoral thesis of G. Lagneau, "Les Institutions publicitaires, Fonction et genèse" (Paris: Université René-Descartes, 1982).

52. Reproduced in G. Sand, *Correspondance (July 1847–December 1848)* (Paris: Garnier, 1971), vol. 8, 664.

53. Ibid., 705–6.

54. W. Benjamin, *Paris, Capitale du XIXᵉ siècle* (Paris: Le Cerf, 1989), 51.

55. Ibid.

5. The Temple of Industry

1. G. Gérault, *Les Expositions universelles envisagées au point de vue de leurs résultats économiques* (Paris: Librairie Société du Recueil général des lois et des arrêts, 1902), 22.

2. G. Kepes, ed., *La Notion de structure dans les arts et dans les sciences* (Brussels: La Connaissance, 1967).

3. Y. Stourdzé, *Pour une poignée d'électrons: Pouvoir et communication* (Paris: Fayard, 1987), 126.

4. Ibid., 127.

5. Cited in W. Benjamin, *Paris, Capitale du XIXe siècle* (Paris: Le Cerf, 1989), 208.

6. F. Braudel, *Civilisation and Capitalism: 15th–18th Century,* trans. revised by Sian Reynolds (London: Collins, 1981–84), vol. 2, "The Wheels of Commerce."

7. P. Baudin, *Expositions internationales de Buenos Aires. Rapport du Commissaire général du gouvernement de la République* (Paris: Imprimerie Nationale, 1912), 88.

8. Ibid.

9. On the influence of positivism in Latin America, see P. Arbousse-Bastide, "Sur le positivisme politique et religieux au Brésil," in *Romantisme. Revue du dix-neuvième siècle,* no. 2 (1979); L. Zea, *El positivisimo en México* (Mexico City: Fondo de cultura económica, 1943).

10. G. and H. Beyhaut, *América latina III. De la Independencia a la Segunda guerra mundial* (Mexico City: Siglo XXI, 1986), 122.

11. Ibid., 112–13.

12. C. Furtado, *Cultura e desenvolvimento em epoca de crise* (Rio de Janeiro: Paz e Terra, 1984).

13. E. Monod, *L'Exposition universelle de 1889. Grand ouvrage illustré historique, encyclopédique, descriptif. Commissaire général de l'exposition* (Paris: E. Dentu, 1890), vol. 3, 24.

14. Ibid., vol. 2, 144.

15. Quoted in Benjamin, *Paris, Capitale du XIXe siècle,* 195.

16. Ibid., 209.

17. Monod, *L'Exposition universelle de 1889,* vol. 2, 360.

18. Ministère des Postes et Télégraphes, *Exposition internationale d'électricité. Rapport administratif,* vol. 1, 3.

19. *L'Illustration,* no. 2994 (14 July 1900), 29.

20. J. London, "The Message of the Motion Pictures," *Paramount Magazine,* February 1915. Translated from the French found in Jack London, *Profession: écrivain* (Paris: 10/18, 1980), 433.

21. C. Chevalier, Introduction, *Exposition Universelle de 1867 à Paris. Rapports du jury international* (Paris: Imprimerie administrative de Paul Dupont, 1868), cdxc.

22. Ibid., dxii.

23. Ibid.

24. M. Chevalier, *Le Mexique ancien et moderne* (Paris: Hachette, 1864), 2d ed., 512.

25. W. Sombart, *L'Apogée du capitalisme* (Paris: Payot, 1932), vol. 1, chapter 6.

26. C. J. Beelenkamp, *Les Lois postales universelles* (The Hague: Mouton and Co., 1910), 526; G. A. Codding, *The Universal Postal Union, Coordinator of the International Mails* (New York: New York University Press, 1964); G. A. Codding, *The International Telecommunications Union* (Leyden, The Netherlands: E. J. Brill, 1952).

27. W. Kleinwachter and K. Nordenstreng, eds., *International Security and Humanitarian Cooperation in the Reunited Europe* (Tampere, Finland: University of Tampere, Department of Journalism and Mass Communication, 1991).

28. Quoted in J. Dury, "Coubertin propose le retour de l'olympisme," *Le Monde,* 22–23 November 1992, 2.

29. See J. Copans, *Critiques et politiques de l'anthropologie* (Paris: F. Maspero, 1974).

30. Ministère du commerce, de l'industrie, des postes et des télégraphes, *Exposition internationale de Chicago en 1893, Rapports publiés par C. Krantz. Congrès tenus à Chicago en 1893* (Paris: Imprimerie Nationale, 1894), 16.

31. Ibid.

32. Exposition universelle de 1900 (Classe 110), *Congrès féministes internationaux tenus au palais des Congrès. Rapport de Mme Vincent, Section du travail. Le "travail des bonnes"* (Paris, 1900), 6–7.

33. Monod, *L'Exposition universelle de 1889,* vol. 2, 283.

34. A. Corbin, *The Foul and the Fragrant: Odor and French Social Imagination,* prepared by M. Kochan, R. Porter and C. Prendergast (Cambridge: Harvard University Press, 1986), 209 [French edition 1982].

35. Monod, *L'Exposition universelle de 1889,* vol. 2, 201.

36. Corbin, *The Foul and the Fragrant,* 224. On the uses of the word "hygiene," see *Dictionnaire (Robert) historique de la langue française,* vol. 1.

37. Gérault, *Les Expositions universelles envisagées au point de vue de leurs résultats économiques,* 22–23.

38. M. Malthête-Méliès, *Méliès l'enchanteur* (Paris: Hachette, 1973).

39. J. J. Mensy, "L'énigme du Cinéorama de l'Exposition universelle de 1900," in *Archives Institut Jean Vigo* (Toulouse: Cinémathèque de Toulouse, January 1991).

40. See L. Aimone and C. Olmo, *Les Expositions universelles 1851–1900* (Paris: Belin, 1993)—one of the most interesting books on the subject.

41. Monod, *L'Exposition universelle de 1889,* vol. 1, xxviii.

42. Rastignac, "Courrier de Paris," *L'Illustration,* no. 2417 (22 June 1889), 518.

43. Rastignac, "Courrier de Paris," *L'Illustration,* no. 2413 (25 May 1889), 438.

44. Ibid.

45. Rastignac, "Courrier de Paris," *L'Illustration,* no. 2411 (11 May 1889), 394.

6. The Communitarian City

1. F. Bacon, *The New Atlantis,* in *Ideal Commonwealths* (New York: Columbia University Press, 1901).

2. C. Fourier, *Théorie des quatre mouvements et des destinées générales,* in *Œuvres complètes* (Paris: Librairie sociétaire, 1846), vol. 1, 38. These works were published in facsimile (twelve volumes) by Éditions Anthropos in 1966, from which extracts appear in English in *The Utopian Vision of Charles Fourier: Selected Texts on Work, Love, and Passionate Attraction,* trans. and ed. J. Beecher and R. Bienvenu (Boston: Beacon Press, 1971). This quotation appears on pp. 402–3. On Fourier, see J. Beecher, *Charles Fourier, the Visionary and His World* (Berkeley: University of California Press, 1986); and R. Barthes, *Sade, Fourier, Loyola,* trans. Richard Miller (New York: Hill and Wang, 1976).

3. Fourier, *Théorie des quatre mouvements,* 47.

4. C. Fourier, *Théorie de l'unité universelle* (1822), in *Œuvres complètes,* vol. 3, 458.

5. Ibid., 243–44.

6. C. Fourier, *La Fausse Industrie morcelée, répugnante, mensongère* (1835–36), in ibid., 653.

7. Fourier, *Théorie des quatre mouvements,* 5.

8. C. Fourier, *Pièges et charlatanisme des deux sectes Saint-Simon et Owen* (Paris: Chez Bossange, 1831), 81.

9. Ibid., 2.

10. Ibid., 12.

11. Fourier, *Théorie des quatre mouvements,* 290.

12. Fourier, *Théorie de l'unité universelle,* vol. 3, 143–44.

13. W. Benjamin, "Fourier or the Arcades," in *Charles Baudelaire: A Lyric Poet in the Era of High Capitalism,* trans. H. Zohn (London: New Left Books, 1973), 159–60 [trans. modified].

14. Fourier, *Théorie des quatre mouvements*, 171–72.

15. C. Fourier, "Publication des manuscrits," in *Le Socialisme sociétaire*, ed. H. Bourgin (Paris: Société nouvelle de librairie et d'édition, 1903), 110.

16. C. Fourier, *Le Nouveau monde industriel et sociétaire, ou invention du procédé d'industrie attrayante et naturelle distribuée en séries passionnées* (Paris, 1829), 291–92.

17. C. Fourier, *Le Nouveau Monde amoureux* (Paris: Anthropos, 1967) (vol. 7 of *Œuvres complètes*).

18. See D. Hayden, *Seven American Utopias: The Architecture of Communitarian Socialism 1790–1975* (Cambridge: MIT Press, 1976).

19. S. Debout, Préface to Fourier, *Le Nouveau Monde amoureux*.

20. V. Considérant, *Déraison et engouement pour les chemins de fer* (Paris, 1838), quoted by W. Benjamin, *Paris, Capitale du XIXᵉ siècle* (Paris: Le Cerf, 1989), 650.

21. É. Cabet, *Voyage en Icarie. Roman philosophique et social* (Paris: J. Mallet and Co., 1842), 2d ed., 20.

22. É. Cabet, "Communisme," in *1845: Almanach icarien, astronomique, scientifique, pratique, industriel, statistique, politique et social* (Paris: Le Populaire), 154–71.

23. C. Rihs, *Les Philosophes utopistes* (Paris: Marcel Rivière, 1970), 186–205.

24. Cabet, "Communisme," 161.

25. Cabet, *Voyage en Icarie*, 32.

26. Ibid., 197–98.

27. Ibid., 20.

28. Ibid., 369.

29. Ibid., 565.

30. Ibid., 215. See also É. Cabet, *History and Constitution of the Icarian Community*, trans. Thomas Teakle (Iowa City: State Historical Society of Iowa, 1917).

31. J. Rancière, *Nights of Labor: The Workers' Dream in Nineteenth-Century France*, trans. J. Drury (Philadelphia: Temple University Press, 1989), 365.

32. É. Cabet, *Cabet et les publications du "Populaire"* (Paris: EDHIS, 1974). For a parallel history, see D. Thomson, "La presse de la classe ouvrière anglaise au XIXᵉ," in *La Presse ouvrière*, studies presented by J. Godechot (Paris: CNRS, 1966).

33. K. Marx and F. Engels, *The Communist Manifesto* (1848), trans. S. Moore (Chicago: Regnery Gateway, 1982), 74–77.

34. P.-J. Proudhon, *Le Manuel du spéculateur en bourse* (Paris, 1857), 4th ed; quoted in H. Peyret, *Histoire des chemins de fer en France et dans le monde* (Paris: SEFI, 1949), 22–23.

35. P.-J. Proudhon, *Carnets de P.-J. Proudhon* (11 March 1847) (Paris: M. Rivière, 1961), vol. 2, 41.

36. P.-J. Proudhon, *Des réformes à opérer dans l'exploitation des chemins de fer* (Paris, Garnier Frères, 1855), 113.

37. P.-J. Proudhon, *Idée générale de la révolution au XIXᵉ siècle*; in English, *General Idea of the Revolution in the Nineteenth Century*, trans. John B. Robinson (London: Pluto Press, 1989).

38. C. De Paepe, *Les Services publics, précédés de deux Essais sur le collectivisme, Notice biographique de B. Malon* (Brussels: J. Milot, 1895), 148. The first version of this lecture dates from the 1870s. On the extensions of the debate in France, see P. Brousse, *Services publics*, (Paris: Éditions de la Revue Socialiste, 1892), and also *Entre Marx et Bakounine, César De Paepe*, correspondence annotated by B. Dandois (Paris: F. Maspero, 1974); T. Paquot, *Les Faiseurs de nuage. Essai sur la genèse des marxismes français (1880–1914)* (Paris: Sycomore, 1980).

39. De Paepe, *Les Services publics*, 145–46.

40. P. Kropotkin, *Mutual Aid—A Factor of Evolution* (Montreal: Black Rose Books, 1989). On his trajectory, see P. Kropotkin, *Memoirs of a Revolutionary,* ed. James A. Rogers (Gloucester, Mass.: P. Smith, 1967).

41. C. Darwin, *The Origin of Species* and *The Descent of Man* (New York: Modern Library, 1995), 913.

42. P. Tort, *La Pensée hiérarchique et l'évolution* (Paris: Aubier, 1985). The analysis in this paragraph is indebted to this author.

43. É. Reclus, *Nouvelle géographie universelle* (Paris: Hachette, vol. 1 [1875]), 7.

44. P. Kropotkin, *Champs, usines et ateliers ou l'industrie combinée avec l'agriculture et le travail cérébral avec le travail manuel* (Paris: P. V. Stock, 1910), 399; in English, *Fields, Factories and Workshops, or Industry Combined with Agriculture and Brain Work with Manual Work* (London: Thomas Nelson and Sons, 1912 [New Brunswick, N.J.: Transaction Publishers, 1993]), 416–17.

45. On the scientific trajectory of P. Geddes, see P. Boardman, *Patrick Geddes, Maker of the Future,* intro. L. Mumford (Chapel Hill: University of North Carolina Press, 1944); and H. E. Meller, *Patrick Geddes; Social Evolutionist and City Planner* (London and New York: Routledge, 1990).

46. F. Le Play, *Les Ouvriers européens,* vol. 1, *Instruction sur la méthode d'observation* (Paris, 1855); in English, *On Family, Work and Social Change,* ed. and trans. C. B. Silver (Chicago: University of Chicago Press, 1982).

47. P. Geddes and V. Brandford, *The Coming Polity* (London: Williams and Norgate, 1919), 186. On the influence of Le Play, see also Geddes and G. Slater, *Ideas at War* (London: Williams and Norgate, 1917).

48. P. Geddes and S. Dewey, *Guide to Paris, the Exhibition and the Assembly* (Edinburgh: Outlook Tower, 1900), 226–27.

49. On P. Otlet's work, see *Traité de documentation. Le livre sur le livre (1934)* (Liège: Centre de lecture publique de la Communauté française de Belgique, 1989).

50. L. Mumford, *Technics and Civilization* (New York: Harcourt, Brace and World, 1963; original edition 1934).

51. M. McLuhan, *The Mechanical Bride: Folklore of Industrial Man* (New York: Vanguard Press, 1951).

52. On this evolution, see J. W. Carey, "McLuhan and Mumford: The Roots of Modern Media Analysis," *Journal of Communication,* vol. 31, no. 3 (summer 1981).

53. S. Butler, *Erewhon* (1872) (London: Penguin English Library, 1979), 199.

54. Ibid., 203.

55. Ibid., 222.

56. P.-M. Moreau, *Le Récit utopique, Droit naturel et roman de l'État* (Paris: PUF, 1982), 52.

57. Y. Zamyatin, *Islanders, and the Fisher of Men,* trans. S. Fuller and J. Sacchi (Edinburgh: Salamander Press, 1984), 39.

58. See Y. Zamyatin, *Le Métier littéraire, suivi de Cours sur la technique de la prose littéraire* (Lausanne: L'Age d'homme, 1990), 92; in English, see Y. Zamyatin, *Soviet Heretic: Essays by Yevgeny Zamyatin,* ed. and trans. M. Ginsburg (Chicago: University of Chicago Press, 1970).

59. Zamyatin, *Islanders,* 15.

60. F. Lyssenko, Introduction to the French edition of *Islanders, Les Insulaires* (Lausanne: L'Age d'homme, 1983), 10.

61. Y. Zamyatin, *We,* trans. Mirra Ginsburg (New York: Viking Press, 1972), 31.

62. Ibid., 112.

63. Ibid., 157.

64. I. Kremniov (A. V. Chayanov), *Le Voyage de mon frère Alexis au pays de l'utopie paysanne* (Lausanne: L'Age d'homme, 1976), 33. [This work is not translated from Russian into English.]

65. Ibid., 80.

7. The Hierarchization of the World

1. L. Houllevigue, "Le problème de l'heure," *La Revue de Paris* (15 August 1913). For a history, see D. S. Landes, *Revolution in Time: Clocks and the Making of the Modern World* (Cambridge: Belknap Press of Harvard University Press, 1983).

2. I. Wallerstein, *Historical Capitalism* (London: Verso, 1983).

3. F. Braudel, *La dynamique du capitalisme* (Paris: Flammarion, 1985), 107.

4. F. Braudel, *Civilisation and Capitalism: 15th–18th Century*, trans. revised by Sian Reynolds (London: Collins, 1981), vol. 3, *The Perspective of the World*, 534.

5. Figures given by J. A. Hobson, *Imperialism* (London: Nesbit, 1902), 19.

6. E. Canetti, *Crowds and Power*, trans. C. Stewart (London: Penguin Classics, 1962), 200.

7. P. Bata, "Les câbles sous-marins des origines à 1929," *Télécommunications*, no. 45 (October 1982).

8. J. O. Boyd-Barrett and M. Palmer, *Le Trafic des Nouvelles. Les Agences mondiales d'information* (Paris: Alain Moreau, 1981).

9. D. Smythe, *Dependency Road: Communications, Capitalism, Consciousness and Canada* (Norwood: N.J.: Ablex, 1981).

10. "Le télégraphe à La Mecque," *L'Illustration*, no. 2985 (12 May 1900), 307.

11. J. and A. Sellier, *Atlas des peuples d'Orient* (Paris: La Découverte, 1993). On the role of telegraph lines in the Ottoman Empire, see Y. Bektas, "La télégraphie au service du Sultan ou le messager impérial," *Réseaux*, no. 67 (1994).

12. M. Dauvers, *Rapport sur les chemins de fer de l'Inde (1864–1865)* (Paris). Quoted under "Chemins de fer," in P. Larousse, *Grand dictionnaire universel du XIXᵉ siècle* (Paris: Administration du Grand dictionnaire universel).

13. M. Tesler, *La telefonía argentina. Su otra historia* (Buenos Aires: Editorial Rescate, 1990).

14. R. Napp, *La République argentine. Ouvrage écrit par ordre du Comité central argentin pour l'exposition de Philadelphie* (Buenos Aires: Imprimerie du "Courrier de la Plata," 1876), 310–11.

15. G. and H. Beyhaut, *América latina III: De la Independencia a la Segunda guerra mundial* (Mexico City: Siglo XXI, 1986), 56. See also G. Pendle, *Paraguay: A Riverside Nation* (London: Royal Institute of International Affairs, 1954).

16. See A. Mattelart and H. Schmucler, *Communication and Information Technologies: Freedom for Choice for Latin America?* (Norwood, N.J.: Ablex, 1985).

17. C. Funtanellas, ed., *United Fruit Co.* (Havana: Editorial de ciencias sociales, 1976).

18. M. Chevalier, *L'Isthme de Panama* (Paris: Imprimerie H. Fournier, 1844), 71 (partly taken from *La Revue des Deux Mondes* of 1 January 1844).

19. See the article "Mexique" in *La Grande Encyclopédie* (Paris: Société anonyme de la Grande Encyclopédie, 1885). See also S. Ortiz Hernán, *Los Ferrocarriles de México. Una visión social y económica* (Mexico City: Ferrocarriles Nacionales de México, 2 vols., 1987–88).

20. A. D. Chandler, *The Visible Hand: The Managerial Revolution in American Business* (Cambridge: Belknap Press of Harvard University Press, 1967).

21. J. A. Hobson, *Imperialism: A Study* (Ann Arbor: University of Michigan Press, 1988; original edition 1902).

22. V. I. Lenin, *Imperialism, the Highest Stage of Capitalism* (New York: International Publishers, 1939), 15.

23. Ibid., 10.

24. R. Luxemburg, *Œuvres I et II* (Paris: F. Maspero, 1964).

25. Quoted in J. P. Nettl, *Rosa Luxemburg* (London: Oxford University Press, 1966), vol. 2, 533.

26. H. Arendt, *The Origins of Totalitarianism* (New York: Harcourt, Brace and Company, 1951), 124.

27. Ibid., 152.

28. G. Convents, "Documentaries and Propaganda before 1914: A View on Early Cinema and Colonial History," *Framework*, no. 35 (1988), 104 [trans. modified].

8. Symbolic Propagation

1. F. Véron, *Lestablissement de la congregation de la propagation de la foy et des missionaires généraux des prélats de France, pour conférer avec les ministres, et precher aux portes de leurs temples, & és places publiques, par toutes les provinces de cette monarchie, au salut des devoyez et pour le repos de l'État* (Lyons: Chez Claude Armand, 1624). This document also includes in an appendix the text of the papal bull of 1622.

2. Quoted in J. Leflon, *Histoire de l'Église. La crise révolutionnaire (1798–1846)* (Paris: Bloud and Gay, 1949), vol. 20, 512.

3. Text reproduced in B. Pelet, *Opinions de Napoléon* (Paris: Firmin-Didiot, 1833), 43.

4. On the history of the work and its press, the best sources are once again the anniversary issues of *Annales* and *Les Missions Catholiques*, See, for example, Monsignor le Roy, "Cinquante ans! Nos souvenirs et nos espérances," *Les Missions Catholiques*, Lyons, 3 January 1919. For a detailed study of a missionary press, see J. Pirotte, "Périodiques missionnaires belges d'expression française, reflets de cinquante années d'évolution d'une mentalité" (Louvain: University of Louvain, *Recueil de travaux d'histoire et de philologie*, 1973), 6th series, no. 2.

5. R. P. Brou, "Aperçu général sur les missions des Pères de la Compagnie de Jésus" (1823–1923), *Les Missions catholiques*, 23 May 1924. See also I. and. J. L. Vissière, eds. *Peaux Rouges et robes noires. Lettres édifiantes et curieuses des jésuites français en Amérique au XVIIIᵉ siècle* (Paris: Éditions de la Différence, 1993).

6. See Leflon, *Histoire de l'Église*.

7. Monsignor Dupanloup, *Lettre pastorale de Monseigneur L'Évêque d'Orléans en la fête de saint Mathieu*, 1859, no. 16.

8. Monsignor Le Roy, "Cinquante ans!" 5–6.

9. See M. Cheza, "Évolution de la presse missionnaire," *Vivant Univers* (Namur, Belgium: September–October 1984).

10. Monsignor Le Roy, "Cinquante ans!" 7.

11. Ibid., 7–8.

12. "Enc. Mirari vos," *Acta Gregorii Papae* (Rome: Poliglotta Vaticana, 1901), vol. 1, 172.

13. G. Berthoud et al. *Aspects de la propagande religieuse* (Geneva: Droz, 1957).

14. S. Simon, "L'exception culturelle mobilise la francophonie," *Libération*, 18 October 1993.

15. P. Foncin, "Alliance Française: Conférence faite à Bordeaux le lundi 1 décembre 1884 à l'École professionnelle," *Bulletin Alliance Française*, 1 November 1885–1 January 1886, 16.

16. C. Gide, *Lutte de langues à la surface du globe. Rôle de l'Alliance Française* (Nîmes: Imprimerie Clavel et Chastanier, 1885).

17. Foncin, "Conférence faite à Bordeaux le lundi 1 décembre 1884 à l'École professionnelle," 14.

18. Gide, *Lutte de langues à la surface du globe,* 8.

19. Ibid., 14.

20. Foncin, "Conférence faite à Bordeaux le lundi 1 décembre 1884 à l'École professionnelle," 15.

21. A. Schleicher, *Die Darwinsche Theorie und die Sprachwissenschaft* (1863); English translation in A. Schleicher, E. Haeckel, and W. Bleek, *Linguistic and Evolutionary Theory: Three Essays,* ed. Konrad Koerner (Amsterdam and Philadelphia: J. Benjamin, 1985).

22. J. Schlanger, *Les Métaphores de l'organisme* (Paris: Vrin, 1971), 125.

23. Foncin, "Conférence faite à Bordeaux le lundi 1 décembre 1884 à l'École professionnelle," 14.

24. Ibid., 22.

25. F. Colonna, "Enseignement des indigènes et enseignement du peuple au XIXe siècle," *Revue française d'études politiques africaines,* no. 109 (January 1975).

26. See especially F. Furet and J. Ozouf, *Lire et écrire: l'alphabétisation des Français de Calvin à Jules Ferry* (Paris: Minuit, 1977); H. Le Bras and E. Todd, *L'Invention de la France* (Paris: Pluriel-Hachette, 1981).

27. H. G. Wells, *Anticipations of the Reaction of Mechanical and Scientific Progress upon Human Life and Thought* (London: Chapman and Hall, 1902), 215.

28. Ibid., 90.

29. Ibid., 89–90.

30. Sir G. O. Treveylan, *The Life and Letters of Lord Macaulay* (London and New York: Longmans, Green and Company, 1909), 291.

31. T. O'Hifearnain, " 'Capuchon, lame et langue.' L'Irlandais et l'Europe continentale au XVIIe siècle," in *L'Irlande et ses langues,* ed. J. Brihault (Rennes: Presses universitaires de Rennes, 1993), 34.

32. See in this respect the aforementioned analyses by Y. Zamyatin in *Le Métier littéraire, suivi de Cours sur la technique de la prose littéraire* (Lausanne: L'Age d'homme, 1990).

33. For a history of these links, see G. Martinière, *Aspects de la coopération franco-brésilienne* (Paris: Éditions de la MSH/PUG, 1982).

34. Cited in ibid., 75.

35. F. Braudel, "Unité et diversité de l'autre Amérique," *Cahiers des Annales* (Paris: A. Colin, 1949), 66. This book represents an amended and corrected edition of issue no. 4 (1948) of the journal *Annales (Économies, Sociétés, Civilisations).*

36. L. Febvre, "Introduction: L'Amérique du Sud devant l'histoire," in *Cahiers des Annales,* ibid., ix.

37. J. Cruz Costa, "Conflits d'idéologie. Philosophes et philosophies en Amérique latine," in ibid., 179–80. For a general view on this "return effect" in other realms, see J. Leenhardt, P. Kalfon, and A. and M. Mattelart, *Les Amériques latines en France* (Paris: Gallimard, 1992).

38. N. J. Spykman, *America's Strategy in World Politics: The United States and the Balance of Power* (New York: Harcourt, Brace and World, 1942), 233.

39. On the English school of documentary, see P. Virilio, *La Machine de vision* (Paris: Galilée, 1988), 60–62; P. Rotha, *Documentary Film* (London: Faber and Faber, 1936; revised 1939).

40. See P. Paranagua, ed., *Le Cinéma brésilien* (Paris: Centre Georges Pompidou, 1987).

41. J. Rigaud, *Les relations culturelles extérieures. Rapport au ministre des Affaires étrangères* (Paris: La Documentation française, 1980), 66.

42. H. Hauser, *Les Méthodes allemandes d'expansion économique* (Paris: Librairie A. Colin, 1915), 200.

9. Strategic Thought

1. H. von Moltke, *Die Operativen Vorbereitungen zur Schlacht,* quoted in M. Peschaud, *Les chemins de fer allemands et la guerre* (Paris: Charles Lavauzelle and Company, 1927), 5.

2. See P. Virilio, "L'Empire de l'emprise," *Traverses,* no. 13 (December 1978).

3. See the analyses of General Von Caemmerer, *L'Évolution de la stratégie au XIXᵉ siècle* (Paris: Librairie Fischbacher, 1907).

4. G. Chaliand, "Introduction: Guerres et cultures stratégiques à travers l'histoire," in Chaliand, ed., *Anthologie mondiale de la stratégie* (Paris: Laffont, 1990).

5. J. De Guibert, *Essai général de tactique (1770),* in *Écrits militaires* (Paris: Copernic, 1977). A chapter is published in Chaliand, ed., *Anthologie mondiale de la stratégie;* see pp. 745–46.

6. Baron de Jomini, *L'Art de la guerre ou nouveau tableau analytique* (Brussels: Meline, Cans and Company, 1838), 26.

7. Quoted in Peschaud, *Les chemins de fer allemands et la guerre,* 11.

8. J. Colin, "Les transformations de la guerre" (1911), in Chaliand, ed., *Anthologie mondiale de la stratégie,* 1092. See also Baron Ernouf, *Histoire des chemins de fer pendant la guerre franco-prussienne* (Paris: Librairie générale, 1874). On the development of the telegraph in the United States and the influence of the army in the Civil War years, see R. B. Du Boff, "The Rise of Communications Regulations: The Telegraph Industry, 1844–1880," *Journal of Communication,* vol. 34, no. 3 (summer 1984).

9. Quoted in E. Mead Earle, "Adam Smith, Alexander Hamilton, Friedrich List: The Economic Foundations of Military Power," in *Makers of Modern Strategy, from Machiavelli to the Nuclear Age,* ed. P. Paret (Princeton, N.J.: Princeton University Press, 1986), 255.

10. E. d'Eichtal, *L'Économiste Frédéric List, candidat à l'un des concours de l'Académie des sciences morales et politiques* (Paris: Éditions de la Revue politique et littéraire et de la Revue scientifique, 1913), 7.

11. Quoted in ibid.

12. F. List, *The National System of Political Economy,* trans. Sampson Lloyd (London: Longmans, Green and Company, 1885).

13. Ibid., 174.

14. R. Gonnard, *Histoire des doctrines économiques,* (Paris: Librairie générale de droit et de jurisprudence, 1941), new edition (original edition 1921), 619.

15. L. Kapeller, "Le trafic international dans l'Europe sans frontières," *Signal,* 2d issue of October 1941: 42, 44.

16. F. Ratzel, *Géographie politique* (Geneva: Éditions régionales européennes, 1988), 17–18.

17. Ibid., 19.

18. Ibid.

19. H. Arendt, *The Origins of Totalitarianism* (New York: Harcourt, Brace and Company, 1951), 166.

20. Ratzel, *Géographie politique,* 318.

21. Ibid., 323.

22. Ibid., 25.

23. Ibid., 17.

24. See M. Korinman, "Avant-propos," in F. Ratzel, *La Géographie politique: Choix de textes et traduction de l'allemand par E. Ewald* (Paris: Fayard, 1987).

25. R. R. Palmer, "Frederick the Great, Guibert, Bülow: From Dynastic to National War," in *Makers of Modern Strategy*, 114–15.

26. B. Barret-Kriegel, "L'intellectuel et l'État," *L'Arc*, no. 70 (1977).

27. J. Fichte, *Discours à la Nation allemande* (Paris: Aubier 1975), 173; in English, *Addresses to the German Nation,* ed. R. F. Jones and G. H. Turnbull (New York: Greenwood, 1979).

28. Ibid.

29. Barret-Kriegel, "L'intellectuel et l'État," 62.

30. See Arendt, *The Origins of Totalitarianism.*

31. Korinman, "Avant-propos," 23.

32. See K. Haushofer, *De la géopolitique* (Paris: Fayard, 1986).

33. A. T. Mahan, *Naval Strategy: Compared and Contrasted with the Principles and Practice of Military Operations on Land* (Boston: Little, Brown and Company, 1911), 138–39.

34. H. F. Graff, ed., *American Imperialism and the Philippine Insurrection, Testimony of the Times: Selections from Congressional Hearings* (Boston: Little, Brown and Company, 1969), vii.

35. Ibid., 42.

36. A. Negrón de Montilla, *La americanización en Puerto Rico y el sistema de instrucción pública 1900–1930* (Rio Piedras: Editorial Universitaria, Universidad de Puerto Rico, 1977).

37. E. Pantojas G., "La iglesia protestante y la americanización de Puerto Rico 1898–1917," *Revista de ciencias sociales,* Rio Piedras, vol. 18, nos. 1–2 (March–June 1974).

38. *L'Illustration,* no. 2881 (14 May 1898), 353.

39. See in particular V. Gribayédoff, "La femme américaine et la guerre," *L'Illustration,* no. 2886 (18 June 1898).

40. C. de Varigny, "Les États-Unis et la doctrine Monroe," *L'Illustration,* no. 2885 (11 June 1898).

41. G. Le Bon, *Enseignements psychologiques de la guerre européenne* (Paris: Flammarion, 1916).

42. M. Malthête-Méliès, *Méliès l'enchanteur* (Paris: Hachette, 1973), 199–200.

43. P. A. Paranagua, ed., *Le Cinéma cubain* (Paris: Centre Georges Pompidou, 1990).

44. To retrace the history of these debates, see Baron L. de Staël-Holstein, *La Réglementation de la guerre des airs* (The Hague: Martinus Nijhoff, 1911).

45. Ibid., 32.

46. G. B. Davies, "Doctor Francis Liebers' Instructions," *American Journal of International Law* (1907): 12–27.

47. Baron de Staël-Holstein, *La Réglementation de la guerre des airs,* 51.

48. *Kriegsgebrauch im Landkriege,* quoted in J. Cuvelier, *La Belgique et la guerre* (Brussels: H. Bertels, 1924), vol. 1: *L'Invasion allemande,* preface by H. Pirenne, 395.

49. F. E. Smith, *International Law as Interpreted during the Russo-Japanese War* (London: T. Fisher Unwin, 1905), 82.

50. Quoted in Baron de Staël-Holstein, *La Réglementation de la guerre des airs,* 51.

51. D. S. Landes, *The Unbound Prometheus: Technological Change and Industrial Development in Western Europe from 1750 to the Present* (Cambridge, England: Cambridge University Press, 1969), 423.

52. P. Virilio, *La Machine de vision* (Paris: Galilée, 1988), 105–6. By the same author, see *Logistique de la perception Guerre et cinéma I* (Paris: Éditions de l'Étoile-Cahiers du Cinéma, 1984).

53. N. Wiener, *Cybernetics or Control and Communication in the Animal and the Machine*, 4th printing (Cambridge: MIT Press, 1985), 11–12.

10. The Portrayal of Crowds

1. A. Quételet, *Sur l'homme et le développement de ses facultés, ou Essai de physique sociale* (Paris: Bachelier, 1835), vol. 2, 251.

2. Ibid., vol. 1, 21.

3. Ibid., 276.

4. A. Quételet, *Du système social et des lois que le régissent* (Paris: Guillaumin, 1848), 70.

5. Quételet, *Sur l'homme*, 24–25.

6. On this early history of moral statistics in Great Britain, see Y. Levin and A. Lindesmith, "English Ecology and Criminology of the Past Century," *Journal of Criminal Law and Criminology*, no. 27 (March 1937). For some examples of studies inspired by nineteenth-century moral statistics, see J. Mayhew and J. Bibby, *The Criminal Prisons in London and Scenes of Prison Life* (London: C. Griffin and Company, 1862); J. Fletcher, *Summary of Moral Statistics of England and Wales* (London: author's edition, 1849).

7. Quételet, *Du système social*, 89.

8. G. Canguilhem, *Le Normal et le Pathologique* (Paris: PUF, 1966), 185.

9. F. Ewald, *L'État Providence* (Paris: Grasset, 1986), 147.

10. Ibid., 148.

11. É. de Girardin, *La Politique universelle* (1852). I consulted long extracts from this book reprinted under the word "Assurance" in the *Grand dictionnaire universel*, vol. 1 (1865), 819.

12. Ibid. for this quotation and the following one.

13. L. Bourgeois, *Rapport portant approbation du Traité de Paix de Versailles, 28 juin 1919, Sénat 1919, Session ordinaire* (Paris: Imprimerie du Sénat, 1919), 118.

14. L. Bourgeois, "L'assurance contre l'invalidité et la défense nationale" (1909), in *La Politique de la prévoyance sociale* (Paris: Bibliothèque Charpentier, E. Fasquelle, 1919), vol. 2, 326. On the chronology of social insurance regimes, see J. Doublet and G. Lavau, *Sécurité sociale* (Paris: F. Alcan, 1902), ix–x.

15. L. Bourgeois and A. Croiset, *Essai d'une philosophie de la solidarité (Conférences et discussions. École des hautes études sociales)* (Paris: F. Alcan, 1902), ix–x.

16. Quoted in M. de Ryckere, "Le signalement anthropométrique," in *Troisième congrès international d'anthropologie criminelle, août 1892, Bruxelles, "Biologie et Sociologie"* (Brussels: F. Hayez, 1893), 93.

17. M. Foucault, *Discipline and Punish: The Birth of the Prison*, trans. A. Sheridan (London: Penguin Books, 1977), 282.

18. A. M. de Guerry de Champneuf, *Essai sur la statistique morale de la France* (Paris: Crochard, 1833). On the place of this author in the history of this science, see M. C. Elmer, "Century-Old Ecological Studies in France," *American Journal of Sociology*, no. 39 (July 1933). (As the title of the article indicates, the founders of "human ecology" in the United States invoked as precursor in their field the research of specialists in moral statistics such as Guerry and Quételet.)

19. *Comptes rendus des séances de l'Académie des sciences, séance du 1 juillet 1907, Rapport présenté par les professeurs d'Arsonval, Chauveau, Darboux, Troost et Dastre,*

vol. 145. On the chronology of the use of photography for judicial purposes, see A. Rouillé, *La Photographie en France. Textes et controverses. Une anthologie de 1816 à 1871* (Paris: Macula, 1989). On Lavater and Töpffer, see D. Kunzle, *The History of the Comic Strip*, vol. 2: *The Nineteenth Century* (Berkeley: University of California Press, 1990); T. Groensteen and B. Peters, eds., *L'Invention de la bande dessinée* (Paris: Éditions Hermann, 1994). (This last book includes Töpffer's essay.)

20. A. Bertillon, *Anthropological Descriptions: New Method of Determining Individual Identity, Conference Given at the International Penitentiary Congress at Rome, 22 November 1885, Address of M. Herbette* (Melun, France: Administrative Printing, 1887).

21. F. Galton published three books on the subject: *Method of Indexing Finger Marks* (1891); *Finger-Prints* (1892); *Finger-Print Directories* (1895). The last was published by MacMillan in London. In a first article, the London scientist had provided insight into the direction of his research ("Personal Identification and Description," *Journal of the Royal Institution*, May 1888).

22. Numerous studies exist in Spanish on this contribution; see, for example, J. Vucetich, *Proyecto de ley de registro general de identificación* (La Plata: Universidad Nacional de La Plata, 1929); L. Reyna Almandos, *Dactiloscopia argentina. Su historia e influencia en la legislación* (La Plata: Universidad Nacional de La Plata, 1932). In French, see *Comptes rendus des séances de l'Académie des sciences* (note 19).

23. L. Reyna Almandos, "Métodos de identificación judicial. La dactiloscopia y la defensa social," *Revista Ciencias sociales* (La Plata, 1911): 9.

24. *Comptes rendus des séances de l'Académie des sciences,* 31. This report was published in its entirety, in French but with an introduction in Spanish, by L. Reyna Almandos, under the title *Bertillon y Vucetich juzgados por la Academia de ciencias de Paris* (La Plata: Universidad Nacional de La Plata, 1928).

25. See especially E. Locard, "Les services actuels d'identification et la fiche internationale," *Comptes rendus du VIᵉ congrès international d'anthropologie criminelle, Turin, 28 avril-3 mai 1906* (Turin: Bocca, 1907).

26. C. Lombroso, *L'Homme criminel, étude anthropologique et médicale* (Paris: F. Alcan, 1887).

27. *Comptes rendus du VIᵉ congrès international d'anthropologie criminelle* (Paris: F. Alcan, 1887).

28. G. Lanteri-Laura, *Histoire de la phrénologie. L'homme et son cerveau selon F. J. Gall* (Paris: PUF, 1970), 172.

29. C. Lombroso and R. Lashi, *Le Crime politique et les révolutions par rapport au droit, à l'anthropologie criminelle et à la science du gouvernement* (Paris: F. Alcan, 1892; original Italian edition 1890), vol. 2, 333.

30. M. Magitot, in *Actes du deuxième congrès international d'anthropologie criminelle, Biologie et sociologie, Paris, août 1889* (Paris: G. Masson, 1890), 239.

31. H. Fournial, *Essai sur la psychologie des foules. Considérations médico-judiciaires sur les responsabilités collectives* (Lyons-Paris: Storck-Masson, 1892).

32. E. Ferri et al., "Polemica sulla *Psychologie des foules,*" in *La Scuola positiva nella Giurisprudenza Civile e Penale,* 1895, vol. 5.

33. S. Sighele, *Psychologie des foules: Essai de psychologie collective* (Paris: F. Alcan, 1901), 10. Second edition entirely reset.

34. G. Le Bon, *Psychologie des foules* (Paris: PUF, 1991), 4th ed., 6.

35. Few writers on the psychology of crowds mention Fournial's contribution. One of the most complete studies of the issue is the doctoral thesis of J. Van Ginneken, "Crowds, Psychology and Politics 1871–1899," University of Amsterdam, 1989.

36. E. Ferri, *I nuovi orrizonti del dirrito e della procedura penale* (Bologna: Zanichelli, 1884).

37. Sighele, *Psychologie des foules,* 10.

38. S. Sighele, "Le crime collectif," in *Comptes rendus des travaux de la cinquième session. Amsterdam, 9–14 septembre 1901,* ed. J. K. A. Wertheim Salomonson (Amsterdam: Congrès international d'anthropologie criminelle), 75–76.

39. Ibid.

40. Ibid., 248.

41. Sighele, *La foule criminelle,* 241.

42. Ibid., 248.

43. S. Sighele, *Littérature et criminalité* (Paris: Giard and Brière, 1908), 182–83.

44. E. Sue, *Les Mystères de Paris,* vol. 1, 6; originally published in *Journal des débats,* 19 June 1842.

45. Sighele, *Littérature et criminalité,* 193.

46. Ibid., 209–10.

47. G. Le Bon, *Lois psychologiques de l'évolution des peuples* (Paris: F. Alcan, 1894), 140.

48. Ibid., 8.

49. Ibid., 47.

50. Ibid., 55–56.

51. Ibid., 17.

52. G. Le Bon, *The Crowd, A Study in the Popular Mind,* 2d ed. (Dunwoody, Ga.: Norman S. Berg, 1977), 20.

53. Ibid., 17.

54. Le Bon, *Psychologie des foules,* 14.

55. See J. C. Beaune, *Le Vagabond et la Machine. Essai sur l'automatisme ambulatoire* (Paris: Champ Vallon, 1983).

56. D. Bernard and A. Gunthert, *L'Instant rêvé: Albert Londe (1857–1917)* (Nîmes: J. Chambon, 1993).

57. Le Bon, *The Crowd,* xvi.

58. Ibid., 152.

59. Ibid.

60. S. Freud, "Group Psychology and the Analysis of the Ego," in *The Complete Psychological Works of Sigmund Freud,* trans. J. Strachey in collaboration with A. Freud (London: Hogarth Press and the Institute of Psychoanalysis, 1955), vol. 18 (1920–22), 69–74.

61. G. Tarde, "Les crimes des foules," in *Troisième congrès international d'anthropologie criminelle, août 1892, Bruxelles,* 73–80.

62. G. Tarde, *L'Opinion et la Foule* (Paris: F. Alcan, 1901), 5.

63. Ibid., 7.

64. Ibid., 6.

65. Ibid., 13.

66. Ibid., 23.

67. G. Tarde, *On Communication and Social Influence, Selected Papers,* ed. T. N. Clark (Chicago and London: University of Chicago Press, 1969), 286.

68. Tarde, *L'Opinion et la Foule,* 49.

69. Tarde, *On Communication and Social Influence, Selected Papers,* 317.

70. Tarde, "Les crimes des foules," 73.

71. W. Bagehot, *Physics and Politics, or Thoughts on the Application of the Principles of a "Natural Selection" and "Selection" to Political Society* (London: King, 1867).

72. M. Chanan, *The Dream That Kicks: The Prehistory and Early Years of Cinema in Britain* (London: Routledge, 1980), 273.

73. G. Tarde, *Les Lois de l'imitation. Étude sociologique* (Paris: F. Alcan, 1895), 2d ed., viii (original edition 1890, with numerous chapters published in the form of articles between 1882 and 1888); in English, *The Laws of Imitation*, trans. E. C. Parsons (New York: Henry Holt, 1903).

74. Tarde, *Les Lois de l'imitation*, xii.

75. Ibid., 245.

76. R. Löwie, *History of Ethnological Theory* (New York: Holt, Rinehart and Winston, 1937), 106–7.

77. G. Tarde, quoted in E. d'Eichtal, "La Psychologie économique," *Revue Philosophique* (5 May 1902): 529.

78. G. Tarde, *La Philosophie pénale* (Lyons-Paris: Storck-Mason, 1890), 118.

79. W. Thomas and F. Znaniecki, *The Polish Peasant in Europe and America* (Boston: Badger, 1918), 5 vols.

80. See F. H. Matthers, *Robert Park, and the Chicago School* (Englewood Cliffs, N.J.: Prentice-Hall, 1967); R. E. Park, *The Collected Papers of R. E. Park* (Glencoe, Ill.: Free Press, 1955).

81. C. Javeau, "Georg Simmel: un aperçu," *Les Cahiers du Grif*, no. 40 (spring 1989).

82. C. S. Peirce, *The Collected Papers of C. S. Peirce*, ed. C. Harsthorne and P. Weiss (Cambridge: Harvard University Press, 1932), vol. 2, 228.

83. See A. Coulon, *L'École de Chicago* (Paris: PUF, 1992).

84. C. H. Cooley, *Human Nature and the Social Order* (New York: C. Scribner's Sons, 1902); *Social Organization* (1910). See also C. H. Cooley, *Sociological Theory and Social Research* (New York: Henry Holt and Company, 1930).

85. See A. and M. Mattelart, *Rethinking Media Theory: Signposts and New Directions*, trans. J. A. Cohen and M. Urquidi (Minneapolis: University of Minnesota Press, 1992), Part II, "New Paradigms."

86. Tarde, quoted in d'Eichtal, "La Psychologie économique," 532.

11. The Pace of the Human Motor

1. É.-J. Marey, "La station physiologique de Paris," *La Nature*, no. 536 (8 September 1883): 227; in English, "The Physiological Station of Paris," *Science*, no. 2 (30 November 1883): 679. For an illustrated discussion of Marey's work, see M. Braun, *Picturing Time: The Work of E.-J. Marey (1830–1904)* (Chicago: University of Chicago Press, 1992).

2. Marey, "The Physiological Station of Paris," 711 and 679.

3. É.-J. Marey, *La Machine animale, Locomotion terrestre et aérienne* (Paris: F. Alcan, 1886), 4th ed., 26; in English, *Animal Mechanism: A Treatise of Terrestrial and Aerial Locomotion*, 3d ed. (New York: Appleton, 1884).

4. É.-J. Marey, *La Méthode graphique dans les sciences expérimentales et principalement en physiologie et en médicine* (Paris: G. Masson, 1885), 2d expanded ed., 111.

5. É.-J. Marey, *La Chronophotographie* (Paris: Gauthier-Villars, 1899), 5.

6. É.-J. Marey, "Exposition d'instruments et d'images relatifs à l'histoire de la chronophotographie," in *Musée centennal, Exposition universelle internationale de 1900 à Paris* (Paris: 1900), 2. On the relations between Marey's early experiments and those of Muybridge, see Marey, *La Chronophotographie*, 6–8.

7. P. Bachlin, *Histoire économique du cinéma* (Paris: La Nouvelle édition, 1947).

8. Marey, *La Chronophotographie*, 26.

9. Ibid., 39–40.

10. Marey, in *Musée centennal, Exposition universelle internationale de 1900 à Paris*, 25.

11. Ibid.

12. Marey, *La Méthode graphique dans les sciences expérimentales*, 1.

13. Ibid., 77.

14. Marey, "La station physiologique de Paris," 226.

15. G. Demenÿ, *Mécanisme et éducation des mouvements* (Paris: F. Alcan, 1904).

16. Marey, *La Machine animale*, 47.

17. É.-J. Marey, "Du moyen d'économiser le travail moteur de l'homme et des animaux," in *Comptes rendus des séances de l'Académie des sciences*, 22 August 1874 session.

18. C. Frémont, "Les mouvements de l'ouvrier dans le travail professionnel," *Le Monde moderne*, February 1895.

19. Marey, *La Machine animale*, vii–viii.

20. F. W. Taylor, *Shop Management* (New York: Harper and Brothers, 1927), 366.

21. Quoted in A. D. Chandler, *The Visible Hand: The Managerial Revolution in American Business* (Cambridge: Belknap Press of Harvard University Press, 1967), 272.

22. F. W. Taylor, "Notes on Belting" (1893). See note 24.

23. F. W. Taylor, *Scientific Management, Comprising Shop Management. The Principles of Scientific Management, Testimony before the Special House Committee*, with a foreword by H. S. Person (New York: Harper, 1927), v. This volume includes both principal works by Taylor and the "Hearings before the Special Committee of the House of Representatives to Investigate the Taylor and Other Systems of Shop Management."

24. H. S. Person and the Taylor Society, eds., *Scientific Management in American Industry* (New York: Harper and Brothers, 1929), 2.

25. Taylor, *Testimony*, 88.

26. F. B. Gilbreth, *Motion Study* (New York: D. Van Nostrand, 1911).

27. G. Lanteri-Laura, *Histoire de la phrénologie. L'homme et son cerveau selon F. J. Gall* (Paris: PUF, 1970), 152.

28. Ibid., 171.

29. Taylor, *Shop Management*, 152.

30. Taylor, *Testimony*, 238.

31. See, for example, J. M. Lahy, "L'étude scientifique des mouvements et le chronométrage," *La Revue socialiste*, December 1913; "Le système Taylor: peut-il déterminer une organisation scientifique du travail?" *La Grande Revue*, 25 December 1913.

32. A. Gramsci, "Americanism and Fordism" (1929), in Q. Hoare and G. Nowell Smith, (eds)., *Selections from the Prison Notebooks of Antonio Gramsci* (New York: International Publishers, 1971), 286.

33. Chandler, *The Visible Hand*, 122.

34. C. S. Mill, "Business Press Traces Its Ancestry to Colonies," *Advertising Age*, vol. 47, no. 16 (19 April 1976).

35. G. Kolko, *Railroads and Regulation* (Princeton, N.J.: Princeton University Press, 1965), 239.

12. The Market of Target Groups

1. H. Juin, *Lectures du XIXᵉ siècle* (Paris: 10/18, 1976), 112.

2. See the issue devoted to Eugène Sue in the journal *Europe*, November–December 1982.

3. A. Gramsci, *Notas sobre Maquiavelo, sobre politica y sobre el Estado moderno* (Mexico City: J. Pablos, 1975), 323–24.

4. M. de Certeau, *La Culture au pluriel* (Paris: Bourgois, 1980), 2d ed., chapter 3, "La beauté du mort," 55. All the quotations on the subject are taken from this work.

5. Ibid., 56.

6. K. Marx and F. Engels, *The Holy Family,* in *Collected Works,* vol. 4 (New York: International Publishers, 1975), 201.

7. Ibid. [trans. modified].

8. M. B. Palmer, *Des petits journaux aux grandes agences. Naissance du journalisme moderne* (Paris: Aubier, 1983), 26 and 29.

9. R. Gubern, *El lenguaje de los comics* (Barcelona: Peninsula, 1974).

10. Juin, *Lectures du XIXe siècle,* 117.

11. N. Atkinson, *Eugène Sue et le roman-feuilleton* (Paris: Librairie ancienne et moderne A. Nizet et M. Bastard, 1929).

12. A. Gramsci, *Literatura y vida nacional* (Mexico City: J. Pablos, 1976), 139.

13. J. Baudrillard, *Pour une critique de l'économie politique du signe* (Paris: Gallimard, 1972), 207; in English, *For a Critique of the Political Economy of the Sign* (Saint Louis: Telos Press, 1981), 169.

14. See A. and M. Mattelart, *Le Carnaval des Images* (Paris: INA-La Documentation Française, 1987); in English, *The Carnival of Images: Brazilian Television Fiction* (New York: Bergin and Garvey [Greenwood Press], 1990).

15. P. Lafargue, *Le Droit à la paresse* (1880) (Paris: F. Maspero, 1976), 121; in English, *The Right to Leisure,* trans. James Blackwell (Glasgow: Labour Literature Society, 1893).

16. Ibid., 153.

17. Reprinted in P. Kropotkin, *La Conquête du pain* (Paris: Stock, 1908).

18. É. de La Boétie, *Le Discours sur la servitude volontaire* (Paris: Payot, 1993), 29; in English, there are at least three editions, including *The Politics of Obedience: The Discourse of Voluntary Servitude,* trans. H. Kurz (Montreal: Black Rose Books, 1975).

19. Ibid., 30.

20. "Transcription du *Discours de la servitude volontaire* (1836)," by C. Teste, in ibid., 203.

21. See the presentation of La Boétie's book by M. Abensour and M. Gauchet, in ibid.

22. T. Veblen, *The Theory of the Leisure Class* (New York: Modern Library, 1943).

23. A.-M. Thiesse, *Le Roman au quotidien. Lecteurs et lectures populaires à la Belle Époque* (Paris: Le Chemin Vert, 1984).

24. P. Lavrov, *La Propagande socialiste; son rôle et ses formes* (1887) (Paris: Bureaux des Temps Nouveaux, 1898); in English, "Socialist Propaganda: Its Role and Forms," in *Communication and Class Struggle,* vol. 2: *Liberation, Socialism,* ed. A. Mattelart and S. Siegelaub (New York: International General, 1983).

25. *Lenin about the Press,* ed. M. Saifulin (Prague: International Organization of Journalists, 1972).

26. G. Lagneau, *Les Institutions publicitaires, Fonctions et genèse* (Paris: Université René-Descartes, 1982), ix.

27. Ibid., 235.

28. T. Fleming, "How It Was in Advertising: 1776–1976," *Advertising Age,* vol. 47, no. 16 (19 April 1976), Special Bicentennial Issue.

29. J. Habermas, *The Structural Transformation of the Public Sphere: An Inquiry into a Category of Bourgeois Society,* trans. T. Burger and F. Lawrence (Cambridge: MIT Press, 1992), 4th printing, 60.

30. *1909 JWT "Blue Book" Defined Role of Advertising*, New York. Reproduced in facsimile in *Advertising Age*, vol. 35, no. 49 (7 December 1964) (special issue commemorating the centenary of J. Walter Thompson).

31. Ibid.

32. Q. J. Schultze, "Professionalism in Advertising: the Origin of Ethical Codes," *Journal of Communication*, vol. 32, no. 2 (spring 1981).

33. "How Advertising and Advertising Agencies Started and Grew in the United States: A Brief History," *Advertising Age*, vol. 35, no. 49 (7 December 1964).

34. See. G. Miracle and T. Nevett, *Voluntary Regulations of Advertising* (Lexington, Mass.: Heath, 1987).

35. "M. Bleustein-Blanchet on the Future of Advertising in Europe," *Advertising Age (International)*, vol. 48, no. 23 (30 May 1977): 59.

36. See A. Mattelart, *L'Internationale publicitaire* (Paris: La Découverte, 1989); in English, *Advertising International: The Privatisation of Public Space*, trans. M. Chanan (New York and London: Routledge and Comedia, 1991).

37. "Thompson Tightens Organization," *Advertising Age*, vol. 35, no. 49 (7 December 1964): 198.

38. J. J. Honomichl, "Since First Straw Vote in 1824, Research Grows," *Advertising Age*, vol. 47, no. 16 (19 April 1976).

39. H. S. Person and the Taylor Society, eds., "Research for Merchandising and Selling," in *Scientific Management in American Industry* (New York: Harper and Brothers, 1929).

40. H. H. Maynard et al., *Principles of Marketing* (New York: Ronald Press, 1932), quoted in C. Paradeise and R. Laufer, *Le Prince Bureaucrate, Machiavel au pays du marketing* (Paris: Flammarion, 1982), 74.

41. S. J. Paliwoda, *International Marketing* (London: Heinemann, 1986), 1.

42. M. Blanchard, *Essentials of Advertising*, quoted in D. J. Boorstin, "The Rhetoric of Democracy," *Advertising Age*, vol. 47, no. 16 (19 April 1976): 58.

43. S. Ewen, *Captains of Consciousness: Advertising and the Social Roots of the Consumer Culture* (New York: McGraw-Hill, 1976).

44. Boorstin, "The Rhetoric of Democracy," 64.

45. J.-C. Passeron, in C. Grignon and J.-C. Passeron, *Le Savant et le Populaire. Misérabilisme et populisme en sociologie et littérature* (Paris: Gallimard-Seuil, 1989), 90.

46. *Public Opinion Quarterly*, vol. 1, 1937.

47. I have recounted the history of the relation between war and the media in *Mapping World Communication: War, Progress, Culture*, trans. S. Emanuel and J. Cohen (Minneapolis: University of Minnesota Press, 1994), Part I.

48. E. Mayo, *The Human Problems of an Industrial Civilization* (New York: McMillan, 1933).

49. See the parallels between the two men developed by M. Pollak, *Une identité blessée. Études de sociologie et d'histoire* (Paris: A. M. Métailié, 1993).

50. R. K. Merton, "Manifest and Latent Functions," in *Social Theory and Social Structure* (1949), (New York: Free Press, 1968 enlarged edition), 101 n. 49.

51. A. R. Radcliffe-Brown, "On the Concept of Function in Social Science," in *Structure and Function in Primitive Society* (London: Cohen and West, 1952), 179ff.

52. Quoted in R. Löwie, *History of Ethnological Theory* (New York: Holt, Rinehart and Winston, 1937), 223.

53. Radcliffe-Brown, "On the Concept of Function in Social Science," 181.

54. H. R. Lasswell, "The Structure and Function of Communication in Society," in *The Communication of Ideas*, ed. L. Bryson (New York: Harper and Brothers, 1948).

55. Merton, *Social Theory and Social Structure*.

Epilogue: New Organic Totalities?

1. On this evolution, see A. and M. Mattelart, *Rethinking Media Theory: Signposts and New Directions*, trans. J. A. Cohen and M. Urquidi (Minneapolis: University of Minnesota Press, 1992), chapters 3 and 4.

2. A. Mons, *La Métaphore sociale* (Paris: PUF, 1992), 9.

3. J. Ruffié, *De la biologie à la culture* (Paris: Fayard, 1983), 354 and 356. This book is also referred to in *Rethinking Media Theory*.

4. R. Petrella, "Vers un 'techno-apartheid' global," *Les Frontières de l'économie globale*, Manières de voir no. 18, *Le Monde diplomatique*, May 1993.

5. P. Schwebig, *Les Communications d'entreprise* (Paris: McGraw-Hill, 1988). See also H. Landier, *L'Entreprise polycellulaire* (Paris: Entreprise moderne d'édition, 1987).

6. A. Mattelart, *Mapping World Communication: War, Progress, Culture*, trans. S. Emanuel and J. Cohen (Minneapolis: University of Minnesota Press, 1994), 209.

7. G. Béney, "La citoyenneté au risque de l'écologie globale," IFDA *Dossier* (Nyon, Switzerland), no. 79 (October–December 1990): 78.

8. See A. Mattelart and M. Palmer, "Shaping the European Advertising Scene: Commercial Free Speech in Search of Legitimacy," *Réseaux, French Journal of Communication*, vol. 1, no.1 (spring 1993).

9. J.-P. Le Goff, *Le Mythe de l'entreprise* (Paris: La Découverte, 1995), 2d ed., 280.

10. See M. Pagès et al., *L'Emprise de l'organisation* (Paris: PUF, 1979).

11. See chapter 6 and the section titled "Samuel Butler and Machine Evolution."

12. F. Guattari, *Chaosmose* (Paris: Galilée, 1992), 15 and 17.

Index

Compiled by Eileen Quam and Theresa Wolner

335

Armand Mattelart was born in Belgium. Since 1983 he has been Professor of Information and Communication Sciences at the Université de Haute-Bretagne (Rennes 2), France, and codirector of the postgraduate program at Paris III (Nouvelle Sorbonne) Rennes 2. From 1962 to 1973 he was a professor of the sociology of communication at the Catholic University of Chile, Santiago, and a United Nations expert in social development. In 1975 he directed a feature-length film on Chile, *La Spirale*. Between 1975 and 1982, he taught at the University of Paris VII and VIII. He has carried out numerous research projects in Europe, Latin America, and Africa. He has authored or coauthored nearly thirty books, translated into many languages, on culture, politics, the mass media, and communication theory and history, including *Mapping World Communication: War, Progress, Culture* (University of Minnesota Press, 1994), *Advertising International: The Privatization of Public Space* (1991); and, with Michèle Mattelart, *The Carnival of Images: Brazilian Television Fiction* (1990) and *Rethinking Media Theory: Signposts and New Directions* (University of Minnesota Press, 1992).

Susan Emanuel has been a producer of educational television programs for the BBC and a lecturer in film and television studies at the University of Bristol, Yale, and MIT. She has a doctorate in communications from Rennes University in France and has translated works by Pierre Bourdieu and Armand Mattelart. She lives with her family outside Boston and in Brittany.